Universal Ton

DUKE UNIVERSITY PRESS

DURHAM AND LONDON

2021

Universal

The Life and Music of William Parker

Cisco Bradley

Tonality

© 2021 DUKE UNIVERSITY PRESS

All rights reserved

Designed by MaTT Tauch

Typeset in Arno Pro and Space Grotesk
by Westchester Publishing Services

Library of Congress Cataloging-in-Publication Data
Names: Bradley, Francis R., author.
Title: Universal tonality : the life and music of William Parker /
Cisco Bradley.
Description: Durham : Duke University Press, 2021. |
Includes bibliographical references and index.
Identifiers: LCCN 2020027300 (print) | LCCN 2020027301 (ebook)
ISBN 9781478010142 (hardcover)
ISBN 9781478011194 (paperback)
ISBN 9781478012719 (ebook)
Subjects: LCSH: Parker, William, [date] | Double bassists— United
States—Biography. | Jazz musicians—United States— Biography. |
Composers—United States—Biography. | Free Jazz— United
States—History and criticism.
Classification: LCC ML418.P268 B73 2021 (print) |
LCC ML418.P268 (ebook) | DDC 787.5092 [B]0—dc23
LC record available at https://lccn.loc.gov/2020027300
LC ebook record available at https://lccn.loc.gov/2020027301

Cover art: Photograph by Jimmy Katz. © Jimmy Katz.

To my parents

SUSANNA LOUISE (REMPLE) BRADLEY (b. 1946), teacher, and
CHARLES CRANE BRADLEY JR. (b. 1944), pacifist and social worker,
who selected trombone for me to play in sixth grade,
which led me to jazz

III. Toward the Universal

Acknowledgments

First and foremost, I must thank the subject of this book, William Parker, for opening up his life to me. I first encountered Parker's music in 2006 when I was a graduate student at the University of Wisconsin–Madison. I purchased a copy of his quartet record, *Sound Unity* (2004), at the Jazz Record Mart in Chicago. Upon first listening to it, I found that it opened up worlds of sound to me, and it sent me on a journey through his monumental work over the decade that followed. I never could have guessed upon first hearing his music that I would have the honor of later writing a book about his life and work. In 2011 I moved to Brooklyn to join the faculty at the Pratt Institute and began attending concerts around the city, first encountering Parker in a duo with tenor saxophonist Charles Gayle at the Clemente Soto Velez Cultural Center on January 2, 2012. Over the two years that followed, I saw him play in different formats many dozens of times, whenever the opportunity arose. Finally, on the day before Halloween in 2014, I approached Parker after a trio performance with Andrew Barker and Michael Foster at Iglesia de la Santa Cruz Church about an interview for my website, www .jazzrightnow.com. For that interview he talked about music as a healing force, while connecting it to an intricate cosmology of existence in such a way that left me transfixed. I realized then what a profound story Parker had to tell.

Just over a year later, on November 24, 2015, I sent Parker an email stating, "I find your work incredibly inspiring and I have been thinking about writing a longer piece on your life and work. What I was thinking is a biographical account that covers your evolution from your earliest years up to the present work you are doing, highlighting your major periods as an artist. Please let me know if you have any interest in this." Parker, who was on tour, replied later that same day: "This sounds interesting, I am in Europe. But let's stay in touch. I have some ideas." We finally found time to meet in January 2016, and contrary to my assumption that it would take some time to get off of the ground, he made it clear that he wanted to move forward quickly and suggested weekly meetings "until we are finished." Over the succeeding three years we conducted twenty-one interviews, and he handed off old boxes of family papers, photos, writings, magazines, press clippings, memorabilia, and other ephemera for me to dig through. Parker's confidence and trust through this project have been one of the great honors of my life.

There are many people who have helped make this book happen. Parker's wife, dancer and arts organizer Patricia Nicholson Parker, and their daughter, Miriam Parker, both did extensive interviews that helped me understand Parker as a person, a husband, and a father, and how he had changed over the decades they had known him. Interviews with pianist Matthew Shipp and multi-instrumentalist Cooper-Moore were also essential. Many other people from the community of musicians also took time to do interviews, often extensive, and everyone I spoke to did it not out of obligation but out of a genuine respect for Parker. These people include Steve Swell, Leena Conquest, Andrew Cyrille, Milford Graves, Hamid Drake, Dave Sewelson, Dave Burrell, Jackson Krall, Jason Kao Hwang, Rob Brown, Joshua Abrams, William Hooker, James Brandon Lewis, Luke Stewart, and Steven Joerg.

A number of scholars deserve mention. Foremost among these is Rick Lopez, whose sessionography of Parker's work was invaluable to this book. It is no understatement to say that this book would have been nigh to impossible to write without him first blazing the trail. His tireless commitment to the intricate details of Parker's sessions (and those of a number of other musicians) has been monumental and has moved the whole field of study forward. Lisa Y. Henderson is another scholar worthy of great praise for her groundbreaking study of free Black communities in North Carolina, which opened the entire story of Parker's origins. After a phone call, she graciously sent me a copy of her hard-to-find master's thesis. In a related matter, thanks are due to Malinda Maynor Lowery and Warren Milteer, who both helped me navigate sources and literature on histories of Native Americans and free people of color in North Carolina. I also wish to thank Jeff Schwartz for supplying me with some obscure Albert Ayler references. Additionally, thanks are due to Ras Moshe Burnett, whose collection of free jazz in the period 1965–75 may be the most extensive anywhere.

There are a number of scholars, writers, and thinkers who provided me feedback that was immeasurably helpful. The three anonymous referees with Duke University Press gave me deep insights and helped me improve the manuscript, its organization, and many of my arguments. I also received feedback on early drafts from three of my colleagues at the Pratt Institute: Macarena Gomez-Barris, Ann Holder, and Zhivka Valiavicharska. I also wish to thank Pratt for providing me with a sabbatical leave for the 2018–19 academic year, during which time I completed the manuscript.

Three other writers also provided me with notable feedback: Luke Stewart, Jordannah Elizabeth, and John Morrison. Luke is a rare combination of presenter, musician, and scholar, one who has exhibited a strong commitment to the furtherance of the music in the next generation. Jordannah and John are two of the cutting-edge thinkers on this music currently writing today. Jordannah founded the "Feminist Jazz Review" column on www.jazzrightnow.com, the first of its kind, and has written a number of groundbreaking reviews and conducted some key interviews with emerging and established artists. John brings a broad perspective and expertise on hip hop, jazz, and other forms of music that always seem to peel back layer after layer of understanding.

I wish to thank my high school band teacher, Michael Tentis, for opening the world of jazz to me. It has never left my ears. I wish to make a special thanks to my wife, Jennie Romer, a passionate human being dedicated to justice and decency, whose strength and determination is a constant source of inspiration. Finally, I wish to thank our daughter, Juliette, for reminding me what we live for. The world would be a different shade of color without her laughter, creativity, and daring.

"Flowers Grow in My Room": Realizing a Vision

All I have is my sincerity.
If you don't believe me, I have failed.　　　　—— **William Parker**

On May 31, 1998, William Parker stepped onto the stage of an elegant Italian opera house at the Verona Jazz Festival for a highly anticipated performance. The Little Huey Creative Music Orchestra, his sixteen-piece big band, was with him, and this was their most high-profile performance to date. In fact, it was their first performance outside of New York City. Rumors of Parker's prowess had circulated around Europe since the 1980s, when he had visited regularly with the Cecil Taylor Unit, and Parker had also brought his own bands on tour when there were opportunities to do so. But at the Teatro Nuovo opera house in Verona on this day, Parker achieved what had seemed impossible: to bring his big band to a European festival.

For the performance in Verona, Parker had composed a suite of pieces titled *Mass for the Healing of the World*, a song for world peace. The opening part, "First Reading (Dawn Song)," began with low rumbling brass and bass that possessed a vocal quality of deep chant with sparse piano casting rays of light across the darkness of the other sounds. Tympani added an urgency to the music as the other members of the band began to coalesce and build toward a collective unity. Inside, Parker was bursting with ideas and mental energy as the performance unfolded. His wife, dancer Patricia Nicholson, had choreographed the piece for the dancers who accompanied it, one of whom was their daughter Miriam. Parker later wrote that "all the players lifted up off of the bandstand and the dancers moved with grace and beauty throughout the space, what might be called clouds of sound filling with shape and deflating, bellowing and rocking, maintaining a sense of tension and release leading up to the Voice of dawn pushing and parting the river, how can it not sing. . . ."

The second part, "Hallelujah," unveiled the arc for the suite, in the form of an instrumental Black mass or shout service, which set up the subsequent parts.[1] As Parker wrote in his diary shortly after the event, chronicling his thoughts at the time,

> Hallelujah consequences the shifting of sound, everyone is blowing. Cooper-Moore is climbing as the road is laid down, we try to accompany the leaps across the stage, but where are we? Listen to Kono, each trombone sound circling the lifting of the legs and the little dramas and subtle poems that mirror drunk rain drops tilted and spread—really no need for metered time. We are now gone, we are stretching, and we have included a large chunk of music history all in one step. Triplets uneven though transcending notes to sounds, colors, dancing above all the lost yesterdays, here now gone. Three, four things happening at the same time, homage and reflection. Verona, Verona we are here. Trumpeter Richard Rodriguez comes down to the lobby of our Hotel and asks the receptionist "Where is the ghetto?" We are here, sizzling Verona. Love with all your heart, Romeo has gone full circle, this is now the house of the blues if only for a minute.[2]

Parker's performance in Verona catapulted him onto the world stage as one of the premier bassists, composers, and bandleaders of his generation. In the more than twenty years since, Parker has toured Europe multiple times each year and has performed in Africa, South America, the Middle East, and East Asia. Appearing on more than 150 records and having won prestigious awards, Parker is widely regarded as one of the most influential jazz artists of his generation.

Vision

Parker's journey to many of the world's premier jazz stages began from humble beginnings as a poor kid growing up in the South Bronx in the 1960s. In December 1967, when William Parker was fifteen, living with his parents and older brother in the Claremont Housing Projects, he had a powerful vision that would define his life. He wrote about it in his diary:

> One day flowers began to grow in my room. Beautiful flowers, their petals were made from the poetry of life. Flowers made from music, dance, painting. Made of happy children who live in a place where there has never been or will there ever be war. A place where every human being is encouraged to shine as bright as possible and not be penalized for it. These flowers are made of the absence of famine and human brutality. I did not ask for these flowers, nor to my knowledge do I water or care for them. They continue to grow and I continue to pick them, they are changing my life.[3]

To Parker, the flowers represented creative talents that he had been granted, and he felt called to bring them out into the world and to share them with others. It took him years to nurture his talents to full fruition, to overcome poverty, and to build a community of like-minded artists, but this vision has guided him through his career.

Parker's vision came at a critical moment for him, when he was beginning to engage with the upheaval of the late 1960s. He had a deep longing for something that would connect him to a bigger world and explain the world that he saw decaying all around him. He found an answer in newly formulated, cutting-edge Black television programming that connected him to everything from political and social movements of the time to influential figures of the Black Arts movement such as Amiri Baraka, Larry Neal, Nikki Giovanni, and James Baldwin. Radio programs also brought Parker into contact with the new cultural attitudes of the civil rights and Black Power eras. These discoveries opened his mind to himself and to reimagining the world and his place in it.

Parker then threw open the doors to all kinds of groundbreaking art that was taking place in the late 1960s. Film entranced young Parker, and he consumed French New Wave, Ingmar Bergman, and avant-garde figures such as Stan Brakhage who opened his mind to worlds very different from his own experience. A self-study of film soon followed to the point where Parker considered making films of his own. But ultimately it was the musicians of the free jazz era, especially John Coltrane, Ornette Coleman, Albert Ayler, and Cecil Taylor, who were an intense source of light for Parker and sent him on a trajectory toward being a musician himself. Jazz poets such as Baraka, Joseph Jarman, and Archie Shepp were also some of the most powerful voices of the time to Parker. The death of Ayler, on the eve of Parker's first public performances, compelled him to commit to the music and to "carry on the work."[4] The music was more than just sound to him; it was a spiritual journey toward salvation, truth, and human compassion, and it would set him on a quest that would define his life.

Parker entered the music scene at the age of nineteen in 1971, just as the loft scene in downtown Manhattan was exploding with activity. He frequented many of the key venues of the time such as Studio We, Studio Rivbea, Ali's Alley, and the Firehouse Theater. He quickly developed a reputation as one of the most talented young bassists on the scene and found gigs such that he was often playing five or more nights per week in his early years. Within a few years he established connections with Don Cherry, Billy Higgins, Sunny Murray, Milford Graves, Bill Dixon, and many others. Through early collaborations with dancer and choreographer Patricia Nicholson, he developed a growing body of compositions intended for groups ranging from solo projects to big band. In 1974 he got his first big break, playing with pianist Cecil Taylor at Carnegie Hall. Taylor had been left as the central free jazz figure in New York after the deaths of John Coltrane and Albert Ayler. Parker would go on to be Taylor's bass player from 1980 to 1991, playing extensively throughout North America, touring in Europe, and appearing on numerous high-profile recordings. Parker was able to form new associations with European players through his work as Taylor's sideperson, and these meetings fostered later collaborations and records. Parker's work with Taylor constituted some of the most important moments in Taylor's sixty-plus-year career and anointed Parker as one of the principal standard-bearers for the music in the next generation.

After leaving Taylor's band, Parker began leading his own projects more prominently by 1994, founding two key ensembles: In Order to Survive and the Little Huey Creative Music Orchestra, both of which recorded a series of groundbreaking records. In Order to Survive was a regular working band where Parker finally was able to refine and record his compositions, some of which he had been working on for more than two decades. The band also was the site of Parker's growing political consciousness through art that was intended to transform society around it. In Order to Survive's four records came to define the sound of the 1990s and reinvigorated free jazz as an art form. Little Huey Creative Music Orchestra emerged as the definitive big band of the era, expanding far beyond the work of Duke Ellington and Cecil Taylor. The band's seven records, released between 1994 and 2006, form a monumental body of work. Parker's big band was also the closest thing the New York scene had to a community band, giving young and emerging musicians a chance to prove themselves while firmly establishing Parker as the leader of the community. Both bands propelled Parker onto the world stage as a composer, bandleader, and performer and established him as one of the most prominent figures in the second generation of free jazz musicians.

Then, in 2001, Parker released *O'Neal's Porch*, with a quartet that included trumpeter Lewis Barnes, saxophonist Rob Brown, and percussionist Hamid Drake, which marked a drive toward a more universal sound in his music. Other bands followed, including the Raining on the Moon Quintet, where they were joined by vocalist Leena Conquest. This work, in particular, drove Parker to develop his theory of universal tonality, that master musicians from any part of the world can meet and, without any preparation, play and communicate with one another in their own musical languages on a profound level. Parker's understanding of improvisation as the method for tapping into this deep and barely explored universal musical cosmos is the crowning achievement thus far in his long career. His work over the past two decades has explored this limitless realm and has left an unparalleled body of work that places the free jazz tradition at the head of the table of world music.

Parker also developed tribute projects to Curtis Mayfield and Duke Ellington, two artists he admired as a young man. The tribute to Mayfield was particularly crucial as it provided a propitious encounter between Parker and Amiri Baraka, a poet who had had a profound effect upon him as a young man. Baraka joined the band's world tour and fused some of the work from the last years of his life to one of Parker's most visionary projects. Both tribute projects also allowed Parker to pay homage to figures who had affected him deeply, both as an artist and a thinker. Parker established himself as a significant solo bassist as well, and in recent years he has composed extensively for vocalists and other formations. Parker's full body of work makes him a major contemporary composer, with more than four thousand individual works to date. Despite the fact that Parker has been prolific in documenting his own work, the vast majority of his compositions have yet to be recorded.

Challenges

At a young age, Parker developed a profound sense of himself and the world he inhabited. Born into poverty in the housing projects of the South Bronx, the son of African American migrants from the U.S. South, he fought against social stigmas that from an early age spoke loud and clear: you have no value. In the face of that, he not only came to value his own talents, but over the years he also established himself as a visionary and daring artist. Despite Parker's immense accomplishments, he has never received the full attention of the jazz establishment press, nor has his work been the focus of any book-length work. This book is the first in-depth study of Parker's life and work, drawn from extensive interviews conducted with the artist as well as with his collaborators, friends, and family.

The lives of figures such as William Parker are often left untold for a number of reasons. First of all, the majority of jazz critics through the years have disregarded free jazz as an art form, writ large. Free jazz emerged in the late 1950s and early 1960s as a movement in the music that would push back against the limits imposed by regular rhythms and tempos, chord changes, and tones of the bebop era; it aimed, in particular, toward creating something new. The music took many forms and soon became a nationwide and, indeed, a global phenomenon while evolving rapidly and embracing new influences, theories, formations, and instruments.

From its earliest beginnings largely up to the present time, a majority of the journalists writing on jazz have attacked the very legitimacy of free jazz, despite the fact that abstract visual art in the same time period was often heralded as genius.[5] Much of this hostility comes from a mischaracterization of free jazz as either outside of or adjunct to the "mainstream" jazz tradition. What is considered central and what is peripheral is, of course, a political decision, though one that has often had a catastrophic impact on the practitioners of free jazz. If one can imagine a large oak tree representing all of the different musics to emerge from or be inspired by jazz, many journalists and musicians have attempted to focus on only a few branches as legitimate while discounting others. Failing to see free jazz as an entity of its own or placing it outside of the historical trajectory of jazz cultural narratives has been a weapon that cultural conservatives have wielded against it since its inception.

The fact that free jazz was, especially in its early years, a revolutionary Black music also impacted how it was received. In its different forms, free jazz critiqued capitalism, racism, Western imperialism, Christian dogma, and consumerism. Many critics ignored its political affiliations or misconstrued them, and only a small number of Black critics, such as Amiri Baraka, praised the music and saw it as a key component in leading the community to a future society based upon revolutionary principles.[6] Yet free jazz constituted the biggest innovation in jazz since bebop in the 1940s. The lack of receptive cultural commentary has been matched by a silence or even disdain among scholars as well. Even for many of the most profound musical figures of the generation prior to Parker, such as Cecil Taylor, Albert Ayler, Don Cherry, Muhal Richard Abrams, Bill Dixon, and Joseph Jarman, a pervasive silence still remains.

In the drive for inclusivity in the American cultural dialogue, antiestablishment, working-class Black artists calling for revolutionary change have often been cast out in favor of figures who integrated themselves into the cultural milieu less abrasively. Parker's body of work is a bold art of resistance, taking aim at many of the hallmarks of capitalism, modernism, pop culture, Eurocentrism, and materialism. But he has not stopped at critique; he has also contributed extensively to the process of memory making through his music and poems restoring, augmenting, or unearthing histories, biographies, and legacies of figures who range from world famous to unknown. Parker has striven to preserve the memories of members of the music community as well as build solidarity with oppressed peoples whose struggle he views as akin to his own.

Parker's success stands in direct challenge to the oft-repeated narrative of a working-class Black figure who "escaped the projects" to great success, allowing them to leave their old world behind. In contrast, Parker has been a community builder and a justice seeker throughout his life, believing his art and that of his collaborators to be imbued with transformative power to make the world a better place. Parker has never forgotten where he came from. His refusal to let others make a caricature of him and his fierce individuality that has stood in the way of commodifying his music have resulted in a dignified, monumental body of work. At an early age, Parker chose to stay true to his artistic vision and to shirk easy attention from critics or promoters. The years of struggle eventually paid off, but it was not an easy journey.

Parker is one of the most influential figures in the second generation of free jazz players. Born after World War II and entering the music scene in the 1970s, after some of the great figures such as Coltrane and Ayler were already dead, Parker picked up the mantle of the music and has carried it for nearly five decades. He has been a leader within this generation of musicians and has pushed far past the initial burst of free jazz in the 1960s. Parker's leading role in expanding and furthering the music has been monumental, even as music critics, record companies, and the jazz establishment worked to commercialize the music and place money and power behind increasingly conservative, less innovative artists and institutions.

Approaches

The context of Parker's music is embedded deep within his own identity and community, so this fact requires us to consider the historical roots of its formation to understand the work itself. Thus, this book tells Parker's story within the long arc of African American diaspora history, traced through his own ancestry. One major yet obvious obstacle in this endeavor is the silence that pervades the history of enslaved peoples and their descendants. Prior to emancipation, the paucity of perspectives from enslaved peoples and the lack of biographical details in the written record present a monumental challenge in telling that story without it being one that is merely seen through white eyes.[7] Recent scholarly work on the ethnicity of enslaved peoples in the Americas, oral histories of enslaved and indigenous peoples, and DNA evidence from Parker together help us form the early phases of the narrative told here. Resistance and the fight for dignity and sovereignty against hostile and violent power structures are the threads that run through these histories.

After emancipation, the written record changed considerably, but it still left out Black perspectives in bureaucratic documents that simultaneously served as mechanisms to categorize, divide, and control people of color. Erasure continued through many emancipated lives, such as Parker's great-grandfather, William "Bill" Parker (b. ca. 1850), who disappears from the record in Goldsboro, North Carolina, abruptly in the late 1870s. Was he lynched while still in his twenties as so many were after the collapse of Reconstruction? Did he die young because of accident, disease, or neglect? By 1880, there is no further trace of him in any record, although his two young orphaned sons remain. The disappearances of lives and the records of them are what scholar Christina Sharpe observes as the normatization of Black death in the historical record.[8] Sharpe argues that, in many ways, these "conditions of Black life as it is lived near death, as deathliness, in the wake of slavery," remain largely unchanged up to the present time.[9]

The strength of Parker's family, even after some migrated north in the 1930s, has preserved a greater visual and written record and is a testament to their efforts to tell their own stories. These records have survived only because the family maintained their own archives and passed them down through the generations, thus allowing us to illuminate lives that would have otherwise been obscured in the record. From that point forward, I weave the personal with the rich literary, artistic, and musical legacies of Harlem and the Bronx that gave birth to the subject of this book.

Parker's impeccable memory and storytelling ability, traits that everyone observes of him, make him the best source to speak of his own experience, and the twenty-one in-depth interviews that I conducted with him over the span of four years form the backbone of this book. Further interviews with Parker's family, close friends, associates, and students allow a multifaceted understanding of him as a person, thinker, artist, composer, performer, community leader, husband, father, and visionary.

Much of the second half of the book weaves together Parker's personal narratives with liner notes, previously published writings and interviews, and diaries to give a full picture of the artist. His liner notes, in particular, are revealing of his vision and motivations, although they have been almost entirely ignored by music critics over the years. The notes reveal a deep concern for history and memory, for the legacy of his elders and contemporaries, and for the political consciousness that has been the sustaining fuel for his long career. Parker's published writings open up lines for understanding his broader philosophy of music and art. And his diary entries unveil the intimate and enduring relationship he has had with the music and the community of practitioners.

Outline

Part I analyzes Parker's origins, early years, and key influences. Because Parker and his ancestors collectively survived the Middle Passage, slavery in the American South, the false promises of Reconstruction, and life in a northern ghetto, this book has as its starting point contemporary debates on what has been termed the "afterlife of slavery."[10] The threads of resistance passed down to him through action and word form a backdrop to his work as an artist.

Chapter 1 traces his family's origins from West Africa across the Atlantic via the slave trade to North Carolina and South Carolina. Employing a combination of DNA evidence, oral history, public records, letters, and family ephemera, we follow the story of his ancestors: enslaved and free Black peoples in the Carolinas who formed families with displaced Native Americans and poor white settlers on the frontier. The collapse of Reconstruction and the renewal of white supremacy in the South eventually pushed Parker's parents to migrate north to witness the 1930s Harlem Renaissance, where jazz was the cultural vanguard of the time.

Chapter 2 takes an intimate look at Parker's childhood in the Morrisania neighborhood of the South Bronx in the 1950s and 1960s prior to and during the economic collapse of the area and the rise of mass poverty and urban blight that swept through African American communities and neighborhoods. His home was a sanctuary filled with jazz that sparked the early phases of his imagination and creativity. His father's dream, for Parker to grow up to play in the Duke Ellington Orchestra, though unfulfilled, served to chart a path for young Parker as he navigated an alienating educational system, a rapidly deteriorating urban landscape, and the resulting poverty. In this environment, Parker found beauty, community, and fleeting moments of solace that allowed him to rise above despair.

Chapter 3 turns to the cultural, intellectual, and spiritual forces that transformed young Parker into an artist. By examining his coming of age in the era of the Black Power and the Black Arts movements, we see how his particular articulation of resistance to social marginalization and alienation manifested in an interest in avant-garde music and film. Via television and radio, Parker found the radical voices of his time who were speaking of Black liberation, art, aesthetics, and a revolutionary future society that would be founded on those principles. In his teenage years, poets were the truth tellers to Parker, and we examine some of the specific works that made a deep impact on him. His self-study of film was also foundational as he eventually moved toward music.

Part II examines the process by which Parker got his bearings on the music scene and how he built a reputation for himself prior to emerging as a bandleader in the 1990s. Parker paid his dues as a sideperson, playing with some of the most prominent figures of the time. Through these years of work, he refined his musicianship so that once the opportunity arose, he was ready to lead his own bands.

Chapter 4 analyzes his earliest professional work, primarily situated in Manhattan's loft scene of the 1970s. As a young musician, Parker was self-taught and learned a great deal on the bandstand while finding opportunities to play with many of the luminaries such as Cecil Taylor and Don Cherry while still in his early twenties. Work with the Music Ensemble, Jemeel Moondoc's Ensemble Muntu, Daniel Carter, and others allowed him to build a community of like-minded artists.

Chapter 5 follows Parker's professional collaborations with and eventual marriage to dancer Patricia Nicholson, their mutual interest in socially aware art, and their mutual struggle against the impoverished conditions of the 1980s. Their collaborations formed the first workshop-type space for Parker to present his own compositions. Parker and Nicholson's relationship and financial struggle became the sustaining force that propelled Parker along in his early years as a musician.

Chapter 6 then turns to examine Parker's biggest break: being hired by pianist Cecil Taylor, with whom Parker worked continuously from 1980 to 1991. This period witnessed Parker gaining recognition as a sideperson, and he reached new audiences, especially in Europe. Forming associations with European players was key for the further development of Parker's music. Taylor was the closest thing Parker ever had to a consistent mentor, and he carried on much of the wisdom he gleaned from the experience into his own work that followed.

Part III focuses on Parker's work as a bandleader. Finally, from the 1990s onward, he found opportunities to lead and record his own bands with regularity. His compositions, some of which dated to the early 1970s, were finally brought to light, and he eventually formed ever-more-ambitious ensembles to showcase his work.

Chapter 7 examines Parker's most active band of the 1990s, In Order to Survive, and the social and artistic context from which it emerged. The band featured a shifting cast of musicians, including Cooper-Moore and Rob Brown, who faithfully assisted Parker in the realization of his work. Chapter 8 illustrates Parker's big-band work with the Little Huey Creative Music Orchestra and his theory of the Tone World. Little Huey has been, in many ways, his most personal and revealing work to date, and a springboard for his storytelling.

Chapter 9 then examines his work of the 2000s, the William Parker Quartet and the Raining on the Moon Quintet, which substantially built his global profile and his drive toward a universal sound. In particular, Parker's collaborations with Hamid Drake became the launching point for a whole range of music. His work with Leena Conquest constituted the first substantial work with a vocalist and set Parker on a new trajectory of composing lyrics in addition to the other aspects of the music.

Chapter 10 examines his tribute projects to Duke Ellington and Curtis Mayfield, his solo work, and a number of bands that are lesser known.

Chapter 11 discusses his most recent work. Having won awards and having played on so many great stages, Parker was finally able to release music in the 2010s that he had recorded as early as the 1970s. The final chapter also considers his legacy, drawn from interviews with his contemporaries, collaborators, friends, and mentees, and his impact on the music and the community of artists who continue to play free jazz in New York City and beyond.

In articulating his own artistic vision, Parker wrote the following:

It is the role of the artist to dance, sing, shout and whisper about all that is wonderful, beautiful and majestic. To mirror and project the present and future, to tell us the stories inside little children's hearts (giving us a view beyond the horizon). Communicating by the language of stone, wood, soil, the language of happiness, sadness and joy. It is the role of the artist to incite political, social and spiritual revolution. To awaken us from our sleep and never let us forget our obligations as human beings. To light the fire of human compassion. When this inner flame is burning, people are uplifted to another state, their vision and senses are doubled, they see, hear and feel things they never did before. The heat of the earth, the cry of living beings. This fire is stoked by conviction, caring, communication with others. The idea is to live strongly within this vision without compromises even after being met by a cold grey world that could care less about vision, a world that makes insensitivity and murder of idealism and individualism a standard. It is the role of the artist to become a human being to see that the only art is the art of living, the artist must quickly make the transformation to human being and in the same breath come to realize he or she is a vehicle through which light passes. We can flow and sing with this reality.[11]

I. Origins

One

Enslavement and Resistance: From West Africa to the Carolinas to Harlem

In the early days of my visitation,
Black hands tended me and cared for me . . .
Black minds, hearts and souls loved me . . .
And I loved them because of this.
In the early days of my visitation,
Black hands tended me and cared for me;
I can't forget these things.
For black hearts, minds and souls love me—
And even today the overtones from the fire
of that love are still burning.

—— **Sun Ra**

William Parker was a child of the Harlem Renaissance. His home was filled with the music of Duke Ellington and other jazz legends, and it was his father's dream for him to grow up to play in Ellington's orchestra. Parker's parents had both come from the rural American South and were part of the early phases of the Great Migration, which witnessed between one and two million African Americans migrating to northern cities such as New York, Philadelphia, and Chicago between 1910 and 1940.[1] Out of this movement

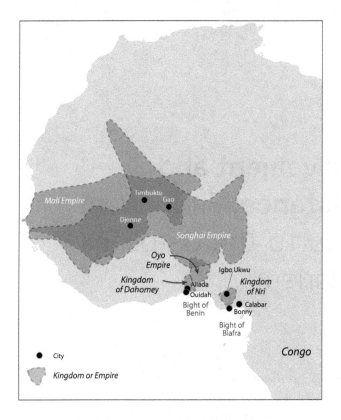

Mali Empire

Timbuktu
Gao

Djenne

Songhai Empire

Oyo
Empire

Igbo Ukwu

Kingdom
of Dahomey

Alláda
Ouidah

Kingdom
of Nri

Bight of
Benin

Calabar
Bonny

Bight of
Biafra

Congo

● City

Kingdom or Empire

of people—the single largest internal migration in U.S. history—the Harlem Renaissance was born. Harlem became the unparalleled hub of African American culture, a center for musicians, artists, and writers, and it propelled jazz onto a national stage.

But before arriving in Harlem, Parker's ancestors had long histories that trace back through years of struggle in the Americas that together inform a history that made Parker who he is. His mother's people were sharecroppers and descendants of enslaved people in South Carolina.[2] His father's family mostly comprised enslaved and free Black people in North Carolina, who formed families with Native Americans of the Waccamaw tribe as well as a few poor white settlers living on the Appalachian frontier. Prior to setting foot in America, Parker's deep roots trace back to West and Central Africa.

African Origins

In the seventeenth or eighteenth centuries, approximately 90 percent of Parker's ancestors, whose names were not recorded, were captured and sold into slavery along the coast of West and Central Africa stretching from what is now Senegal to the Congo. The region is marked by a series of rivers connecting the interior to the coastlines and sprawling deltas. Nearly half of his African ancestors came from what is now Nigeria, mostly of Igbo origin, and can be traced back to at least the seventh century in the Kingdom of Nri.[3] Nri, which was located to the east of the Niger River, is famous for its bronze, clay, and terracotta sculptures depicting its priest-kings as well as natural fauna in the region.[4] The archaeological record has also left us remnants of intricately designed Igbo pottery and colorful textiles, most notably preserved at the great palace ruins at Igbo-Ukwu.[5] Surviving glass and carnelian beads indicate that Nri was part of long-distance trade networks that connected to places as distant as Venice and India.[6]

Nri rose to greater power around the ninth century with the rise of iron technology and reached its greatest influence between the twelfth and fifteenth centuries.[7] In that period, unbaked clay sculptures were often constructed to honor the sacred Earth—intentionally made to be ephemeral—while there was also a deep belief in water-related gods of the rivers, lakes, and seas. Music had a sacred and political function, and kings often had a retinue of musicians and other performers who accompanied them in all official activities of state, with a large, prestigious drum being the central feature, often with other smaller drums or other instruments also included in these ensembles of political ceremony.[8] The Igbo phrase for musical instrumentalist, *oti egwuloku egwu*, translates as "one who beats music into life." As one art theorist stated, for the Igbo, "The artistic meaning of life is a unity of earth (Ala), man and death: earth as the environment for life, man as society—the meaning of life—and death as the infiniteness of life."[9]

Olaudah Equiano (ca. 1745–97) was an Igbo who was captured and enslaved, survived the Middle Passage, and later attained freedom and wrote of his life in one of the most famous slave narratives ever published. He was born in Isseke, in what is now southeastern Nigeria, and described the music of his people:

> We are almost a nation of dancers, musicians, and poets. Thus every great event, such as a triumphant return from battle, or other cause of public rejoicing, is celebrated in public dances, which are accompanied with songs

and music suited to the occasion. The assembly is separated into four divisions, which dance either apart or in succession, and each with a character peculiar to itself. The first division contains the married men, who in their dances frequently exhibit feats of arms, and the representation of a battle. To these succeed the married women, who dance in the second division. The young men occupy the third; and the maidens the fourth. Each represents some interesting scene of real life, such as a great achievement, domestic employment, a pathetic story, or some rural sport; and as the subject is generally founded on some recent event, it is therefore ever new. This gives our dances a spirit and variety which I have scarcely seen elsewhere. We have many musical instruments, particularly drums of different kinds, a piece of music which resembles a guitar, and another much like a stickado. These last are chiefly used by betrothed virgins, who play on them on all grand festivals.[10]

In describing food that was consumed at public festivals and at other times, Equiano notes that their principal dishes contained bullocks, goats, and poultry: "To make it savory, we sometimes use also pepper, and other spices, and we have salt made of wood ashes. Our vegetables are mostly plantains, eadas, yams, beans, and Indian corn."[11] Equiano also mentions the consumption of pineapples, dried fish, palm wine, and tobacco, and the use of cotton cloth for richly dyed clothes, especially with bright-blue designs. Men and women adorned themselves with perfumes that they manufactured from aromatic wood.[12]

Nri culture was guided and maintained by ritual specialists who traveled throughout the region wielding staves of peace. These practitioners' duty was to purify the Earth from human crimes and to teach others of their healing arts and practices.[13] Nri kings were often selected, after an interregnum, from this body of ritual practitioners, based on the perceived manifestations of their supernatural power. This system of leadership also reflected a broader adherence to the idea that titles and positions of power were earned, not inherited. At the same time, much of the political power remained local and was administered through a system of republican democracy, where councils of village elders made decisions collectively, giving rise to the phrase Ìgbò ènwē ézè, best translated as "the Igbo abhor monarchical power."[14] Women often held positions of significant social prestige.

Nri's power began a slow decline from the fifteenth century onward, and in the last quarter of the seventeenth century Nri collapsed under the pressures of militarism spurred on by the Atlantic slave trade.[15] From that point through the early nineteenth century, many thousands of Igbo were captured and sold at ports such as Bonny or Calabar along the Bight of Biafra, which encompassed one-half of the Niger River delta.[16] Enslaved Igbo were commonly taken across the Atlantic to places such as Trinidad, the Leeward Islands, Jamaica, and western New Granada (today Colombia), as well as to Virginia.[17] Moved later to North Carolina, these Igbo-descended people likely constituted the majority of Parker's paternal relatives.

Nearly one-fifth of Parker's ancestors came from farther west along the West African coast in what is now Benin, Togo, Ghana, and Cote D'Ivoire. Most of the people from this region were either Aja or Yoruba speakers, captured during the rising periods of warfare that consumed the region from the mid-seventeenth century onward. As power shifted there, as elsewhere, from an interior agrarian state—in this case, Allada—to the coastal trading state of Whydah, spurred to power by its importation of increasingly deadly European guns, many people were captured during the resulting wars.[18] Subsequently, the kingdom of Dahomey, armed with the latest European firearms, conquered Whydah in 1727.[19] The interior reach of Whydah and the control it had been able to wield over its conquered populations led to many thousands of people from the area being sold into slavery along the coast.[20] European firearms then became the fuel cast upon the fire of warfare between Dahomey and the Yoruba-speaking Oyo Empire to the east. Through this process, Dahomey became one of the most prominent West African slave-exporting states.[21] Taken to the Bight of Benin—one of the most exploited regions connected to the slave trade—people were then sold and taken to colonial America, likely constituting some of Parker's maternal ancestors in South Carolina.[22]

Farther to the north and west along the African coast, nearly another one-fifth of Parker's ancestors may be traced to the great Empire of Mali, which had emerged as the most powerful state in West Africa in the thirteenth to sixteenth centuries.[23] Founded by Sunjata Keita (ca. 1217–1255), about whom a great literary epic was preserved by griots, most people there spoke Mandinka and practiced Islam.[24] The trade and learning centers of Gao, Djenné, and Timbuktu were Mali's greatest cities, the last of these annually drawing tens of thousands of students from across West Africa to its famous university at its peak in the fifteenth century.[25] In the latter part of that century Mali began to be challenged by its neighbors such as the Songhai Empire, and in the seventeenth century Mali splintered into a number of kingdoms that became engulfed in a similar rising tide of bloodshed spurred by the importation of European rifles and muskets.[26] Roughly one-third of Mandinka speakers were enslaved through this violent process and sold downriver to the coast, where they were transported to the Americas. These Mandinka speakers were likely the first of Parker's African ancestors to arrive in the Americas.[27]

In West Central Africa, approximately one-tenth of Parker's ancestors came from Cameroon or the Congo. Much less is known of their history, but that region was the origin of more enslaved people than any other part of the continent, including many people taken directly to South Carolina, thus forming the ancestry of some of Parker's maternal relations.[28]

Only eight in ten enslaved people survived the horrors of the Middle Passage, where disease, shortages of food and water, and death at the hands of captors claimed millions of lives over the centuries.[29] Mortality was even higher after arrival, when enslaved people faced the conditions of a new diet, new diseases, and the extreme brutality of slavery. Upon arriving on the North American mainland, many of Parker's people first lived in Virginia before being moved to North and South Carolina. Igbo were among the largest ethnic groups there, joining earlier enslaved people who were primarily from the Gambia in West Africa. Most of these ancestors arrived in Virginia in 1700–60, during which time 59,000 Africans arrived via the Atlantic trade. It was also during that period that Virginia's system of enslaved labor was firmly established along the Chesapeake Bay, near the estuaries of the James and York rivers. By 1790, because of internal population growth, there were nearly 300,000 people of African descent living in Virginia.[30]

Peoples of African Descent in Virginia and the Carolinas

Among all African peoples, the Igbo in particular gained a reputation as being resistant to enslavement: it was inimical to their spiritual beliefs, deeply set republican ideals, and intense sense of equality among adults. Disproportionately high numbers of enslaved Igbo attempted to escape, refused to work, or fomented revolts, with prominent involvement by women.[31] Other enslaved Igbo, uprooted from their homeland, where physical and symbolic connection to the land and all it represented—family, ancestors, sustenance—was central to their identity, sometimes chose to commit suicide in defiance of enslavement.[32] As one enslaved Igbo person who escaped and wrote about the phenomenon of suicide rationalized it, "They are universally of the opinion, and this opinion is founded in their religion, that after death they shall return to their own country, and rejoin their former companions and friends, in some happy region, in which they will be provided with plenty of food. . . ."[33]

Thus, death in this way bore the metaphysical meaning of regeneration and renewal. Enslaved Igbo also developed a reputation for building strong communal support systems in opposition to the violent and harsh conditions of slavery, such that an observer wrote, "The newly arrived find help, care, and example from those who have come before them."[34] In a figurative sense, Sun Ra echoed this process in the poem extract that opens the chapter.

The Igbo also had a deep impact upon the culture of enslaved Africans that developed in Virginia and other North American colonies. In many cases in Virginia they were the first enslaved people to arrive in particular areas or plantations and thus set down "the basic patterns of material, social, and ideological culture of enslaved communities . . . people made do with what they had at hand to fashion what they needed to sustain themselves, to forge connections among and between each other, and to make sense of their new worlds."[35] Many enslaved people bore the same names as their ancestors, and others were named after the towns and cities of their origins. Many of the vegetal parts of African American soul food may be traced back to the Igbo, especially dishes that include yams, black-eyed peas, and greens.[36]

In Virginia, and later in North and South Carolina, Parker's ancestors carried with them the culture of their origins, which they contributed to the making of an emerging African American culture. When rare opportunities arose for enslaved people to attend heavily regulated social gatherings between plantations, they would meet for music or dance, where instruments such as the banjo, an adaptation of the Malian xalam, were often used alongside drums of various types. Musicians also played other instruments based on African antecedents such as the kazoo, jug, panpipes, one-string fiddle, one-string bass, one-string gliss zither, mouth bow, and washboard, as well as a growing number of European instruments including the four-stringed fiddle.[37] These rare moments of music and community served as a refuge from the intense horrors of enslavement.[38] Out of this trauma of enslavement, displacement, and oppression, the blues were born and came to form the backbone of American music in the centuries since, especially gospel, jazz, soul, rhythm and blues, rock and roll, and hip-hop.

At some point between 1775 and 1810, if Parker's ancestors were not already in the Carolinas, they were forcibly relocated there.[39] His mother's family was concentrated around Orangeburg, South Carolina, while his father's side lived in the counties of Wayne, Duplin, Durham, and Robeson in North Carolina.

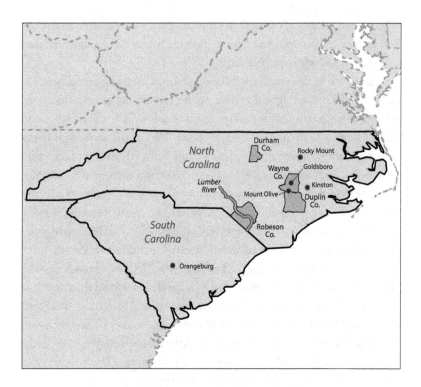

Also around that time, they converted to Christianity—his mother's ancestors becoming Methodists and his father's people becoming Baptists, although his father's progenitors were less religious.[40] In the nineteenth century, Parker's forebears emerge with greater visibility into the historical record.

Parker's mother, Mary Louise Jefferson (1913–1996), came from Orangeburg, South Carolina. Orangeburg was established in 1704 as a fur trading post and remained a small settlement until after the American Revolution. With the invention of the cotton gin, Orangeburg rapidly opened large stretches of land for cultivation, and enslaved Africans, brought from coastal South Carolina or down from Virginia, were forced to work the land. Enslaved people soon came to form the majority of the population of Orangeburg and in 1860 made up two-thirds of the population of the county.[41] It seems likely that Parker's ancestors first set foot in the area around the turn of the nineteenth century.

Mary Louise's paternal relations—the Jeffersons and Washingtons—are difficult to trace prior to the Civil War because they adopted those surnames after emancipation. Her mother's side of the family, however—the Glovers—were enslaved on the plantation of Thomas W. Glover, one of

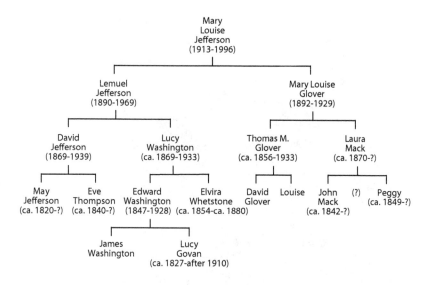

Mary
Louise
Jefferson
(1913-1996)

Lemuel
Jefferson
(1890-1969)

Mary Louise
Glover
(1892-1929)

David
Jefferson
(1869-1939)

Lucy
Washington
(ca. 1869-1933)

Thomas M.
Glover
(ca. 1856-1933)

Laura
Mack
(ca. 1870-?)

May
Jefferson
(ca. 1820-?)

Eve
Thompson
(ca. 1840-?)

Edward
Washington
(1847-1928)

Elvira
Whetstone
(ca. 1854-ca. 1880)

David
Glover

Louise

John
Mack
(ca. 1842-?)

(?)

Peggy
(ca. 1849-?)

James
Washington

Lucy
Govan
(ca. 1827-after 1910)

the wealthiest planters in Orangeburg. Of the earliest figures in the family, David and Louise Glover, little is known. Their son, Thomas M. Glover (1856–1933), lived to see emancipation but tasted the bitterness of the false promise of Reconstruction.[42] He lived out his days as a sharecropper with a life not terribly different from that of the old days. He married Laura Mack, possibly the daughter of John and Peggy Mack, sharecroppers in Amelia Township in Orangeburg County.[43] Thomas and Laura had eight children. The eldest, Mary Louise Glover (1892–1929), married Lemuel Jefferson (1890–1969), and the couple and their offspring also worked as sharecroppers. It was backbreaking work, and even by age fifty, it appears that Lemuel was in failing health; as one of his children wrote in a letter, "We should be able to take care of our father because he ain't able to do much work."[44] Lemuel was the only grandparent who lived to meet Parker when, as a boy, his mother would bring him back down to Orangeburg nearly every summer. Parker remembered Grandfather "Lem" often talking of the buckra, the white bosses, as he would sit on his porch with his shotgun.[45]

Lemuel Jefferson and Mary Louise Glover's daughter Mary Louise Jefferson (1913–1996) was the eldest surviving child, and because of her mother's early death, she filled the role of mother to her younger siblings from her mid-teens onward. She later worked as a domestic servant for a while in the South and had a short-lived marriage. But in the 1930s she and two of her sisters moved north to New York and settled in Harlem. Some family letters

Figure 1.1 Lemuel Jefferson (1890–1969), Parker's maternal grandfather, in Orangeburg, South Carolina, 1967.

survive that their father and siblings wrote to them from Orangeburg, often urging them to return.[46]

Much more is known about Parker's paternal side of the family. Parker's father, Thomas Dortch Parker (1913–1976), came from Goldsboro, North Carolina. Goldsboro was the seat of Wayne County, where the Parker family had dwelled for several generations, after moving there from neighboring Duplin County. Up until the building of the railroads in the 1830s and 1840s, the economy of Wayne County was driven primarily by hog and cattle farmers, many of whom relied upon enslaved people for labor and production.[47] Still, most farmers could not engage in a cash-crop economy because of high transportation costs. Railroads definitively transformed local markets and linked the region to the coast, the interior, and regional cities, where local goods could be sold at greater profit.

The railroad between Wilmington and Raleigh cut through Wayne at Weldon and was completed in 1840.[48] By 1856, the North Carolina Railroad, moving out from Charlotte, intersected the Wilmington-Weldon line at Goldsboro. Although slave labor was used in Wayne County from early in its history,

Figure 1.2 Mary Louise
Glover (1892–1929),
Parker's maternal
grandmother, in
Orangeburg, South
Carolina, ca. 1920.

Figure 1.3 Lemuel Jefferson (1890–1969) with Parker's aunt and cousin, led by
the family mule "Hattie," in Orangeburg, South Carolina, early 1950s.

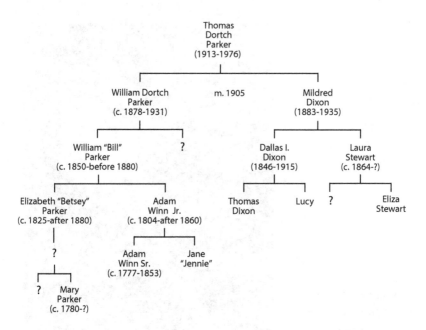

the terrain did not allow for large-scale plantations. By the time that cotton production became a major industry in the 1850s, rice cultivation was in decline and tobacco was grown for home or local consumption only. As Lisa Y. Henderson notes, "Wayne County was located southeast of the best tobacco land, southwest of good cotton-growing soil, and due north of the swampy expanses that rice required."[49] That left most Wayne County farmers to primarily cultivate beans, corn, peas, and sweet potatoes. Once railroads began crisscrossing the county, farmers found new and distant markets for their goods.

Native Americans, Maroons, and the Free Black Community

Wayne County had a significant pre–Civil War free Black community of which the Parkers were a part. The community experienced significant growth in the 1830s (230 percent) and by 1840 comprised 464 individuals split among 77 separate households headed by men and women.[50] By 1860, Wayne had the ninth highest free Black population of North Carolina's eighty-six counties and accounted for about 5 percent of the state's overall free Black population.[51] Many free Black people in the area had been long-time residents and had accumulated enough wealth to rent or buy their own land, first appearing in significant numbers in real estate deals in the 1830s.[52] Some of the most notable families also moved there around the same time or just prior, such as the Winn family, who soon formed families with the Parkers, coming north from Duplin County.[53]

The position of free Black people in North Carolina before the Civil War was a precarious one. Free Black people could own property and move from place to place, but they could not attend public schools like white residents. The rising prominence of free Black people in the 1830s began to draw hostility from the white population. After several free Black people were implicated in an aborted slave revolt in neighboring Duplin and Sampson counties in 1831, having been inspired by Nat Turner's recent uprising in Virginia, white petitioners began calling for the exile of all free Black people from the state.[54] Furthermore, the free Black population lost its right to vote across the state in 1835, again as a reaction to Turner and the fear of additional uprisings. In Wayne County in the 1830s there was the collusion of prominent landowners in the area kidnapping free Black people—especially children—and enslaving or selling them, while other free Black residents were regularly "harassed by challenges to their freedom."[55]

The earliest figure in the family who can be identified in the record is Parker's great-great-grandmother Elizabeth "Betsey" Parker (b. ca. 1825), a woman of English and possibly Irish ancestry.[56] She had been orphaned at an early age, grew up in poverty, and was raised primarily by her paternal grandmother, Mary Parker (b. ca. 1780). Betsey Parker's parents' names are not known, and nothing more is known of her origins or that of her grandmother. Once she reached adulthood, Betsey headed her own household for the rest of her life, having a long relationship with Adam Winn Jr. (b. ca. 1804), who, together with his father, Adam Winn Sr. (ca. 1777–ca. 1853), were among the most prominent free Black people in eastern North Carolina prior to the Civil War.[57] Adam Winn Sr.'s exact origins are unknown, but oral history and DNA evidence make clear that at least a portion of his ancestors or those of his wife Jane ("Jennie") could be traced back to the Native American Waccamaw tribe, although African ancestry made up the greater part of their heritage.[58]

The Waccamaw were Siouan speakers who had been pushed inland from the South Carolina coast by European incursions and conflicts with other tribes in the seventeenth century, and then were displaced again into what is now the southeastern part of North Carolina in the century following.[59] Through this process, the Waccamaw came into closer contact with other Siouan-speaking Native Americans such as the Cheraw, Pedee, and Saponi, as well as other indigenous groups such as the Tuscarora (Iroquois speakers from the eastern piedmont), Hatteras (Algonkian speakers from the North Carolina coast), and a number of other small groups from the North Carolina–Virginia border region. These groups, diverse and eclectic in origin, came together in 1735–87 in the area of Drowning Creek (also known as the Lumber River) in what would later become Robeson County, North Carolina.[60] They chose the area because it was firmly removed from the reach of colonial governments, and as one historian illustrated it, they "could live outside of English control and nurture their community."[61] Oral tradition indicates that there was a fusion of certain numbers of diverse peoples who eventually coalesced to form the Lumbee Indians, a tribe that has never received official recognition by the United States government despite being the largest U.S. tribe east of the Mississippi River. English became the lingua franca of these communities.[62]

Adam Winn Jr.'s free status, his Waccamaw blood, and the family's close ties to the Native Americans of Robeson County suggest that his ancestors escaped slavery somewhere farther east and found refuge in a maroon community either directly affiliated with or near the indigenous settlements there. It is likely that his grandparents were the first to arrive in the region, around the 1750s or 1760s, when the community of refugees, displaced Native Americans, and Africans who had escaped slavery converged to form settlements in the region that were, at least at that time, beyond the control or infringement of the American colonial government and its military detachments. The "low-lying swamps of lazy, rippling black water" of Robeson, especially Burnt Swamp Township to the west of Lumberton, seem to be the most likely place where the family first settled in the region.[63]

Maroon communities like the one that the Winn family was a part of were consciously set well apart from white communities, such that "once the scouts had selected a site that provided concealment, inapproachability, invisibility, and sustainability, the community could settle down." Such communities were often made up of people "who had come together at different times, from different places, with different stories. Some joined alone; others were couples, families, or friends."[64] Often after maturing their crops, the initial surveyors and settlers would then return to retrieve other family still enslaved on plantations and farms. For the Winn maroons, they found asylum within or near the Native American groups of the area with whom they built family, community, and solidarity outside of or against white society, for a time.[65]

Although no description of the Winns' maroon community exists, there are surviving accounts that bring such communities to life in other parts of North Carolina, namely the Great Dismal Swamp of the eastern part of the state, and these communities persisted until well after emancipation.[66] Abolitionist and writer Frederick Douglass noted that the community there comprised "uncounted numbers of fugitives," although more recent historians have estimated their total numbers to be around 2,500 people. The numbers no doubt fluctuated in the nearly two centuries that maroons inhabited those areas.[67] Eighteenth-century observers noted that many maroon communities lasted for generations, with children and grandchildren of those who formed maroon communities there being born free of white society.[68] Some maroon communities grew substantial enough to have their own preachers who led worship in the communities or traveled between settlements through the waterways of the swamp.[69]

In places like the Burnt Swamp, people would construct houses or even temporary settlements on stilts. When axes were not available for fashioning timber into home-construction materials, they built homes out of mud, sticks, and bark.[70] Over time, the maroon communities grew and strengthened in numbers and came with knowledge of house building and agriculture that they used to sustain themselves. Within the swamp, maroons moved around freely in bark canoes, hunting wild game, especially during the summer, when many animals migrated deeper into the wettest parts of the swamp.[71] Fashioning their own bows and arrows, log traps, and deadfalls, they hunted bears, beavers, deer, ducks, frogs, muskrats, opossums, otters, partridges, quail, snakes, squirrels, turtles, and wild hogs and cattle. In the winter, maroons often grew corn and sweet potatoes, and raised hogs and a variety of fowl.[72]

Wetlands in the Drowning Creek area were home to hardwood trees, with lower densities of pond pine and Atlantic white cedar, all of which were obtained for local use and valuable in trade.[73] The waters, streams, and certain portions of the swamp were inhabited by redfin pickerel, which were harvested and eaten by the inhabitants.[74] The landscape in the Burnt Swamp was filled with pocosins, which were wide, shallow basins constantly rejuvenated from water sources underneath and were particularly fertile and rich in resources ranging from plants and rare medicinal herbs to peat for fuel.[75] Maroons and Native American inhabitants of the area manufactured bark, herbs, and roots they found there into medicines, such as the sweet-smelling Carolina jessamine, which could be used to cure jaundice, reduce fever, eliminate pain, and treat respiratory problems.[76] Those who were unable to acquire cloth through trade or manufacture their own leather had to rely upon clothing made from animal skins, fur, and bark, which they made to look like leather for the purpose of camouflage.[77]

How the Winn family acquired their wealth remains a mystery, but it seems that they either had a leadership position within the maroon community or developed some means for a profitable business within it. Some free Black people in Wayne County and neighboring areas worked in the turpentine trade, but they could have as well earned it via farming or acquired it through some inheritance. Regardless, in the second decade of the nineteenth century, Adam Winn Sr. emerged from obscurity and began buying property to eventually establish himself as a significant figure. Although most free Black people of North Carolina lived in poverty, Winn was a bold exception to this. Little is known of his early life other than the fact that he had at least five sons and a number of nephews who were also counted among the free Black community in the area, many of whom left prominent descendants who, after the Civil War, worked as justices of the peace, commissioners, postmasters, carpenters, blacksmiths, and farmers.[78] Members of the family also later founded the Winn Chapel Church and the first school for Black children in Wayne County.[79]

Around 1819, Adam Winn Sr. began acquiring property in the Mount Olive area of Duplin County and neighboring Wayne County. He and his son, Adam Jr., had acquired more than 700 acres by 1836.[80] Most of their acquisitions were in agricultural swampland and swamp pastureland because the Winns were familiar with the potential yields from their experience in the maroon community. Then, in 1837–38, Adam Winn Jr. was forced to sell some land to the Wilmington & Raleigh Railroad (which is now part of the Seaboard Coast Line), although this yielded a clear profit. Through this process, he became one of the most prominent free Black people of the area, buying and selling land, crops, and livestock with many white landowners and businesspeople. In 1850 he owned 1,900 total acres assessed at $3,800, which at the time was quite a sum.[81] However, mounting debts and consistent legal opposition began to undermine his position in the 1840s, and at some point in the 1850s he lost everything. Records are not clear about exactly how Adam Jr. met his undoing, but it appears that wealthy white landowners conspired to sue him for debts, using courts and a biased legal system to bring about his downfall.

At the same time, Adam Winn Jr.'s personal life was quite complex. For one, he was a slave owner himself.[82] Although he never married, he carried on long-term relations with at least three women concurrently and fathered

Figure 1.4 America Young (1820–1900), sister-in-law of Adam Winn Jr. (1804–?), Parker's great-great-great-aunt, Wayne County, North Carolina.

at least twenty-four children. His earliest family was with one or more enslaved women (one of whom was named Venus), and he had at least seven sons and four daughters through these unions in 1830–46. These children remained enslaved, and some were used as collateral in his business ventures in the late 1840s or even sold in the 1850s to offset his mounting debts.[83] Simultaneously, Winn also maintained households with Betsey Parker and Susanna "Larkey" Newell, producing six and seven children with them, respectively. The children of these unions took their mothers' surnames and were born free.[84] The mothers of Winn's children were all quite aware of his other relations, for they lived on neighboring plots of land. Betsey Parker is usually designated as "white" in records where race is indicated, although in the 1870 census she was classified as "mulatto," along with her children. According to similar records, Susanna Newell was white.[85]

Betsey Parker and Adam Winn's son William "Bill" Parker (b. ca. 1850), Parker's great-grandfather, appears not to have lived to the age of thirty, leaving two orphans to be raised by their grandmother Betsey.[86] The younger of the two orphans was Parker's grandfather, William Dortch

Parker (ca. 1878–1931). The status of the family had fallen considerably following Adam Winn's financial ruin, the general economic collapse of the former Confederate states following the Civil War, the early death of Bill, and the political environment after Reconstruction.

Social disruptions to the free Black and enslaved communities of Wayne County and neighboring regions brought on by the Civil War began when the Union army took the coastal town of New Bern from the Confederates on March 14, 1862. From that point on, free Black and enslaved peoples began to regard New Bern as a haven and began fleeing there such that by January 1865, more than seventeen thousand people of African descent had relocated to Union-held parts of North Carolina.[87] Still, many enslaved people of the area around Goldsboro were not content to wait for freedom, and evidence of a coming insurrection spread, discovered via a messenger caught in Robeson County aimed at uniting enslaved and perhaps Native peoples, although it never materialized.[88] Another, more effective campaign was waged by the Lumbee Henry Berry Lowry against the Confederates, and after the end of the Civil War, it evolved into a fight against the reassertion of white supremacy.[89]

Goldsboro, because of its importance as a railway center, was a strategic target, but it was not until General William Tecumseh Sherman's Carolinas campaign that the town was captured in March 1865. Goldsboro also experienced an influx of African American residents, and between 1860 and 1880 the African American population nearly doubled in the town, increasing from 6,188 to 12,124 (shifting from 41.5 percent of the total population to 48.6 percent). Goldsboro's railroads and the resurgence of the cotton industry in the state brought new opportunities to the region, but the benefits of these were reserved entirely for white residents.

Reconstruction and the Undermining of Emancipation

Reconstruction brought divided politics to Wayne County and much of eastern North Carolina. African American Republican candidates did carry a number of state congressional seats in the area in the 1870s and included one U.S. Congressman, John Adams Hyman, but the Democratic Party machine remained resilient. Goldsboro twice hosted the congressional district Democratic nominating convention, in 1872 and 1880, although the local African American newspaper, the *Goldsboro Star*, voiced consistent support for the Republicans.[90] Having never been really united even during the Reconstruction Era, the North Carolina Republican Party was in full disarray by the 1880s. Black representation in state government hit its peak then, but quickly diminished, and by the turn of the century, laws were put in place to prevent African Americans from voting, which simultaneously dismantled the Republican Party as an effective political force.

Without representation, and facing laws and a legal system set to marginalize and terrorize African American citizens, the gains of Reconstruction were quickly undone.[91] In 1881 public schools were established for African American children for the first time in Goldsboro, but the taxes to support them were segregated along racial lines. Hamstrung by the narrow tax base of the impoverished African American community, these schools struggled to provide education, and after support was increased to schools for white children in 1901, the already struggling schools for Black children fell further behind.[92] Between 1888 and 1900 the resurgent Democratic Party found its center based around a newly articulated ideology of white supremacy. One of the ways that this new white political consciousness coalesced locally in the Goldsboro area was in the formation of new newspapers such as the *Caucasian*, based in the nearby town of Clinton; the paper bore the official slogan "Pure Democracy and White Supremacy."[93]

Set against the backdrop of the post-Reconstruction period, William Dortch Parker, or Dortch as he appears in all public records, must have struggled considerably. We unfortunately know very little of his early life. After having been orphaned by age two, he and his older brother Scott were raised first by their grandmother Betsey and, after her death, by their father's sister, Polly Parker (b. ca. 1852), who never had children of her own.[94] By the time that Dortch was in his mid-teen years, he had fathered a son, Willie, and he later married the child's mother, Hessie Bennet, in 1897.[95] What happened to Hessie is unknown, but in 1905 he married a second time to Mildred Dixon, and they went on to have four daughters, Lauretta, Bessie Lee, Polly, and Millie, as well as one son, Thomas. Of these children, all grew healthy into adulthood, except Polly, who died in infancy.

By 1910, Dortch was employed as a wagon driver for a department store, H. Weil & Brothers in Goldsboro, which had been founded by Herman Weil, a Jewish immigrant from Oberdorf, Bavaria, who had arrived and founded the business there in 1858. Weil's business became one of the most successful in Goldsboro.[96] During Dortch's employment there, the company included a dry goods store, a brickyard, and an ice plant. Dortch worked for Weil all his life as a porter and laborer, and although his job supplied only meager

Figure 1.5 H. Weil & Brothers, Center Street, Goldsboro, North Carolina, ca. 1920, where Parker's paternal grandfather, William Dortch Parker (ca. 1878–1931), worked in 1910–30. Courtesy of University of North Carolina Library.

wages to support a family, by 1930, just before his death, Dortch owned a home of moderate value.[97]

Dortch's wife, Mildred, was the daughter of Dallas I. Dixon, an enslaved person from Durham County who, after emancipation, moved to Goldsboro and worked first as a railroad hand. By 1880, he was a brakeman, a skilled-labor position that must have garnered additional income.[98] In that capacity his primary responsibility was braking the train at the conductor's signal, but he was also tasked with ensuring that the couplings between cars were sound, lining switches, and relaying signals to other crew members. He traveled about the region, riding in the caboose, as was customary for brakemen at the time. Because Goldsboro had become a regional rail hub, his work could have taken him northwest to Raleigh, north to Halifax, south to Wilmington, and east perhaps all the way to the coast.[99] Despite his holding this position for a number of years, Dallas's success did not last. By 1900, he had been reduced to a day laborer. A decade later, he worked as the janitor for the Baptist church that he regularly attended, while he lived two doors down from Mildred and Dortch in Goldsboro.[100] His death certificate notes that he was the sexton of the church, where he would have been tasked with its upkeep and with acquiring supplies for its congregation, and he may have also overseen the maintenance of its graveyard.

Music in the Wayne County Area

It is difficult to determine exactly what music the Parker and Dixon families would have experienced in their lives in the early decades of the twentieth century. However, it is possible to reconstruct bits and pieces of the African American music culture of eastern North Carolina in those years. Goldsboro had a reputation for a strong gospel tradition that dates back to the nineteenth century.[101] Thus, it was in churches that much of the region's music was taught, maintained, and passed down from generation to generation. Music was public, it was central to Christian worship, and it often served as a focal point for both sacred and secular gatherings.

Guitar playing was particularly popular, as was the piano, bass guitar, washboard, tambourines, drums, and even rarer instruments such as the ukulele.[102] When standard drum kits were not available, musicians would play on whatever they had. As one Goldsboro resident described it, "We would get some of those old lard stands and some of those old big, whitewash pots. We would get some of those old canning jars. We would get some old pieces of tin like they used on roofs . . . and we'd take five-gallon buckets and set all of the stuff up around us."[103] Then people would break tobacco sticks in half and use them to play the assembled percussion instruments accompanied by whatever other instruments they had. The same resident recalled his grandmother "had an extraordinary gift of rhythm with her hands and her feet. She would clap her hands and move both of her feet at the same time. She could make her hands sound like drums, her feet would sound like the beating of a bass drum, her hands could sound like the melody of a snare or bongos . . . and she could do it so powerfully and so loud."[104]

Many families revolved around music. As one longtime resident recalled, "We would play music from morning to late at night. Sometimes my mom would sing while we played."[105] Family reunions often involved people gathered around a porch on a hot summer's day, with numerous guitars, a bass guitar, tambourines, and whatever drums were available, while people sang spirituals, gospel songs, or folk music. Music often inspired dance at such events in what people called "foot shouting."[106]

Other than sacred music, the blues was the most common type of music in the area. Chick Wooten, who later toured with the doo-wop band the Corsairs, recalled the blues musician A. J. Percy, who was active in the Goldsboro area in the 1920s and 1930s. Percy "had a really heavy voice, was humpbacked, and his vest rode way up his back. He used to sing that song, 'Rock Me, Mama,' and he could really pull it down."[107]

Jazz arrived in the area as a locally practiced art form by at least the mid-1930s, although traveling bands had passed through at an earlier date. One of the earliest bands mentioned in local newspapers was Lee Darden and his band the Harlemites, formed in 1934, which were described as "the hottest band in town."[108] They played regular engagements at local clubs, casinos, and for African American dance halls, as well as touring on a circuit that ran from Raleigh to New Bern. The region was also home to J. Tim Brymn (1881–1946), an early ragtime composer from nearby Kinston, and the monumental pianist Thelonious Monk (1917–1982) from Rocky Mount, although they made their names—and their music—in New York City.[109]

Leaving North Carolina

In the 1920s, when Dortch and Mildred's son Thomas Dortch Parker (1913–1976) was growing up, the Ku Klux Klan (KKK) was gaining strength in North Carolina. Having garnered an initial following during the Reconstruction Era, the KKK had dwindled by the turn of the century. *The Clansman* (1905), a novel by Baptist minister and onetime Goldsboro resident Thomas Dixon Jr., ignited a nostalgia for the organization among some white people, and it became the inspiration for D. W. Griffith's deeply racist film *Birth of a Nation* (1915). The film, which reached a nationwide audience, sparked a resurgence of the KKK in the South and spurred substantial growth in northern cities, with the Klan gaining approximately four million members nationally by the mid-1920s. North Carolina also saw a considerable increase in Klan membership through the decade, especially in white communities that were located near African American population centers such as Raleigh and Durham to the north of Wayne County.[110]

One night, not long after his father's death, in 1931, Thomas Parker was out walking and got stalked by members of the KKK. The story he told—the only thing he ever told his son about life in the South—mentioned men in white sheets and that he ran through a graveyard and escaped to a road and never looked back. He hitchhiked all the way to New York City in the weeks that followed, joining his older sister Bessie, who had already settled in Harlem. Later, Parker recounted that his father never talked about Goldsboro and never returned to North Carolina ever again, not even for his mother's funeral in 1935. When asked, Thomas said, "I didn't leave nothin' down there."[111] Parker never recalled his father reminiscing or talking about growing up, food, family, or anything else. Thomas arrived in New York making a clean break with his past and was determined to start a new life.

Harlem Renaissance

The Harlem Renaissance was the most vibrant cultural center produced through the process of the Great Migration.[112] In 1914 the African American community in Harlem numbered just 50,000 people. By 1920, their numbers had swelled to 80,000, and a decade later the community had grown to 200,000.[113] Through this fusion of diverse peoples from across the southern United States, the Harlem Renaissance—a cultural wave of poets, writers, musicians, dancers, performers, and other artists—was born.

Thomas likely arrived in Harlem a few years before Parker's mother, Mary Louise, did. Both had prior short-lived marriages. Thomas had married a woman named Viola, and in 1935–40 they lived together at 126 Bradhurst Avenue with a view of what is now Jackie Robinson Park.[114] One of the first jobs that Thomas got was as a house painter. Mary Louise Jefferson had married a man named Benny Pratt, another Orangeburg native, but they separated by 1939, and she moved north.[115] After arriving in New York City with her sisters Carrie Lee and Alberta ("Bert)," she lived for a number of years in Harlem at 425 West 146th Street and worked as a seamstress.[116]

Both of Parker's parents were witness to the power of the Harlem Renaissance, replete with clubs, restaurants, churches, and public spaces that had achieved a cultural dynamism for African Americans unparalleled up to that point in their history. By the time of the Parkers' arrival in the 1930s, the African American parts of Harlem stretched from West 111th up to West 151st streets and from St. Nicholas Avenue to Lexington Avenue, with the exception of the area around what was then known as Mount Morris Park (today Marcus Garvey Park).[117] The area of greatest cultural activity was between West 131st and West 144th streets and between 8th Avenue (today Frederick Douglass Boulevard) and 5th Avenue.

On 7th Avenue (today Malcolm X Boulevard) between West 131st and West 135th, there was a stretch of clubs where jazz and blues were regularly performed.[118] The Band Box Club, at 161 West 131st Street, for instance, hosted regular jam sessions until it closed in 1935. Across the street, the Barbecue boasted "the best ribs" as well as the first jukebox in all of Harlem.

HARLEM RIVER

Thomas Parker residence, 1935–40

Mary Louise Jefferson residence, 1940

ST NICHOLAS AVENUE

BRADHURST AVENUE

SEVENTH AVENUE

LENOX AVENUE

146TH STREET

142ND STREET

Cotton Club

140TH STREET

Savoy Ballroom

Capital Palace
101 Ranch Club

138TH STREET

Renaissance Casino and Ballroom

135TH STREET

Lincoln Theater

Hot-Cha Bar and Grill

Bamboo Inn

133RD STREET

Pod's and Jerry's Catagonia Club

Lafayette Theater

Joplin's Boarding House

The Corner

Band Box Club

131ST STREET

The Barbecue

Connie's Inn

127TH STREET

Alhambra Ballroom

Apollo Theatre

125TH STREET

Hollywood Cabaret

124TH STREET

Both clubs were situated near "the Corner," where musicians played outside, busking for donations from passersby. Down the street near 8th Avenue, the widow of the famous ragtime player Scott Joplin ran a boardinghouse where the likes of pianists and composers Jelly Roll Morton (1890–1941), Eubie Blake (1887–1983), and Willie "the Lion" Smith (1893–1973) lived at various times.[119] Up 7th Avenue at West 132nd, the Lafayette Theatre, known as "the House Beautiful" and the first major New York theater to desegregate, was a 1,500-seat auditorium that had included groundbreaking work with Black actors already in the 1920s, Duke Ellington's New York debut in 1923, and early performances by pianists Fletcher Henderson (1897–1952) and Bennie Moten (1894–1935) and drummers Chick Webb (1905–1939) and Zutty Singleton (1898–1975).[120] Most famously, in 1936 the theater featured the play *Voodoo Macbeth*, Orson Welles's adaptation of the Shakespearean classic, set with an all-African American cast. The basement beneath the Lafayette Theatre was a performance space for the Hoofer's Club, which included trend-setting tap dancers such as Bill Robinson (1878–1949) and Chuck "Honi" Coles (1911–1992).

On 7th Avenue between West 133rd and 135th was another string of important cultural centers.[121] Pod's and Jerry's Catagonia Club had been a popular speakeasy during Prohibition and featured acts such as Willie "the Lion" Smith until it closed in 1935. At the Hot-Cha Bar and Grill on the corner of 134th, the young Billie Holiday (1915–1959) was discovered in the early 1930s and by the late 1930s was signing contracts with major American record labels such as Columbia Records, bringing more widespread attention to the Harlem music scene. Farther north, at the corner of 138th Street, the Renaissance Casino and Ballroom featured music, dancing, and Harlem's first great basketball team, the New York Renaissance, which was the most dominant professional basketball team in the United States during the 1930s, playing many local games as well as across the country.[122]

On the northern periphery of the Harlem hotspots was the Cotton Club at 644 Lenox Avenue at West 142nd Street. Managed by notorious mobster Owney "the Killer" Madden, the club featured some of the most important jazz acts of the period, including pianist-composer Duke Ellington's breakthrough performances in 1927–31.[123] At the same time it was under pressure from Ellington that the club was desegregated during his tenure as house bandleader. Ellington was followed by Cab Calloway's Brown Sugar revue (1931–34) and saxophonist Jimmie Lunceford's orchestra (1934–36), before the club moved down to Midtown Manhattan to appeal to a different audience.

Where exactly in all of this activity Thomas and Mary Louise each placed themselves is not known. They were far from being connected to the class of African American notables that had risen to fame in Harlem at the time. We do know, though, that Thomas in particular developed his love for jazz in the live setting during these years, long before he ever owned his own record player at home. He frequented the jazz clubs when he had enough money to do so, and it was there that his dream for his children to grow up to be musicians was born.

Jazz ultimately brought Thomas and Mary Louise together. One night in 1943 they met while dancing in the Savoy Ballroom on Lenox Avenue at West 140th Street. It was a popular hotspot in a culturally vibrant part of Harlem that inspired "Juke Box Love Song" by poet Langston Hughes (1902–1967):

> I could take the Harlem night
> and wrap around you,
> Take the neon lights and make a crown,
> Take the Lenox Avenue busses,
> Taxis, subways,
> And for your love song tone their rumble down.
> Take Harlem's heartbeat,
> Make a drumbeat,
> Put it on a record, let it whirl,
> And while we listen to it play,
> Dance with you till day—
> Dance with you, my sweet brown Harlem girl.

Harlem nightclubs in the 1920s–1940s featured many dances that African Americans had brought with them from juke joints and other dance halls in the South, and many dances could be traced back to African roots.[124] During those years the Savoy was one of the premier places for men and women to meet publicly for entertainment, dancing, and courting. In addition, the Savoy had been one of the leading points of genesis for new dance forms, most famous for the Lindy Hop in the 1920s, and by the 1940s, the dance hall's innovators had developed the jitterbug, among other swing dances.[125] Mary Louise would often go there with her sister Carrie Lee and Carrie Lee's husband, Joseph "Uncle Joe" Edwards. One such evening while Mary Louise was there, she met Thomas. After dancing together, they struck up a romance and were soon a dedicated couple.[126] By the end of 1944, they moved across the river to the Bronx, ready to start a family.

Two

Struggle, Beauty, and Survival: Childhood in the South Bronx

once as a child

i walked two

miles in my sleep.

did i know

then where i

was going?

—— **Sonia Sanchez**

William Parker—or Billy as his family called him when he was young—was born on January 10, 1952, at the Bronx-Lebanon Hospital on Fulton Avenue. He was the second of two boys, arriving just fifteen months after his older brother, Thomas Jr., who grew up as Tommy. Billy's birth came more than two months premature, and he arrived with a clubfoot and a heart murmur. As an infant and toddler, he underwent a series of operations to correct his foot and grew to be a very healthy, athletic youth. His brother got his father's formal name, but Thomas Sr. was actually called "Bill" within the family, so in a way, Parker was named after his father as well, not to mention his grandfather and great-grandfather.

The Bronx was home for young Parker for the first twenty-three years of his life. The various apartments that the Parkers would later call home were located in or near the neighborhood known as Morrisania. When the Parkers moved into the neighborhood in the mid-1940s, Morrisania had already seen waves of Irish, German, East European, Jewish, and Italian immigrants pass through it. African Americans were often confined to the least-desired housing, near the rail yards or railroad tracks.[1] At the time of the Parkers' arrival, the Black population numbered about 25,000 people. The Claremont area, comprising the blocks right around where the Parkers eventually lived, became the most concentrated Black community in the entire Bronx, especially in the areas between East 169th Street and Claremont Park.[2] In what eventually became termed "urban blight," concentrated areas of poverty and poor-quality housing emerged in these areas, often along train lines, near factories, or in polluted or peripheral areas along the waterfront.[3]

The Parkers were a part of a wave of Black migrants from Harlem from the 1940s to the 1960s who were attracted to the area by the robust church communities, racially integrated schools, and a modestly successful business district that contained some of the most vibrant music venues in all of New York City.[4] The move north was generally considered to be a "step up" to better and more spacious housing.[5] A similar influx of Puerto Ricans settled in the Bronx at the same time; thus, by 1950, there were approximately 160,000 African Americans and Puerto Ricans living in the Bronx, nearly all of them in the South Bronx. This trend continued such that a decade later there were more than 350,000 African Americans in the Bronx, and more than three-quarters of them lived in the South Bronx.[6]

For a time in the 1950s the neighborhoods were generally safe, with strong communities that looked out for each other. There was a sense of optimism. Black neighborhoods were expanding into four- and five-story row-house walk-ups that were hardly elegant but were an improvement from the areas adjacent to the rail yards and polluted waterfronts where most Black residents had been confined in earlier years. Despite all of the challenges that they faced, "Morrisania [was] a dynamic, cohesive, fundamentally hopeful black community . . . in the 1930s, 1940s, and 1950s."[7] One resident described Morrisania in those years as a "viable community of hardworking people who had hopes and dreams for the future."[8] Another resident stated that despite de facto segregation and all the other challenges that the community faced, "Men who didn't have college degrees could get jobs. They weren't the greatest jobs, and certainly not the highest paying, but it was enough to keep a family going and to maintain a small sense of hope that better days were coming."[9]

The Parker family's first home was located down the hill from the Bronx-Lebanon Hospital at 1351 Washington Avenue, where they lived in a tene-

Figure 2.1 Parker family on roof of tenement house at 1351 Washington Avenue, Bronx, 1952. Father holds Parker's brother, Thomas; infant William is swaddled in his mother's arms.

ment house.[10] When Billy was still quite young, the building burned down, and the family moved temporarily into the Melrose Houses, a public housing project at 304 East 156th Street. These were newly built public housing buildings that totaled 1,891 units and more than 5,000 people in a neighborhood where more than 22,000 people were concentrated in public housing.[11] After another set of public housing projects, the Claremont Houses, were built around 1964, they moved back into their old neighborhood at 450 East 169th Street, near Washington Avenue. It was part of a vast stretch of public housing south of Claremont Park that was built during that time; each building was sixteen stories high with nine apartments per floor, altogether holding tens of thousands of people. In 1969 Parker made a passing reference to the conditions of the projects in his diary: "No mice right now but broken elevators and dirty halls."[12]

Although the projects originally included many Jewish and Italian families, within a year of the Parkers' arrival, only the African American families remained. Everyone else—except Billy's friend Joey Buller's family—left for the north Bronx, Westchester, or Long Island as a part of widespread white

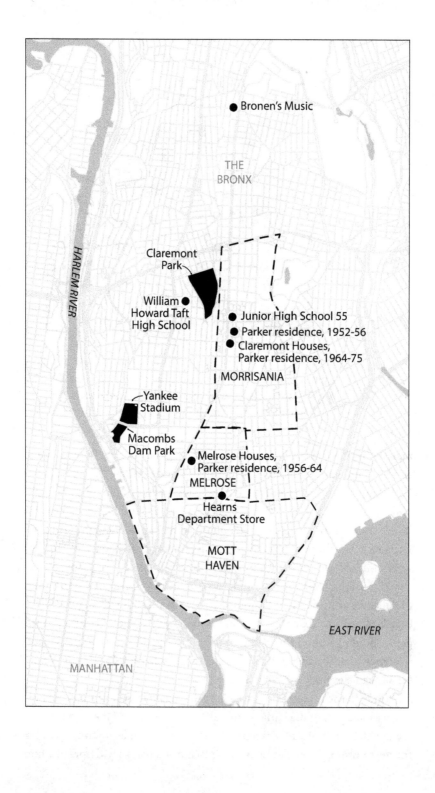

● Bronen's Music

THE
BRONX

Claremont
Park

William ●
Howard Taft
High School

● Junior High School 55
● Parker residence, 1952-56
● Claremont Houses,
Parker residence, 1964-75

MORRISANIA

Yankee
Stadium

Macombs
Dam Park

● Melrose Houses,
Parker residence, 1956-64

MELROSE
●
Hearns
Department Store

MOTT
HAVEN

HARLEM RIVER

EAST RIVER

MANHATTAN

flight to the suburbs. Together with wide swaths of lower Mott Haven, lower Morrisania, and western Melrose, the public housing projects that the Parkers inhabited became the face of intense urban poverty in the South Bronx.[13] Tens of thousands of people moved from the Bronx to Westchester or Nassau counties in New York and to Bergen and Essex counties in New Jersey. One local Christian minister observed that Claremont, where the Parkers would live most of their years, was "one of the most highly deprived socioeconomic areas in the Bronx."[14] "The projects could define who you were only if you let them" Parker stated. "People could leave to go to work, but there were no facilities, nothing positive to do, no cultural centers to help people to thrive. They pushed us all together, Blacks and Puerto Ricans, and there was nothing there to empower people."[15]

Thomas Sr. originally worked as a pinsetter at a bowling alley and then worked for a time in a bakery. But in 1948 he got a long-term job as a furniture polisher and repairman at Butler Furniture on East Broadway in the Bronx.[16] Aside from fixing old or damaged furniture brought to the shop, he could also repair anything damaged during shipping.[17] At the time that Mary Louise met Thomas, she worked as a seamstress, making bags of all kinds—garment, lingerie, linen, and laundry—for the Arnel Company on Fourth Avenue.[18] Their combined crafts enabled the couple to refurbish old furniture for their home, which they kept in immaculate condition, covered in gold-colored upholstery.[19] After working as a full-time parent, Mary Louise resumed paid work in 1958 as a teaching aide with the school lunch program in the Bronx public schools, a position that she held until retiring because of ill health in 1975.[20] Through the 1950s and early 1960s the family survived on about $3,500 per year, living in poverty.[21] In 1962 Thomas got a job at Morris Pall & Son, just a few doors away from his previous job, and his earnings increased. Together the Parker couple grossed approximately $7,000 most years through the 1960s.[22]

The family remained in poverty but managed to direct its small amount of expendable income toward pleasures for the children. When they needed to do shopping, they went to Hearns Department Store on the corner of Third Avenue and 149th Street. Parker could recall no Black-owned businesses in the area where he grew up. Although there were small restaurants along the commercial district, the Parkers never visited them because they had no means to do so. Instead, Billy created a whole world of toy trains and imagined going from city to city, while checking the *World Book Encyclopedia* to learn the distances between each stop. On special occasions, Billy and Tommy would go to Yankee games, where they could get bleacher seats for

Figure 2.2 William and Thomas Parker, brothers, at 145th Street near St. Nicholas Avenue, Harlem, ca. 1955.

seventy-five cents.[23] As Billy and Tommy got older, their father gave them what little extra money he had so that they could buy jazz records.

Mary Louise organized many of the family's social events. She didn't have friends, but she had family.[24] Being the eldest of ten children, that was her social world, and she spoke to her siblings and in-laws on the phone nearly every day. Her best friend was Thomas's sister Bessie Smith, who was like a second mother to Billy. On weekends, Aunt Bessie would come over, "and she'd start talking with my mother. They wouldn't stop talking until Sunday night when Aunt Bessie left, talking about the carpet, the curtains, ways to fix up the house."[25] Parker composed a poem in honor of these memories:

> *It is another Friday afternoon*
> *aunt Bessie is over for*
> *the weekend*
> *I am looking out the window*
> *the horizon is white-violet*
> *the smell of hot rolls*
> *fills the air*

Figure 2.3 Parker's parents,
Mary Louise and Thomas,
late 1960s.

> *there is talk about*
> *furniture, making curtains*
> *my mother knits me a*
> *colorful hat like the*
> *one Don Cherry wears*
> *Don can't wait to taste*
> *the rolls*[26]

With a close-knit family came a lot of pride. When Billy went to school, his mother said, "When they ask what your father does for a living, tell them he's an interior decorator." She insisted on branding his work as a furniture repairman in another way: "It was the insecurity of living in poverty. If my father had been a janitor, they would have told me to tell people he was a sanitation engineer."[27]

The South Bronx of the 1950s in which young Billy Parker grew up was a place in transition. Great changes were being wrought upon the physical landscape of the borough. Most famously, the Cross-Bronx Expressway, designed by strong-arm urban planner Robert Moses, was built between 1948 and 1972. Moses saw the South Bronx as a crossroads for commuters coming from Westchester and beyond, rather than a community with its own integrity.[28] Unlike previous parkways built in the borough, the Cross-Bronx Expressway split "a dozen solid, settled, densely populated neighborhoods."[29] The highway destroyed neighborhoods, led to the forced eviction of thousands of Bronx residents, undermined local businesses, and pushed significant numbers of working-class residents further into poverty.[30] As one Black resident recalled, "The Cross-Bronx Expressway had a negative impact on neighborhood life and the economy of the South Bronx. It took out a lot of those blue-collar employment opportunities" and played a role in the deindustrialization of the South Bronx that destroyed the local economy in such a way that Black residents were disproportionately affected.[31] Between 1947 and 1976, New York City lost a half-million factory jobs, and the loss was particularly acute in the Bronx. Between 1970 and 1977, three hundred companies left the Bronx, taking tens of thousands of jobs with them.[32] Unlike in Manhattan, where white, middle-class activists led by Jane Jacobs managed to thwart Moses's plans, outcries in the Bronx were pushed aside, despite organized vocal resistance to the city planning. The devastation of the South Bronx was to be largely ignored by the city, and it was now possible for thousands of white commuters living in the suburbs to bypass the area completely.

The building of the expressway further destabilized neighborhoods that had once been among the most diverse in the city. White residents found ways to leave the South Bronx. This process of white flight was immortalized by the Temptations in their song "Run, Charlie, Run" in 1972. The idea emerged that it was best to move farther and farther north in the Bronx.[33] Although some better-educated Black and Puerto Rican families also left, this resegregation of the community along class and racial lines left a fractured community of primarily Black and Latino communities that plunged into poverty.[34] Hemmed in by vulgar automobiles, abandoned by businesses and job opportunities, and vacated by white flight to the suburbs, the South Bronx became the face of African American urban poverty and the system of structural violence that maintained it.

Heroes

The Parkers' apartment served as an escape from the growing problems faced by South Bronx residents. Parker's mother cooked the family a full breakfast every morning of biscuits, chicken livers, eggs, corn bread, and other southern fare. She would also bake chocolate cakes and sweet potato or apple pies two or three times a week. They were poor, but she did what she could with what money they had, raising the two boys with staples of the food she had grown up on in South Carolina. Parker later reminisced about the food the family ate growing up, mentioning chocolate cake, apple pie, sweet potato pie, peach cobbler, fish, greens, and corn bread in his diary. Mary Louise also sewed all of the clothes for the family and made quilts for their beds.[35]

The Parker home was always filled with music, and Thomas Sr. loved jazz. In the beginning the radio was their sole means for hearing whatever the latest jazz hits were at any given time. When Billy was still quite young, though, his father bought a small box record player and would send the boys to the store with a few dimes to acquire 45s. Over the years they managed to build up a good collection of soul music and many issues on the Motown label (founded in 1960) and subsidiary labels such as Gordy Records and Soul Records. They also purchased jazz records through record clubs, where they would pay a dime to get ten LPs. One tradition was that when Thomas Sr. came home from work, he would put on records by Duke Ellington (1899–1974), the most popular of which was his recordings at the Newport Jazz Festival in 1956.[36] The kids would play "dance contest" and were particularly inspired by Paul Gonsalves's twenty-seven-chorus solo in the middle of "Diminuendo and Crescendo in Blue."[37]

Saturdays were family time for the Parkers because Thomas was off work that day. They would spend the whole day listening to the growing collection of records that he had assembled. Other than Ellington, the family listened to Ben Webster, Coleman Hawkins, the ballads of Johnny Hodges, Eddie "Lockjaw" Davis, and the lesser-known Willis "Gator-Tail" Jackson. When they got older, records such as Ellington's *Soul Call* and *Far East Suite* were mainstays, as well as Jackson's *Together Again, Again*, with Jack McDuff on organ, and Ella Fitzgerald's collaboration with Ellington, *Ella at Duke's Place*.[38] As Parker later recalled, "We didn't have a lot of records, so we listened very deeply to the ones we had. If my father was having a few drinks with his friend Mr. Rayford, a television repairman . . . sometimes we listened to the same record all day!"[39]

Although it would take many years for young Parker to articulate in words why he was drawn to music, he recalled that it was his father's influence via records that made him realize "that there was a tremendous power in music. It was the thing that accompanied the great ceremonies in life. By ceremony I mean the sun rising and setting, ocean waves moving towards the shore as birds take off in flight."[40]

He was also drawn to music through more lighthearted means. For Christmas one year, Billy and Tommy got a Fanner 50, a set of toy guns made by Mattel to be used in such games as cowboys and Indians. But the Parker kids never used them for their intended purpose. Instead, they pretended they were trumpets and played jam session. "I'm Walnut Jones," one of them would say, "and I've been soloing for three weeks now," and then the other would grab an imaginary microphone and introduce his character.[41] Parker and his brother thought musicians had a certain allure because they dressed nicely and had an aura of style and success about them.[42] Parker also used a broom as a bass, working the handle with the rhythms and scales he played in his head. Between playing imaginary instruments and dancing to the tunes in their heads (or to records they played along to), the boys built their first relationship with music and performance.

Saturdays were young Parker's day to wander, if he did not have any other commitments. He would walk down Melrose Avenue, go to Third Avenue, and, if he had money, buy a record and come home and listen to it. He also had a small notebook in which he wrote poetry or diary entries about things that he was then observing. He also encountered things that opened up his eyes. One refuge for Billy was the Bronx Botanical Garden.[43] It was an escape from the deteriorating urban landscape that was otherwise overwhelming. He found the colors of the flowers very stark and fascinating, and loved the feeling of peace that he got when he was there. Flowers would have symbolic meaning to Parker throughout his life as sources for inspiration and truth, and this began with his occasional visits to the gardens as a boy.

In the gardens and in other parts of the Bronx, Parker found magic, things that lit the flame of his imagination or that served as escapes from the toil of the day to day. He recalled seeing magic in "the clouds, in the people, in the sounds of kids playing in the playground. I just had to grab things where I could find them because I was in the dark. I didn't know which way was up."[44] But things would come along that would pop out. Sometimes he did not even remember or think about them until many years later. Parker wrote:

> It's as if
> I loved you
> More than
> I could see
> Yet the Sky Is Still Dancing[45]

"I always hear people talk about the magic of Harlem. For me, I felt that way about the Bronx," Parker said.[46] The alertness to seeing magic in the things around him, first manifesting during his childhood growing up in the Bronx, is something that Parker has continued to carry with him his entire life.

The neighborhood that Billy Parker grew up in had music as the central, unifying feature. Figures such as jazz trumpeters Henry "Red" Allen (1908–1967) and Jimmy Owens (b. 1943), vocalist Maxine Sullivan (1911–1987), pianists Valerie Capers (b. 1935) and Eddie Palmieri (b. 1936), Latin jazz percussionist Ray Barretto (1929–2006), and many others were prominent figures in the local scene. As the economy improved in the 1950s, venues such as Kenny's,[47] Club 845, Blue Morocco, Goodson's, and Hunts Point Place ("the Apollo of the Bronx") proliferated along Prospect Avenue, Boston Road, Westchester Avenue, and Southern Boulevard, featuring Afro-Cuban music, jazz, rhythm and blues, and calypso, while drawing eager audiences of Black and Latino residents.[48] Although the Harlem jazz scene generally overshadowed the Bronx scene, after the Harlem clubs closed for the night, Bronx players would retreat to the Boston Road Ballroom for late-night sets.[49] Beyond the clubs, music happened outside on street corners, in church choirs, and in public school bands. Later in the 1970s and 1980s, after public school budget cuts severed the lifeblood of jazz from this community, the neighborhood's next generation of innovators would give birth to hip-hop.

Parker's father also had other heroes. One was Geronimo (1829–1909), the Apache leader who led many raids against the U.S. along the Mexican border and who Billy's father talked about all the time. He also kept a scrapbook with pictures of sports figures like Willie Mays and fighters like Joe Louis, Sugar Ray Robinson, and Muhammad Ali, as well as commercials or newspaper articles that featured Black people in general. In many ways, these were measures of success, people to admire and to emulate.[50] His father was friends with Floyd "Stumpy" Brady, a trombonist in the Count Basie Orchestra, which gave Thomas Sr. an eye into what the life of a working musician was like.[51] But above all, Parker's father loved Ellington. And it was not until years later that Parker reflected that "it was my father's dream for my brother and me to grow up to play in the Ellington Orchestra. He never said that then. It was too big of a dream. But now reflecting back, I can tell that's what he wanted most of all."[52]

When Billy was ten or eleven years old, Thomas Sr. saved up money and bought him a trumpet (and an alto saxophone for his brother) that he obtained from a pawnshop. "I loved those old instrument cases, the smell of them," Billy later reminisced. He began with mail-order trumpet lessons that his father had seen advertised in a magazine. A company sent him a new lesson each week, but the impersonal nature of it did not really motivate him to take the lessons all that seriously. So eventually Billy went with his brother to the New York School of Music on 149th Street in the Bronx. Later, Tommy studied with a teacher named Fats Green, "who kind of looked like Cannonball Adderley," but stopped after a short while.[53] In junior high school, Billy switched to trombone, but he still had not really found his calling in music. He did play a cello for a couple years in junior high or early high school, which would eventually spark an interest in the bass.[54]

As Billy and Tommy got older, their father would sometimes give them a couple of dollars on Saturdays to go buy records at Hearns Department Store. By 1960, monaural records were being replaced by stereo recordings, so all of the mono records were cheap, ranging from $1.49 to just $0.29. On their excursions the two boys would buy their father a record or two and then get ones for themselves. At first, they bought mostly records on the Verve label, but soon they discovered Atlantic Records. "They looked different," Parker recalled, "but for a long time we'd just look at them in the store. Then, eventually, we began buying them."[55] Through this process they stumbled upon John Coltrane (1926–1967) and Ornette Coleman (1930–2015). In particular, Coleman's groundbreaking *Free Jazz*, with the Jackson Pollock painting on the cover, stunned them both.[56] Although their father did not have an interest in that music, the Parker brothers listened to it on an inexpensive record player that they had in their room.[57]

When he ran out of money one time, Billy asked his mother for twelve dollars for his class ring. He used it instead to buy the Jazz Composer's Orchestra self-titled double record.[58] Mary Louise kept asking, "When is that ring gonna come?" and he would reply, "I don't know what happened, Ma." Years later, Parker sheepishly remarked, "That's how I would do. I'd get money to buy something and buy a record. I couldn't help it. I really had to hear what they sounded like."[59] He did the same thing buying football equipment. He would also buy cheaper clothes, save fifty cents on one thing, twenty-five cents on another, and after a while be able to buy a few more records. The summer before his senior year, he had a summer job in a mail room and used whatever he earned to buy records. His appetite as a listener was insatiable.

In high school one year, Billy became friends with a guy named Manny, who always came to class with drumsticks sticking out of his back pocket. Once in a while they would talk about music. One day, Manny had a magazine in his pocket along with his sticks. Billy asked to see it, and it was his first time reading *DownBeat*, which at that time still covered avant-garde jazz. Soon after, he read a review that Dan Morgenstern wrote about saxophonist Albert Ayler (1936–1970), something to the effect that "the group sounded at times like a Salvation Army band on LSD."[60] And at the time, Billy thought, "Wow, what does that sound like? Man, that must be some sound."[61] Inspiring music, amid the social maelstrom of life in the South Bronx, was the saving grace of Parker's childhood.

Struggling in the South Bronx

In the mid-1960s the South Bronx neighborhood where the Parkers lived got considerably more impoverished. At the same time the institutions that might have otherwise offered opportunities for better lives remained hostile to African Americans. Education in particular was a difficult environment for many children. On the one hand, it theoretically posed as an avenue to opportunity, but the institutions themselves were not designed for Black students to succeed. Parker and his brother attended William Howard Taft High School, at Sheridan Avenue and 172nd Street, which had a student body that had been mostly white from the time of its founding in the 1940s up to the early 1960s. Parker recalled his first day at the school as frightening.[62] He wrote in his diary during his sophomore year there that "I do not like school, I am shy and enjoy the world inside my head. The world inside is never cold, it does not engage me or take my lunch money. It does not steal my basketball or threaten to beat me up if I wear the wrong color shirt." He believed that he needed something to latch on to in order to feel comfortable, and "eventually that became art and music."[63]

The twofold forces of white flight and the creation of specialized magnet schools that often drew high-performing students left Taft High School quickly unintegrated, with a primarily African American student body and deprived of adequate resources to serve an impoverished community. Parents often organized to demand equal resources for their children, especially when the differences were so stark.[64] And even though *Brown v. Board of Education* was a landmark case in 1954, the schools of the Bronx were often becoming more segregated at that time as demographics in the neighborhoods changed.[65] Students had to take a test to get into the good schools, which resulted in most poor kids attending underfunded and inadequate schools. Though for a few years, Taft High School was highly integrated in the early

1960s, many white residents soon transferred their children to neighboring districts, thus reinstituting de facto segregation again by the mid-1960s, just like the public housing projects.[66]

The lack of Black teachers was also a consistent problem for Parker and his classmates. One Black Bronx student later wrote of the transformational moment when she had her first Black teacher: "I instinctively connected to her. The feeling was one you might have with a relative you knew would not harm you. I guess I felt secure."[67] But most students did not have such an opportunity.[68] As pianist Cooper-Moore put it in colloquial terms, "When you're in ghetto schools, teachers do triage on you. Some kids are worthy, some aren't worthy. Kid A is going to jail, kid B is going to be dead before the age of fifteen, maybe we will focus on kid C."[69] Although Parker always did well in school, he still never felt connected to the education, and he felt the constant pressure to conform. He recalled many kids his age being pushed to the brink of despair at the situation around them.

For Parker, one incident epitomized his feeling of alienation at school and the explicit racism that festered there. He wrote about it years later in the liner notes of his record *In Order to Survive*:

> In 1964, I was attending Junior High School 55 in the South Bronx. One morning instead of going to math class the boys in my 7th grade class were escorted to the school auditorium. We were going to listen to a lecture given by guidance counsellor Mr. Peseroff. The subject matter of the lecture was our future careers. I waited with great anticipation to hear what choices of work would be available to me. To my surprise the entire talk centered on not how we would succeed within the society, but how we would fail. We were flat out told that we were not going to make it. That our future destiny was to be messengers, janitors or stock boys. We were told that we would be pushing racks of clothing through the 34th Street garment district. There was no encouragement to be doctors, lawyers, engineers, teachers, or priests. At twelve I was told that I had no future. The crime committed by our guidance counsellor that day was one against the nascent hope that was stirring inside of us looking for confirmation.[70]

Junior High School 55 was the school for kids from the Claremont projects. Peseroff also told them "to get their parents to sign them into a vocational high school." Even then, the purpose was not so that the kids could have become auto mechanics or electricians but rather that "you aren't ever going to be anything in life."[71] These were the kinds of social forces that led one observer to state around that time, "The whole atmosphere [of the

South Bronx] is geared to crushing a person's spirit, and most people don't have the kind of strength to resist."[72]

At the same time, Parker said, "There is this idea that we are being held down by ourselves, by our parents." His mother in particular did not set a high bar for him to reach. Mary Louise had dropped out after sixth grade, and Thomas Sr. had left after eighth grade. "My grandfather couldn't read or write," Parker explained. "My parents could read, but quit school early. They just wanted me to finish high school. That seemed like a big accomplishment to them. And then my mother always wanted me to get a government service job like postal delivery. That was seen as the dream because it was stable, it was reliable. That's what they wanted me to do."[73] Parker's uncle, Lemuel Jefferson Jr., "could play the electric bass and really sing the blues," and he performed with his son Larry, who played the bass and sang. The husband of Parker's Aunt Bessie, Smitty Smith, was supposedly related to the alto saxophone player Talmadge "Tab" Smith (1909–1971).[74] So Parker's family had some familiarity with the lives of musicians, although his mother wanted him to pursue something with more certainty.

Mary Louise bore the legacy of growing up in the segregated South, however, and she discouraged the two boys from leaving their neighborhood: "I remember my mother had this extreme fear of venturing very far away. She said we belong in the Bronx and we don't go downtown." Once, when his high school Spanish teacher, Vincent Vassallo, invited the class for tea at his apartment on West 73rd Street in Upper West Side Manhattan, his mother would not let him attend. She told him, "Oh, you can't go there. They're not gonna let you in. They're gonna have a doorman and he's not gonna let you into the building." Parker further recollected, "When my mother came to New York, she never met any white people. She never had any white friends. No white person came to our house, ever. She was from the South and that's how she was brought up. You stay in your place. You don't go into other neighborhoods. You shop at Black businesses, you go to Black theaters and so forth. She thought we weren't supposed to mix."[75]

By the late 1960s, the situation in Morrisania had reached an intense level. Businesses were leaving, undercutting the availability of local jobs. Then arson led to the burning of a huge number of properties. More than half of Morrisania's housing stock was destroyed by the early 1970s, and it was one of the epicenters for the burning of the Bronx, where a fifth of the total housing was destroyed and a quarter of the population left.[76] One resident described the situation: "There seemed to have been a fire every night in various areas around me. The burning of stores and that sort of thing.

The streets were becoming dirtier; the garbage wasn't being picked up as it should be—the people were becoming such that they didn't care one way or another."[77] Other residents recalled the experience of watching the neighborhoods burn as they rode the elevated subway trains along Third Avenue or Jerome Avenue during morning commutes.[78] Fires destroyed residences and pushed the neighborhood further into poverty for those who remained. The burning also chased out the Black audience that had once frequented the jazz clubs at the heart of the neighborhood, which bankrupted all of the small music venues for which the area had been famous during the previous two decades.[79]

Survival

Although music was always present in his life, Billy grew up with a wide range of interests. A self-identifying introvert, he found sports to be his connection to the community, drawing him out of his shyness. Through sports he met a number of characters in the neighborhood: the Downs brothers, the Berry brothers, John Daly, and Paul Butler, all basketball players. Puerto Rican Frankie, Little Timmy, Big Timmy, Alonzo, and Scoop were the guys who just hung out around the projects, checking stuff out.[80]

Then there were the neighborhood personalities like a guy everyone called Pusshead, who, if one was not careful, would steal basketballs, coats, or shoes. One guy had a mother who was mentally ill and would routinely carry his little brother up to the roof of the projects and threaten to throw him off, so they would have to call the cops. Then, of course, there were the tough guys who carried knives or other weapons who one had to avoid or placate somehow. Parker described the experience of growing up in the projects: "It was like a maze. If you could get through from ten years old to eighteen, those years from junior high through high school, without being shot, stabbed, beaten up, bullied . . . or doing those things to others, you were very lucky because it was a breeding ground for things like that."[81]

Day-to-day life had many potential dangers, some catastrophic. Out on the street, Parker might encounter people who wanted to fight, people who would pull knives, or police who would stop and harass him. He just did his best to avoid those situations, to block out the emotional and psychological impact, and keep going.[82] And although some other kids became good friends, some who were desperate might double-cross a friend or neighbor. One night, some of the same people who Billy played basketball with tried to rob the Parkers' apartment. "People were pretty desperate at the time and things started to get pretty rough," Parker recalled. "Every once in a while, I would get into a scuffle, a tight spot, but I was lucky. I always managed to get out of it without too much collateral damage." His brother, Tommy, was not so lucky—he got stabbed once and had to be hospitalized. Although he survived, the attack was a constant reminder of the unpredictable day-to-day existence that kids faced in the neighborhood. There were also physical boundaries one did not cross: "We'd never go across the street to the Patterson projects, because that was someone else's turf and we'd get beat up if we went over there. So, we stayed close."[83]

In the 1960s crime escalated astronomically in the South Bronx as the community fell apart, poverty became concentrated and institutionalized, and opportunities for residents eroded dramatically. Assaults more than quadrupled between 1960 and 1969, and burglaries increased more than sixteen times over. Heroin also hit the South Bronx in the mid-1960s and devastated Morrisania, although Parker never saw the drug personally.[84] Other people witnessed the fallout. "From what I could see," one resident said, "there was a major epidemic happening."[85] In the beginning it was just a few isolated cases, but soon addiction to heroin afflicted large numbers of people, and this played a direct role in the escalating violence. "Mostly young men [were affected]. It started in the early 60s, but it was in the mid-60s when I really started to notice it," one resident stated.[86] Often, street gangs were organized to eliminate drug dealers from communities. "I started hearing about folks that I grew up with getting thrown off rooftops because they were dealing. For the first time, I started to feel fear, not only for myself, but for the whole community," another community member recalled.[87]

Athletics was one way that people tried to get out of life in the projects, especially through baseball, basketball, or football.[88] Like a lot of kids, Billy and Tommy spent considerable time on the basketball courts in the park near the projects. Boys from the neighborhood would meet there every day, and games would go on from mid-morning until sundown from spring until autumn. Once in a while Thomas Sr. would come down and watch. If it was a hot summer day, he'd give the brothers a little money and say, "Get everyone an ice pop."[89]

Billy and Tommy both played a lot of football, too, and joined the Buddy Young Football League, which had teams in the Bronx, Harlem, Brooklyn, and East Orange, New Jersey.[90] The league was named for Claude "Buddy" Young (1926–1983), an early African American professional football player who was best known for his years as a running back with the Baltimore Colts and was at the forefront of desegregating the National Football League and paving the way for other Black athletes.[91] The league itself had been founded in 1965 by Harlem-based photographer, journalist, and youth worker Carl Nesfield, who looked to imbue young minds with leadership skills via football.[92] Building a league in the impoverished areas of New York's Black communities had its challenges, and the league faced regular funding shortages.[93]

Football was relatively new to Harlem as a pastime for youth, and because of the equipment and space required, it was expensive. The league looked to community organizations for funding and support, such as the United Block Association (UBA), a technical resource for block associations in Harlem with which Nesfield was affiliated, but it also appealed to popular figures.[94] The most famous of these was Jimi Hendrix, who, just weeks after doing his famous Woodstock concert, performed on a four-foot wooden stage outdoors at the conclusion of "a rambunctious block party" in his old neighborhood at the corner of Lenox Avenue and 139th Street for a benefit to support the UBA on September 5, 1969. Hendrix's Gypsy Sun and Rainbows played a set that included "Fire" and "Machine Gun," as well as "Voodoo Chile," which he introduced as "the Harlem national anthem." His participation had been arranged by Hendrix's friends Arthur and Albert Allen, the activists known collectively as the Ghetto Fighters.[95] At the event, Hendrix said, "Sometimes when I come up here, people say, 'he plays white rock for white people, what's he doing up here?' Well, I want to show them that music is universal—that there is no white rock or black rock."[96] Although the audience was famously resistant to his music, he did still draw many to the venue that one observer described as "neighborhood residents and a handful of young white rock fans."[97]

By 1968, eight hundred boys and young men between the ages of eight and twenty participated in the league.[98] The Parker boys played their games every Saturday and Sunday through the fall season in Macombs Dam Park, across from Yankee Stadium in the Bronx, or at other football fields in Harlem. The league was racially integrated, but as Parker characterized it, the white players "were white street cats, white people who were cool with Black people. There were some Puerto Rican kids. It wasn't about Black or white. If you could play, you were accepted. I liked being around people who were different, but who were right."[99] Recruiters would come from local colleges and see the players there; if they were good, they might get signed. Parker even played against John Brockington (b. 1948), who went on to play for Ohio State and had a distinguished professional career with the Green Bay Packers in the 1970s. Billy played free safety and punter and was very good, even being voted most valuable player one year. He was skilled enough that he could have tried to get a college scholarship. The team itself was very good, too: "We played against the semi-pro teams and we did okay." But as Billy was finishing high school and began to feel the call to music, he remembered thinking, "Once I committed, I decided I am going to really do music, that is what I am going to concentrate on. I pretty much dropped everything else."[100] He also observed at the time that many of his friends began having kids around age sixteen or seventeen, and he avoided that if for no other reason than he was shy, but he also had other things he wanted to do before having a family.[101]

The summer before his senior year of high school, the wife of one of his teachers, Vincent Vassallo, got him a job in the mail room at Touche Ross, an accounting and auditing firm. For a while, he used the money to buy records: "I tried, but I couldn't stay there. I felt bad. I thought I had let my teacher and his wife down. But that's the way it was. I couldn't do it."[102] A deep consciousness of himself and his potential as an artist had been stirring within him for a number of years, finally coming to the surface.

Through the 1960s and 1970s, the Parkers stayed in their neighborhood. Some of Billy's cousins moved to the North Bronx and settled on Needham Avenue. Parker recalled other families moving out and buying houses or renting elsewhere. The Parkers were never able to afford to move out. Thomas Sr. lost his job in November 1969, and the fragile family finances collapsed. As Parker, then seventeen, wrote in his diary, "My father lost his job, my mother is spending many hours a day applying for welfare."[103] In 1973 some thieves broke into the Parkers' apartment and beat up Thomas Sr., an attack from which he never fully recovered, either physically or spiritually. On June 16, 1976, Thomas Sr. went to the Bronx-Lebanon Hospital feeling short of breath. He waited hours and faced racist questions such as "What drugs are you on?" despite never having used drugs of any kind.[104] Hours passed with little concern for his condition when a doctor who had not been assigned to his case happened to pass by. He checked Thomas's breathing with his stethoscope and concluded that he suffered from a collapsed lung. Later that night, before receiving any of the proper treatment he needed, Thomas's condition triggered a heart attack. Parker never got to say goodbye. He had moved down to the Lower East Side, was living on food stamps, and did not have $1.50 to pay for the carfare to the Bronx. By the time he heard from his mother, it was too late. Parker pawned some BYG records to take a taxi to console her, and the two organized a funeral. Parker wrote these words in memory of his father:

One day the drum of my father
would no longer speak
and
there was no sweet laughter blowing from the
rooftops
bodies die
spirits live.[105]

To add to the family tragedy, just two years later Tommy Parker died of a suspected drug overdose, and although he had moved to an apartment on 137th Street in Harlem, "He never really made it out."[106] Parker's brother was buried alongside their father in the Bronx's Woodlawn Cemetery.

Three

Consciousness: Art, Politics, and Self in the Mind of a Young Man

Black music has been the vanguard reflection of black feeling and the continuous repository of black consciousness.

—— **Ron Wellburn, 1971**

The Black Arts Movement is radically opposed to any concept of the artist that alienates him from his community.

—— **Larry Neal, 1968**

"Living in the projects was not really conducive to a poetic life, but at the same time, it was really a postcard for poetics," Parker mused many years later:

> In the Bronx, we always had the sky. In between the projects—those concrete mountains—was light. As a kid, I remember first noticing it when I was out collecting bottles on the street. We could get two cents for glass bottles, so we would walk around and pick them up. I looked up and I saw the light from the sky shining through creating a silhouette of the buildings. It was then that I realized light reaches people wherever they are. Somehow, if you are fortunate enough, you turn and look over your shoulder at some point and notice it is there.[1]

Still, as a teenager Parker was filled with the anxiety of poverty and the social marginalization that stemmed from it. Questions of deep longing reverberated around in his head: How am I going to get out of these projects? How am I just going to pay rent? What am I going to do, and how am I going to do it? He was not sure what to expect on a day-to-day basis, how things would go, where his path ahead might lead: "But things would happen every day, self-discovery that would take away the worry. Things would happen that reassured me that I was on the right track, even if the path was not clear to me as I went forward. I would just get up and see what the next step was going to be."[2] The seeds for his self-realization were planted at an early age and were nurtured to fruition through a threefold process of self-respect, spirituality, and an autodidactic hunger for art and knowledge.

Black Power, Personal Sovereignty

The Black Power movement instilled a sense of newfound pride in Parker as he grew up. His mother had raised him to feel ashamed about certain aspects of being African American. As a boy, she made him put clothespins on his nose when he slept to try to make his nose smaller. As poet Amiri Baraka (1934–2014) would write at that time in the poem "An Agony. As Now," "I am inside someone / who hates me. I look / out from his eyes."[3] Parker recalled feeling social pressure to straighten his hair with Conkolene, a product whose slogan was "If your hair is short and nappy, Conkolene will make you happy." Or in a related way, as Parker's daughter Miriam elaborated, "My father's family raised him with the idea that to deal with racism, you have to be small and not get in the way."[4]

In 1968 author Julius Lester began hosting a radio show on WBAI on which he featured free jazz, and Parker recalled first hearing Marion Brown's *Afternoon of a Georgia Faun* on the show.[5] WBAI's commitment to cultural and political commentary had grown out of a broader national movement within the Pacifica radio network in Los Angeles, San Francisco, and New York. Lester hosted a program called "The Great Proletariat Cultural Revolution," which gave voice to the Black Power movement and issues broadly concerning African Americans.[6] He urged people to not just be "empty followers" but to think for themselves. It woke Parker up when Lester asked, plainly, "Who told you your hair was bad?" And Parker began to face the self-hate that had been instilled in him. Some of his growing self-respect was also spurred by public figures who already were in the limelight, such as when entertainer Sammy Davis Jr. quit straightening his hair or when the "Godfather of Soul" James Brown wrote the song "Say It Loud—I'm Black and I'm Proud!"[7]

The Parker family would sometimes buy copies of the newspapers *Muhammad Speaks*, sold on the streets by members of the Nation of Islam. The paper featured speeches by Elijah Muhammad, which Parker recalled often bore such themes as "the White man is the Devil." But the message did not resonate with him. Many of his sports heroes—Bart Starr, Ray Nitschke, Johnny Unitas—were white, and he did not see them as the Devil. "But what I saw as the Devil was the mistreatment of people, the disrespect shown to Black people. The Vietnam War. Those things were clearly wrong."[8]

One negative repercussion for the Black community that young Parker observed in the late 1960s was what he referred to as "the Black narcissistic attitude." He was surrounded by people who thought that how you look is more important than how you feel, that there was still a prevailing focus on how to assimilate into society rather than striving to be true to oneself. He thought of his resistance to this as "maintaining my own sovereignty as a human being." Blackness then was about "the way we walk, the way we talk, rather than how that would come to be commodified later on." Still, he also resisted accepting a "uniform for Blackness—hoodie, sneakers, low-hanging pants, or whatever it is at any given time, since it changes and is different from place to place."[9] He was committed to doing what he felt as an individual rather than accepting some cultural prescription or blending in with the crowd.

Revolutions in Sound, Word, and Image

Parker's greatest exposure to Black Power and cultural pride, however, came through art and music. Black music was central to Black identity and cultural formation. As Amiri Baraka wrote at the time, "Rhythm and Blues is part of 'the national genius,' of the Black man, of the Black nation. It is the direct, no monkey business expression of urban and rural (in its various stylistic variations) Black America." The totality of it was self-evident: "Identification is Sound Identification is Sight Identification is Touch, Feeling, Smell, Movement."[10]

The fusing of culture and politics at the time seemed natural, given the civil rights, Black Power, and Black Arts movements that were then intersecting. The civil rights movement had begun in Alabama and other parts of the American South in the mid-1950s as a struggle against Jim Crow laws, demands for equality under the law and equal opportunity, and efforts to end threats to Black life such as police brutality and lynching. The Black Power movement had emerged primarily in the urban North and West in places such as New York, Chicago, the Bay Area, and other cities in the early to mid-1960s and demanded Black political and cultural autonomy or separation, as well as realized political power. Writer Larry Neal (1937–1981), who first articulated the idea of the Black Arts movement, characterized it as the "aesthetic and spiritual sister of the Black Power concept."[11] As Baraka later reflected,

> Black art, in the sense that we first used it, meant not only an art that was an expression of Black life, but revolutionary art. The theater we spoke of was revolutionary theater, a theater that was black by color in that it was created by black people; black by culture, in that it was an expression of African culture; but also black in terms of its consciousness, that it wanted to create a political statement that would benefit black people. A theater that is revolutionary in that it seeks to transform reality; revolutionary in that it is a weapon in the arsenal of world revolution.[12]

Parker first encountered these various cultural, social, and political movements via television when he lived in the Claremont public housing projects of the South Bronx in the late 1960s. Beginning in 1968, after the assassination of Dr. Martin Luther King Jr. there was a rise in Black television programming for the first time on a wide scale, led by Black artists, producers, and writers. New York's *Inside Bedford-Stuyvesant, Positively Black,* and *Like It Is* got perhaps the most attention and broadest viewership, but major urban centers followed suit.[13] These television programs were invaluable to Parker in that they exposed him to a wide variety of art and politics in the Black community to which he would have otherwise had no access. Guests on television shows discussed, often in raw language, issues such as electoral participation, economic self-help, cultural nationalism, community policing, armed revolution, affirmative action, collective agriculture, separatism, and other strategies to address the challenges then experienced by Black society.[14]

The first television program that Parker recalled having a major influence on him was *Soul!*, a nationally broadcast series that appeared on Channel 13, New Dimensions in Television (WNDT), based in New Jersey. The project was initiated by producer Christopher Lukas, who had previously been involved in making a one-episode special called *Talking Black*, which one journalist described as "essentially an exploration of the new consciousness of blackness as a positive concept among Negroes."[15] Propelled forward by the first project's initial success, Lukas proposed to create a regular show that "would offer the best African American artists to a television audience." Once approved, Lukas hired theater producer Ellis Haizlip (1929–1991) as the program's curator and host.[16] For the thirty-nine episodes that made up its first season, beginning in fall 1968, *Soul!* was broadcast locally on a weekly basis and was subsequently distributed nationally. It was fantastically popular, such that when Parker tuned in to the program, he was part of the estimated 65 percent of Black New York City television viewers who watched it regularly.[17]

As the initial press release described the show, "The format of *Soul!* resembles some of the popular late-night programs—segmented, lively, informative and entertaining. Appearing on the show will be top stars and up-and-coming young talents from the black community. There will also be pertinent features dealing with all aspects of the social, cultural and artistic life of the black population."[18] In practice, the show aimed to bring the best African American artists, musicians, and other cultural figures to New York to speak with Haizlip in open dialogue and to perform their work live. Filmed on a vibrantly lit, multicolored stage, from innovative angles, the show featured a range of contemporary ideas, fashions, hairstyles, and foods, while the focus was on a broad range of art, poetry, and music.[19] The inaugural episode featured an interview with the revolutionary Last Poets, and later episodes brought a range of figures from mainstream cultural figures such as Sidney Poitier and Harry Belafonte; Black Power leaders such as Stokely Carmichael, Louis Farrakhan, and Kathleen Cleaver; musicians such as Odetta, Gladys Knight, and Earth, Wind, and Fire; and literary figures such as Amiri Baraka, Sonia Sanchez, and Toni Morrison.[20] *Soul!* "imagined the dawn of a new world."[21] Haizlip wrote many years later that the program's title was "a place-holder for an as-yet-unknown word—and world—would attempt to envision."[22] In a festival that Haizlip organized in 1972 titled Soul at the Center (held at Lincoln Center in New York City), he linked music inextricably to personal and collective identity and even more so to a sense of being: "Haizlip pursued the notion that sonic reflection was not only inevitable but also desirable . . . people need[ed] ambient vibrations to locate themselves, to know where they were and (in a collective sense) where they were heading."[23]

Through *Soul!* Parker became familiar with Amiri Baraka. At the age of sixteen, Parker would never have been able to predict that he would later share a stage with Baraka. Parker had been drawn to the show by a performance of multi-saxophonist Rahsaan Roland Kirk and soon became familiar with interviews that Haizlip, or guest hosts such as poet Nikki Giovanni or musician and record producer Curtis Mayfield (1942–1999), were conducting with Black musicians, writers, and other artists and intellectuals. The program became the primary avenue by which viewers such as Parker could access Black avant-garde arts performances that were not available locally.[24] The presentation of such an interactive, stimulating, and diverse Black public sphere in which artists could speak about the state of the country and the Black community was profound for Parker. In many ways *Soul!* was ahead of its time, not only breaking barriers for Black television but also casting light on Black female artists in a way never done before, and for igniting conversations about Black homosexuality that would not be outmatched for decades. Baraka, in many ways, was the epitome of the type of guest that Haizlip invited to the show, one who possessed a blend of the art and politics, made particularly effective through his dynamic performing style. Baraka read a number of his poems, including this one:

> All these me's together
> we need to get on outside ourselves . . .
> all these me's . . . need to hook up, hook up and form a we.

For much of the episode, Haizlip and Baraka were seated near a coffee table that held the guest's collected works between carved bookends and an African mask. Baraka critiqued the white literary scene of New York, commented on contemporary political and arts movements, and talked about the importance of the sanctity of Black families. For one, Baraka noted, just the act of a Black man and woman living together and raising children together was revolutionary in post-slave society, for enslaved people had been denied the protection of legal marriages: "Black people achieving health and normalcy . . . that will be revolutionary."[25] Baraka encouraged both the studio and home audiences to be active participants in their own liberation on all fronts: economic, physical, and psychological: "You work eight hours for white folks. Can you work one hour a day to liberate yourself?" This all came right at the time that Baraka was being vaulted onto the national stage as one of the major voices of the Black Power movement and liberation struggles.[26] As Devora Heitner commented, "*Soul!* unabashedly posited musicians, actors, and poets as experts on the state of Black people, of Black liberation,

Figure 3.1 Ellis Haizlip and Amiri Baraka on *Soul!*, late 1960s.

and of the political and aesthetic contribution of new cultural forms to Black identity and to the world at large."[27]

Another show, *Positively Black*, also influenced Parker. The show hosted figures "reading heavy poetry and talking about civil rights and movements in places like Newark and Bedford-Stuyvesant."[28] Parker recalled that his only encounter with any aspect of African culture as part of formal education was reading *Things Fall Apart* by Nigerian novelist Chinua Achebe in high school, but that still felt quite divorced from his own experience.[29] *Soul!* and *Positively Black* opened up a whole world to him. So Parker began buying small books by poets such as Larry Neal, Don L. Lee (later known as Haki R. Madhubuti), Gil-Scott Heron, James Baldwin, Nikki Giovanni, and Kenneth Patchen.

Early Awakenings

Avant-garde music was profound for Parker. What became known as avant-garde jazz, free jazz, or new Black music represented a complete rejection of chordal restrictions, and "as the music grew, it was evident that it was an insurrection against European musical bondage." Many of its early practitioners combined a keen spiritual sensibility or sociopolitical consciousness with dynamic creative energy. Emerging around 1957 in its earliest manifestations, the music was ahead of its time before the rebellious 1960s cultural wave that engulfed the United States and the globe.

Within circles of Black writers and critics, there was considerable public debate about the meaning of the new music. Critic Ron Wellburn noted that the "new aesthetic for black music was founded on feeling: black music was to give spontaneous expression to black feeling. Self/spirit became the focal point, individually and collectively."[30] Other writers at the time saw "the new music" as the latest expression of Black identity. For instance, A. B. Spellman saw its emergence as based on "a similarly revolutionary impulse" to how bebop first developed, and he criticized Eurocentric periodizations of the music that divided jazz into "primitive, baroque, rococo, classical, romantic, and atonal periods." Spellman argued that the music was "the imminent maturation and self-assertion of the black man in an oppressive American society."[31] French critics and theorists Philippe Carles and Jean-Louis Comolli were among the very few white critics of the time who seemed to recognize the political nature of the music and the cultural dynamics that produced it: "[The new music] purported to testify to the oppression of black Americans, to express their revolt, and even to play a role in their revolutionary struggle."[32]

Having encountered Ornette Coleman's record *Free Jazz* as a kid, Parker was already well-versed in avant-garde jazz at an early age.[33] Coleman had remained relatively unknown in many jazz circles until he performed with trumpeter Don Cherry (1936–1987) at the Five Spot in New York City in 1959. From there, his recordings went off like bombs, drawing some rare praise but generally facing considerable criticism. Coleman did not adhere to standard rules of twelve- or sixteen-bar blues, and he had a particularly spontaneous approach to playing. As one critic put it, "He starts any particular idea wherever he chooses, wherever he feels it, and the ideas often overlap choruses; he does not observe the conventional chorus break."[34] Another, more figurative response to Coleman noted that his music had been "described as raw, shrill, beautiful, repulsive, provocative, but rarely boring and always extremely personal."[35] But when Parker saw a poster advertising Coleman's record *At the "Golden Circle" Stockholm* with the trio standing in the snow and the caption that read "Ornette Coleman comes out of retirement. Plays at the Village Vanguard but he's added trumpet and violin," it was a turning point.[36] Parker was filled with excitement, intrigued even more about making music: "It wasn't until I got into the avant-garde that I really began to see some light, some heavy light within all of the confusion of my life. I realized then that I didn't want to pursue sports, I didn't want to be hip, and definitely not try to fit in. That was my path because that was something I could do and I felt comfortable in that area of music."

The music spoke to Parker and others in ways that no other music did at that time. As Baraka wrote, "The 'new' musicians are self-conscious. Just as the boppers were. Extremely conscious of self. They are more conscious of a total self than the R&B people who, for the most part, are all-expression." He added, "At its best and most expressive, the New Black Music is expression, and expression of reflection as well. What is presented is a consciously proposed learning experience. It is expanding the consciousness of the given that they are interested in, not merely expressing what is already there, or alluded to. They are interested in the unknown. The mystical." Baraka went on to argue that the New Black Music would be the music of the future: "It will include the pretension of The New Music, as actuality, as summoner of Black Spirit, the evolved music of the then evolved people."[37]

Jazz, and the free jazz of the 1960s in particular, had a profound effect upon practitioners across other artistic disciplines within the Black Arts movement.[38] For Parker, we see this in his earliest artistic yearnings, inspired by the poetry of the period. Poetry spoke to his soul, lifted him up from his circumstances, and made him feel like he was part of a broader community of people facing similar challenges. It came to occupy the void that a racist education left him seeking to fill, searching for something familiar to grab hold of, to firmly plant his feet upon to move forward in life.

Jazz Poetry

Music and poetry sometimes came already together.[39] One particularly strong example of this in Parker's coming-of-age moment was Baraka's recitation of "Black Dada Nihilismus" on New York Art Quartet's self-titled album.[40] The poem accompanied the song "Sweet," by Roswell Rudd:

> I
>
> Against what light is false what breath
> sucked, for deadness.
> Murder, the cleansed
>
> purpose, frail, against
> God, if they bring him
>   bleeding, I would not

forgive, or even call him
black dada nihilismus

[...]
the blacker art. Thievery (ahh, they return
those secret gold killers. Inquisitors
of the cocktail hour. Trismegistus, have

them, in their transmutation, from stone
to bleeding pearl, from lead to burning
looting, dead Moctezuma, find the West

a gray hideous space

[...]
in their bedrooms with their drinks spilling
and restless for tilting hips or dark liver
lips sucking splinters from the master's thigh

Black scream
and chant, scream,
and dull, un
earthly
hollering. Dada, bilious
what ugliness, learned
in the dome, colored holy
shit (i call them sinned

or lost
     burned masters
          of the lost
               nihil German killers
                    all our learned
art, 'member
what you said
money, God, power,
a moral code, so cruel
it destroyed Byzantium, Tenochtitlan, Commanch
[...]

As writer and Black Panther leader Eldridge Cleaver wrote of this poem, "I have lived those lines."[41] The poem spoke similarly to Parker. Baraka unveils a far-reaching vision in the poem, rejecting Christianity and denouncing European imperialism and colonialism in the Americas and the legacy of those intrusions. Some critics, unable to contextualize the work and missing some of its deeper meaning, denounced Baraka as normalizing a language of violence or even denigrating the art form with political rhetoric or acts of barbarism.[42] Baraka was digging deep into the violence, immorality, and trauma that Black Americans were enduring. As one writer observed of the poem, "The language of fragments, violence, and exasperation registers a despair of human history. [Baraka] is searching the darkness of a terrible freedom for a new principle of order—a new God and a new humane moral code; and he is searching still for a style which could give poetic shape to a seething mass of sensations. . . ."[43] Baraka's work with the New York Art Quartet was a landmark in recording poetry and jazz together and one that Parker found particularly potent, an inspiration for combining the art forms, or employing the tradition of jazz poetry that grew out of it, in his later work.

Another poetry-music integration that was similarly important for Parker was Joseph Jarman (1937–2019) reading the poem "Non-cognitive Aspects of the City" on the record *Song For*:[44]

> *[. . .]*
> *where Roy J's prophecies become*
> *the causes of children*
> *once quiet black blocks of stone*
> *encasements/of regularity*
> *sweet now*
> *intellectual dada*
> *of vain landscapes*
> *the city*
> *long history*
> *upheaval*
> *the heath valueless in its norm*
> *now/gravestone or gingercakes*
> *the frail feel of winter's wanting*
> *crying to leaves they wander*
> *seeing the capital vision*
> *dada*
> *new word out of the*
> *twenties of chaos*
> *returned in the suntan jar*

fruits of education/with others
non-cognitive—
these motions
embracing
sidewalk heroes
the city—each his own
where no one is more
alone than any other
moan, it's the hip plea for
see me, see me, i exist
exit the tenderness for power/black
or white
no difference now/the power/city

[...]

Could have spirits
among stones
uppity   the force   of
becoming
what art was
made to return
the vainness of our
pipes, smoking
near fountains, the
church pronouncing
the hell/of where we are
[...]

Parker found the work astonishing both in creation and in form. Like Baraka's recording with the New York Art Quartet two years previous, it was a part of the interdisciplinary work that was emerging within the Black Arts movement with politics, music, and poetry cross-pollinating. Parker, whose first practiced art form was poetry, was fascinated at the dictional power of the piece and its union to music that elevated its impact.

Parker had many sources of inspiration, but certain records were of particular importance. A short list of deep influences includes Coltrane's post–*A Love Supreme* period, including *Om, Meditations,* and *Live in Seattle;* the music of Frank Wright; the music of Albert Ayler; and Archie Shepp's *Fire Music* period.[45] In the liner notes of *Fire Music,* Shepp (b. 1937) wrote,

"We have to get into the lives [of the people,] which is one way of saying we have to get more and more into our own lives and know who we are so that we can say all that's on our minds."[46] Demonstrating this, Shepp wrote that the track "Hambone" was inspired by a character on New York children's television who was "both a mime and a practitioner of 'urban folk motifs.'"[47] Another example of Shepp's storytelling is "Los Olvidados" (The Forgotten Ones), which was inspired by Shepp's work as a counselor and music teacher with Mobilization for Youth, a publicly funded program that served communities on Manhattan's Lower East Side.[48] Parker considered all of these records to be cosmic music. Describing the impact, Parker wrote, "This music was the lifeline for many people because it had a cathartic effect on us. It was a wake-up call to our inner being." As he elaborated, "It was at first glance about inciting a spiritual revolution that is arousing the listeners of the music to begin to think and live in terms of their own spirituality. The definition [of the spirit] must be a living entity whose only justification is love and compassion for all."[49]

Parker found Shepp's poetry particularly poignant when paired with music, especially "Malcolm, Malcolm, Semper Malcolm," which Shepp recorded just days after the assassination of Malcolm X in February 1965:

> A Song is not what it seems
> A tomb perhaps
> Bird whistled while even America listened
> We played, but we aren't always dumb
> We are murdered in amphitheaters
> On the podium of the Audubon, the earth
> Philadelphia 1945
> Malcolm! My people, dear God!
> Malcolm!

The young Congolese writer Emmanuel Boundzéki Dongala, later a renowned chemist and novelist, described the poem: "It takes more than outright anger to compose the thrilling eulogy that Shepp did for Malcolm X . . . a work of tenderness and fury, of love and hatred, of passion and political vision. . . ."[50]

Parker was also struck by Shepp's work "The Wedding," seeing it as reflecting his own reality:

> We sat ten abreast
> On logs that stretched the entire length

Of the room
I knelt and kissed the ring on the Baptist's hand
"Thank you Jesus!" sister Beatrice said, "Praise him!"
This from the steely Black men
Whose corned haunches ached from the cold
Pearly May got down on her knees
So that the weight of the baby was shifted to her thighs
While outside, Black junior advanced on Panamanian red
And Hector stuck a spike straight into the ball of his eye
The buttered knife's cold of Lexington's flaws
Lay cleft between Hecate's breasts
And men's buttocks shivered
With the peculiar rhythms of bullocks to flies
They had been born in a Christian climate
And capitalism had picked them clean
[...]

Shepp's work is a biting critique of a society that had repeatedly betrayed its own principles, spoken to a generation that was full of revolutionary spirit. Dongala noted that "Shepp is giving an explicitly social dimension to jazz where it existed only implicitly. His saxophone is no longer a simple instrument, it's a weapon he believes in and it's not the only weapon he has."[51] For Parker, Shepp woke him up to "the revolution of music and the written word" that was happening in the late 1960s and 1970s.[52]

Parker looked beyond the music to other poets for inspiration as well. He was deeply impacted by the work of Nicaraguan poet and priest Ernesto Cardenal (b. 1925). Parker had the opportunity to see Cardenal read his poetry at St. Mark's Church-in-the-Bowery on East 10th Street.[53] The reading was in Spanish, but Parker recalled, "I didn't need to know Spanish to be moved by his words and feel his compassion for life."[54] "Hora o" (Zero Hour), in particular, spoke to Parker:

Noches Tropicales de Centroamérica,
con lagunas y volcanes bajo la luna
y luces
de palacios presidenciales, cuarteles y tristes toques de queda.
[...]
El palacio de Carías apedreado por el pueblo.
Una ventana de su despacho ha sido quebrada,
y la policía ha disparado contra el pueblo.

y Managua apuntada por las ametralladoras
desde el palacio de bizcocho de chocolate
y los cascos de acero patrullando las calles
¡Centinela! ¿Qué hora es de la noche?
¡Centinela! ¿Qué hora es de la noche?[55]

Parker considered Cardenal a revolutionary who was "totally committed to freedom and justice."[56] Cardenal's sense of urgency and justice, a theme that also emerged from a number of other of his seminal influences, spoke strongly to Parker.

First Creations: Writing

Poetry then turned him on to avant-garde playwrights such as the Polish theater director and theorist Jerzy Grotowski (1933–1999). Grotowski is considered to be one of the most influential figures in contemporary experimental theater, in which the performance is intended to enact a change upon an audience. In particular, Grotowski detected problems in modern life that theater could address:

> Theatre—through the actor's technique, his art in which the living organism strives for higher motives—provides an opportunity for what might be called integration, the discarding of masks, the revealing of real substance: a totality of physical and mental reactions. . . . Here we can see theatre's therapeutic function for people in our present-day civilization. It is true that the actor accomplishes this act, but he can only do so through an encounter with the spectator . . . in direct confrontation with him. The actor's act . . . is an invitation to the spectator. This act could be compared to an act of the most deeply rooted, genuine love between two human beings. This act . . . we call the total act.[57]

This sincerity, this openness and honesty, further compelled Parker to see the act of live musical creation as a transformative act for both performer and audience member.

Parker saw a long television program on CBS one Sunday morning that displayed the work of Grotowski, and it was the movement of the bodies across the stage that most caught his attention.[58] For Parker the sound and the movement were the dialogue of the drama, and the language and the silence were the shape, "all coming out of nature, the greatest teacher."[59] This way of thinking artistically inspired him to think differently and to feel comfortable in that difference. In all of the musicians, poets, filmmakers, and theater directors that Parker experienced, the common appeal was how they challenged prevailing norms, standards, and ways of thinking in the face of oppressive power structures or hegemonies of thought.

Parker's first period of active creativity was writing words, and he began composing poetry while in his early teens. The distribution of his writings to the public also seemed perfectly possible, inspired by the Black poets of the time who were often publishing, at least initially, with small presses. Because of all of the storefront publishers, community organizations, and Black cultural activism, publishing was actually fairly easy to do at the time. Parker set to work with pen and paper, writing "prose poetry," scenarios, and descriptions of cinematic images that he hoped to make a reality. He eventually signed a contract with Amuru Press, but the publisher went out of business soon after, before the collection ever went to press, so the poems were never printed at the time. Some of the material appeared many years later in *Music and the Shadow People* and in *Mayor of Punkville*.[60]

Film

Parker's fascination with words, ideas, and music also led him to begin a self-study of film by French directors Francois Truffaut (1932–1984) and Jean-Luc Godard (b. 1930), and Swedish director Ingmar Bergman (1918–2007), as forays into understanding human feeling and emotion. As film critics turned directors, both Truffaut and Godard had called for a fresher cinema that was situated more in the moment.[61] Truffaut's first feature-length film, *400 Coups* (400 Blows), dealt with the feeling of being alive, with spontaneity, and with the fleeting moments of life. Godard, on the other hand, used close-up shots to isolate people, free from distractions, and to emphasize the beauty of people or objects. In a way, Truffaut and Godard presented cinema as not just capturing real life but dwelling within it.[62] In a certain sense, these French New Wave directors caused movies to become a much deeper part of the human sensory experience than they had been before that time. Parker thought of their films as "all of these things together were making a big sandwich for me, a layer of this, a layer of that. And for me, the meaning of it all was always about the people, the kids growing up in the projects, poor people, the disenfranchised. It wasn't about being into art or telling people that I knew about the hip writers or filmmakers."[63]

Bergman woke Parker up to the broad spectrum of realities that people inhabited in other times and places. Bergman did much to make film personal, intended to have the intimacy be more like that of the theater, dealt with deeply impactful themes of human sense, touch in particular, and took an unblinking look at pain and death. The first of Bergman's films that Parker encountered, *Shame* (1968), is a film about the impact of war on the lives of a couple, Jan and Eva Rosenberg. The two are musicians—violinists—who had formerly held first chair in an orchestra that no longer existed and had retreated to an island where they run a small farm. Interestingly, however, *Shame* was the first full film that Bergman had made that had no music in it— its absence is felt deeply. As Bergman explained, "They have worked the land a long time, these violinists. They still have their instruments, but it would take years for them to learn to play them again. Their hands are ruined. Theirs are lives that no longer have music in them."[64] *The Passion of Anna* (1969) also had an impact on Parker. Both films opened his mind to images he just would not have encountered in the Bronx: "Seeing different landscapes, different spaces, different perspectives, my mind began to glow."[65]

When Parker's interest in film was first sparked around 1964, one of the first he recalled liking was *The Loneliness of the Long-Distance Runner*, directed by Tony Richardson (1928–1991), a key figure in the English Free Cinema movement of the 1950s, which proclaimed that "implicit in this attitude is a belief in freedom, in the importance of people and in the significance of the everyday."[66] The film was based on a novella and screenplay written by Alan Sillitoe (1928–2010) and is one of a number of writings by the author that dealt with the theme of rebellion against an unfair or unjust social or political system.[67] The main character, a teenager named Colin Smith, played by Tom Courtenay, lives outside of London and is rebelling against the system. During a tough period for Smith when his father had died and his mother got remarried, the boy robs a bakery. After getting caught, Smith is forced to go to an all-boys school, where it is soon discovered that he has a talent for running long distance. So the response is "we will put you on the track team and you will be one of us."[68] At the climax of the movie, however, when Smith is competing against a major rival in a pivotal race, he loses on purpose to defy the establishment. It was as if to say, "You're not getting me. I'm not going to sell out to serve your interests." In another sense, the film is about how a "man keeps his integrity while under the physical and legal authority of those whom he despises."[69] The themes resonated deeply with Parker at a critical stage as he was coming of age.

When he could get his hands on a copy of the *Village Voice*, Parker would voraciously read the "Movie Journal" column of critic Jonas Mekas (1922–2019), who was a vocal supporter of avant-garde film. By early 1971, Parker felt pushed to seek out contemporary experimental film, and he soon found himself going to the Anthology Film Archives regularly, where a ticket was only $1.50 and he recalled "I was often the only or one of only a few in the audience."[70] No filmmaker fascinated Parker more than Stan Brakhage (1933–2003). As a young adult, Brakhage had refused to have his vision corrected using glasses and became fascinated with the multitude of visual variations he could bring to "normal" vision. It was Brakhage's explorations of conceptualization through various forms and techniques that appealed to Parker. Brakhage's common practice of making silent films caused the visual experience to be even stronger.

Brakhage had revolutionary ideas about many aspects of film, ranging from color to perception to composition. In his early collection of essays, *Metaphors on Vision*, he laid out much of his theoretical approach to perception in film: "Imagine an eye unruled by man-made laws of perspective, an eye unprejudiced by compositional logic, an eye which does not respond to the name of everything but which must know each object encountered in life through an adventure of perception. How many colors are there in a field of grass to the crawling baby unaware of 'Green'? How many rainbows can light create for the untutored eye? How aware of variations in heat waves can that eye be? Imagine a world alive with incomprehensible objects and shimmering with an endless variety of movement and innumerable gradations of color."[71] He added, in another essay, "My eye, turning toward the imaginary, will go to any wave-lengths for its sights. I'm writing of cognizance, mind's eye awareness of all addressing vibrations."[72] For Brakhage, the act of seeing was supposed to be a personal one and one that emancipated one from common ways of seeing, always in pursuit of an "adventure in perception."[73] His challenge to the orthodoxy of perception was a powerful and transformational force for Parker, encouraging him to trust his own ways of processing his senses. It freed him up to rethink existing ways of seeing, hearing, and so forth. In 2012, with a long career in progress, Parker would state that *Metaphors on Vision* and Brakhage's films were "perhaps my greatest influence."[74]

Brakhage's epic *Dog Star Man* (1961–64) had a monumental impact on Parker. Brakhage, like Parker, experienced poverty, and for a while the film-

Figure 3.2 Stan Brakhage (1933–2003).

maker even switched, out of necessity, from a 16mm camera to an 8mm and shot some of his most critically acclaimed work with it, including *Dog Star Man.*[75] Jonas Mekas, whom Parker read incessantly, declared, after seeing parts 2 and 3 of the film, that they were "absolute masterpieces" and, speaking to the experience of the film, stated that it was a "visual symphony that flows through you and lifts you and polishes you and opens up and makes you more receptive to other subtle movements, colors, experiences."[76] As Mekas also wrote, "Brakhage's *Dog Star Man* [was where] the real revolution took place [in the sixties]. The film explodes the conventional narrative form and brings to the narrative film an intensity and complexity not known to cinema before."[77] Brakhage worked on the film to explore what he called "closed eye vision" or, rather, the "image transformations the emotions impose on physical events," using the techniques of multiple exposure and overpainting.[78] Brakhage challenged his audience to reconsider the definition of "good composition" by underexposing or overexposing the film or by stretching objects out of shape using unusual lenses. The film dealt with myriad concepts: the prelude was composed of a long metaphor about connections between human beings and corporeal existence, abstractions, and the cosmic.[79] In some ways, *Dog Star Man* investigated, via surrealist sensibility, an interest in the unconscious, especially dreamlike states of mind.[80] The main character, Dog Star Man, and the sun, solar flares, and the imagery of burns are all featured intensely in the film. In later parts of the film, fusions of male and female anatomy, sometimes creating androgynous forms, multi-sexed beings, human anatomy being rearranged, and eventually a live

Figure 3.3 Jonas Mekas (1922–2019).

birth, together form a commentary on the totality of humanity, its experience, and the deepest possible connections between people.

Brakhage's *The Art of Vision* (1965) was, in many ways, the coming to fruition of many of the ideas that had begun in *Dog Star Man*, though in a more deconstructed manner, or as Parker thought of it, "*Art of Vision* was basically *Dog Star Man* unraveled, taking the superimpositions out."[81] The film ran for over four hours and was intended to be consumed in a manner that allowed audience to enter and exit, or to even show it at home while one did other things in the home. As Mekas explained, "Like looking at a piece of tapestry, then looking at somebody in the room, or at the window, then looking again at the tapestry."[82] Mekas considered the work "a towering contribution."[83] Brakhage further explored the possibilities of superimposition, first with four layers, and then gradually eliminating them one by one until just one remained, as one critic interpreted as "a gradual peeling apart of the richness of life."[84] Another critic boiled the film down to an investigation into "the skill of making seeing."[85] For a young Parker, Brakhage's films blew open his mind to seeing in new ways and revolutionized his senses, his point of view, and what he even thought was possible through the act of artistic creation. Parker would later discover that the concepts he encountered in Brakhage "translated directly to music on the bass" in terms of harmonics, color, and image.[86]

The film *Little Stabs at Happiness* (1960), directed by Ken Jacobs (b. 1933), was also influential for Parker. For one, he sensed Jacobs's "staunch aversion to 'order and determination,'" as one critic later described it. Jacobs aimed to "undermine every lure of aesthetic mastery, every potential 'tyranny' exerted by film images on their viewers, while producing some of the most confoundingly gorgeous, soul-rattling experiences available to motion pictures."[87] Parker continued to read Mekas, who heaped considerable praise on the film and considered it to be one of the works that made up "the real revolution in cinema today," finding that it "opened up sensibilities and experiences never before recorded in the American arts. It is a world of flowers of evil, of illuminations, of torn and tortured flesh; a poetry which is at once beautiful and terrible, good and evil, delicate and dirty."[88] Jacobs came from very challenging working-class origins in Brooklyn, but he had established himself as an experimentalist, one who embraced shadow plays, double-screen films, projected performance pieces, and all manner of unconventional films.[89] Parker found these scenes overpowering in their concept and daring in their orchestration.

The film *Mass for the Dakota Sioux* (1964), directed by Bruce Baillie (b. 1931), was similarly important for Parker.[90] The film is dedicated to the Dakota Sioux and quotes proverbs and statements about them, although it contains no images of the Sioux. At the same time, the urban shots, often presented through overexposed takes, or even double- or triple-exposed scenes with trains, cars, motorcycles, and people on the streets, seem as much of a commentary on contemporary life as it was about the Sioux.[91] Subsequent shots of commercials that were then being aired on television and one of a military parade are certainly critiques of modern life. Baillie shot the film in a very low-fi manner, one that paralleled Parker's own early experiments in film. As Baillie declared, "In 16mm you should use the camera like a pencil. That way film making can become personal, like handwriting."[92] Both the approach to filmmaking and the allusions to indigenous peoples in the Americas spoke to Parker, and later in his career he would make his own gestures toward solidarity with indigenous peoples in his own work.[93] Parker wrote in 2012 that "independent cinema was at the core of my existence," referring to himself as a young man. Parker added that these films "taught me to see beyond the horizon."[94]

Parker also had a fascination with Hollywood movies, attracted to the bigger-than-life characters that were portrayed. He incessantly watched films directed by John Ford, Billy Wilder, Nicholas Ray, Sidney Lumet, Richard Brooks, and John Frankenheimer. But Parker was especially attracted to the films of Kenneth Anger (b. 1927), which were often rerun at the Film Anthology Archive in the early 1970s.[95] The one that most caught Parker's eye was *Fireworks* (1947), the earliest of Anger's films to survive, an experimental film that was filmed in his parents' home in Beverly Hills, California, and explored issues of sexuality, homophobia, and death and rebirth, some elements of which were banned from public viewing by censorship laws.[96] Anger summarized *Fireworks* as "a dissatisfied dreamer awakes, goes out into the night seeking a 'light' and is drawn through the needle's eye. A dream of a dream, he returns to bed less empty than before."[97] When the film was debuted at the Coronet Theatre in Los Angeles in 1958, it sparked an obscenity trial, although the film was eventually declared to be art and not pornography. Parker was young, and *Fireworks* and other films made him dream big and imagine life beyond his own experience and the place where he grew up.

Parker's obsession with film inspired him to do his own photography and filmmaking. At age eighteen or nineteen, he got a Fujica Single-8 camera, which allowed him to back-wind the film.[98] He was very interested in doing superimpositions and immediately began experimenting. The main sites for filming were the Claremont projects themselves, the buildings and the people that lived there, including a film he made of his mother and other relatives. Parker also looked to nature, filming "clouds and trees" and any other natural wonder he could encounter in the urban setting of the Bronx.[99] Unfortunately, when he was living at 141 1st Avenue in Manhattan in an insecure building, his apartment was looted and all of the film was stolen. Yet his creativity was not bound into genres or even disciplines: "There were no walls between writing, film, music . . . it was as if there was a room filled with sound, and another with words, one with images, and so forth. But the carpet in all of these rooms was imagination—it linked everything together. One inspired the other."[100] Perhaps in another life Parker would have become a filmmaker.

Musical Purpose

When Parker encountered individual poems, songs, films, and other works of art, he regarded the most potent of them as experiences of transformative power: "I would read them or hear them or see them, but I was careful not to over-indulge, since one can wear them out and you feel their power diminish. So, I would often experience one of these and that was like putting it up on my shelf. I kept it with me, I could recall it from memory and at certain moments, take it down from the shelf to experience it again."[101] Cecil Taylor's record *Conquistador!* was perhaps the most potent experience of all, and even fifty years later, Parker recounted its resulting transformations, the experience of sonic trance, and how it would break him out of the mold.[102] He carried with him Jonas Mekas's statement "Who cares about good art, bad art when the world is dying?"[103] This taught Parker that art was not for art's sake. Art had greater meaning, it built connections between people, and it could be a fierce cry for justice.

For Parker, all of these social and artistic ideas represented a form of enlightenment: "I began to think about what I was going to do and how I might bring this enlightenment to people."[104] He felt confident because he could always rely on the message of "my fathers, John Coltrane, Albert Ayler . . . and the politics of Charles Mingus, 'Fables of Faubus'":

> *Oh, Lord, don't let 'em shoot us!*
> *Oh, Lord, don't let 'em stab us!*
> *Oh, Lord, don't let 'em tar and feather us!*
> *Oh, Lord, no more swastikas!*
> *Oh, Lord, no more Ku Klux Klan!*
> *Name me someone who's ridiculous, Dannie.*
> *Governor Faubus!*
> *Why is he so sick and ridiculous?*
> *He won't permit integrated schools.*
> *Then he's a fool! Boo! Nazi Fascist supremists!*
> *Boo! Ku Klux Klan (with your Jim Crow plan)*
> *Name me a handful that's ridiculous, Dannie Richmond.*
> *Faubus, Rockefeller, Eisenhower*
> *Why are they so sick and ridiculous?*
> *Two, four, six, eight:*
> *They brainwash and teach you hate.*
> *H-E-L-L-O, Hello.*

Mingus's lyrics referred to Orval E. Faubus, the governor of Arkansas, who to resist segregation had deployed the National Guard to prevent Black teenagers from going to high school in Little Rock in 1957. The song became a rallying cry against the systematic oppression and exclusion of African Americans at the time when it first appeared on the record *Mingus Ah Um*.[105]

Parker also listened a lot to Curtis Mayfield in the 1960s and 1970s. Mayfield composed politically conscious songs about a wide range of issues, especially drug abuse in Black ghettos. Mayfield's soundtrack for the film *Super Fly* (1972) gained wide recognition because it broke with the music of many other Blaxploitation films of the time in that it did not glorify pimps and drug culture but rather shed light upon the state of life in impoverished Black communities. As Mayfield's son observed, Curtis sang about "the dynamics of power—who has it, who needs it, who is denied it."[106] Parker was inspired by the film to avoid being self-destructive and to question the present reality. Again, he felt called to deconstruct prescriptions of "what we were supposed to be doing as Black people, and instead to break the mold. I just couldn't accept things the way they were."[107] He had begun to play improvisational music by that time, and the freedom it afforded him in the practice of art making matched the freedom he sought in day-to-day life.

Some influences for Parker were drawn directly from personal experiences or interactions. One significant one was from a high school English teacher, Mr. Slotkin. He would ask the students to write essays in which they defined virtue, justice, truth, love, and other concepts like that. To inform their opinions, they read many classics, the most influential of which was Plato's *Dialogues*, one that focused on whether divination could be taught or if it was a virtue. In one of the dialogues, the character Ion returned from a poetry festival and was questioned by Socrates about why Ion, who was famous for reciting Homer, could not recite other poets as effectively. The dialogue concluded with Ion claiming that it was a virtue, that his ability to recite Homer was a gift, not something he could have just learned through practice. For Parker, this pushed him to think about what gifts he possessed, what he might strive to learn, and how to nurture his talents to fruition. He almost never had anyone drawing these things out of him: he was on his own, and it was up to him to discover himself, to recognize his abilities, and to bring them to the world. "That's kind of what saved me," Parker remarked many years later.[108]

With all of the art, music, writing, and politics that Parker was experiencing, and the resulting personal enlightenment, he felt increasingly alienated from his formal education. "School couldn't match all of the other information, the images, the words, the movements, the music I was encountering, it wasn't even in the ballpark," he thought. The art, politics, and self-transformation "were like a river of light and I was soaking up all of that stuff."[109]

Inner Dimensions

Parker also sought out spiritual transformations. Together with his brother, he began practicing yoga during junior high school, following the TV instructor Richard Hittleman. Waking up early, they would do a yoga class at

7 AM before going off to school. Hittleman had been the major early conduit for bringing hatha yoga into American homes via television.[110] For Parker, yoga was both a physical and a spiritual practice that helped him develop concentration, poise, and an inner calm to face the noise around him.

Parker's Aunt Elvira, his mother's sister, was a Jehovah's Witness. When she came to visit, the Parker apartment would often empty out. She liked to talk about religion, and nobody had the patience for it except young Parker. Rather than focus on some of the typical hallmarks of her faith, she would just talk with Parker about the Bible and the New Testament in particular. She would pick out passages, and they would discuss them. She also referred to the Watchtower publication *From Paradise Lost to Paradise Regained*. The tangible idea of paradise on Earth had some appeal to Parker as a voice of liberation that resonated with so much else that was happening in the mid- to late 1960s. By the time he was in high school, Parker was reading the New Testament on his own, "and I always found the right passage, the one that was needed to give me some kind of strength to hold onto life, no matter what I was facing."[111] Parker never became a regularly practicing Christian, but passages from the Bible gave him enduring strength in the uncertain world he inhabited: "While living in the Claremont projects, I was trying to learn about spirituality, compassion, how to love people unconditionally. That was the only part of religion that I was interested in, I was never concerned with how to get eternal life, just how to live."[112]

An experience that reached even deeper into Parker's growing spirituality was hearing John Coltrane's record *A Love Supreme* toward the end of high school.[113] The music and the intention to uplift and bring people closer to God called strongly to young Parker. As Coltrane wrote, "During the year 1957, I experienced, by the grace of God, spiritual awakening which has led me to a richer, fuller, more productive life." Coltrane went on to include a prayer with passages such as "Thought waves—heat waves—all vibrations—all paths lead to God," as a taste of his Universalist spirituality that he would continue to develop until his early death in 1967. The graphic included in one of his records in which Buddhism, Hinduism, Christianity, and the religion of ancient Egypt are shown to all converge on the same cosmic center also made a strong impression upon Parker. In direct reference to its spiritual components, Baraka stated, "John Coltrane, Albert Ayler, Sun Ra, Pharoah Sanders, come to mind immediately as God-seekers. In the name of energy sometimes, as with Ayler and drummer Sunny Murray. Since God is, indeed, energy."[114] Adding, in reference to Coltrane in particular, Baraka added, "The music is a way into God. The absolute open expression of everything."

Nobody had a greater spiritual impact upon young Parker than Albert Ayler. Ayler's music bore heavy influence from gospel and Negro spirituals, and it was laden with spiritual and religious references. Ayler's unique brand of religious march songs resonated with older forms of Black American religious and spiritual music that reached all the way back to field shouts and hollers.[115] Ayler's release of *Spirits* (1964), *Bells* (1965), *Spiritual Unity* (1965), and *Love Cry* (1968) established him as one of the most powerful avant-garde jazz voices of his generation, fusing key elements of the Black music tradition with his own unique voicings and concepts.[116] Parker found some of his deepest spiritual yearning manifested in Ayler's statement that bore the title of one of his last records, *Music Is the Healing Force of the Universe.*[117] The song included these lyrics:

> *Music is the healing force of the Universe*
> *It is a being*
> *Always here*
> *A feeling*
> *Open up your door and let it come in*

It was then that Parker "became aware that music was healing and when it was vibrating on a high level, it could really change and reshape your life. The spirit of the vibration could be passed from musician to listener."[118]

Parker was deeply impacted by Ayler's death in 1970. He wrote an extended piece about Ayler's influence in his diary:

"THE DEATH OF ALBERT AYLER"

Albert Ayler was found in the East River on November 25, 1970. After hearing of his death, I broke in tears. I felt a great sadness, and there was an irony about the event; for the past year my life was in the process of being changed. Albert Ayler's music was very important in the movement of that change. Unlike many others, Albert was very direct in speaking to me. I never met him personally, but each time I listened to his music, I was able to hear the inner song speaking to me. He spoke of dancing flowers and the Holy Spirit, of divine prayer. How we should all learn to love God . . . to seek truth, the truth of the spirit.

Albert never sang of how he lost his baby or how good it was, he was singing about the salvation of man through heavenly means. A person I thought to be a true messenger carrying out the real reason for playing music (living). I had been enlightened by all of this to another level of seeing.

... Albert has gone to the Father, and he is missed like we miss all of our loved ones. How I wish they could live on and on, we certainly need them in this world. But we must let them go, we must carry on the work.[119]

Parker later said that "it was the aesthetic of the music of John Coltrane and Albert Ayler that changed me, that taught me how to find my sound."[120]

Parker developed a practice of nonviolence. His mother had raised him to strike back when he was threatened, saying, "Don't let nobody hit you; if they do, hit them back." But he often questioned her, "Why should I hit back?" and she would say, "This is the Bronx; you've got to do that." But at some point in his teen years, Parker began what he considered to be a lifelong training in compassion for others that would demand that he find another path.[121] In 1970, when he turned eighteen and received his draft card, Parker declared himself a conscientious objector. To make this official, he had to go to a hearing before the draft board. Most people brought a religious officiant who would bolster their claims, but Parker just went by himself. When he was asked why he did not want to serve in the army or go to fight in the Vietnam War, he replied, "I don't believe in killing people."

The officer asked, "Are you afraid to die?"

Parker replied, "No."

Long pause. "OK, you can go."

"That was the happiest day of my life."[122]

Embracing the Avant-Garde

Around 1970, Parker began going to see free live concerts in branches of the New York Public Library, especially at the Countee Cullen Branch at 135th Street in Harlem. One of the first bands he saw there was led by Charlie Haden (1937–2014), whom Parker had first heard on WBAI radio. Haden had gained legendary status as early as 1959, doing innovative bass work with Ornette Coleman on *The Shape of Jazz to Come* and subsequent records.[123] In 1970, just prior to the concert Parker attended, Haden released his iconic record with the band Liberation Music Orchestra, which he had founded in response to American involvement in the Vietnam War, while the government simultaneously ignored civil rights, poverty, drug addiction, and so many other problems at home. The combination of Haden's innovative bass playing and progressive, humanist politics appealed to the eighteen-year-old

Parker. After the performance, Parker approached Haden and introduced himself, telling him he wanted to become a bass player, even though he had only just acquired his first bass. Haden told him to listen to records and play along, telling him that is how he had learned to play bass as a teenager. Haden continued to be an inspiration for Parker, who observed Haden in a live performance at the time: "One night, every solo he took was fantastic. That was a period when he was especially digging into the bass with such strong playing."

Parker did once visit an office of the Black Panthers on Boston Road in the Bronx, where the party had its Ministry of Information. He wanted to try to get the people there interested in music, especially Charlie Haden's Liberation Music Orchestra and some of Archie Shepp's music, but they showed no interest. Still, Parker continued to listen to politically conscious music, such as Shepp's *Attica Blues* when it came out in 1972.[124]

Parker turned to the avant-garde precisely at a moment when some would say it was coming undone. The fire behind "new Black music" in the 1960s began as the most influential development in jazz since the emergence of bebop in the early 1940s, but it gained a wider cultural relevance because it was being embraced by key cultural figures within the Black Arts movement.[125] Nevertheless, the avant-garde would face monumental challenges from the late 1960s onward: the combination of industrial capitalism and consumer culture would propel other forms of music to the forefront, and the music industry itself would often work to stamp out this insurgent art form.[126] But Parker, who had seen its transformative power in his youth, would forge ahead, convinced both that it would provide a mode for his own artistic expression and that it held solutions to distinct social and cultural ills. Parker responded to a higher calling than artistic creation: he would come to regard himself as kind of a shaman, a practitioner of spiritual healing via music. That realization would carry him for the decades that followed, pushing him to overcome any obstacle in his path and rarely feel weary in his endeavors. Many years later, he would reflect, "The training takes a lifetime. You do it all your life. It is the ability to see about tomorrow." For Parker, the most profound truths are "right in front of our faces, though the answers to what we need may change at every given moment. That is why we need to make music that is right there in the moment."[127]

After graduating high school in 1970, Parker tried to attend Manhattan Community College. He went for one day but found it so alienating that he never went back. "I had nobody to talk to at the time who might have said, 'try it again, go one more day,'" he regretfully recalled later. "It would have been valuable to go and get a bigger perspective on the world than the limited one I had then." Parker had felt alienated from education at an early age, and that sense never really dissipated: "I never heard a voice coming out of school that said anything that I could relate to. The voices I heard were from the streets and the oral histories of the people. I could imagine everything school should be but was not." Parker could not muster the motivation to attend college: "Nobody told me, you can study music in college and play music. All I thought about was playing music, at the time, and I just felt schooled out."[128] Some years later he considered studying jazz at Lehman College but again decided against it. It would remain an ambition throughout his life to get a bachelor's degree, one that he considered once every decade or so, but his eventual success as a musician pulled him in other directions.

II. Early Work

Four

The Loft Scene: Art, Community, and Self-Determination

The school of music I wanted to be associated with was the black music revolutionary spiritual school. At the same time, I had to be open to the unknown school that would reveal itself as time went on.

—— **William Parker**

What are the Blues? They're a vulnerability, an openness, a rawness.

—— **Cooper-Moore**

First Bass, First Gig

Long before Parker ever owned his first bass, he would stand with a broomstick in his hands and play along to records in his father's collection. He would thump, pluck, and sway back and forth, his fingers feeling the rhythms and his heart measuring out time. When he finally got his first instrument, in some ways it already felt quite natural.

Parker's first bass did not last long. He had bought it at a pawnshop for $60 and played it a little. But then it fell over accidentally, and the neck snapped off, right as he was getting more serious about playing it. So in 1969 he went to Bronen's Music Store on Webster Avenue at the corner of East

188th Street in the Bronx. Bronen's had a long history in the borough, having been founded in 1915, and it had a reputation for giving good deals to people from the neighborhood.[1] Even after it was destroyed by fire during the blackout of July 17, 1977, the owner later remarked, "Despite what happened, we loved the people. We decided to stay and rebuilt."[2] Parker spotted a Czechoslovakian wood-carved Juzek bass at Bronen's for $100. Juzek basses, as well as violins, violas, and cellos, were made by the Czech designer Janek "John" Jůzek (1892–ca. 1965) and had been used widely in the United States since the 1920s.[3] Juzek instruments were commonly purchased or rented by public schools, so it was an ideal instrument for an aspiring student.[4] Parker's father had unfortunately lost his job, however, so family finances were extremely tight. Parker paid Bronen's for the instrument in installments of four or five dollars every few weeks, and over the span of about eight months, and at least twenty payments, he acquired the bass.

After getting his long-anticipated instrument, Parker was standing on Webster Avenue waiting for a bus to go back home. A guy approached him and asked, "You a bass player?"

Parker's first reaction was "Who's he talking to?"

"No, you," the man said, pointing.

"Yeah, I'm a bass player," Parker replied, a bit coy.

"Cool. I gotta band, but we need a bass player. Come down to this place on Amsterdam Avenue," the man replied, showing him the address. "Next Sunday for a jam session."

Parker thought to himself, "It's Monday. I have until next Sunday to learn how to play." This encounter happened just after he had first talked with Charlie Haden, so he followed his advice and went home and furiously practiced all week, playing along to records with every waking breath. Parker's bass was notoriously difficult to play. As German bassist Peter Kowald (1944–2002) would later point out, after becoming good friends with Parker in the 1980s and 1990s, "William Parker's bass (especially the old one) is the most difficult instrument to play that I ever put my hands on: because of the distance above the finger board, pressing down the strings requires such an effort."[5]

When Sunday came, he went to the appointed place. The guys in the band were excited. "The bass player is here!" They began to hit it right away in front of a small audience. The leader of the band would call out a tune. "'Straight, No Chaser. Key of F.'"

At the time, Parker said "I didn't know the difference between F and B flat or anything else. I just played. I had been playing all of those tunes and always had a good feel. They gave me solos and everything, but I had no chops."

Before long, his fingers were "red bubbles of blood," and he wondered, "How am I gonna get out of here?" So he looked down and said, "Man, what time is it?"

"Oh, it's about 8 o'clock."

"Man, I'm sorry guys, I got another gig in a half hour."

"Oh, OK. You comin' back next week?"

"Sure." He waited a few days for his fingers to heal and then kept practicing.

Jazzmobile

The Saturday after his first gig, Parker went to Jazzmobile on 125th Street in Harlem to get free music lessons. Jazzmobile had been founded in 1964 by pianist, composer, and educator Dr. William "Billy" Taylor (1921–2010) and philanthropist and arts administrator Daphne Anstein.[6] The goal of the organization has been twofold: to present jazz to the public and to educate the next generation of musicians. In the summer of 1965, Jazzmobile had presented a considerable amount of music by free jazz luminaries such as John Coltrane, Pharoah Sanders, Albert Ayler, Archie Shepp, Sun Ra, and Cecil Taylor as part of a "floating street-corner multi-arts festival that filled Harlem with music, dance, poetry, and painting."[7] But by the time that Parker arrived in 1971, Jazzmobile was not presenting or teaching free improvisation.

When Parker attended the instructional program, it ran for most of the day. Because the lessons were free and there were few other institutions that were accessible, especially to working-class residents of Harlem and the Bronx, the classes were overloaded with eager students clamoring to learn music. When Parker first arrived, the program did not have enough practice rooms, so he was initially assigned to a bathroom as a practice space for his first lessons. On Parker's first day, Paul West, the director of the program, tuned up his bass and gave him the fingering chart for "Honeysuckle Rose" in half position. "Work on this. I'll be back."

Parker worked and worked on the piece, and he lost track of time. Eventually, a knock came on the door, and it was the janitor coming to clean. It was half an hour after the program was supposed to end. Parker had played the piece all day, had lost himself in the music, and had not thought once of lunch, fatigue, or anything else. The music was opening up to him. The next week, Parker went back, and bassist Richard Davis (b. 1930) gave him lessons. Davis was one of the most-recorded jazz bassists of the 1960s, having worked with Miles Davis, Eric Dolphy, Andrew Hill, Sam Rivers, Pharaoh Sanders, and others.[8] Davis's work spanned all the various types of jazz as well as classical music; thus, he brought peerless experience to his brief episode of teaching at Jazzmobile.[9] Davis had a large ensemble in which aspiring students played, so Parker got some of his first big-band experience there.

By the time that he was studying at Jazzmobile, Parker was playing along to a lot of avant-garde jazz records, especially Albert Ayler and Archie Shepp, but whenever he mentioned it to his teachers at Jazzmobile, the reply was, "No, no, no. We don't teach that here. Not here." But he did meet some musicians who were also hip to free music, most importantly the tenor and soprano saxophonist Hassan Dawkins.[10] Dawkins had come from Los Angeles with his two daughters, and Parker had actually met him earlier in the South Bronx, but connected more deeply with him at Jazzmobile. Dawkins lived on Clay Avenue in the Bronx, right near Claremont Park, close to where Parker lived with his parents. One day, Dawkins found a contrabass clarinet that someone had left behind on a subway platform, so he began playing that instrument, too. Parker described Dawkins's playing as "a tenor player out of the Archie Shepp school, but who had his own voice." Soon after, they got hooked up with drummer Freddie J. Williams and began to play together. Williams medicated on Thorazine (a common medication for schizophrenia) and slurred his speech. Whenever he walked, Williams counted his steps. Parker considered him "an idiot savant, he was a very good drummer with a fast right, could keep time, play fills, and always performed on a set of pancake drums that were easy to transport." Dawkins would pick them both up in his yellow Volkswagen Beetle, which was just big enough to transport a bass and a drum kit, and they would practice and go to gigs together.[11]

Based on his early experiences of learning music at Jazzmobile and elsewhere, Parker would later compose a "Blueprint for a Music School," in which he would advocate for a different sort of structure and approach:[12]

Study One

1. Open Improvisation (improvising without any verbal communications)
2. Preset Improvisation (improvising with verbal communications)
3. Drones and echoes, the practice of one sound played continuously; the secondary sound that is bounced back into the face of the first sound

Vibration of Sound

1 The importance of sound, how it vibrates and why
2 The effect of sound on the human nervous system
3 Room with continuous sound (24-hour jam session that never stops, students can enter and play at any time of day)

Compositional Possibilities

The reason for composition, the goal of the composer
The redefinition of all music terminology to fit the needs of the composer

1 What is composition for 100 different musicians?
2 Harmony in infinite parts
3 Melody . . . resolved . . . unresolved . . . partials
4 Phrases . . . phrasing . . . contour . . . shape
5 Groupings
6 Clusters
7 Inclusion of sound

Intonation

What is intonation?
Non-Western intonation (untampered intonation)
A440
In tune/out of tune?
Ear training
Listening in real time (present time)
Learning to respond to sound in present time
Options of response
The world is dying. Which way do we go?
(The world is dying. Do we have time to do anything that is not real?)
Rhythm and the world
World music/music people, music culture
The shaman's song
American Indian culture and music
Healing through sound

Parker also critiqued the common music school approach to create clones of past musicians. He asked, "If you spend your life trying to be Charlie Parker, who will be you? We fail musically when we try to be something other than ourselves. The problem is that we go to music school, and music school is never interested in developing the music inside." Instead, Parker advocates for the opposite approach: "Musical instruction should consist of training the senses to act as a filter or conduit for sound, to know how to react to the music that flows through us, to learn to manipulate a musical instrument in order to turn sound into tone, not in a serendipitous way, but through an exact intuition that is bursting with reason, purpose, and knowledge, allowing one to play the right sounds at the right moment to tap into an inspiring magical music."[13]

Parker stayed at Jazzmobile as long as he could. Although the brand of jazz it was teaching did not really speak to him, he did learn his fundamentals there. He also thought, "Well, I know one thing. I have to really be one with this bass. No matter what I play on it, I have to learn the bass and be one with it."[14] Parker had a few teachers, but he was mostly self-taught. As his friend Cooper-Moore would say many years later, "I have a musical education that I have been trying to get away from for fifty years. William is who he is because he had nobody telling him what to do but him. It's as if he said to himself, 'what is in me? How do I get it out of me?' He's one of the gifted ones."[15] So Parker left the school and began gigging with all kinds of different people. The year 1971 was a flurry of small performances with folk singers, dancers, poets, a Cuban folkloric group, even a ventriloquist, all in different situations in the Bronx and Harlem.[16]

One of the first Bronx venues where he appeared regularly was a place called The House That Jazz Built, run by vocalist Maxine Sullivan and named after a film, written by Douglas Bronston and directed by Penrhyn Stanlaws, that had been released in 1921.[17] Parker played there many times with Sullivan as well as pianist Dill Jones and drummer Lewis McMillan, and it constituted his first regular experience on the bandstand. Sullivan, originally from a small town in western Pennsylvania, had a career that spanned nearly sixty years, with her first known sessions with her uncle's swing band the Red Hot Peppers in the early 1930s through to her release of seven records in the final two years of her life.[18] Sullivan was a mentor of a different kind for Parker, someone with immense confidence and stage presence who had been in the industry for a long time and who loved to encourage young talent.[19] The venue was also frequented by well-known figures such as pianists Elmo Hope (1923–1967) and Bertha Hope (b. 1936), raising its status as a jazz club, although Elmo had passed away by the time that Parker began playing there. Bertha Hope's career, far less documented than her husband's, began in the 1950s, when she played in her native Los Angeles and other parts of the West Coast. She made her first known recordings in 1961 as part of Elmo Hope's band and in that year moved to New York City, where her reputation increased. However, her first opportunities to record as a leader did not come until the 1990s, when her career had an upturn and she toured in Europe and Japan.[20]

When Parker was playing at The House That Jazz Built in the early 1970s, it was a particularly difficult time for the people of the South Bronx, especially in that area, and many buildings were burned down, leaving the club as the last standing building on the block. During the day, Parker would often play with Sullivan and then go down into the East Village at night.[21] Around 1973, when Parker began to play more in the East Village, he could still not afford the $0.35 subway fare, so he would walk all the way from his parents' apartment in the Claremont Houses at 450 East 169th Street with his bass strapped to his back.[22] He would first walk to Yankee Stadium, cross the Macomb's Dam Bridge, and then walk down Frederick Douglass Boulevard through Harlem. From there, he would walk all the way to the West Village and then to the East Village, often to 1st Street between Avenues B and C. He would eat wheat germ out of a jar and drink apple juice that he would pack for himself, but often fasted out of necessity on nothing but water. Despite the physical hardship, his spirits were high. He would do "mental composing" while he walked, occasionally stopping to scribble down a few notes in a small notebook that he carried in his pocket. He enjoyed seeing parts of the city that he had never visited before, and it further opened his mind to everything that New York City had to offer. The return trip was "a little scary," but if he had to do it, he was usually energized enough from playing that he could make it back. Oftentimes, what meager pay he had gotten from playing at pass-the-hat gigs allowed him to use the subway. Despite the fact that his mother disapproved of his pursuing music, when he arrived home at four o'clock in the morning, dinner was always waiting for him.[23] Then he would arise the next day and do it all over again if he had another opportunity to perform.[24]

Parker also continued to build ensembles and rehearse in the Bronx with large groups, such as the Aumic Orchestra, which he convened in 1972 at the Third World, a Black cultural and music center founded by playwright Ben Caldwell (b. 1937) in 1968.[25] Caldwell had been born in Harlem and emerged as a significant dramatist of the Black Arts movement, best known for his plays *The Militant Preacher* (1967), *Hypnotism* (1969), and *The World of Ben Caldwell* (1982).[26] His work "uniquely satirize[d] not only the racism and naivete of whites, but also those African Americans who either [sought] to emulate whites . . . or anchor themselves to stereotypes."[27] Caldwell exposed African American self-hatred and self-deception, creating a commentary that mirrored many of Parker's own thoughts throughout the period. Caldwell had worked with Amiri Baraka in the mid-1960s and had lived for a time in Newark before moving to the Bronx.[28] Caldwell was at the center of a tight Bronx community of Black creative artists, and he made the Third World a flashpoint for new Black art in the South Bronx at that time.[29] The center presented plays, hosted poetry readings, and had regular concerts for creative artists.[30] It also functioned as a fertile space for community building; Parker met multi-instrumentalist Marshall Allen (b. 1924), leader of the Sun Ra Arkestra at an event there in 1972.

The Third World was the first home for William Parker's music and the space where he presented his first substantive works as a bandleader for the ambitious Aumic Orchestra. The band consisted of twenty-two musicians, including three drummers and four bassists.[31] The band's only performance was on March 25, 1973, including people who were already or were soon to be frequent collaborators: Hassan Dawkins on tenor saxophone and bass clarinet, Daniel Carter (b. 1945) on soprano saxophone and flute, and Roger Baird and Freddie J. Williams on drums.[32] Parker had met Carter on one of his excursions to the East Village, and the two would go on to collaborate for the rest of their careers. The one other noted participant was trombonist Bill Lowe (b. 1946). He had gotten his start playing with South African expats in London in the 1960s before moving to New York, and during his career he appeared as a sideperson on more than forty records playing trombone, bass trombone, and tuba, but later achieved his greatest influence on the music as a professor of jazz at Northeastern University.[33] The other personnel remain relatively unknown: Kwame Lucumi (tenor and alto saxophone), Linton Gayle (tenor saxophone, flute), Charles Harris (tenor saxophone, clarinet), Mike Clark (alto saxophone), Trent Powell (clarinet, flute), Tony Joseph and Rick Murian (flute), Robert Williams and Tom Brown (trumpet), Joe Mato and Herb Kuan (bass), Darry Barnes (marimba), and Wade Barnes (drums and percussion).[34] Lucumi was a friend of Parker's who lived in the Amsterdam-Phipps public housing projects near Lincoln Center. Lucumi was interested in Egyptology, and he and Parker would talk about that and

Figure 4.1 Parker, late 1970s. His patched bass exemplifies the poverty he endured at the time. *Credit*: ©Raymond Ross/ CTSIMAGES.

other aspects of African history and culture before or after they played music together.

Aumic Orchestra (with Aum sometimes spelled Om) was a certain kind of sacred music, though not aligned with any particular religion. Aumic Orchestra was inspired by the recordings of the Jazz Composer's Orchestra.[35] The orchestra had been founded in 1965 by American pianist Carla Bley (b. 1936) and Austrian trumpeter Michael Mantler (b. 1943) to further orchestral avant-garde jazz and had been directly inspired by the Jazz Composers Guild, which was founded the previous year. Bley and Mantler also founded JCOA Records and the nonprofit organization Jazz Composer's Orchestra Association in 1966. The main product of the organization was the big band, which released a series of records that included *Communion* (1966), a 1968 double album, and a group of records in the 1970s that featured a series of different soloists, including Bley, Canadian poet and lyricist Paul Haines, trumpeters Don Cherry and Clifford Thornton, trombonists Roswell Rudd and Grachan Moncur III, and violinist Leroy Jenkins, before

Figure 4.2 Poster for Aumic
Orchestra's performance at the
Third World, Bronx, 1972.

disbanding in 1975.[36] Aumic Orchestra was also inspired by bassist Alan Silva's recordings of the Celestial Communication Orchestra on the BYG label.[37] Both of these sources of inspiration were not musical in nature but rather the concept of having the big band's music shape and define itself in the spirit of John Coltrane's *Ascension* (1965), yet without ever imitating a particular style. For the performance at the Third World, they were not able to rehearse until the day of the show. Hassan Dawkins recorded the performance on a reel-to-reel tape, but the tape has probably not survived. Beyond exhibiting Parker's first attempts as a bandleader, and of a big band no less, the significance of Aumic Orchestra is that it provides a rare snapshot of what was happening in the creative music community in the South Bronx in the early 1970s, which was otherwise poorly documented.

Parker began playing more and more in the East Village and began to meet people who ascribed to a similar aesthetic, such as multi-instrumentalists Daniel Carter and Gunter Hampel (b. 1937), vocalist Jeanne Lee (1939–2000), and drummer Rashied Ali (1933–2009). Carter, in particular, was among his most important early collaborators and friends; he shared related artistic visions and finally offered Parker a safe community where he could create, grow, and be himself. "I didn't feel weird or out of place. I felt special. I felt like I fit in with the community and the creativity. I found a home there like I'd never found anywhere else," Parker recalled.[38] Artist lofts were just then opening up to the music, and they became a haven for Parker as he situated himself in the community of artists.

The Loft Scene

Much of lower Manhattan between the 1950s and 1970s was composed of aging buildings, many of which were no longer being used for their original purpose of manufacturing, leaving behind often empty or partially empty postindustrial areas. The Bowery, SoHo, and especially the Lower East Side became the home to artist lofts after a long period of declining businesses, white flight to the suburbs, and uncertain city planning. When artists first began moving into those neighborhoods, they dwelled there illegally because significant parts of those neighborhoods were not zoned residential. Artists moved there because large, open spaces were ideal as studios, rehearsal spaces, and performance spaces, creating a kind of artist colony in lower Manhattan, where rental rates had fallen so low that artists could actually afford them.[39]

Within the jazz community the loft scene grew out of the Black Arts movement of the 1960s, which was centered on a desire for cultural autonomy and sovereignty in the face of a music business that was often exploitative. This vision was articulated by music critic Ron Wellburn: "Black culture cannot be separated from economic or political considerations; nor can black music be separated from its related creative/expressive forms. For the 1970s and beyond, the successes of political, economic, and educational thrusts by the black community will depend on both an aesthetic that black artists formulate and the extent to which we are able to control our culture, and specifically our music, from theft and exploitation. . . ."[40]

When Parker first began to play in clubs on the Lower East Side, he became aware of the New York Musicians Organization, formed by drummer and percussionist Juma Sultan, saxophonists Noah Howard and Archie Shepp, pianist Dave Burrell and Karl Berger, and bassist Wilbur Ware, which was political and advocated for self-determination.[41] The idea was to refuse to be a servant of the music industry and rather try to create their own work much like their predecessors Charles Mingus (1922–1979) had done with the Jazz Composers Workshop in the 1950s, Bill Dixon (1925–2010) and the Jazz Composers Guild had done in 1964, and the Association for the Advancement of Creative Musicians had done on the South Side of Chicago beginning in 1965.[42]

Dixon, in particular, was an inspiration for Parker. From his first entrance into the music scene, Parker would aim to maintain his own autonomy as an artist. Dixon understood the problem that faced avant-garde musicians. Feeling locked out of the many jazz clubs that featured mainstream, popular acts like Woody Herman, Dizzy Gillespie, and Gerry Mulligan, Dixon had endeavored to create his own scene.[43] Dixon explained his motivations: "I did the October Revolution . . . for a simple reason. I had a point that I had to prove to people. All these writers—Dan Morgenstern, Martin Williams, etc.—were telling me that this music I saw wasn't worth anything, that no one could be interested in it. I knew people could be interested in anything if it was presented to them in the proper way."[44]

Key figures such as drummers Milford Graves (b. 1941) and Rashied Ali had both been involved in the Jazz Composers Guild and were to be integral to the burgeoning loft scene of the 1970s. The loft scene began to emerge as early as 1968, but events in 1972 galvanized a new community. That year, producer George Wein elected to move the Newport Jazz Festival to New York City, but it featured few New York–based musicians and few Black artists. James DuBoise and Juma Sultan (b. 1942) of Studio We called a meeting at University of the Streets, where the community formulated a list of ten demands:

1   That a minimum salary be guaranteed to the bands.
2   That musicians have determination as to what location they will play.
3   Black musicians to be consulted regarding total activity coordination of the Jazz Festival. A committee for such purpose to be set up through Black Musicians United.
4   That each day of the Festival, there be a major activity in Harlem.
5   That during the Festival, a day be set aside to honor Marcus Garvey and the formal Community dedication of Marcus Garvey Memorial Park [then Mt. Morris], with his "Black Is Beautiful" theme.
6   From the funds received by the Urban League, renovation of the Marcus Garvey Building, 204 Lenox Avenue, housing the Music Workshops and the Black Indepth Thinking Classes dedicated to rehabilitation of Addicts with a stress on Musicians and providing promises for the Black Musicians to create and teach.
7   Liaison between the Urban League and Community based program on the wants and needs of the Black Musicians. The pilot project development to be in Harlem.
8   That the Urban League set aside, on a quarterly basis, funds for a School of Music in Harlem.
9   That free tickets to the Festival locations outside of Harlem, and within Harlem, if tickets are required, be dispersed in needy area.
10 That there be 100% support to the above demands.[45]

Much of the focus of their demands was on increased participation, stability in pay, and forging a more direct relationship between the festival and Black communities of Manhattan. Their proposals were rejected across the board.

In response to their proposals being rejected, DuBoise, Sultan, Noah Howard, Rashied Ali, Milford Graves, and other musicians decided to create a rival festival of events throughout New York City, with the intention of outnumbering the conservative Newport events. After considerable effort and planning, the loft organizers featured more than 100 events that included more than 250 performances involving more than 500 musicians across three of the city's boroughs. Events were held at a wide variety of venues, including some of the emerging Lower East Side lofts such as Studio Rivbea, Ali's Alley, and University of the Streets; other lower Manhattan locations such as Slug's Saloon, uptown at the Harlem Music Center, and in the Bronx at the Third World; in city parks such as Tompkins Square Park in the East Village and Mount Morris Park in Harlem; and even at the Prospect Park Bandshell in Brooklyn.[46] Their festival featured a variety of established figures such as saxophonists Archie Shepp, Clifford Jordan, and Dewey Redman; drummer Milford Graves; pianist Andrew Hill; trombonist Roswell Rudd; as well as a heavy concentration of aspiring avant-garde jazz musicians such as saxophonists Anthony Braxton and Arthur Doyle, the loft managers Rashied Ali and Sam Rivers, and Sultan's Aboriginal Music Society.[47]

Out of the experience of creating the counter-festival, some of the organizers formed the New York Musicians Organization with the aims of continuing their work.[48] The following year, they again organized a counter-festival that included major figures such as Sun Ra, but Wein found room to compromise by offering them the Alice Tully Hall to book for the Newport festival.[49] This caused division within the organization, with Rashied Ali taking the stance that they should not cooperate with Wein. Rivers was booked for the Newport festival, but to show his support for the organization, he still booked Studio Rivbea for events simultaneously. Despite the fact that the organization soon fell into disarray, it nevertheless put the spotlight on Studio Rivbea, Ali's Alley, and other key lofts and encouraged the proliferation of loft spaces in lower Manhattan over the five years that followed.[50]

By the time of all of the loft organizing in 1972 and 1973, Parker was already establishing himself on the scene on the Lower East Side. By the 1950s, artists had been attracted to the East Village for its cheap rents, and in the 1970s and 1980s the substantial squatter community reached its peak in the area.[51] In the early 1970s, when Parker first frequented the neighborhood, the lofts were the center of the scene in which he was interested in taking part. Many of the musicians also lived in the neighborhood, so it was easy to go from one loft to the next or to practice in an apartment or loft space when one convened a band. An organic community of artists had formed there, drawn by inexpensive rents and the opportunity to present their work to audiences. Musicians did not need to make a lot of money to survive or create their art if they were squatting or paying very low rents, so people scraped by and often relied upon one another. The Lower East Side would remain a rustic artists' neighborhood well into the 1990s, at which time developers placed the area in their crosshairs as part of a broader program to gentrify Manhattan.

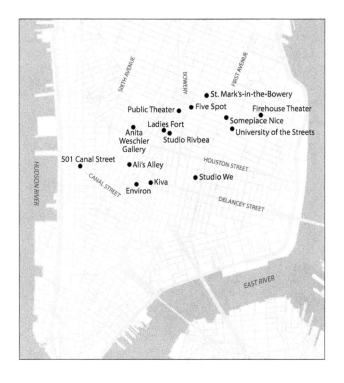

The Music Ensemble

Around 1972 or early 1973, Daniel Carter and drummer Roger Baird began playing a duo together. They had met one day at Studio Rivbea. Carter had pulled from his saxophone case some composed music he had been working on and showed it to Baird. Then they began playing. After about five minutes, Carter put the compositions back in his case and just improvised with Baird. Carter later admitted that that moment sent him on a musical trajectory that he followed for the rest of his life. The two played regularly at Baird's basement studio near West 4th Street and 6th Avenue. Parker joined soon after and eventually invited violinist Billy Bang (1947–2011), born William Vincent Walker, to join as well as his friend Malik Baraka (d. 1982). Baird's early impression of Parker was that "he was a man of few words and of a lot of musical heart."[52] The quintet eventually called themselves the Music Ensemble. The band would then invite others to occasionally get involved such as alto saxophonist Kazutoki Umezu, trumpeters Dewey Johnson and Arthur Williams, bassists Earl Freeman and Herb Kahn, and

Figure 4.3 Daniel Carter, 1970s. *Credit*: ©Raymond Ross/CTSIMAGES.

drummer Rashid Bakr. As Bang wrote of the group, "The Music Ensemble was more than a working group of set musicians. It was closer to being an alliance of musicians that shared similar approaches to alternative and creative music; and adventure into shared collective music."[53]

Malik Baraka, originally named Gregory Barnes and brother of drummer Wade Barnes, was a new collaborator. Baraka was a musician with whom Parker would do consistent work in the mid- to late 1970s. Parker first met Baraka at the Muse, a children's museum in Bedford-Stuyvesant, Brooklyn, where they watched Reggie Workman, Jimmy Garrison, and Ron Carter all play the same bass, producing completely different sounds.[54] Later, Parker, Wade Barnes, and Baraka played at the same venue, where Baraka played a cornet and "played some of the most angelic trumpet I have ever heard to this day," according to Parker.[55]

Billy Bang was originally from Mobile, Alabama, but had moved north to the Bronx with his mother when he was still a child. Bang had first performed on bongos and dancing in New York City subways before briefly considering a career in classical music.[56] But before he became serious about it, he volunteered for service in the Vietnam War. After returning, he was recruited by a chapter of the Black Panthers for his weapons expertise. Bang went with a group to buy guns that they intended to use to rob a bank in Baltimore. They bought the guns from a pawnshop, but while they were there, Bang noticed a violin in the back and bought it for $25. Then they left. Another member of the group of Panthers, Bilal Abdur Rahman, had observed Bang's interest in the instrument and was a saxophonist himself. So when it came time to make plans to meet, Rahman told Bang the wrong time intentionally to keep him out of trouble.[57] As it turned out, all of the others were arrested; Bang later said, thankfully, "I bought the violin instead of a gun."[58] Bang and Parker finally crossed paths at the Third World, where he spotted Bang wearing a cape and carrying his violin in a knapsack.[59] Parker and Bang forged a friendship and a musical partnership during their time together in the Music Ensemble that thrived for decades until Bang's death in 2011.

The Music Ensemble played what they called "everyday music," which they derived from meeting every Friday at Baird's house over the course of about two years. To generate their ideas when they practiced, they would just meet up, unpack their instruments, and see what happened. Someone might begin by reciting poetry or reading from a book; another member of the band might start hitting a bell; one might start playing a line. Malik Baraka sometimes began by reading a book for a half hour, then playing something on his trumpet, and then going back to the book. As Parker wrote of Baraka, "Malik would listen maybe the first 2 or 2 and ½ hours, waiting for the spirits to call, waiting for the right moment to pick up his trumpet. When Malik did play, he would blow 3 or 4 choruses; then he would go back to listening. He was never worried about playing in a style; music was the style."[60] Baraka once stated, "The sound: it just comes through when it is ready."[61] Baird played little bells and an extended drum kit, making all kinds of sounds. Sometimes Parker and Bang would work out lines, but a lot of the time they played spontaneously. Baird recalled a session with bassist Earl Freeman that was particularly exciting: "He'd sort of re-created the bass. He played a fretless electric Fender bass and made it sound like some other kind of reality." Bang noted, "Our music was generally never written down or notated on paper. In the beginning I was uncomfortable, because I

THE LOFT SCENE

Figure 4.4 Parker, Billy Bang, and Zen Matsuura in front of Neither/Nor, East 6th Street, New York, June 3, 1986. *Credit*: ©Alan Nahigian.

always wanted to know where our root was. What color were we in? Later I realized the unimportance of my personal concept, and understood that the Ensemble was intuitively working for a unit feeling. It was an unadulterated journey, searching for the beauty of unity in sound. Simple and pure."[62]

Practice sessions often went as long as four hours, running from 7 PM until 11 PM or later. They practiced almost daily in 1973–75. Their practices were like theater and were a kind of "on the spot music." Musically, their performances went far away from jazz and might be broadly described as a mix of the Art Ensemble of Chicago and the folk jazz group Oregon.[63] Bang qualified it: "It was my New York version of Chicago's AACM, without the protocols and/or hierarchy."[64] The group was critical in the development of the musical talents and aesthetics of its various members and has been said to have contained "the seeds of ensembles such as Other Dimensions in Music and Test" that took form in the late 1980s and 1990s.[65] Many of the bands playing improvised music at the time were doing so over some kind of external musical structure. The Music Ensemble was one of the few bands in New York at the time that was playing improvised music entirely free, intuitively and instinctively. As Baird reminisced, "My feeling of connection to the universe was heightened greatly during some of the music we played. Occasionally time itself would stand still and each musical fragment would hang suspended in a timeless framework. Experiencing the moment with a total clarity, playing would be effortless and joyful."[66]

The Music Ensemble played quite a few performances in the East Village and the West Village, often in lofts of that time, none of which were documented. Its first documented performance, which took place at Kingsborough College in Brooklyn on April 24, 1974, was broadcast on WKCR-FM, Columbia University's student-operated radio station.[67] After the Columbia University student uprising of 1968, the station had shifted to presenting "The Alternative," and jazz, especially avant-garde jazz, had come to have a significant place in its regular programming.[68] A recording that Baird compiled from the Kingsborough performance along with excerpts of a concert on February 15, 1975, at Holy Name School Auditorium came out many years later as a self-titled release, the only publicly available recording of the group.[69] Another live performance that was not recorded occurred at the Open Mind, a bookstore in Soho, where guest Jerome Cooper (1946–2015) played upright piano instead of his customary drums.[70]

With so much continued interest from the core band members, the Music Ensemble decided to rent studio space at the Anita Weschler Gallery at 510 LaGuardia Place in the West Village for $200 per month.[71] Weschler used the space during the day, and the Music Ensemble played there at night. By June 1974, it was holding public performances in the space, such as the three-day residency, June 14–16 of that year, when the group presented its music for two sets each night at 9 and 11. In 1976 the band played a regular series of gigs at Someplace Nice at 97 St. Mark's Place on the Lower East Side.[72] Someplace Nice was a storefront cultural center that evolved into a restaurant run by "revolutionary thinker" John Dahl.[73] It was the perfect home for the music and for Parker. Dahl would often talk to Parker about the lack of Black businesses in the neighborhood. In the summer, Dahl ran a lunch program "that kept my family alive when we had no food," Parker reflected. "Dahl was on the level of Malcolm X."

The Music Ensemble faded away by 1977, however, as many of its members got more focused upon other projects or when some felt the need to pursue music performance opportunities that were more lucrative to support their families.[74] Baird and Parker played together in numerous other bands in 1973–76 and had a reunion in 1995 that also included Carter. Baird has appeared on a few records over the years, both within improvised music and in other areas. Bang went on to have a prolific career, with more than twenty records as a leader and many more as a sideperson, although perhaps his most revealing albums were his two Vietnam-related projects that dealt with his personal demons and the post-traumatic stress disorder that he endured from his battle experience.[75] Bang and Parker continued to play together: Bang's Survival Ensemble, 1976–78; Billy Bang Sextet, 1984–86; various trio, quartet, and quintet formations through the years; and particularly a duo format during the final years of Bang's life.[76] Carter's career is too prolific to summarize here, but Parker and Carter later played together in Other Dimensions in Music and innumerable other formations, short-lived and long-lived groups, and have been lifelong friends. Unfortunately, Malik Baraka got heavily into drugs and died young on December 26, 1982.[77] About a week after Baraka's death, Parker wrote in his Sound Journal that "Malik was a human being and musician who was able to allow music to flow through him. He realized that he was the instrument, not the pocket trumpet that he played. He deeply touched my life and others with his song and vision."[78]

More than a decade after the Music Ensemble stopped playing, trumpeter Roy Campbell founded the band Other Dimensions of Music with Parker, Carter, and drummer Rashid Bakr. "In some ways, Other Dimensions was an extension of the Music Ensemble, though of course Campbell was not a part of the earlier band," Parker observed. "With Other Dimensions, sometimes in one set, we played the whole history of jazz music with all kinds of rhythms, moods, question marks, and answers went in that music. That's how I learned to anchor avant-garde music, how to push things, and not to be afraid to play anything. We would play melodies or rhythms, we did not worry about whether it was avant-garde enough or not."[79]

Juice Quartet

One of the first lofts that Parker frequented was the Firehouse Theater, which was run by Alan Glover, better known as "Juice." Juice was a tenor and soprano saxophonist, and he soon invited Parker to play in the Juice Quartet, an ensemble that also included pianist Kasa Allah and percussionist Juma Sultan.[80] Sultan had previously gained attention as a member of Jimi Hendrix's band, which had played at the 1969 Woodstock Festival. At times the Juice Quartet also featured other drummers, such as Phil King, Abu Kali, and Ali K. Abuwi. Cooper-Moore (b. 1946), then named Gene Ashton, who co-ran Studio 501 Canal, remembered meeting Parker soon after he moved to the city in the summer of 1973, when he played a gig with Parker at the Firehouse: "William was really shy and never said a word. I had never seen such a skinny person in my life, and with such beautiful eyes."[81]

The Firehouse Theater often held weekend performances, so it began to build a community of performers and audience members. By July 1973, the Juice Quartet was playing regularly at the space, appearing on a bill for the New York Musicians Festival and on two sets a few days later at the Firehouse Theater.[82] It was there that Juice worked out his approach to music and the band worked out its sound. After a couple of years of being less active, the Juice Quartet had a rebirth when Juice got a Comprehensive Employment Training Act (CETA) artist job in 1978–79. The CETA Artists Project was a federally funded program to hire visual, performing, and literary artists in 1978–80 and was the largest of its kind since the Works Progress Administration of the 1930s.[83] CETA has been recognized as a major launching point for many artists in the late 1970s, and for Parker it was a bright spot in his early career.[84] It gave him the first financial stability of his life, if only from a very modest hourly wage. It allowed him to help support his family and to focus on developing more works as an artist. Some of the money he made from that job went to producing his first record as a leader, *Through Acceptance of the Mystery Peace*, on Centering Records in 1980.

Juice asked Parker to perform with the Theater for the Forgotten, which performed in prisons. The theater company consisted of approximately fifty artists and performed the work *"Piece of the Apple," A New York Miniature*, which including music composed by Juice, poetry by Arnold Mayer, and direction by H. M. Koutoukas. They premiered the work in public spaces; as a flyer indicated, "This surrealist event will premiere in Grand Central Station, Lower Level West. . . . Each of the other boroughs will receive premiere performances of this production."[85] As promised, they performed the work in February 1978 at the West Brighton Branch of the Public Library in Staten Island; Junior High School 36 in the Bronx; the Italian Senior Citizens Center in Elmhurst, Queens; and the Coney Island Hospital in Brooklyn. The reunion of Parker with Juice prompted an independent concert by the quartet at Columbia Presbyterian Amphitheatre in Long Island City, Queens, as well.[86] The theatrical production returned with a series of outdoor performances between June 10 and August 25, 1978. According to Juice, "I found some hand-written notes that says we performed for more than 30,000 people" through the course of that summer.[87] Parker's last performance with Juice, called October Harvest, was at the Symphony Space Theatre in October of 1979, before two brief reunion concerts with Parker's big band Little Huey Creative Music Orchestra in 2005.[88]

Other Encounters

The Firehouse Theater was a cultural center and a community hangout spot. While Parker worked the venue, he also made a number of key connections. Once, while playing a duet with Juice's son Omo, drummer Billy Higgins (1936–2001), who had just arrived, slyly took the boy's place at the drum kit when Parker had his eyes closed and jumped right in. The two played spontaneously together for an hour. Afterward, Higgins complimented Parker by saying, "Oh, man, you have a nice feel." This chance meeting struck up a sustained musical relationship between the two, and they would continue to play duo regularly. Not long after their initial meeting, Higgins invited Parker out to his apartment on St. Mark's Avenue in Brooklyn, where they would practice together. Parker later remarked, "I learned a lot playing duos with Billy—just keeping time and dancing with the time. That was a very important period of development for me."[89] At Higgins's apartment, Parker met saxophonist Clifford Jordan and pianist Chris Anderson, with whom he collaborated in later years.

The same day that Parker met Higgins, he also met pianist Andrew Hill (1931–2007), who lived around the corner from the Firehouse Theater. Hill and Parker began to play together shortly after that time. Parker also met tenor saxophonist Charles Brackeen (b. 1940) and drummer Rashid Sinan there. Hill, Brackeen, and Sinan all lived on East 9th Street. Each of Parker's chance meetings led to short- or long-term musical associations as he got to explore concepts, ideas, and approaches with other musicians who were also interested in free music. In addition, Parker met bassist Wilbur Ware (1923–79) at the Firehouse Theater. Ware lived just around the corner, and Parker soon after began to study with him formally. Ware taught Parker to trust himself and seek out his own answers in the music.[90] Parker's close friend, fellow bassist Peter Kowald, would later observe that "it may be that Wilbur Ware's huge sound, his way of turning things upside down, and Jimmy Garrison's flow in William Parker's early years were important points of departure for his way of playing."[91]

Parker played many sessions at the Firehouse Theater and gained a community at the space. On a typical day, he practiced there with the Music Ensemble from 10 AM until 1 PM. After finishing, he would then go with his bandmates over to Studio We at 193 Eldridge Street, run by James DuBoise and Juma Sultan. The former factory space had functioned as a studio for pianist Burton Greene from the mid-1960s and was subsequently taken over by DuBoise after Greene went on tour in Europe. Studio We had begun presenting weekend concerts in 1969 and was one of the key spaces that launched the loft era.[92] The first festival occurred in July 1970, when Studio We hosted "Three Days of Peace Between the Ears," which inspired both Sam Rivers and Rashied Ali to open their lofts. Both of them played at the festival and saw its potential.[93]

Following the loft's significant role in the New York Musicians Festival in 1972, however, Studio We began to get a lot more attention, and the six-floor building eventually contained a recording studio, multiple rehearsal spaces, and even a restaurant in addition to the concert venue. As critic Ed Hazell noted, "With five floors devoted to music (one floor housed visual artists), Studio We was an important crossroads for the new music. Working bands rehearsed there, musicians met, and jammed there, forming new friendships that resulted in new bands."[94] Daniel Carter recalled playing there almost immediately after arriving in New York City in 1970, attending regular jam sessions and performances. To add to all of the artistic activity, classes in African languages and culture were also offered.

Thus, Parker entered into an eclectic cultural milieu at Studio We, and when he spent afternoons there, he would hang out with other artists who frequented the space, such as pianist Dave Burrell (b. 1940), saxophonist Archie Shepp, drummer Ali K. Abuwi, and pianist Sonny Donaldson. Parker even wrote about a particularly riveting performance there by the Charles Sullivan Quartet in the spring of 1973: "Every song soared higher than the one before. It was one of those afternoons that continually flowered and blossomed from start to finish." He further elaborated, "I would meet and play with musicians like Ronnie Boykins, Sonny Donaldson, Hassan Hakim, Earl Cross, drummers like Freddy J. Williams, Clemson Parker, Harold Smith, Ali Abuwi, Eugene Davis. These musicians will most likely not be remembered in jazz history books. They have secured a position in the book of 'Mysteries' which will document the contributors to spiritual equilibrium."[95] Parker often played at Studio We with Sultan's band Aboriginal Music Society, which had formed, like a number of bands of the period, as a fusing of Black revolutionary ideals and a desire for creative autonomy.[96] Parker also began to play in the We Music House and eventually became a member of the musicians' collective that ran the space.

Parker and other musicians would then commonly hang out at Studio We for a few hours and then, around 7 PM, go over to Studio Rivbea, which had one of the most active scenes of any of the lofts, presenting music seven days a week. Studio Rivbea, located at 24 Bond Street, was run by multi-instrumentalist Sam Rivers. The space was well situated—the landlady was painter Virginia Admiral and mother to actor Robert DeNiro, who was then just emerging, and the building was also home to photographer Robert Mapplethorpe, who occasionally photographed Rivers and sometimes took the elevator down to check out the music.[97]

Studio Rivbea had started as a rehearsal space in 1968, but by 1970, Rivers was presenting concerts there on the weekends. Spurred on by the success of the first New York Musicians Festival in 1972, Rivers began programming music in the space seven days a week and invited groups of varying sizes to perform live.[98] Funding from the New York State Council for the Arts allowed Rivers to offer regular programming and to support spring and summer festivals. Despite the casual atmosphere, "Rivbea drew a loyal crowd, quite happy to sit on pillows, low mattresses, park benches, or the hard floor, and to mix informally with musicians while sipping coffee, tea, or soda."[99]

This studio and other lofts became "the major showcases for jazz performances of all types in New York" and often drew elated coverage in the mainstream New York press as well as the national and international press.[100] Journalist Les Ledbetter described the scene there in 1974:

> Packed into the studio's basement were local cognoscenti, college students from around the country and other knowledgeable music fans from as far away as Sweden, France, and Japan. Some were very young; some were obviously veterans of earlier jazz scenes; a few were foreign visitors who spoke little or no English, and a few were other musicians who had come to listen or join in. And all demonstrated a devotion to jazz that created instant camaraderie and an easy-going atmosphere that provided a fine milieu for the lesser known performers who experimented with the directions and boundaries of jazz. . . .[101]

The concerts were often akin to a salon-style presentation, with ample time for discussion, interaction, and feedback from the audience.

It was at Studio Rivbea that Parker began to play much more regularly, even becoming the house bassist for an extended period, and began to establish himself on the music scene there just as the space itself was gaining greater visibility. By 1974, he was often playing there multiple times per week with different bandleaders or collaborators such as saxophonist Charles Brackeen, baritone saxophonist Charles Tyler (1941–1992), and alto saxophonist Jemeel Moondoc (b. 1951). At the same time, he was playing with a band led by Rashied Ali at Hilly's on the Bowery, the venue run by legendary club owner Hilly Kristal (1931–2007), "a big, hairy, scruffy, Jewish ex-

Figure 4.5 Parker and Rashid Bakr with Ensemble Muntu, Studio Rivbea, New York, July 4, 1976. *Credit*: ©Tom Marcello.

marine."[102] The space would soon after change its name to CBGB (Country Bluegrass Blues) and give birth to punk music in 1974.[103]

Parker quickly became acquainted with other key parts of the loft scene. Up the block from Studio Rivbea was a place called Ladies' Fort, run by Joe Lee Wilson. In addition to booking regular concerts, Ladies' Fort had a reputation for serving cheap food, which was crucial because most loft performers like Parker had very little money.[104] Another crucial loft was Ali's Alley, run by Rashied Ali, on the ground floor underneath his loft apartment at 77 Greene Street.[105] Ali's Alley had more of a nightclub vibe to it than most other lofts, with table seating, a full bar, and a soul food menu. Its slogan was "Good Vibes, come with neighbors, children, lovers present ex or future, husbands and wives, good vibes."[106] Ali was regarded as the epitome of the self-reliant artist at the time, carrying his records to gigs, forming his own label (Survival), and running his own space.[107] Ali's Alley was often curated to give an artist or a band a week of gigs so that they could really dig into their material. Artists made modest amounts of money because of the policy that the money that came in through door fees all went directly to the musicians.[108] For avant-garde artists like Parker, it was a haven where they could present their work through consistent booking and walk away with at least some money in their pockets. There were lots of other lofts in the area, some with names, some more informal or lesser known.[109] The most important thing for Parker was that each room had something different to offer and that each one provided an opportunity to learn something new or make a new acquaintance and encounter a new musical approach, idea, or concept.

While frequenting the loft scene, Parker met avant-garde drumming legends Sunny Murray (1936–2017) and Charles Moffett (1929–1997), and trumpeter Raphe Malik (1948–2006). Ornette Coleman ran a space called Artists House, where Parker played with tenor saxophonist Frank Lowe and where they recorded *Black Beings*, Parker's first appearance on a record.[110] The loft scene began to have a national draw, bringing in aspiring musicians from other areas such as bassist Wilber Morris, cornetist Lawrence "Butch" Morris, and reedist David Murray from the West Coast; trombonist Joseph Bowie from St. Louis; trumpeter Lester Bowie, multi-instrumentalist Joseph Jarman, and saxophonist Luther Thomas from Chicago; and, later on, multi-instrumentalist Henry Threadgill's band Air.

Ensemble Muntu

Of all of Parker's early sideperson work, nothing was more active or played a greater role in his development as a musician than his involvement in Jemeel Moondoc's band Ensemble Muntu. The ideas behind Muntu had their origins in the time that Moondoc spent and played with Cecil Taylor (1929–2018) at Antioch College in 1971–73, when Taylor forged groundbreaking curriculum on Black music.[111] The course emphasized the impact of African musical, linguistic, and cultural origins; the African American experience as enslaved peoples in the United States; and Black Christian churches as spaces of resistance before and after the Civil War. Alongside similarly innovative curricular work by Bill Dixon at the University of Wisconsin and later Bennington College, Taylor was on the forefront of an emerging narrative around the idea of Black music. The ideas of John Coltrane's *Ascension* and *Meditations* were still quite pervasive at the time, and Milford Graves was developing Bäbi music and Frank Lowe was working on *Black Beings*. So, for Moondoc, who was engulfed in all of this, the fusion of music, history, and spirituality became central to his artistic vision:

> Muntu is about the transition and survival of an old world culture connected to me by birth. Muntu is about me traveling back centuries into an ancient

world known to me only through my ancestors. This connection is spiritual, and embraces the living and the dead. When performing music, the execution of contacting ancestors requires a religious belief. This process can be an outer body experience causing one to be possessed, but can also bring into the room the spirits of ancestors known and unknown. The intent of the performance is not to merely entertain, but to uplift, and awaken the listener's spiritual powers.[112]

Moondoc left Antioch together with pianist Mark Hennan and moved to New York City in July 1973. Upon arrival, Moondoc began organizing Ensemble Muntu with Hennan, soon adding trumpeter Arthur Williams, whom they had met at Antioch and who introduced Moondoc to drummer Rashid Sinan. Williams was a middle-register player capable of dark textures and who was intrigued with the sound of Dizzy Gillespie. Parker described Williams as a musician who "played a full animated palate of sounds using space and force."[113] Not long later, Moondoc heard Parker play at Studio Rivbea, and the two struck up an artistic relationship from their very first encounter. Moondoc's first impression of Parker was "the first time I ever played with William, it was a truly amazing musical connection. Parker's sound is big, deep and dark, and he has big ears. We played together with ease and freedom of movement. William can swing and drive, he can strut and dance on the bass . . . it was this incredible freedom."[114] Muntu began immediately rehearsing, most commonly without the piano, at Sinan's tiny tenement apartment on East 10th Street.[115]

Gigs were a necessity for a band in which everyone was living hand-to-mouth. Ensemble Muntu rehearsed through fall 1973 and then debuted its work in New York with a string of Thursday nights in December at Studio Rivbea. The gigs created just enough buzz to get more gigs on the loft circuit. For Parker, Muntu was his first band to play regularly and to stay together for an extended period of time. Rashid Bakr (born Charles Downs, 1943) replaced Sinan on drums by February 1974 as the band continued to work the loft scene with dates at Studio Rivbea's summer festival in June of that year, on radio programs, in church performances, at Ali's Alley and Studio Rivbea in March through May 1975, and five weeks at Sunrise Studio in August 1976.[116] Sunrise Studio was run by percussionist Mike Mahaffey.[117]

By 1976, Moondoc was beginning to think about recording a record. To this end, the group continued to play the loft circuit with dates at Environ in February and the Loft Jazz Festival of that year, back at Sunrise Studio, and then a host of lofts including Environ, Studio Rivbea, Ali's Alley, Piano

Magic, the Brook, and Jazzmania through the summer, fall, and winter.[118] Its music was also broadcast on the radio, on WNYU on February 10 of that year for a performance held five days prior and a live broadcast on WKCR on February 29. Thus, by April 1977, the group was fully prepared to record *First Feeding* (Muntu Records, 1977). The record got some positive reviews in jazz publications, one of which referred to Moondoc's sidepeople as "sleeping giants."[119] As critic Barry McRae wrote in the *Jazz Journal*, "Parker is a supple bassist and Bakr a dynamic drummer who keeps up the tension at all tempos. . . ." Moondoc remarked, "That record got us a long way—from the unknown to the semi-known, and that's a long way."[120]

For Parker, all of the regular performing not only allowed him to hone his abilities with his instrument but also caused him to gain considerable confidence as a player. At times he experienced major breakthroughs in his soloing. One night at Studio Rivbea, he picked up his bass like a saxophone and was playing it in a way that his subconscious ideas were pouring out as he plucked. He began to see colors and began to formulate cross-sensory connections between sound and color that had a deep impact upon his future artistic vision. During another performance, at Environ, Parker emerged with a brilliant bowed solo that worked as counterpoint to everything that the band had been doing.[121] These experiences continued to propel Parker forward as a player.

First Feeding gave Moondoc and Ensemble Muntu enough attention that they played regularly in the lofts through 1977; a two-night performance at Damrosch Park at Lincoln Center; three residencies at Ali's Alley, the first in October 1977; and then two in March and then in April 1978; and numerous other loft performances throughout those two years. All of these performances made it finally possible to take the band to Europe—Parker's first international tour—in October 1978, with dates in the Netherlands and France over the course of six weeks.[122] Several of the performances received very positive reviews, which propelled the band further ahead. Of the regular sidepeople, only Parker had been able to join Moondoc in Europe. The tour arrangers provided a drummer to take Bakr's place, and Williams had elected not to go on the tour for personal reasons. During the tour, Moondoc came to appreciate the open sound that the quartet had without piano and, after returning, decided to keep Parker and Bakr, and soon added Roy

Figure 4.6 Jemeel Moondoc and Parker with Ensemble Muntu, Studio Rivbea, New York, July 4, 1976. *Credit:* ©Tom Marcello.

Campbell Jr. on trumpet.[123] By mid-December, the revamped band had another residency at Ali's Alley.[124] The addition of Campbell was to have a big impact on Parker; he developed an understanding of Campbell and a desire to collaborate with him for years to come.

Ensemble Muntu recorded its second record, *Evening of the Blue Men* (Muntu Records, 1979), the following March during a live set at St. Mark's Church and released it before going on a Canadian mini-tour that summer.[125] It turned out to be the pinnacle of Muntu's live performances. In December, Cecil Taylor asked Parker and Rashid Bakr to join his unit, and Moondoc's band never really recovered. As Moondoc remarked, "Muntu basically disintegrated when William and Rashid went with Cecil. I couldn't compete against Cecil. So, I had to do something else. I had to abandon my Muntu dream."[126] Though both musicians continued to play with Muntu when they were available, their attentions had been drawn elsewhere. In a way, Ensemble Muntu was "one of greatest artistic success stories" of the loft era.[127]

After 1978, as the lofts began to decline as the music shifted to the Public Theater and other downtown clubs, the music scene itself began to evolve considerably. Grassroots arts funding in the United States reached its peak under President Jimmy Carter but was one of the first things slashed from the budget under Ronald Reagan. A new phase of hardship was in store for the musicians trying to make a living in New York, and the situation for Parker was no different. Even in the mid-1970s, Parker was barely able to make ends meet. In June 1975, when trumpeter Don Cherry (1936–1995) invited him to play for a week at the Five Spot, he made $500, the first time he made any real money for a gig.[128] Most of the time, door gigs paid very little. Nevertheless, the community of artists gave Parker a feeling of buoyancy as he emerged onto the scene, developed relationships, and began to make a name for himself.

In 1977 or 1978, Malik Baraka suggested to Parker that they try to get his brother Thomas back into music. Thomas Parker played the alto saxophone; admired Jimmy Lyons, Archie Shepp, and Marion Brown; and had formerly studied with tenor saxophonist Budd Johnson, as well as Sonny Red and "Fats" Green. The Parker brothers had done some recordings on reel-to-reel tape with the pianist Ronald White in the Bronx. White lived on Brook Avenue and came out of the Monk school of piano players. The tapes that they made are now lost. White died young, still in his twenties. As Parker remarked, "If you could make it past thirty years old in the Bronx, you could make it. But a lot of people didn't get to thirty."[129] So after White's death,

Figure 4.7 Parker with Don Cherry at the Five Spot, New York, June 1975. *Credit*: ©Michael Ullman.

Thomas Parker had drifted away from music, and Malik Baraka and Parker tried to pull him back into their group, adding Baraka's brother Wade Barnes. First, they put a deposit down on a saxophone for Thomas at the Bargain Spot, a pawnshop on 13th Street and 3rd Avenue, for about $25. Parker was working his CETA artist job, so he had a little more money than usual. But the night after that, Parker came down with appendicitis in the middle of a gig at Ali's Alley, and he had to be rushed to the emergency room.[130] They were never able to get the saxophone, and his brother died soon after while William was still in the hospital recovering.[131]

Five

"Music That Will Give People Hope": Centering Dance Music with Patricia Nicholson

Music is invisible to the naked eye.
If you want to look at music,
go find a beautiful lake with wonderful trees
that is placed against a lovely blue sky.
That is the closest thing to music
that we can see.

—— **William Parker**

On Thursday, December 20, 1973, Parker was playing with Ensemble Muntu in a residency at Studio Rivbea and working on a composition of his, "Late Man of This Planet," a dreamlike dirge.[1] After the concert ended, a young dancer named Patricia Nicholson (born Patricia Wilkins, 1949) approached him and complimented the work, stating directly, "I am looking for music that will give people hope."[2] She had been trying to find improvising musicians with whom to work. Earlier that day, she had been at Ornette Coleman's loft on Prince Street for a performance, and then a friend had brought her over to Studio Rivbea. Parker responded positively and directly to Nicholson's statement, thinking that what she was seeking was worthwhile. As Nicholson later recalled, "I went looking for the music, and I found

William."[3] After a brief conversation, Nicholson and Parker exchanged phone numbers. Parker eventually called her back on New Year's Day from Webster Bowling Alley, near his home in the Bronx. They spoke about their mutual interests, and Nicholson hired him to put a band together that would work with her dance improvisations.

A month later, they began rehearsing. From the very beginning, Parker struck Nicholson as frightfully shy. He was very intense during rehearsals, performing with deep sincerity and conviction, but when the band took a break to discuss ideas, Parker could not muster up a single word. Nicholson felt drawn in by this exceedingly quiet though seemingly "fragile" individual. When they spoke casually, he would often reply, "No response. No response," leaving Nicholson confused.[4] Eventually, Parker arrived at one of the rehearsals with a notebook filled with writings.[5] In lieu of communicating verbally, he showed her the poetic prose he had been composing. Those writings opened up a world of communication between them. Nicholson instantly fell in love with his writing. The two of them began talking via phone, which seemed to work better for Parker. He would pull the phone into the bathroom of his parents' apartment to get privacy, and they would talk for an hour at a time. When they did meet in person, Nicholson regarded Parker as a very gentle individual, but also one who was often joking or pulling pranks on her in playful ways. He had very particular tastes, never ate any red-colored food, and only ate a small range of dishes.

William and Patricia's relationship developed as they worked together. Nicholson's projects focused on improvised music and dance "as a form of prayer."[6] For Nicholson, this drove to the root of her interest in "transcendence, transformation, and healing."[7] And from the very beginning, Parker displayed that the music was his "through line": it was what held everything else in his life together for him. Their shared artistic interests and deepening romance led them to marry in early 1975, and their first child, Miriam, was born later that year and named for the wife of one of Parker's favorite poets, Kenneth Patchen. A son, Isaiah, would follow ten years later. Nicholson, a woman of Jewish and European Catholic heritage, was accepted into the family by Parker's parents, although he once admitted they assumed she was "white trash" for marrying him.[8]

Parker's marriage and the birth of their first child came just before he lost his father and his brother. But even then there was tension within the family and some hesitancy on his parents' part. His father elected not to attend the wedding, feeling uncomfortable in that setting. Parker's brother's death in 1978 was particularly difficult for him to deal with, and Nicholson helped Mary Louise organize the funeral arrangements, although Parker did organize a festival honoring his brother shortly after he was released from the hospital.[9] After Parker and Nicholson wed, they moved together to the Lower East Side, first to an apartment at 141 1st Avenue, above a fresh fish market. Although Nicholson wanted to live in the Bronx, Parker knew that the music scene he was aiming to be a part of was there, and his friends and collaborators Billy Bang and Daniel Carter already lived in the area. Many musicians who met Parker in his early years there recall the persistent smell of fish in the apartment, wafting up from the store. Nevertheless, this became a launching point for both Parker and Nicholson to get more involved in the arts communities in the neighborhood.

"Music That Will Give People Hope"

As Nicholson and Parker's collaborations grew, Nicholson named the project Centering Dance Music Ensemble. "For me the group was about being exactly in the middle of right now. It's finding the center of now," Nicholson explained. "The concept of art and life not being separate is a concept that William and I both shared absolutely."[10] At first it was her concept and group, but by the first performance the music was definitely Parker's, while Nicholson led the dancers. But one of the central ideas was that dance and music were unified within one artistic mode of communication and performance. Centering Dance Music Ensemble began to perform in different formations. Appropriately, their first gig was back at Studio Rivbea on March 17, 1974, in a duo format where they performed excerpts from a piece titled "The Ghosts Garden." At the time that they first conceived of the piece, it was a time of searching for both of them. For Parker, he was still experimenting with the process of composing, and each piece presented him with the challenge of turning ideas into reality. But he struggled through it and began to gain confidence and skill as a composer. He was self-taught, so he developed his own process for making this music come alive.

In many cases, Parker's early compositions had lives of their own and grew significantly over the span of years or even decades. "The Ghosts Garden" is a good example of this. The piece continued to evolve and resurfaced at a performance Parker and Nicholson did at a residency in May and June 1985.[11] By that time, it had expanded into a suite (*Fire Cycles*) with a rather prophetic message:

ERUPTION: Cancerous Sores erupt over the surface, the sad Earth weeps.

IBE: I believe you will allow my children to live that you will sing a song to make the sun rise.

SMOKE: Smoke fills the hallways of the Ghost House. Wake up! Wake up!

DECEPTION: They lived from the beginning the foundation was built on lies.

FLAME: A mountain of flames.

TEARS: The earth is a ghost garden it grows flames as spirits look for tears.[12]

By 1990, Parker and Nicholson had adapted the piece for small orchestra, including violinist Billy Bang and tubist Dave Hofstra (b. 1953) on a performance in December.[13] Throughout the piece's evolution, there was "a pull towards the ancient now ancestral markings and the concrete now that is fading," Parker wrote. The reference to ghosts is meant to illustrate the juxtaposition of eternity and loss. In a very distant way the piece was inspired by the Lakota Sioux ghost dance, "but only from the periphery," Parker noted. "The goal was to achieve transformation through music, dance, and poetry."[14]

Nicholson led Centering Dance Music Ensemble in its various formations and engaged in free improvisation dance, reacting, interacting, juxtaposing the sounds of the musicians. Parker worked as the music director under Nicholson's guidance, and he hired musicians for the projects. As it evolved, Nicholson remained the bandleader, while Parker workshopped his compositions. This was a very important step in Parker's development; it functioned as his first consistent outlet to feature his own work.[15]

Nicholson's focus was often to keep the band together, but Parker was always pushing to try something new and hated performing the same piece more than once. Nicholson said, "We need to repeat and refine these pieces," but Parker replied, "No, we should never repeat anything. If it's done once, it's over. We need to move on to the next thing."[16] Parker further elaborated, "Music, I realized then, was like food. You have to serve it fresh. Monday's composition is for Monday. You can't do Monday's composition on Tuesday. You can't serve leftover music. It lasts as long as it's played and then it dies and you have to start over again and do another one. So, that philosophy pushed me to make every concert a different concept." The late 1970s, before he became a high-profile sideperson in other bands, was a crucial period of development for Parker as he began to expand his vocabulary as a player. As he composed and played, he would stumble on new concepts or ideas and make a mental note, and one such idea might lead to half a dozen other ideas, concepts, or even compositions.[17]

Partially influenced by his interest in film, Parker saw color in sounds. He considered compositions to be an arrangement of sound and silence, resulting in a "sound painting" or, in other words, "sound painted over a canvas of silence." For Parker the possibility of such creations were limitless, and "any sound that exists in the universe can be used in a sound painting." As Parker established himself as a composer, he found that he could communicate his work by writing notes down in the conventional way but that he could also use symbols, shapes, colors, graphs, and other figures to convey meaning or intention. Once musicians heard one player in an ensemble create a sound, they could repeat the sound, complement the sound, or choose not to react: "When a sound painting takes on a life of its own, going places that were not intended in the original design of the composition, we have discovered music." Thus, for Parker, deviation from the composition or prescribed idea was necessary for artists to engage in music. Parker also viewed musical possibilities as limitless: "Music cannot be limited to symbols on paper the same way a photograph of a human being is not the real human being. Music lives in a world separate from the musician, a world of which we have only touched the surface."[18]

Centering Dance Music Ensemble, 1974–1980

Centering Dance Music Ensemble was very active, especially in Parker and Nicholson's early years together, 1974–80. They presented "Nascent: A Piece for Dance and Music," a piece for a thirteen-piece big band and four dancers at Holy Name Auditorium in April 1975. The band included Baird, Bang, and Baraka from the Music Ensemble, but the other band members were new collaborators for Parker: Alan Braufman (flute, alto saxophone), Michael Clark and Kappo Umezu (alto saxophone), Art Bennet (soprano saxophone), Mary Drivers (oboe), Nancy Ancrum (flute), Jeffery Nussbaum (trumpet), John Marshall (pocket trumpet), Frank Clayton (bass), and Ellen Christi (voice), as well as dancers Godrun Keith and Alexandra Strauss in addition to Nicholson.[19] Parker referred to the piece as "the beginning of my *Rite of Spring*," referencing the well-known Igor Stravinsky orchestral ballet, but only figuratively.[20] The same band performed another composition, "Rainbow Light," in November 1976 at St. Mark's Church-in-the-Bowery, though with Nicholson, Leslie Levinson, and two other unidentified dancers.[21]

The earliest audio recording by Centering Dance Music Ensemble dates to October 24, 1976, a suite titled *Dawn Voice*.[22] The music came from Parker's reaction to a photograph of morning sunlight coming through trees given to him by clarinetist Rozanne Levine (b. 1945), which he included in the flyer to advertise the show.[23] Indeed, the opening section, titled "Illuminese/Voice," evokes images of light, arching ever upward, and the brightening of a world, a world waking up to itself. Levine's pristine clarinet is the bold lead voice, supported by Malik Baraka and John Mingione on trumpets and Billy Bang and Ramsey Ameen on violins over Parker's bass lines. Occasionally, Ellen Christi's vocals add bursts of energy—concentrated sparks of light—onto the musical canvas, eventually cresting with an extended vocal solo over bass drone. The suite had many folk elements and bore images of farms and mountains. Despite having lived all his life in the intense urban environment of New York City, many of the most powerful prevailing images in Parker's mind at the time were "horizons, sunrise, sunset, hills, valleys, streams, light coming through the trees. . . . Blue music . . . by blue, I mean like the sky—more peaceful, ethereal."[24] Parker then provided counter to these narratives and themes with dissonances on his bass.

Parker described *Dawn Voice* in an interview done many years later:

> The idea was to have a pastoral piece, almost like a Mass that had a canopy over its dynamics—a tent that would keep a certain dynamic level, a tent that would let light in. The light would manifest as sound, sometimes as movement, sometimes as poetry. . . . That's what it's about—canopies of light and movement and shadows. This was about beauty and light turning in on itself. Also the idea was like you were watching a film with different sections, except you were listening to it. So it was pure poetic vision, without so much of a dramatic plot or anything; it had different musical sections.[25]

As Nicholson notes, "Just like William, I used structure."[26] *Dawn Voice* contained a lot of choreographed lines. The floor of the church where they performed was actually tilted, so when they performed the section of the suite called "Falling Shadows" with diving movements, Nicholson recalled that "it made me feel very precarious."[27] Levine, who played clarinet in the suite, noted that "the musicians had to be really responsive to what the dancers were doing. And the dancers, as much as they could within the structures that Patricia had choreographed, had to be responsive to what we were doing in the moment."[28] The sound-movement communication was riveting and required immense in-the-moment focus.

The final part of the bigger *Dawn Voice* suite, "Face Still, Hands Folded," referenced Parker's father in the open casket at his funeral in 1976. Parker accompanied Billy Bang's magnificent violin solo with a poem in honor of his father:

> However I see
> I hear it
> The Voice
> The only voice I hear
> I begin
> A crown of thorns
> A dance
> A rose
> This earth guided by rhythms of sunlight
> Oceans of blue sky
> Spaces of joy
> To fill a heart with happiness
> And each morning the wind blows
> I am a broken leaf falling from the tree
> Afraid to feel the ground
> I see
> I hear
> The wind blow
> My face beside the water
> I begin
> Very real and gentle, all those lights
> A sense of existence
> Of praise
> Another day to see
> To feel
> What is due respect of this life
> Displayed upon the lighted shadows
> At dawn
> A way to see the world amidst the tears
> A smile for tomorrow
> The chance of the practical life
> Flower pot sitting on the window sill

Brown rice in the jar
Water boiling for tea
Sweet potato pie hot from the oven
Sitting on the table
Collard greens
Corn bread
No books
No role to play
Human beings
No poet
No dancer
No culture
The trees are bright blue
And the sunset is in the stars
The universe inside this world
Inside a man's heart
And discovery of life
Of that which is alive
Right now I am frail
In front of death
The sense of time passing
From childhood until now
There is wonder
How much can we do in a lifetime?
The lake sits still
And ordinary flowers sit on the lake
Life is short
And there is no room for heroes
Those flowers are gentle and just wish to be
Every branch and every leaf
And every flower is filled with wonder
Now who shall bring the shadows?
And who shall greet the rainbow?
The poet, the soldier, or the prophet?
I believe
And I feel
And I hear
The Voice
And there goes my life[29]

Figure 5.1 Patricia Nicholson, Terry Sprague, and Parker, Environ, New York, 1978. *Credit*: ©Raymond Ross/ CTSIMAGES.

At another performance at St. Mark's Church in December 1976, reedist John Hagen, Rozanne Levine, Malik Baraka, percussionist Toshiyuki Tsuchitori, and dancer Leslie Levinson joined Parker and Nicholson in the suite *Document Humanum*.[30] Levine recalled the performance as "very ensemble oriented" and noted that "solos were always in service to the dance and the overall piece. It was different than pure jazz because we were all subsumed into doing a music-and-dance piece. We were parts of the whole." Nicholson often hired dancers Levinson, Terry Sprague, and Pam Read during that time period, among others. Together they continued to build upon the idea of their performances as a form of prayer or meditation, and it seems no accident that they most commonly performed in churches at that time. Levine added that "whenever we got together it was a feeling of worship, that we were getting together in a church and doing a celebration or worshiping something greater than ourselves. That spirit permeated those concerts."[31]

The year 1977 was the busiest of Parker and Nicholson's early work together, with five performances spaced evenly throughout the year. Prolific as ever, they continued to generally perform each new piece just once while continuing to work in different formations of both musicians and dancers.

Figure 5.2 Parker and Patricia Nicholson, Environ, New York, 1978.
Credit: ©Raymond Ross/CTSIMAGES.

Duo performances in March and November, both at St. Mark's Church-in-the-Bowery, showcased their most intimate work. The first duo concert featured "Cathedral of Light," which was a piece that Parker had developed as early as 1975 in a duo with violinist Billy Bang and one that he would return to in 1997–99 as a solo piece.[32] In July 2008 he performed an extended solo version of the piece that ran for over fifty minutes, at Somewhere There, a club in Toronto, which was recorded and released by Barnyard Records.[33] Parker and Nicholson also played two dates with midsize ensembles at the loft Environ in April and June of 1977, *Liberation Folk Suite* and *Sun Garden*.

Parker and Nicholson's other collaborative performance in 1977 occurred in August at the Someplace Nice Music Festival, the first festival Parker ever played a significant role in organizing. Although detailed information about the bills at the festival have not survived, it spanned across the four weekends during the month, including some weekday concerts, and included a range of music and dance-music performances. On August 28 the climax of the festival featured Parker and Nicholson with reedist John Hagen and trumpeter Arthur Williams playing a piece called "Commitment," among others. By this point, Parker was being even bolder in his imagery, drawing direct influence from his teenage interest in film. As he wrote, "What I liked about [Francois] Truffaut and [Jean-Luc] Godard and Stan Brakhage was that they had a body of work. They made many films, and each film they made was complete. That's what I wanted to do with the compositions."[34]

"Commitment" was one of the first pieces Parker composed and played that dealt with his concept of bass as drum set.[35] By that time, Parker had been listening intently to Milford Graves, especially his solo work, the record *Bäbi*, and his recordings with Albert Ayler, as well as drummer Beaver Harris's work with Archie Shepp. Drummers Rashied Ali and Sunny Murray were also quite influential on Parker's thinking at the time. Graves, Harris, Ali, and Murray were like "orchestras" in and of themselves.[36] In playing "Commitment," Parker regarded the G-string as his hi-hat or a ride cymbal, D-string as a snare or tom, the E-string as a gong, and the A-string as a lower tom.

Simultaneously, Parker had been listening to Alhaji Bai Konte (1920–ca. 1983), a Gambian jali (praise singer) and kora player. Parker's mother-in-law, Kathleen Wilkins, happened to know Marc Pevar and Susan Pevar, who had produced Bai Konte's record *Kora Melodies from the Republic of Gambia* and had given her an LP copy that she passed on to Parker. Parker had only had limited opportunities to hear contemporary music from the African continent up to that point, so to him it was "miraculous music."[37] Bai Konte's style of playing inspired him to think of ways to play the bass without stops, like a harp.[38] In this manner he was playing only overtones on the open strings, not dissimilar from a drum. And though he had never played drums extensively, Parker had some experience playing in drum circles at public parks, where he exhibited an ability of "naturally fast hands" and had developed a certain sense of African rhythms.[39] Parker was also thinking deeply about the work of bassists Lewis Worrell (b. 1934), Donald Garrett (1932–1989), and Henry Grimes (b. 1935): "I could hear some gospel and some deep church stuff in what they were doing and I was relating to it. This constituted the first 'no note' concept with just sound and rhythm."[40]

Added to the rest of his developing concepts, one day it came to Parker, when he was practicing arco technique (bowing), that each string was a band of light and the bow was a prism. To Parker the harmonics were different colors in the light spectrum, and "each of those colors has an effect on people."[41] With that breakthrough in the understanding of his instrument, the bass came alive for him in an entirely new way. Combining his two main concepts at the time—pizzicato bass as trap drum set and arco work with strings as bands of light—set Parker on a productive path forward, reaching deeper levels of understanding his instrument and its limitless possibilities.

Centering Dance Music Ensemble's later works continued to build upon its innovations with new material. *Corn Meal Suite*, first filmed at an unidentified venue in 1978, was another important piece developed by Parker and Nicholson. At that time the group included tenor saxophonist Bilal Abdur Rahman, alto saxophonist James Lott, alto saxophonist and flautist Will Connell Jr., bassist Jay Oliver, and either Takeshi Zen Matsuura or Rashid Bakr on drums (the dancers other than Nicholson have not been identified). The piece was performed live twice at St. Mark's-in-the-Bowery on April 10–11, 1978, with trumpeter Arthur Williams replacing Bilal Abdur Rahman, and dancers Suchi Branfman, Leslie Levinson, Pan Read, and Juli Tozer performing improvisations and Nicholson's choreography. The filmed version was screened at the intermission of a trio performance by saxophonist David S. Ware (1949–2012), drummer Denis Charles (1933–1998), Parker, and Nicholson in 1980.[42] The audio was broadcast on WKCR-FM in 1993.[43] In December 1979, Centering Dance Music Ensemble developed its first piece explicitly for children, "On Fire," which debuted at the Children's Dance Theater.

Ware always had a big sound. Parker regarded him as "a natural extension of Coltrane, Ayler, and Shepp, as well as a strong connection to Yusef Lateef and Gene Ammons. But David was also different than all of them. He had a unique sound coming out of a strong spiritual stance that he had developed as early as junior high school."[44] Ware was also close friends with saxophonist Sonny Rollins and often rehearsed with him. Parker and Ware developed a friendship, and in the early 1990s they would reconnect, with Ware later hiring Parker for his quartet in 1996.

For the performance where the film was screened in 1980, Parker assembled a group with new personnel, scaling things down to a trio. By that time, Parker had been playing with Charles for a number of months, and they had developed a good relationship. Charles brought a unique blend of Caribbean-influenced African rhythms into the free jazz tradition, where he "would leave a lot of space and have dialogues with himself."[45] Parker felt that the rhythm section would really open things up for fiery free jazz saxophonist David S. Ware, if only he could get him interested in playing. After his early to mid-1970s work, including a stint in the Cecil Taylor Unit, Ware had become fed up with the music world.[46] Ware had spent some time away from playing while driving a taxi full-time, but Parker caught him at a moment when Ware wanted to return to music. On the loft scene, it was also the bridging of two schools—Parker still in some ways in the Jemeel Moondoc camp—while Ware was connected to Cooper-Moore and the musicians at the 501 Canal Street loft. Ware had already developed an underground reputation as an incredible saxophone player, even though outside of the lofts he remained unknown. Ware would later rise to much greater prominence after 1988, releasing a series of critically acclaimed records as a bandleader.

After a few rehearsals, the Parker-Ware-Charles trio performed at Kiva, a community center run by Asian American poets and activists at 199 Lafayette Street in SoHo on May 9, 1980.[47] The space was sizable, giving Nicholson plenty of room to dance as part of the performance. The musicians were positioned at the center of the room, with Nicholson moving in circles around them, where she was in between them and the audience. Because Kiva generally drew a crowd, Parker was able to offer his band a guarantee of $50—a very unusual occurrence in those days. At the time, Parker recalled that almost no venues in New York were offering guarantees for the kind of music they were playing, but Parker felt that he was getting to the point where he wanted to be able to pay his bandmates. Plus, Ware had been out of the music for a little while, so Parker needed to offer him an incentive. At that time, $50 was substantial; as Parker recollected, "That was half your month's rent."[48]

The trio's music featured bold, dynamic playing by all three figures. The opening track, the twenty-four-minute exposé "Facing the Sun, One Is Never the Same," showcased Ware's considerable talent, Charles's explosive minimalism, and Parker's urgent, driven compositions. The piece built its narrative tension up to peaks of ecstatic expression in the final minutes.[49] The band paid tribute to Albert Ayler with its second piece, "One Day Understanding," which is a variation of an Ayler theme, and it is there that the band reached its cacophonic climax. In the middle of that track, Parker took one of his earliest great solos caught on record, a high-energy arco approach with rapid ascents and descents and multiple overtones, producing a multilayered, shimmering prism of sound. People can be heard voicing their awe from the audience. Then Parker took a two-minute bass solo before resuming as a trio for the fourth piece, "Tapestry," which is a more somber, quiet piece where every sound made an impact. Despite the success of the performance, circumstance would dictate that they would never perform again.

Despite Parker's prolific performances, compositions, and collaborations, the first decade of his work, from when he entered the scene in 1971 until he joined the Cecil Taylor Unit in late 1980, was chronically underdocumented. This was precisely an economic issue. The major record labels were not recording free jazz throughout that time period, so musicians were often resorting to self-production. Although it afforded them some measure of freedom and autonomy from an often exploitative recording industry, the financial rewards were often limited. Parker himself attempted to make a number of records in the time period. For example, he planned to release a debut solo record, *Soliloquy*. He hand-printed record covers and had them set up all over his apartment to dry. But he never could afford to press the vinyl, and unfortunately the original tapes have since been lost.[50] Thus, Parker's first solo recording was irrevocably lost to poverty. Another instance of this was with the collaborative trio Parker had with Ware and Charles. They hand-printed five hundred record covers but were unable to afford to press the LPs at the time.[51] The recording from 1980 lay unheard until it was released as part of Parker's collected early recordings in 2012.[52]

Most jazz musicians struggled in the 1970s and 1980s. In 1971 the National Endowment for the Arts (NEA) budgeted $50,000 for jazz, whereas classical music was earmarked for $3.5 million.[53] Although funding for jazz did rise through the decade, its impact was limited. Many of the available NEA grants were quite small, but some of the earliest recipients included figures such as trombonist Grachan Moncur III and the Jazz Composer's Orchestra Association, who were involved in the same scene as Parker.[54] Some grants supported the creation of new works while others supported tours or education of young and aspiring musicians. Under President Ronald Reagan, the first major cuts to the NEA came in 1982, based on objections to "the general principle of government support for the arts" and as a casualty of rising federal budget deficits brought on by increased military spending.[55] This trend would continue through the 1980s, with major additional cuts in 1995 under the Republican-controlled Congress.[56] There was a shift from public to private funding of the arts, and this often augmented the already top-down structure of most arts funding.[57] Needless to say, working-class Black artists found their opportunities diminished and their aesthetic choices constricted; it caused many to abandon their craft. It was even harder for Black artists to fund their work when it had a radical orientation.[58] In late 1980 Parker was hired by pianist Cecil Taylor, and from that point on he became much busier and toured Europe almost every year, if not multiple times per year, as part of various Taylor-led ensembles. Playing with Taylor afforded Parker paid work, which was scarce in New York City, but despite his work with Taylor, financial challenges continued to mount. Parker and Nicholson nevertheless forged ahead, worked collectively, and continued to scrape by financially while they worked diligently on their music.

Through the early 1980s, Parker and Nicholson collaborated less frequently. One major exception, however, was a performance in June 1982 in the United Nations building at the opening of the second UN Special Session on Disarmament, called to develop and implement a policy of nuclear disarmament. As one of its express aims, this session had to conduct a "review and appraisal of the present international situation in light of the pressing need to eliminate the danger of war, in particular nuclear war."[59] This session had come about after some modest progress at the first session held in 1978 and because of global outcries against the proliferation of weapons that was then happening between the United States and the Soviet Union. Both nations pledged support, although their actions seemed to belie a skepticism at odds with their public rhetoric.[60]

Nicholson had been raised Catholic and had been very involved in the Atlantic Life Community, a network of leftist Catholic antiwar activists that included the prominent Plowshares, an antinuclear weapons protest movement.[61] Plowshares had been founded by two brothers who were Catholic priests—Daniel Berrigan (1921–2016) and Philip Berrigan (1923–2002)—who took inspiration from a passage from the Book of Isaiah:

> And many people shall go and say, Come ye, and let us go up to the mountain of the Lord, to the house of the God of Jacob; and he will teach us of his ways, and we will walk in his paths: for out of Zion shall go forth the law, and the word of the Lord from Jerusalem. And he shall judge among the nations, and shall rebuke many people: and they shall beat their swords into plowshares, and their spears into pruning hooks: nation shall not lift up sword against nation, neither shall they learn war any more.[62]

On September 9, 1980, the Berrigan brothers and six other members who became known as the Plowshares Eight had led a nonviolent action against war machines produced by a munitions facility in King of Prussia, Pennsylvania, and were eventually sentenced to more than ten years in prison. These actions had raised their profile even further as major figures in the struggle against American militarism. The Atlantic Life Community aimed to draw together activists from throughout the northeastern United States, to coordinate efforts, and to build the movement on a larger scale.[63]

By 1982, the anti–nuclear weapons movement had been growing for most of the decade, and its participants had learned from the successes and failures of anti–Vietnam War movements in the 1960s and 1970s. When the second UN Special Session on Disarmament was announced for New York, it became a flashpoint for the movement, which had a strong desire to make its collective voice heard in various ways. In June 1982 a massive antinuclear protest march attracted an estimated one million people to the city.[64]

Because of the devastation that Japan had experienced near the conclusion of World War II, it had produced some of the leading voices calling for the elimination of nuclear weapons. For instance, the mayor of Hiroshima, the first city to have an atomic bomb dropped on it, proposed that cities around the globe work independently from national governments to bring about the abolition of nuclear weapons.[65] For their performance in support of disarmament at the United Nations building, Parker and Nicholson were inspired by the story of Sadako Sasaki (1943–1955), a girl who had lived one mile from where the atomic bomb was dropped on Hiroshima and who later developed leukemia from radiation exposure. In the final months of her life, Sasaki had endeavored to fold a thousand origami paper cranes, an act that had gained notoriety internationally as a symbol of the movement to eradicate nuclear weapons and the threat that they posed to human survival.[66] She said, "I will write Peace on your wings and you will fly all over the world."[67] The life and early death of Sadako Sasaki inspired peace and nuclear nonproliferation movements all over the world.[68]

Nicholson came up with the concept of a children's choir for "A Thousand Paper Cranes," and Parker wrote the music. To this end, Nicholson recruited a thousand schoolchildren to each fold a paper crane; the results were presented on the stage for the performance in the United Nations building. The peace opera, as Parker and Nicholson called it, contained a number of pieces composed by Parker, many with lyrics that he also wrote. Nicholson had come up with the concept and designed all of the choreography. Emily Collins assisted Nicholson in organizing all of the children throughout New York City.[69] The peace opera began with a piece titled "Ashes" that functioned like an opening prayer. A series of other pieces followed that spoke to various forms of injustice and the social cost of violence and warfare. Then the performance reached its peak with "Song of the Cranes," which a children's choir sang:

"SONG OF THE CRANES"

> *For ever more, for ever more (x2)*
> *For ever and ever, for ever and ever*
> *Only tears of joy shall we cry (x2)*
> *For ever and ever, for ever and ever*

Figure 5.3 Children performing the Thousand Cranes project, Sound Unity Festival, New York, 1984. Parker's daughter, Miriam, seventh from left. *Credit:* ©Raymond Ross/CTSIMAGES.

The roots of trees grow deep hold tight (x2)
For ever and ever, for ever and ever
We sing out, we cry out (x2)
All nature is one (x2)
For ever and ever, for ever and ever
Peace on earth, peace on earth
This is our hope, this is our prayer
Peace on earth, peace on earth
This is our hope, this is our prayer
For ever and ever, for ever and ever
With faith and love we cannot fail (x2)
For ever and ever, for ever and ever
Truth is marching in (x2)
For ever and ever, for ever and ever
Filled with love that comes from above (x2)
For ever and ever, for ever and ever
Truth is marching in.

Since Parker's coming-to-consciousness in his teenage years reading film critic Jonas Mekas, he had never drawn a dividing line between art and politics. His work with Cecil Taylor at the time resonated strongly with his desire to make revolutionary art aimed at having an impact upon the world.

When a recording was made of the Cecil Taylor Unit at the Willisau Jazz Festival in 1983, it was released as *Nicaragua: No Parasan* (Nica, 1984), with its eye on the Reagan administration's escalation of U.S. military involvement in Central America, and Nicaragua in particular. Reagan adopted policies that viewed the very existence of a left-wing revolutionary government, the Nicaraguan Sandanista National Liberation Front, as a challenge to the hegemony of the United States in the Western Hemisphere.[70] And it was clear that Reagan intended to use his covert and illegal funding of the counterinsurgency as a test case for his broader doctrine of cultivating military resistance to progressive regimes, especially in the Americas.[71] The political implications were clear and potentially devastating for people in many countries in Central and South America.

Taylor, Parker, and the other members of the band stood in solidarity with the Sandanistas. According to the liner notes for *Nicaragua: No Parasan*, "The Willisau concert was an anthem of colonized African Americans for the volcanic uprising of the Third World, for freedom and peace. Today, there is a threat of Central America's becoming a second Vietnam. We dedicate it to the revolutionary people of Nicaragua, especially the black Sandinistas of the Atlantic coast. The net proceeds, approximately 7,000 franks, go for the support of a music cooperative in Nicaragua."[72] This kind of artistic activism would form the backdrop for work that Parker would do with Nicholson and with bands like In Order to Survive in the 1990s, and would solidify his relationship with the community of artists of which he was a part.

Sound Unity Festival, 1984

Much of Parker and Nicholson's early years of work culminated in the Sound Unity Festival, which they helped organize in the summer of 1984. With a grant from the West German government, Parker, Nicholson, Kowald, and others helped organize the festival in a gymnasium on Second Avenue, featuring 119 musicians playing over the course of five days.[73] Here they performed *A Thousand Paper Cranes* for a second time in front of a new audience. The week-long festival featured many of their closest collaborators and drew performers from Europe whom Parker had encountered during his time touring there with Cecil Taylor. Other bands on the bill included the Jimmy Lyons Quintet, Commitment, Peter Kowald Trio and Quartet, Billy Bang's Forbidden Planet, Charles Tyler Quintet, Jemeel Moondoc

Sextet, Irene Schweizer-Rüdiger Carl Duo, Don Cherry and the Sound Unity Festival Orchestra, and the Peter Brötzmann Ensemble.

The festival was more than a community-building event. As Parker articulated it at the time, "The Sound Unity Festival was the first step in what I see as a three- or four-part plan to organize musicians in New York City to take other steps in their self-determination in gaining wider exposure to their music and helping to build an audience. And what made it different from other festivals is that it showcased a number of musicians that normally don't get hired, that don't get to play on regular festivals here in America." He added an explicitly political commentary: "The rich control everything. You can't separate a poor person from a poor musician. It's all the same syndrome. You have survivors of this music out here for 20 or 25 years. Some have been able to squeeze through by getting teaching jobs."[74] For Parker the festival was an attempt by artists to take matters into their own hands, to demand respect and financial rewards for their labor.

The music of the festival had deep political and spiritual meaning for many of the participants, and the festival was an opportunity to transmit those ideas to a broader audience. Tenor saxophonist Charles Gayle (b. 1939) asked the question:

> How do we rectify the world? Possibly two-thirds of the world is starving or are very bad off. This is the 80s. When we found out that we can eliminate masses of people through one stroke, then there has to be a new way of thinking. If we aren't focusing on the preservation of the human race in its beauty, its fine form, I know we have made a mistake. Anything we do in this Western world that supports the degradation of a people or of nature itself, we need to examine our term "sanity" and what course we are on.[75]

For the film *Rising Tones Cross*, which was made about the festival by Ebba Jahn, Gayle read the following prayer-like poem:

> *To all things. Peace.*
> *To those things. Peace.*
> *For all words and all deeds. Peace.*
> *Harmony for all souls.*
> *For all beliefs. Peace.*
> *The known and the unknown.*
> *The realization of the known and the unknown.*
> *For all things are one. Peace.*
> *In spite of all words and all deeds and all thoughts.*

Figure 5.4 Charles Gayle and William Parker, JVC Jazz Festival, Damrosch Park, Lincoln Center, New York, June 26, 1994. *Credit:* ©Alan Nahigian.

We seek peace for our souls.
There are no other words, there are no other deeds.
We all seek peace.
The realization is a gift of life.
Peace of the soul is realization.
All things we ask for, we ask from ourselves.
If you want peace in your soul,
Know what that is
And know that the other person wants the same peace.
That's it.[76]

Economics of the Avant-Garde

The work of Centering Dance Music Ensemble never received critical acclaim. It was hard to set up gigs with clubs when Nicholson or Parker mentioned that dancers were going to be involved. And when they approached organizations like Dance Theater Workshop, they were not welcomed because free jazz musicians were not typically working in those settings.

The segregation of genres and artistic disciplines was too vast an expanse to bridge. Music critics seemed uncertain how to talk about dance, and dance critics were not used to writing about or listening to improvised music. Similar to dance incorporated into Cecil Taylor's work that Parker was a part of during the same period, it rarely got much attention, despite clear innovations in this fusion art form.

The 1980s were hard times for musicians. With deep cuts to federal arts funding, it became very difficult to function as a working musician in New York City, especially ones working in the avant-garde. Peter Kowald, who moved from West Germany to New York City in early 1984, offered an outsider's perspective:

> You read about it in books, but here you come face-to-face with it: just how culturally insignificant jazz is in the land of its birth in the sense that there's not much money for it. It's not even seen as a cultural achievement although its influences on everything are plain. All the music for TV and films, white rock music, so much here is influenced by jazz. Jazz is behind everything. Yet, the people who seriously practice it have very slight cultural importance here in contrast to Europe. They're paid much worse here . . . such that a lot of people are barely existing. . . . There's not a violinist or any performer in Europe who's so bad off.[77]

The mid-1980s also saw a racial divide in the New York scene, much as in other eras. Kowald again brought his perspective as an outsider, speaking in 1984: "An important revelation of these last five months here is that the white and the black scene are two very different scenes, very distinct both in terms of the musical formations themselves and the audience. I was shocked at how far this thing goes, how this break, this split, is really there and determines a lot of what goes on." Kowald also noted at the time that there were far fewer opportunities for Black musicians because "the promoters, club owners, people who run the places where you can play, they're mostly white. I'm amazed how much I myself could do here when Black [musicians] wouldn't have gotten the gigs." Kowald went on to note distinct aesthetic differences that ran mostly along racial lines: "Free jazz musicians are constantly in touch with their Black roots, even when it is not so audible in their playing. There's simply a link to rhythm and tone structure. Everything that comes from inside [of a person] is always there. I was amazed to see that white [musicians] often play more interesting stuff, but it starts to get boring because so little comes from inside because it's often so conceptual and it can lose its value quickly."[78]

The American recording industry had also turned its back on jazz. Jazz as a commercially successful form of music had been on the decline since the mid- to late 1960s, replaced by rock as the recordings that had mass appeal.[79] Parker himself noted in 1984 that "most of the recording companies that record this music are European. No American company records this music on a regular basis."[80] Europe remained the land of opportunity for jazz musicians and the only place where anyone could make money on a regular basis. As Parker stated at the time, "Personally speaking, most of the money I make off of this music is from touring in Europe." Parker also felt that the music had faced intentional discrimination because it had been identified with the civil rights and Black Power movements of the late 1960s. "This music could have been a very good platform for a lot of peoples' consciousness," he argued, "and it had been very political." Nicholson bolstered these remarks along racial lines: "[The people in power] did not want a serious art form that was Black because it gives too much respectability and inspiration. What they wanted was to get Black people to conform."[81] By the mid-1980s, this was old news, in many ways, but the implications were still playing out, with fewer opportunities for those who were continuing to be involved with the music that had a revolutionary legacy.

Despite their dedication and partly because their work was innovative and defied existing artistic structures and genres, Parker and Nicholson struggled to support themselves as they worked together. They survived on food stamps and other social services, making day-to-day life always difficult, especially after the arrival of their firstborn. They were constantly down to their last ten dollars, unsure of when their next money would appear. Going to the grocery store, they would make a prayer: "'God, please I hope more money comes in soon,'" and then "buy something you don't need and then buy something that you need," Nicholson joked years later.[82]

Around 1984, Parker and Nicholson met Sarah Farley, an old friend of singer Billie Holiday, who had emerged as the leader of the homesteader community organization Local Action for Neighborhood Development (LAND). Through the organization, in 1988 Parker and Nicholson were able to buy their own apartment on East 6th Street in a formerly abandoned building for $250. Kowald, a close family friend by then, described the apartment: "All that was left was a front wall, and through the window openings you could see the sky. The back wall and the floors were simply not there and I can still see William on a long ladder with hammer and chisel, and definitely not in a bad mood."[83] It came with the commitment to work

Figure 5.5 Parker with
son, Isaiah, at home on
East 6th Street, late 1980s.
Credit: ©Patricia Nicholson.

eighteen hours per week on restoring the building and included a loan from the city for new plumbing. While Nicholson was busy with their second child, Parker put in the hours working on building walls, floors, bedrooms, and the like. Later, a grant from the New York Council of the Arts for $7,500 allowed them to buy building materials and to build a kitchen in the unit.[84] It was rugged at first, but they fashioned it into a home for their family where they continue to live to the present day.

The Parker home was filled with art, music, dance, and creativity in many forms. Miriam, Parker and Nicholson's daughter, who has established herself as a dancer in her own right, remarked that "all of my childhood memories are related, in some way, to creativity and bending the norm." She recalled one particularly fond memory of listening to a record of Kenneth Patchen reading his poetry while Parker made the family blueberry pancakes for breakfast while sunlight drifted in through a window: "My dad smiled a lot. He is a very loving person. And he is really great with kids. He would buy records and share them with me, like Michael Jackson's first big record, and of course jazz, Albert Ayler, all kinds of stuff." Miriam's first experiences dancing were with her father.[85]

Parker played practical jokes on his kids, like adopting different personas and doing silly things or pulling pranks. "He's not just a comedian," Miriam laughed. "He's a performer. He used to be shy, but he's become less shy over the years." Miriam delightfully described her father's imagination, his curiosity, his playfulness: "He has a bright, beautiful light inside of him that is irreplaceable. He is also relentlessly supportive of the underdog."[86] The family's food was simple, with things like brown rice and ramen as common staples. Parker made sweet potato pie, collard greens, and roast chicken or turkey for holidays.

What meager support Parker and Nicholson had provided them the time to do their work. Parker felt relieved that he felt no pressure to find a day job. When they discussed their circumstances, Nicholson always said to him, "Don't worry about it. Make the music."[87] Poverty was a continuous burden for them well into the 1990s. Many friends and collaborators credit Nicholson for her stalwart support of Parker. "Not many people are willing to follow their spouse by taking a kind of vow of poverty so that they can create art," pianist Matthew Shipp observed of her.[88] To Cooper-Moore, Nicholson was the bedrock, "creating a whole community for us all to be a part of. It's a pretty amazing thing that, to be a part of something."[89] Making the sacrifice of financial and material well-being allowed Parker to nurture the spark of his creativity into a fully burning flame.

Six

"Music Is Supposed to Change People":
Working with Cecil Taylor

Cecil Taylor's life story is the
history of the new jazz.

—— Steve Lake, 1989

Cecil Taylor (1929–2018) was one of the most influential, powerful, and in-novative musicians of the twentieth century, and his monumental legacy is still unfolding. By the mid-1960s, he had established himself as one of the most profound jazz figures of his generation. Despite the respect he gained from fellow musicians, a few perceptive critics, and audiences around the world, Taylor, like many others of his time, struggled to survive. As Taylor once stated, "That piano has developed from my poverty, not having the money to tune it. Certain things have happened to that piano just because I played it."[1] In the late 1980s, looking back, Taylor remarked that "the thirty years went by very quickly and at the same time I am very fortunate to be alive. Sometimes I wonder how I survived."[2]

Taylor's six-week stint of concerts at the Five Spot in 1957 are now consid-ered to be one of two major genesis points for free jazz as a distinct subgenre of the music.[3] Taylor made a series of definitive recordings. *Looking Ahead!*, released on Contemporary Records in 1959, established his distinct sound and some of the facets of his unique approach to the music that some critics would define as not adhering to chord changes, rhythmic complexity and nonconformity, and freeing the rhythm section from its timekeeping function.[4] In the liner notes, Taylor described the music: "Some people say I'm atonal. It depends, for one thing, on your definition of the term. In any case, I have not yet been atonal on records, including this one, but have been on occasion in live performances. Basically, it's not important whether a certain chord happens to fit some student's definition of atonality."[5]

Unit Structures, released in 1966, is one of the most important and influential recordings of his career, featuring high-energy music that had no equal in its intensity or the scope of its vision at the time.[6] Penning his own liner notes, Taylor wrote about the record in the poetic essay titled "Sound Structure of Subculture Becoming Major Breath/Naked Fire Gestures": "Joint energy disposal in parts of singular feedings. A recharge; group chain reaction. Acceleration result succession of multiple time compression areas. Sliding elision/beat here is physical commitment to earth force. Rude insistence of tough meeting at vertical centers. Time strata thru panels joined sequence a continuum (movements) across nerve centers. Total immersion."[7] One interpretation of the record understood it as a theorization of "an aesthetic renegotiation of performative space and time and in so doing incorporated critiques of European-derived epistemologies and the cultural history of the African diaspora." Put another way, the record was "a critique of U.S. history, culture, and power relations therein."[8]

After the deaths of John Coltrane in 1967 and Albert Ayler in 1970, Taylor carried the mantle of free jazz in many ways, and in the 1970s new opportunities began to open up for him. In February 1970 he was appointed to the faculty of the University of Wisconsin, where he gave a series of workshops titled "Black Music from 1920 to 1970."[9] Taylor's years as a university-level educator had him at the forefront of developing curricula and ideas about Black Music that would further cement his position as the leader of the free jazz community. In 1972–73, Taylor, saxophonist Jimmy Lyons, and drummer Andrew Cyrille (b. 1939) were artists in residence at Antioch College, where they attracted a large number of students eager to learn about their groundbreaking music. Receiving a Guggenheim Fellowship in 1973, being awarded an honorary doctorate from the New England Conservatory, and playing on the White House lawn for President Jimmy Carter began to provide him more financial stability and wider recognition.[10]

By the mid-1970s, European tours were becoming his most steady source of income as New York City collapsed financially and the United States began to defund the arts on a broad scale.[11] On one tour, Taylor recalled, "During the mid-1970s we were doing 10 or 12 concerts per tour, and none of the attendance totals were under 2,000. Then we came back to read the trade papers and a man big in the business saying, 'Well, we cannot present this kind of music on television because the audience will not accept it.'"[12] In 1984 Taylor remarked that "when we were in Europe . . . and had all these concerts, it was kind of difficult for us to return to New York City, because there simply was nothing, absolutely nothing."[13] For decades after, really for the rest of Taylor's career, the disparity of opportunities between Europe and the United States remained, with but a few exceptions.

Meeting Cecil Taylor

Soon after Parker began playing in Jemeel Moondoc's Ensemble Muntu in early autumn 1973, trumpeter Arthur Williams introduced him to Taylor. At the time, Williams had been going to Taylor's big-band rehearsals and invited Parker to come along. Taylor had moved to New York and was attempting to build on the groups he had previously assembled while teaching at Antioch College. Over the months, the rehearsals fluctuated considerably in terms of the people involved. At one point, Parker invited trombonist Joseph Bowie (b. 1953) and saxophonist Luther Thomas (1950–2009)— both originally from St. Louis—to attend the rehearsals. It was a kind of community jam session for those interested in contributing to Taylor's project, although it did not pay well. Musicians participated in the big band to have the experience of working with one of the true masters and visionaries of the era. The big band rehearsed for a few months, primarily at Taylor's apartment at 96 Chambers Street, leading up to the concert at Carnegie Hall on the evening of March 12, 1974.[14]

The big band included many of the prominent free jazz players at the time, as well as a number of lesser-known students of Taylor who had followed him to New York. The ambitious project included alto saxophonists Jimmy Lyons, Bobby Zankel, and possibly Luther Thomas; tenor saxophonists David S. Ware, Hassan Abdullah, Craig Purpura, and Elliot Levin; soprano saxophonist Ken Simon; baritone saxophonist Charles Tyler; bassoonist Karen Borca; trumpeters Raphe Malik, Hannibal Marvin Peterson, Arthur Williams, and Kevin Powell; trombonists Joseph Bowie and Craig Harris; French hornist Sharon Freeman; flautist Carol Poole; guitarists David First and Bud Neuber; bassists Sirone, Dave Saphra, and Earl Henderson in

Figure 6.1 Cecil Taylor big band, Carnegie Hall, New York, March 12, 1974.
Credit: ©Harvey Spigler.

addition to Parker; and percussionists Rashid Bakr, Sunny Murray, Marc Edwards, and Andrew Cyrille.[15] They played one eighty-minute suite titled *Tribe* that included a series of pieces titled "Voice," "To Night," "Being Body," "Black Node," "Suns," "Weight Fall," and the title piece.

Rehearsing and performing with Cecil Taylor's big band taught Parker a considerable amount about freedom and trust in the music. He realized that nobody had an answer to all of the questions raised in the music but that one could rely on the support of the other big-band players. And once one let go of particular certainties, such as the key of a particular section or piece, and instead let the music carry one along, trust grew and strengthened the collective participants. This had a major impact on Parker's approach to big-band music and even on the small-group improvisations that he developed throughout his career.[16]

The Carnegie Hall concert was particularly pivotal because it was the beginning of a long musical relationship between Parker and Taylor. Although the two did not immediately begin playing together in other groups, they remained familiar with each other. Parker reacquainted himself with Taylor in June 1975. When playing for a week with Don Cherry at the Five Spot, he encountered Taylor in the audience after the show concluded.[17] Parker was also connected to Taylor's world through many of their mutual friends and collaborators. Taylor commented on Parker, "Isn't he something?"[18]

Then, in August 1979, Taylor attended a performance by Ensemble Muntu at the Tin Palace, a dingy saloon on the Bowery and 3rd Street.[19] Unbeknownst to Parker, Taylor was looking for a new rhythm section. About a year later, Taylor had an opportunity to do several concerts with saxophonist Jimmy Lyons (1931–1986) at Blues Alley in Washington, DC, an historic jazz nightclub that had been founded in 1965.[20] The concerts were scheduled for December 1980, and after calling two other players who were unavailable, Taylor had his manager, Jim Silverman, call Parker.[21] From the very beginning, Parker and Taylor worked well together, and Parker immediately became Taylor's regular bass player. At the same time, Taylor also added Rashid Bakr as the drummer. Parker knew Bakr well from Ensemble Muntu, leading Moondoc to frequently state that "Cecil Taylor stole my rhythm section."[22] In many ways, Parker's work with Ensemble Muntu had been a training ground for playing with Taylor. When Parker got the call, he was ready.

After the first concert with the Cecil Taylor Unit in 1980, Parker began to rehearse regularly with the band at Soundscape at 500 West 52nd Street, near 10th Avenue, which was generally scheduled right after Taylor got done practicing duo with Ornette Coleman in the space.[23] Parker's first impression of the sessions when hearing the music was that "it looks like Cecil is playing all of the parts!" So he pondered the music for the first hour of the rehearsal until the thought occurred to him: "Of course he's not playing all of the parts. What can I contribute to it?" So he began to hone his ability to listen and respond, to play within and outside of the structures that Taylor and the other musicians laid down. It was the beginning of a new stage of development, playing extensively with a core ensemble that practiced regularly. Through the years it became a form of meditation for Parker, whether rehearsing with the band or practicing the music alone. As he remarked, "When we practiced, everything was beautiful. That's how it was with Cecil. The process."[24]

Jimmy Lyons (1931–1986) had a central and transformative presence in the Unit. He had the ability to lighten up the music, to counterbalance the intensity of Taylor's approach to piano. There was constant call and response that elevated the interplay of horn and rhythms. Lyons had gained a deep understanding and familiarity with Taylor since replacing Archie Shepp as the saxophonist in Taylor's band in 1961. Lyons's dedication to Taylor was so deep that he sacrificed part of his own career as a leader to play with Taylor, regularly turning down gigs of his own if they conflicted with the schedule of the Unit.[25] Lyons was Taylor's "closest and most trusted friend, the two having experienced both the years of struggle and the period of growing success together."[26] As Taylor stated in 1988, "All the music that I write will always be dedicated to Jimmy Lyons . . . he was in many ways my protector, as well as the most reliable, devoted musician I've ever worked with."[27]

Still, Lyons managed to maintain his own approach to the music, with his own identifiable articulation and pedagogy, despite working so many years with someone with such a monumental and pervasive artistic vision as Taylor. Lyons had clearly absorbed a lot of Charlie Parker but really carried forward what he gleaned into a different context and developed an approach to high-energy playing that was all his own. As critic Ekkehard Jost observed, "Lyons' mastery of both the linear-melodic and the energy-oriented styles, along with his ability to employ each purposely as context required, made Lyons the ideal partner for Taylor."[28] Lyons's discipline in practicing and preparing is now legendary. Parker would join Lyons and Karen Borca for practicing and rehearsals in the Bronx in what became a form of meditative practice for hours on end, day after day.

Outside of regular rehearsals by the Unit, the band did not play again until mid-1981, at which point it began to get more work, including a weekend in May 1981 at the Public Theatre in New York, a space that had played a central role in drawing loft jazz bands out into public venues since 1978, marking the end of the active loft scene.[29] The Unit also played a series of afternoon concerts at the Herbst Theatre in San Francisco in October. The following month, the Unit embarked on its first European tour, playing international jazz festivals and club dates in Paris, Milan, London, Zurich, and Freiburg.[30] The date at the International Jazz Festival in Zurich was quite propitious because trumpeter Bill Dixon's two-bass quartet with Alan Silva, Mario Pavone, and drummer Laurence Cook opened the evening and was documented for the now-legendary *November 1981* recording.[31] Taylor's band followed, and it recorded *Calling It the 8th* for Hat Hut Records, the band's first album as a unit.[32]

The record included two long improvisations, the title piece spanning thirty-three minutes, split between the two sides. It opens with Taylor chanting while doing hand rhythms (presumably on top or on the side of the piano), then Taylor, Parker, and Bakr launching in furiously with an extended improvisation. Although there are a few momentary lulls in the action, they are always followed by ascents and sudden bursts that continue to push the action. Lyons appears sparsely but makes the most of open, beautiful lines about a third of the way through the piece, adding an additional layer to an already complex-energy music. Parker's bass lines are incredibly robust, not only pushing the action but also occupying space and giving the music buoyancy. Everywhere in the music, Taylor's keys dance. Only toward the end of the title piece do the players step back, with slower and more deliberate lines before some final vaunted ascents with Lyons reaching high. The second piece, "Calling It the 9th," was a denser yet less compact improvisation with the parts parsed out a bit more than the first.

The day that it recorded, the Unit played at the Freiburger Jazztage in Freiburg, jumping in a Mercedes-Benz and driving to Germany, where the band split a night with pianist McCoy Tyner's band.[33] During the early years with the band, Parker never played with an amplifier. At the time he did not own one and would often just play through a microphone. Unfortunately at live concerts, audiences often could not hear Parker's lines clearly, although Taylor was always able to hear the bassist. In studio recordings of the period, however, Parker's robust lines were clearly audible.

All along the way, Parker learned how to integrate himself into Taylor's music, no small task considering that the pianist had a very strong and resolute vision. Parker had already been playing professionally for a decade and had been practicing five to six hours or more each day during most of those years. So it was never a matter of endurance, which was a baseline requirement to play with Taylor. Much of the learning process continued to come down to trust building and getting to know Taylor and the other players so deeply that anticipation became instinctual. At the same time, Parker became aware of the possibilities to delve even deeper into the music itself: "At that time, I became aware of the fact that if you are playing the bass, which is at the basement of the music, there is a sub-basement, and another sub-level beneath that. You have to keep digging further and further down. If you are playing the melody, which is the top floor of the musical building, there is always another level up from that, and another one beyond that one, and so forth. Really what I mean is that the dimensions and depths of sound have no limit and it was playing with Cecil that taught me that."[34]

Lush Life Concerts, 1981–1982

From December 1981 to March 1982, the Cecil Taylor Unit played a long series of concerts at Lush Life on Bleecker Street in the West Village. It began as a series of quartet gigs that brought back Rashid Bakr on drums on December 26, with full weeks in both January and March following. The Unit was very tight by that time. Parker had gotten very comfortable with the uncertainty of what would happen in the live setting. Much of Parker's growth as a musician had to do with ear training. Taylor would announce that they would begin an improvised piece beginning on F sharp, for example, and then Parker would have to listen and respond as the music grew, expanded, and evolved from that starting point.[35] There were no other cues.

As Taylor remarked before one of the January rehearsals, "Music is supposed to change people. When you dance, you change. When you sing, you change."[36] By the time they played the series of Lush Life concerts, Parker was "giving into the music. It was like relaxing into free fall and letting the air and the wind move you. That's how playing the music was."[37] One critic commented that Parker and Rashid Bakr made up "one of the most attentive and resourceful rhythm teams [Taylor] has employed."[38]

Taylor's music at the time was "drenched in the blues tradition, in the ritual traditions of Africa and the call of the griot."[39] In many West African societies, griots were lore keepers who collected, safeguarded, and passed down oral histories, legends, and collective wisdom from one generation to the next, sometimes allowing for the passage of information over many centuries through a long chain of griots.[40] A number of scholars have recognized the griot tradition as heavily influential in the making of the blues and jazz traditions by African Americans in the United States and elsewhere.[41] Taylor would often begin the performances by talking or chanting, drawing from words of Aztec, Incan, or Egyptian languages.[42] As Parker recalled years later, "When Cecil played, I could see dancers in my head, whether or not they were included in the actual performance."[43] Indeed, at the time Taylor was experimenting with the integration of dancers into his performances, and it was to be the hallmark of many of his projects throughout the 1980s.

The Lush Life performances soon grew into Expanded Unit gigs, featuring the new iterations of Taylor's big band involving various lineups. Taylor included frequent collaborators saxophonist Glenn Spearman (1947–1998), bassoonist Karen Borca (b. 1948), and trumpeter Raphe Malik (1948–2006), among a number of others. Spearman's debut record was *Night after Night,* and he continued to work with his own bands until his early death.[44] Borca is chronically underdocumented despite being a groundbreaking player and barrier smasher.[45] Malik, also underdocumented, recorded three records as a leader in the final years of his life, after appearing on a number of recordings by Lyons, Taylor, and others.[46] The band would rehearse at the

Bell Telephone Building in lower Manhattan, across from the Odeon Café, where they would eat after concluding rehearsal.[47]

Saxophonists Steve Coleman and David Murray were all in the original lineup but got fired after the first week because Taylor felt they were not taking the music seriously. When saxophonist Frank Wright (1935–1990) joined the group at the next rehearsal, "He lifted the whole band up. We could hear the difference between enlightened and illuminated sound and sound that is just sound. Frank had a sound that would just light up the sky."[48] Wright was known for his explosive, high-energy, cacophonic playing. Others involved in the band included Ken Simon (alto saxophone), Charles Tyler (baritone saxophone), Butch Morris and Daniel Carter (trumpets), Craig Harris (trombone), Muneer Abdul Fataah (cello), and Andre Martinez (drums). The Expanded Unit did weekly performances on Sunday nights in March and April at Lush Life with three sets each night at 9:30, 11:30, and 1:15 AM. Of these new inclusions, Martinez became a regular member of the Unit and played and toured with Taylor throughout much of the rest of the 1980s.[49]

The Lush Life concerts were critical in Taylor's own development. Taylor had a series of deep conversations with drummer Andre Martinez around that time which led to a reconceptualization of his own concerts. Martinez had been under contract with Dee Dee Sharp for concerts with her Philadelphia Gamble & Huff Productions that took the form of show productions. Taylor was fascinated by the prospects and developed these ideas in a direction all his own. As Martinez recalled,

> From this point on, Cecil's shows began to change and become more like productions [with] intros, poetry, dance, chanting. . . . Pieces were scored as sections where moments of inspiration and melodic romantic-type melodies took place, encores were shortened, but the power and creative fury remained. It was about show and production, layout and format: intro and dance; followed by chant; then entrance and set theme; followed by a more intense piece; then a few solos; then a medium piece; followed by an all-out piece—then bring it down, then up and out. Then do a small encore, leave, and let them come again for more next time.[50]

The work being refined at Lush Life culminated with performances at Judson Memorial Church on Washington Square Park in the West Village, May 27–28, premiering improvised techniques of noted dancer and choreographer Dianne McIntyre with her troupe, Sounds in Motion, together with the music in a four-part piece titled *Eye of the Crocodile*.[51] McIntyre

(b. 1946) has been a major dancer and choreographer, pivotal in developing new approaches while working with authors, playwrights, and musicians such as Bill Dixon, Max Roach, Abbey Lincoln, and Ahmed Abdullah before beginning her work with Taylor.[52] McIntyre had founded Sounds in Motion in 1972 and later received a grant from the National Endowment for the Arts that allowed her to tour in the United States and Europe.[53] She had founded the only dance studio in Harlem at the time, also called Sounds in Motion, which drew artists, scholars, and activists involved in the "forward movement of Black consciousness."[54] Much like Parker, McIntyre considered her art to be "a functional part of the struggle for survival."[55] To this end, McIntyre shared an interest with her collaborators to reach working-class Black Americans first and foremost, a theme that resonated with Parker.

Cecil Taylor was McIntyre's most consistent early collaborator; they first worked together in 1974. In those early years, Taylor and McIntyre developed their techniques, Taylor and the dancers taking cues from each other, "attentively listening to and watching each other's improvisations." McIntyre regarded one of the keys to their success the fact that "Cecil was a very, very dance-oriented person." The rapid exchanges and revolutionizing the components of an ensemble were groundbreaking in their vision. McIntyre described it as "Cecil and I and the dancers, we all came into be like one body." Elaborating further, McIntyre stated in relation to Taylor's performances, "I realized that music was so special to me that the dance actually became the music, so that the dancer's body became a musical instrument. So it began more and more to merge with the music, and I found that there is no difference between the dancer and the music."[56] Parker, who had done extensive work with Patricia Nicholson, was familiar with the concept of combining improvised music and dance, so he found the project to be quite natural, even as it was boldly innovative.

The Sounds in Motion troupe that McIntyre featured with the Cecil Taylor Unit at Judson Memorial Church included dancers Cheryl Banks and Mickey Davidson, both of whom had performed previously with Sun Ra, as well as Warren Spears and Kevin Wynn. In rehearsals the musicians would play, and McIntyre would walk around in a circle, generating ideas. There was never any talking or trying to do something a second time. She would usher in the dancers, and then the dancers and musicians would enter the world of collective improvisation.

Although New York critics overlooked these innovative integrations of improvised music and dance, when the Cecil Taylor Unit and the Sounds in Motion Dance Company featured their work at a series of performances in Italy and the United Kingdom in March 1983, they drew large and enthusiastic crowds and a positive response from critics.[57] At one beautiful performance space in Cagliari (the capital of the Italian island of Sardinia) on a crystal-clear day, they could see Africa out across the waters when they faced the Mediterranean.[58] Earlier that day, the well-known sculptor and muralist Pinuccio Sciola (1942–2016), from nearby San Sperate, had hosted the whole group for lunch and given one of his works to Taylor to honor the artists.[59] The final concert, at a grand concert hall called the Roundhouse in Camden, England, was a week-long festival that also featured the Gil Evans Big Band, Lester Bowie, Freddie Hubbard, and other jazz players.

The Cecil Taylor Unit stayed in Europe to play additional concerts in Berlin in March and April 1983. Parker had previously met bassist Peter Kowald in New York in 1982, and Kowald later invited him to come to Germany. It was there that Parker met reeds player Peter Brötzmann, drummer Tony Oxley (b. 1938), and trombonist Konrad "Connie" Bauer (b. 1943), all of whom would become key collaborators in later years.[60] The connection with Brötzmann was immediate, and the German saxophonist quickly invited Parker to play concerts with him in New York in April and May 1983.[61] From that point forward, Parker was increasingly drawn into the FMP family of artists centered in Germany, many of whom would become major collaborators in future years.[62] "Parker's ability at crossing over several improvising aesthetics, playing with Europeans and their unique approach to improvising, showing a great deal of flexibility and artistic sense to be able to do that," trombonist Steve Swell would observe many years later.[63] Playing in Europe in the early 1980s allowed Parker to finally begin to make a living from his work, but he remained in relative poverty even in those years.

After Taylor and McIntyre had a falling out, the Unit collaborated with Mickey Davidson, who had been one of the principal dancers in McIntyre and Taylor's previous work and had also collaborated with trumpeter Ahmed Abdullah.[64] Davidson's troupe included dancers Pauline Tagnelie, Leon Brown, and Ron McKay. Taylor brought Davidson's troupe back to Europe for a series of improvised music-dance performances in October and November 1983. The Unit was by then a sextet, including Brenda Bakr on vocals, Rashid Bakr and Andre Martinez on drums, along with Parker, Lyons, and Taylor. Premiering at a festival in Nancy, France, on October 18, Sun Ra opened the night, and the Unit followed, beginning its set with poetry and Bata drums to a crowd of more than four thousand people.[65]

Other dates on the tour followed at the Festival Internacional Jazz de Zaragoza in Zaragoza, Spain, on October 26, and the next night at the jazz festival in Madrid. The Unit returned to France for a performance in Orleans, which was recorded for Radio France on October 29, and then endured a harrowing car ride to Berlin to perform at the Total Music Meeting '83 on the next day at the Berlin Philharmonic. Dates in Mannheim, Germany, and Dornbirn, Austria, prepared the band to record for Hat Hut Records in the Black Forest in Germany on November 10–11, a recording that was never released.[66] After one date in Basel, Switzerland, on November 16, the band returned to the United States, having spent a month presenting its music to enthusiastic and receptive audiences across Europe.

Jazz Wars

While Parker was playing and touring with Taylor, the beginnings of what became known colloquially as the jazz wars erupted. This was the era that witnessed a conservative turn in how establishment granters, promoters, record labels, and writers began heralding a return to the tradition as a reaction to the free jazz trajectories of the music that had erupted since the late 1950s. There had been a number of journalists and critics who had opposed free jazz since the release of *The Shape of Jazz to Come* by Ornette Coleman in 1959, and the fissures gradually became more entrenched within the community, the jazz music industry, and the competition to get arts funding.

But things intensified and became personal in the 1980s. The jazz wars in earnest began with a scathing review written by Stanley Crouch for the *Village Voice* in response to four Lush Life concerts in March 1982.[67] Crouch was a drummer by training, although he had not gotten any attention from the press and had released no records of consequence. He had written positive reviews about some free jazz players such as saxophonist David S. Ware and trumpeter Raphe Malik, but not Taylor's drummer Rashid Bakr. Somehow Crouch had gotten the idea that Taylor was going to hire him, but that never materialized.[68] So, perhaps in retaliation, Crouch wrote a scathing review in which he disregarded much of the jazz avant-garde as "primitive" and "free of musical knowledge" while also attacking Taylor directly for his anti-conservatory approach to playing and orchestration, despite the fact that Taylor was conservatory-trained.[69] Shamefully, the newspaper printed the review. This was part of a broader conservative regression that Crouch was a part of in the 1980s.

Crouch simply did not understand most of the music of the avant-garde, evidenced by his descriptions of it as "violent folk music" and its practitioners as "[a] bunch of pretentious illiterates."[70] Rather than identify and analyze the revolutionary steps forward from existing repertoires, structures, or musical vocabularies, he condemned the music for lacking characteristics familiar to him. Crouch decried much of Taylor's work because it moved away from the blues, without illuminating the new doors the pianist had opened. Attacking the music for what it did not do was flimsy grounds for critique, but the press and a part of the public bought it. Crouch, of course, was not alone, and he echoed misguided criticism that had been voiced since the very inception of free jazz, including charges of "anti-jazz" or simply refusing to see free jazz as music in the first place.[71] Parker recalled trumpeter Lester Bowie referring to him and his associates as "the wild bunch" because they just freely improvised and that in contrast to AACM, there was no perceived intellectualism in the music. This reference was picked up by the press and continued to be used to characterize the music negatively in later years.[72] Matthew Shipp went further to say that much of the jazz establishment and many critics regarded them as "just a bunch of niggers who could play."[73] These kinds of attitudes have continued to haunt the music through the decades.

Crouch attacked the personnel included in the Lush Life big band of March 1982, with special vitriol for rival drummer Rashid Bakr.[74] When Crouch returned to Lush Life for the subsequent April 4 Expanded Unit performance, "All hell broke loose," and Crouch was escorted out by the bouncer before the performance began.[75] Crouch's personal vendetta against Taylor, Bakr, and others by this point was clear, underscored by his homophobic attacks on Taylor that had appeared in his review. Crouch outed Taylor as gay, positing the argument that Taylor's sexual orientation played a role in his inability to swing in the music.[76] However, the unspoken message was that Crouch's outing of Taylor was intended to undermine and destroy the pianist's career. As Taylor later responded, "Someone once asked me if I was gay. I said, 'Do you think a three-letter word defines the complexity of my humanity?' I avoid the trap of easy definition."[77]

The conflict between Taylor and Crouch continued without resolution well into the 1990s. Crouch soon joined forces with fundamentalist figures such as Wynton Marsalis who beckoned a return to the bebop tradition. The establishment—journalism and public funding—tilted hard toward the conservatives. Magazines like *Down Beat* heaped praise upon musicians who were giving bebop a rebirth and paid less and less attention to the jazz vanguard. The legacy of this deep split was, in some ways, solidified with the Ken Burns documentary *Jazz* (2001), for which Marsalis was the senior creative consultant and for which Crouch served on the advisory board and was interviewed extensively throughout the film.[78] The Burns documentary, aimed at establishing a kind of jazz canon, was heavily biased toward conservatives and drastically underrepresented Cecil Taylor among many other avantgarde musicians of the era. As one theorist argues, "Keeping artists like Taylor 'outside' the schema for 'formal history' by way of a generalized indication that certain elements are constant in jazz improvisation and verge on being quantifiable as such is a market-cornering gesture built to ensure the authenticity of one rendition of the construction of tradition."[79] Taylor was not the only target for Crouch's vitriol: the critic would go on to make a career out of attacking prominent, innovative African American artists and writers including Alex Haley, Spike Lee, Cornel West, Amiri Baraka, Tupac Shakur, and Snoop Dogg.[80] Although the jazz wars faded over time, the damage had been done, with a great blow struck against Black revolutionary music, against free jazz, against the continued development of the music into the unknown beyond. Nevertheless, a whole generation of musicians in the 1980s and 1990s, with Parker in the lead, did just that: continued to push forward, to explore these forbidden frontiers, to expand the limitless possibilities of the music.

The Music Goes On: Orchestra of Two Continents

Despite whatever journalistic noise was happening in the background, the Cecil Taylor Unit continued making groundbreaking music through the 1980s. In the fall of 1984, Taylor unveiled his Orchestra of Two Continents. The band combined American and European musicians with the regular quintet of Parker, Lyons, and both Bakr and Martinez on percussion, plus vocalist Brenda Bakr, bassoonist Karen Borca, saxophonists Frank Wright and John Tchicai, as well as European trumpeters Tomasz Stańko and Enrico Rava, and Gunter Hampel on baritone saxophone. Stańko (1942–2018) got his first critical attention as a member of the Krzysztof Komeda Quintet (1963–67), and subsequently with his own quintet from 1968 and a co-led unit with Polish pianist Adam Makowicz from 1975. Rava (b. 1939) was one of the premier Italian jazz players of his generation, gaining recognition through work with saxophonist Gato Barbieri's quintet and in various Steve Lacy–led groups in the 1960s and later work with many established musicians in the 1970s and after. Hampel (b. 1937) was a German multi-instrumentalist best known for his record *8th of July 1969*, but he became less active after the mid-1980s. The music of the large ensemble blended American free jazz informed by the bebop tradition, led by Jimmy Lyons interacting with European free improvisers.[81]

Five years later, Stańko wrote the following:

> When I was working for the first time with Cecil Taylor in 1984 (Orchestra of Two Continents), there was not much time for rehearsals. Yet I noticed that his style of work was very unusual, unconventional, completely different to what most musicians are used to. This caused quite a havoc, a kind of musical anarchy—surprisingly enough evolving toward astounding musical effects combined with happening-like, dance-like, motional elements . . . it would be difficult to find a better word to describe his art than as "magical." He would appear on stage in his unique and beautiful way, a visualized form, color and movement . . . it was impossible to resist falling under the spell of the atmosphere he created . . . swollen with dazzling perfume . . . intoxicating. . . .[82]

For European players who had learned music in very different ways, at times the encounter was startling, as Stańko illustrates:

> In the course of work, when I started getting a better insight into [Taylor's] creative process, into the way Taylor worked the universe of sounds—I realized that it was a very precise and adequate way of conveying the artistic concept and ideas. I remember one of the problems to solve was his system of notation. At first it was causing a lot of up-side-down among the musicians. But shortly—like in a dream everything started getting sense . . . it was as if we discovered a new dimension mysteriously pulsating and floating with measures, lines and phrases of his "winged serpents."[83]

Orchestra of Two Continents' first date, October 15, 1984, was in the historic opera house Oper der Stadt Köln in Cologne, Germany, on a stage used to holding large symphonies and a room that could seat thirteen hundred audience members.[84] Then Taylor's agent for the tour arranged a place for them to rehearse for few days before performing at the Jazzovy Festival Praha 84 at the Czechoslovakian Ministry of Culture for a televised event on October 18.[85]

Taylor's Orchestra of Two Continents' next performance was in Rubigen, near Bern, Switzerland, two days later. The venue, Mühle Hunziken, had the stage in the middle of the room with people all around the exterior as well as above, for there was a prominent balcony that also encircled the stage. It was a packed house with an electric crowd. As drummer Andre Martinez remarked, "[The crowd was] charged and that fueled us."[86] Swiss radio recorded the concert and broadcast it to a national audience.

The band woke up the next day and traveled straight to Milan, where they spent three days in Studio 7 laying down tracks for the record *Winged Serpent (Sliding Quadrants)* for the Italian label Soul Note.[87] The music resembled his Unit work, in some ways, but now had the benefit of seven additional voices contributing to the complexity and layers of the band's sound. The result is a whirling kaleidoscope of sound delivered at top speed. Lyons and Taylor remain the most prominent voices on the record. The second piece, "Womb Waters Scent of the Burning Armodillo Shell," opens with horns making call and response, voicing echoes through the early minutes. "Cun-Un-Un-Ùn-An" begins with chanting from the entire band and Taylor voicing words with rumbling percussion underneath maintaining narrative tension. About midway through the piece, horn-led plunges take over with percussion retreating underneath while the lead voices explore tonal dissonance. The record brilliantly displays Taylor's capabilities with a big band while showcasing many of his own unique qualities as an artist and improviser. He would continue to build on the work later in the decade.

After recording in Milan, the band traveled to Warsaw to perform two days later at the Jazz Jamboree 84, 26th International Jazz Festival. This was a major event, with Ornette Coleman, Michele Rosewoman, Buddy Rich, and many others for an event that was nationally televised.[88] Two more dates in France at Belfort and the jazz festival in Paris completed the tour. The finale took place in the Theatre Musical de Paris, an opera house built in the 1860s that had staged many historic performances, including the debut of Stravinsky's *Petrouchka* in 1911 and symphonies conducted by Tchaikovsky, Mahler, and Strauss around the turn of the century. It had been renovated magnificently in 1979–80 and had the capacity to hold 2,500 people. It was filled for the Orchestra of Two Continents.[89] The ambitious orchestra, having demonstrated its creative power through this series of sensational concerts, was never to be assembled again.

Before flying home, the Cecil Taylor Unit played two sets—now with a two-saxophone lineup of Jimmy Lyons and Frank Wright, Taylor, Parker, and Martinez—back in Milan.[90] Upon returning to the New York, the Unit hit the ground running. Taylor continued to experiment with different lineups, such as a septet with Lyons, Wright, bassoonist Karen Borca, Parker, Martinez, and adding Roy Campbell Jr. on trumpet at Irving Plaza on November 17.[91]

The Unit then reverted to the two-saxophone quintet for a week at the Blue Note in December. Taylor had been skeptical of playing at the Blue Note, having thought that the owner and audience would not understand the music because it was a mainstream venue. But one evening, Taylor and Martinez happened to be walking past the Blue Note, and Martinez dragged him inside to make an introduction. The owner, indeed, had no idea who Taylor was, despite his monumental stature at that point, but fortunately Abbey Lincoln happened to be there and explained Taylor's significance to the owner. "The next thing you know," Martinez replied, "the owner buys us champagne and gives us six nights. Opening the show was Jack DeJohnette."[92] As one critic remarked, "Jack DeJohnette/Cecil Taylor: the jazz club double-bill of the year, perhaps the decade thus far. The drummer will lead Special Edition, the pianist his Unit. Rest up and make a reservation."[93] Aspiring sixteen-year-old saxophonist Ras Moshe happened to be in attendance and recalled that "I skipped school for a week to hang out at the Blue Note when Cecil and Jack were there. I hung out in the dressing room with those cats almost every night, too. It inspired me for life."[94] The club was packed most nights, especially on the weekend of the stint, and many mainstream figures such as Art Blakey, Louis Hayes, and Billy Hart attended the shows.[95]

Werkstatt Berlin, 1988

The formation of the Orchestra of Two Continents in 1984 further elevated a series of important collaborations that Taylor made with European musicians that also provided Parker a number of auspicious encounters with future collaborators. This culminated in Werkstatt Berlin, which formed a major part of a broader cultural festival: Berlin—European City of Culture 1988. According to Nele Hertling, "The basic idea of the 'Werkstatt' was and still is to present not only finished products, but also to encourage working processes and creative processes, to support them and open them up as much as possible for observation or participation by artist colleagues, students, or simply to those interested."[96]

The festival drew musicians, actors, writers, dancers, designers, architects, fashion designers, and others to an eclectic workshop-style gathering intended to push the projects of the various artists forward. The Berlin-based record label FMP became a central partner in the planning of the event and, following Taylor's success at the Workshop Freie Musik (Free Music Workshop) in 1986, elected to feature the pianist.[97] He was invited to spend a month in the city in June 1988 and to rehearse and perform on both sides of the Berlin Wall. Parker joined Taylor there.

Figure 6.2 Cecil Taylor playing solo at Werkstatt Berlin, West Germany, July 16, 1988. *Credit*: ©Dagmar Gebers/FMP-Publishing.

Taylor led a session most nights and through the course of the month worked with nearly two dozen musicians as well as presenting two solo sets that bookended the month-long exposé. The workshops lasted for five or six hours each day, and many of the participants remarked on the incredible stamina Taylor displayed while demonstrating images or ideas, practicing, and exploring the myriad possibilities with each of the musicians and ensemble formations that he encountered over the weeks in Berlin. After hours, younger musicians who were not on official bills flocked to the discotheque Abraxas, where "Cecil Taylor was holding court" into the early hours of the morning through a range of off-the-cuff conversations about music and art. Then Taylor would get up the next day and work with someone new or delve further into a workshop with one of the various groups even more deeply. One observer noted that Taylor was "bubbling over with an infectious enthusiasm that made everybody in the vicinity look at their surroundings anew."[98]

At the center of everything was the Cecil Taylor European Orchestra. It was a big band consisting of Peter Brötzmann, Evan Parker, and Hans Koch on saxophones; Louis Sclavis on soprano saxophone, clarinet, and bass clarinet; Martin Mayes on French horn; Tomasz Stańko and Enrico Rava on trumpets; Christian Radovan, Hannes Bauer, and Wolter Wierbos on trombones; Tristan Honsinger on cello; Parker and Peter Kowald on basses; Gunter Hampel on vibraphone; and Han Bennink on drums. The orchestra often rehearsed for five or six hours a day and culminated with a two-hour performance, split between two hour-long pieces, on July 2, 1988.[99]

Taylor opens this record with chanting. Parker follows with extended bass work paired with percussion. Next, the horns interact as a group, exploring the possibilities of the sound. Soon, the music of the ensemble begins to evolve into smaller groupings, although often with dense, multilayered interactions with multiple encounters occurring simultaneously. At the twenty-eight-minute mark, strings erupt from underneath as the horns dissipate, though after some revealing arco playing, the horns begin to rejoin, selectively, so as not to overshadow. Around the thirty-fourth minute, the piece takes a dirge-like turn that it carries until the final eight minutes, when the music begins to open back up again. One final push includes some of the most triumphant moments, before it diminishes to conclusion. The second piece places more of a spotlight upon the soloists. The music is like a broad mountainous landscape, abundantly filled with multiple peaks and valleys, ascents, steep drops, light and darkness, the visible as well as the unseen.

The music of the European Orchestra remains one of Taylor's greatest accomplishments. As one critic in attendance remarked, "The European Orchestra was a mountain of real invention that vindicated everybody's faith in the idea of large ensemble music like no other before it."[100]

As Tomasz Stańko remarked of his experience with the Cecil Taylor European Orchestra, "I was enriching and deepening more than ever my understanding of art creative process. Complete freedom combined with discipline gave me a new perspective for penetrating the innermost secrets of music. After all, discipline and anarchy have always been the mighty angels of art." He added, "Cecil had a total control over the orchestra de facto composed of a number of very strong musical individualities, each musician being in a way an 'anarchist.' He almost did not use words. Information and disinformation floated and reached us simultaneously—and that, logically speaking should cause chaos—but the effects were actually completely opposite."[101] For participants in the workshop who were encountering Taylor's musical concepts or approach for the first time and required further clarification, Parker served as an adept intermediary.[102]

Werkstatt Berlin 1988 was a watershed moment for the American and European improvised music scenes. It brought together two scenes that had not been fully in dialogue with each other. Furthermore, it allowed Taylor, at the peak of his creative powers, to draw out the best of the European talent at the time. Neither scene would ever be the same. Taylor, long underappreciated in the United States, would find the crowning moment of his career up to that time in Berlin. Identifying many established or recently emerged talents there, Taylor would profoundly influence an entire generation of European players. Taylor closed the month with a solo set; as one critic wrote of it, "The solo performance on July 16 was a reminder of just

Figure 6.3 William Parker at Werkstatt Berlin, West Germany, July 1988. *Credit*: ©Dagmar Gebers/ FMP-Publishing.

how complete and self-contained a universe is the Taylor piano. You want drums? Here are eighty-eight. A fast arpeggio scorched by a thumbnail sounds like the call to arms of a martial snare-roll. The back of his hand flops onto the keys like a gentle cymbal splash. A fist in the lower register has a bass drum's finality. Alternating forearms are throbbing djembes in some West African choir."[103]

Parker said he could have played in more sessions at the Werkstatt but opted out of some of them to open things up for Taylor.[104] Parker was well-paid for his work, he stayed in a decent hotel, and there was a sense of community—it all felt rather remarkable after years of struggling to make ends meet. Parker returned to New York with a renewed sense of purpose and ability, having worked on the world stage.

Feel Trio and Other Cecil Taylor Projects

On September 20, 1985, Jimmy Lyons played his last concert with the Unit at the Afro-American Museum in Philadelphia. He was suffering from a long struggle with lung cancer. The lineup included Frank Wright on tenor saxophone and Steve McCall on drums. Parker recalled the night as "one of the greatest concerts we ever played," with Frank Wright having a particularly inspired performance.[105] Lyons passed away on May 19, 1986, and his death was to leave a massive void in the Cecil Taylor Unit. From that point until the emergence of the Feel Trio in late 1988, personnel fluctuated considerably, with various figures coming into the band in different formations temporarily, including Carlos Ward on alto saxophone, Leroy Jenkins on violin, Arthur Brooks on trumpet, and various percussionists. The varying lineups found their highest profile in a series of nine concert dates at the Knitting Factory between February and June 1988.[106] Jon Pareles described one of these performances: "There were full-tilt rampages and light, twinkling counterpoint among piano, vibraphone and bass; there were liquid, shimmering passages that escalated to a full-group crossfire."[107]

Taylor's duo with Tony Oxley in Berlin in the summer of 1988 was one of the most gripping sets to emerge from the month-long marathon of playing and recording. From that encounter, Taylor formed a new group—the Feel Trio—with percussionist Oxley and Parker, which became the focal point of his small-group work over the following three years. The band solidified its work during a short European tour in fall 1988 at the Leverkusen Jazz Festival and Freiberg Jazz Festival in Germany and at a concert in Nancy, France.[108] Then they returned for a string of American performances the following month, leading up to a week at Sweet Basil in New York City in February 1989.[109] As one critic noted of Taylor's music at the time, "Perhaps more than any other jazz artist, the pianist Cecil Taylor's performances have to be seen in concert."[110]

Taking a break from the Feel Trio, in August of that year the Cecil Taylor Unit, with Andre Martinez and Gregg Bendian on percussion, played two major festivals in Brazil at Rio de Janeiro and São Paulo. The first event occurred in the lustrous Teatro do Hotel Nacional de Rio. The audience's reaction was split, with some people leaving the event while those who stayed "flipped over the music."[111] Composer and multi-instrumentalist Hermeto Pascoal (b. 1936), one of Brazil's most well-known musicians at the time, attended the performance.

Parker and Martinez later trudged through the slums of Rio to go to Gope, a major instrument store, where they bought pandieros and whistles of various kinds. At one point the percussionist from Gilberto Gil's band encountered them there and thought they were taking too great a risk being in such a rough part of town and got them a taxi back to the hotel. But Parker replied, "When the spirit is correct, the forces will protect you. We are dealing with people and they can sense our spirit and honesty."[112] Using their regular instruments and those newly acquired, they jammed with the hotel samba band every day until they left for São Paulo.

The Feel Trio resumed touring through Europe in the summer of 1990, playing the North Sea Jazz Festival, Festival Konfrontationen in Nickelsdorf, Austria, and other dates leading up to a week at Ronnie Scott's Jazz Club in London. A recording was made of the entire week for the short-lived Codanza Records, totaling ten CDs that represented the most extensive documentation of any of Cecil Taylor's regular small ensembles throughout his career. As critic Richard Cook wrote of the performance, "While these ten separate performances are all of a piece, each grown from the same raw materials, there's no mistaking their separateness, their independent existence of each other. There is loud and quiet, forward momentum and contrasting suspension, thickness of texture and lightness of touch, circular movement and linear development . . . light and shade."[113]

Cook also noted that Taylor had worked without a bassist in the 1960s and 1970s, such that it seemed "the bass had a questionable role in this music."[114] But "Mr. Parker has found his own way into this music and has made his voice integral to the workings of the group. His great woody sound is matched with a sensitivity which some might think was not so needed in such a hyperactive and stormy setting, yet following his lines through the course of any of these sets demonstrates how shrewd and reflexively sharp he is, and how skilled at determining what has to be said and done." Although Taylor often took a standard leader's fee when getting paid for earlier performances by the Unit, he always split the pay equally for performances by the Feel Trio because he was so happy with the results. Taylor regularly referred to the trio as a "gathering of family."[115]

After playing for a week at the Blue Note in Tokyo in October 1990, the Feel Trio plus Andre Martinez returned to the United States.[116] Taylor had a New England tour planned, but unfortunately Oxley had to cancel because of back problems.[117] The Unit with Martinez then did the tour instead, playing thirteen concerts across a swath of cities from Maine to Vermont to Connecticut, with key dates at the Strand Theater in Dorchester, Massachusetts; the Hopkins Center at Dartmouth College; the Maine Center of the Arts; the Langston Hughes Center of the Arts in Providence; the Hampden Theatre at the University of Massachusetts; and a number of other places that elevated the profile of the band in the eyes of music scholars and audience members.[118] As Taylor stated, "If I have to name an aesthetic source for what we're doing, it would be what Ellington did. We're working with textures and personalities and sonic densities. But this is a different kind of

Figure 6.4 Cecil Taylor Historical Quartet with Parker, Anthony Braxton, and Tony Oxley (Braxton and Oxley not pictured) at Teatro Valli in Reggio Emilia, Italy, October 13, 2007. *Credit*: ©Luciano Rosetti.

organization. We're not talking about harmonic changes. I'd rather think of the music in terms of areas of specificity that we've developed ourselves." Taylor added, "We can hear more of the world's music than ever before. If Debussy can hear a Balinese gamelan orchestra at a Paris world fair and change his concept, I can learn from Xenakis, Billie Holiday and Duke Ellington. I study architecture, too. Americans think we have a monopoly on certain kinds of expression. I'm not so sure anymore. Different cultures are expressing what they are undergoing as people, and we should listen."[119] The extensive touring from 1989 to 1991 was some of the most prolific playing of Taylor's entire career, and after decades of struggling financially, he finally lived with some stability. The tour has been argued as being integral to Taylor being awarded a MacArthur Foundation "genius" award in 1992.[120]

Despite all of the personnel changes in the Cecil Taylor Unit, Parker remained the constant from 1980 to 1991, almost never missing a gig. After a scheduling conflict for a concert in Oakland in which Parker was unable to play, Taylor called him and said, "We really, really missed you on the gig."[121] After that their work together began to diminish. But it seemed to be a blessing in disguise. Parker had learned an immense amount from the "maestro" and had honed his instincts as a musician and performer. It was now time for him to strike out boldly as a bandleader.

III. Toward the Universal

"It Is the Job of the Artist to Incite Political Revolution": In Order to Survive

Ask a starving child what jazz is
and that child might say jazz
is a hot plate of food.
In the final analysis,
who cares what jazz is
if we have no respect for life,
if the world is dying.

—— **William Parker**

Living in the community of artists in lower Manhattan in 1984, Parker saw many great injustices and yearned for ways to address these grievances. He believed that it was "the job of the artist to incite political revolution."[1] In that year he penned "In Order to Survive: A Statement," which he read publicly in front of the Shuttle Theater on August 25 for the community block association event formed to "stop the gentrification of the Lower East Side."[2] The event came to bear the title of his manifesto, although it was put together by a wide range of community organizations including Sound Unity (which also organized the festival of the same name that year), Plexus, Nuyorican Poets Café, LAND, and the Shuttle Theater.[3] The event was cochaired by writer and painter Richard Bruce Nugent, the last surviving member of the collective that had published *FIRE!!*, the historic Black literary magazine that emerged in Harlem in 1926.[4] According to Thomas Wirth, "Although it lasted only one issue (for financial reasons), *FIRE!!* had been one of the most brilliant achievements of the Renaissance," produced as a cooperative venture of the Black Harlem literati as an incisive and revolutionary cultural outlook.[5] Nugent had continued to be a key force behind a number of African American arts and literary movements through the years and was a stalwart supporter of the organizing then going on among artists on the Lower East Side.[6] Karl Berger, Jemeel Moondoc, and others from the community performed at the event.[7] Parker's statement reads as follows:

In Order to Survive:
A Statement

We cannot separate the starving child from the starving musician, both things are caused by the same things, capitalism, racism, and the putting of military spending ahead of human rights. The situation of the artist is a reflection of America's whole attitude towards life and creativity. There was a period during the 1960s in which John Coltrane, Malcolm X, Duke Ellington, Cecil Taylor, Ornette Coleman, Bill Dixon, Sun Ra, Martin Luther King, and Albert Ayler were all alive and active. Avant-garde jazz contemporary improvised music coming out of the Afro-American was at a peak of creativity and motion.

ABC Impulse was recording Coltrane and Archie Shepp, ESP Disk was recording the music of Albert Ayler, Sunny Murray, Sonny Simmons, Giuseppi Logan, Noah Howard, Frank Wright, Marion Brown, Henry Grimes, Alan Silva, and many other exponents of the music. Blue Note and Prestige Records were recording Andrew Hill, Eric Dolphy, Sam Rivers, Ornette Coleman, and Don Cherry among others. Radio stations such as WLIB, now called BLS, and WRVR, which now plays pop music, were both playing jazz 24 hours a day, including some of the new music of Coltrane, Shepp, Ayler, and Ornette Coleman. There was energy in the air as people marched and protested in the north and south demanding human rights, demanding that the senseless killing in Vietnam stop.

Simultaneously, like musicians before them, the avant-garde became aware of the necessity to break away from traditional business practices. Like musicians' lives being in the hand of producers and nightclub owners who only wish to make money and exploit the musician. The musicians began to produce their own concerts and put out their own records in order to gain more control over their lives. The Jazz Composers Guild, formed by Bill Dixon, was one of the first musicians' organization in the 1960s to deal with the self-determination of the artist. Other efforts had been made by Charles Mingus and Sun Ra as they both had produced their own concerts and records in the 1950s. To follow was the AACM (Association for the Advancement of Creative Musicians) formed about a year after the Jazz Composers Guild, and Milford Graves, Don Pullen, and the record company SRP (Self Reliance Program).

Musicians got together with poets to put out a magazine called *The Cricket*,[8] and all the articles were written by poets and musicians themselves. It was edited by Imanu Baraka, Larry Neal, and A. B. Spellman; advisors on the magazine were Milford Graves, Cecil Taylor, and Sun Ra. Contributors included Roger Riggins, Stanley Crouch, Albert Ayler, and Ishmael Reed. The motto was "Black Music in Evolution."

Just as the music and the movement began to break ground establishing itself, several things happened: Malcolm X was assassinated, Martin Luther King was assassinated, John Coltrane died, and British rock-and-roll began to change the music industry. Not only could records be sold, they could sell posters, books, wigs, dolls, and thousands of electric guitars to the youth of America. They promoted and pushed rock music as the real thing, yet when these rock stars were interviewed they would always cite jazz or blues as the origin of rock. Also at this time there was a sudden increase in the availability of drugs in the black community. Every apparent gain as a result of the civil-rights movement was not given up without fight. All gains were achieved because America had a gun to its head. To question, to speak of change, was never willingly allowed, but the 1960s movement was so strong that it couldn't be denied. They could silence a few poets but they couldn't silence an entire nation.

The 1970s was a period of tranquilization. There was no mass movement to continue the motion set forth by the 1960s, it was a ten-year period of systematically silencing and discouraging the truth. Poets were made to feel like criminals; people were going back in time because it seemed easier than going forward. Record companies began only to record safe music, musicians began to water down their music. The C.I.A. and F.B.I. had files on the music—they knew who was going along with the program, those who bought cars and played electric music—and those whose politics were considered a threat to the existing inertia. The neglect of the poor, the neglect of the arts is no accident, this country is sustained by killing off all that is beautiful, that deals with reality. They will go to any lengths to hold back the truth, to prevent the individual from hearing and seeing his or her own vision of life. Some people are controlled by neglect, while others are controlled by making them stars.

As the 1980s arrived this fire music that talked about revolution and healing had almost vanished—only a few musicians continued to play and develop it. The sleepiness of the 1970s gave birth to a new electronic age of computers and video machines. Wherever human energy could be saved, it was popular music that lost what little identity it had. In listening to today's pop music it's hard to tell whether the group is male or female, black or white. Synthesizers have replaced living musicians. We have all been desensitized. People walk around in a daze sitting back while these blood-thirsty gangsters have free reign of the country and of the people's lives.

Our food sources, our housing sources, are owned and operated by power-hungry people who do not have our best interest in mind, they only wish to make a profit. All of this is not new knowledge, it has been said many times before, the message must be constantly repeated, intellectual knowledge of the problems is not enough, we must feel the blade piercing the hearts of all who are oppressed, jailed, starved, and murdered by these criminals who call themselves leaders who act in the name of peace and democracy.

Since we have little we must band together pooling all our little resources to form a base in which to work. We must learn from all the mistakes of the past, dropping any selfish notions in order for this movement to succeed, in order for it to take root and begin to grow. We must ask the questions: Why am I an artist? Why do I play music? What is the ultimate goal? Am I playing with the same spirit that I played with 10 years ago, or have I just become more technically proficient?

The idea is to cultivate an audience by performing as much as possible on a continuous basis, not waiting to be offered work, rather creating work. Uniting with all those who hear. Those who are willing to go all the way. We must put pressure on those with power to give some of it up (picketing, boycotts, petitions, whatever it takes), and finally we must define ourselves and not be defined by others. We must take control of our lives, building a solid foundation for the future.[9]

....

For Parker this statement was the beginning of his formulation of "a context" that surrounded his music.[10] In his journal, at the same time as he delivered the above manifesto, he wrote that "Black improvised music has had to fight for its life since the first slaves were brought here in 1619. This fight for survival goes on today and will continue to go on until America is transformed." For Parker, "fire music" was essential to the continuance of existence, and "In order to survive" became his motto. "To be effective against America's anti-life policies, we have to be radical in every area of our lives," Parker wrote. "The music we create, how we walk, eat, sleep, and breathe, must all be geared to a new aesthetic, a system that allows and encourages all people to follow their own vision without being penalized for it, a system that puts life ahead of profit."[11]

Parker recognized that playing music was not to make money, not to be a star, not just to put sounds together to be technically or musically "correct" within the frame of some musical pedagogy. Instead, Parker sought to place music at the cosmological center of the community, to make it the lifeblood of the human struggle for dignity, compassion, sustenance, and liberation. By connecting the struggle of artists to the broader community, Parker argued for solidarity against society's most harmful forces: capitalism and racism.

Parker formed a short-lived collective to produce a newsletter called the *Bill Collector*. One day he was talking with drummer William Hooker (b. 1946) and multi-instrumentalist Daniel Carter, and Carter's wife, Marilyn, said that because there were two people involved named William they should call the newsletter the *Bill Collector*.[12] The group put out only one issue, but it did include Parker's manifesto.

In his historical reckoning, Parker held the 1960s to be the golden era of not just avant-garde jazz but of social progress more broadly. The two were inseparable to him: society flourished when its music and art were bold forms of self-expression, maintained through autonomous arts organizations, and created in sync with the needs and interests of the populace and the world at large. From major record labels to the radio waves, the cultural production of the 1960s generation was at its peak, and with organizations like the Jazz Composers Guild, the Association for the Advancement of Creative Musicians, and the Self Reliance Program, the movement seemed unstoppable, at least for a time.

Parker's reference to the *Cricket* is revealing: many of the editors and writers in the magazine influenced his thoughts about the role of music in the community and as a force for social change. As Larry Neal wrote, "Music can be one of the strongest cohesives towards consolidating a Black Nation. . . . Implied here is the principle of artistic and national unity; a unity among musicians, our heaviest philosophers, would symbolize and effect a unity in larger cultural and political terms."[13]

Neal not only sought unity among different practitioners of Black music but also sought to integrate the music into other areas of the Black Arts movement. An editorial written by the editors of the first issue of the *Cricket* echoed these sentiments: "The true voices of Black Liberation have been the Black musicians. They were the first to free themselves from the concepts and sensibilities of the oppressor. The history of Black Music is a history of a people's attempt to define the world in their own terms. They have been the priests of pure wisdom, in essence the voice of a People." The editorial went on to state that "we propose a cultural revolution. This revolution must first take place among Black Artists. We must bring all Black Art back into the community, putting it at the core of the developing black consciousness. The *Cricket* represents an attempt to provide Black Music with a powerful historical and critical tool. In assuming this responsibility, we are saying to the world that no longer will we as Black Men allow the white sensibility to dominate our lives. It is the responsibility of black musicians and writers to finally make a way for themselves."[14] Baraka later echoed this when writing in homage to Neal: "[The *Cricket* was] significant in that for the first time, black people were defining their art, their aesthetic, their social aesthetic and aesthetic ideology, not someone else."[15] In his own manifesto, Parker drew upon these concepts in forming a vision for cultural autonomy, self-determination of working artists, and the role of music in transforming society.

The main issue that Parker grappled with was recognizing both the positive rise of the music in the 1960s and its subsequent tumultuous fall. The assassinations of political and social reformers such as Malcolm X and Dr. Martin Luther King Jr. were matched with the tragic deaths of a number of key musical figures like John Coltrane and Albert Ayler, which occurred simultaneously with the rise of rock and roll; thus, the position of avant-garde jazz as cultural innovator and liberator began to crumble.[16] The music industry began to assert itself as a counterrevolutionary force interested only in "safe music" and the rolling back of honest, revealing art. Parker states emphatically that "this country is sustained by killing off all that is beautiful, that deals with reality" in a mission "to prevent the individual from hearing and seeing his or her own vision of life."[17]

As Parker wrote in his journal at the time that he delivered his manifesto, "Progress has become a process of dehumanization. In America, all of life's resources are controlled by those who have no respect for life," here referring to the rising materialism of the 1980s and degradation of the individual in that mass economy.[18] The hijacking and dismantling of the avant-garde wave by "blood-thirsty gangsters" and "power-hungry people," whom he identifies as a range of individuals that included politicians, corporations, and cultural fascists, had undone so many of the gains of the 1960s.[19] He adds: "The neglect of the poor and minorities is no accident. It is the conscious, calculated plan to keep those who control in power. Anyone speaking the truth is a threat to the system, a system that will go to any lengths to sustain America on the same level, a system that misrepresents life."[20] But to combat this, Parker advocated doing what Bill Dixon, Charles Mingus, and others had done to spark the whole thing to begin with: solidarity among artists, working people, and all those who are oppressed by the system—in Parker's own estimation this would include most people—to push for massive, wide-scale change of the social and moral order.

With all of this context in mind, Parker set about putting a band together. His profile had risen throughout the 1980s when he was playing with Cecil Taylor, and by 1987, his own bands began to get listings in the *New York Times*.[21] However, there was a transition period after Parker left Taylor's band and began to form his own bands. Parker spent those years in the early 1990s fiercely practicing and further developing. "For at least a year, he almost disappeared and he shed it and shed it and shed it. He didn't go to any teacher, he looked into himself. And by the end of it, he had honed his playing even more. Not only could he do that, though, he could play from self. He could play from his spirit and soul and you would feel it," pianist Cooper-Moore observed.[22] Parker's new band, In Order to Survive, comprised different lineups in the early 1990s, when it was first coming together. Trombonist Alex Lodico, who played in the first iterations of the band, was soon replaced by Grachan Moncur III (b. 1937).[23] Drummer Denis Charles, alto saxophonist Rob Brown, Cooper-Moore, and trumpeter Lewis Barnes soon came to fill out the band and solidify its ranks. From the beginning, Parker's idea was to get away from repeating the past and rather to "make music that is happening in the moment and do it according to who we are." Parker wanted to get away from the classic avant-garde sound, "that sound that's cacophonous and everyone's blowing."[24]

Parker selected the five musicians for the band for specific reasons. "Denis Charles was coming out of Art Blakey and Ed Blackwell, but he was mostly playing Denis Charles," Parker observed. Charles had a lot of Caribbean rhythms, and he "had this thing where he would build tension and then release it." At times when Parker wanted more sound, he would add

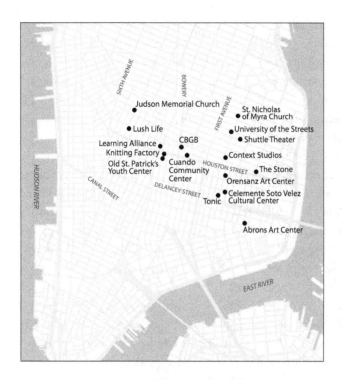

Rashied Ali for a two-drum kit lineup. Rob Brown "could play any melody I had in my head," and Grachan Moncur "could always play counterpoint to that. Lewis Barnes came out of another school of playing, but also one connected to modernism. Cooper-Moore was coming out of church, out of Gospel."[25]

Parker aimed to write a melody or line that was open-ended, a "nice riff that brought up a certain feeling." Then he would add his own bass line underneath that had a groove but also pushed it at the same time. The piano lines were the poetry and "were full of the idea of justice and the idea of spirit. The spirit of Black people, the spirit of the South, the spirit of the blues, the spirit of Harlem, the spirit of the Bronx."[26] Cooper-Moore noted that Parker did not come to composition from the perspective of music theory, like a bookish undergraduate, but rather "he thought, what tones are going to affect people? How am I affected by these tones?"[27] On a more technical level, Parker described their music as "tempered and untempered sounds, metered and non-metered rhythms. It has melody, harmony, counterpoint, and polyphony. Each musician labels and defines the music he or she plays. The music is always more than its definition, just as a human is more than the name one is called. A label is only a handle to open a door; it does not allow us to experience what is behind the door; to do that, we must enter the door and live behind it for many years."[28] Brown noted that from Parker's base composition, "We usually developed an arrangement that was abstract and shifting. In performance, we might stray away from the original, subject to inspiration in the moment."[29] Parker employed both traditionally notated and graphic scores.

Parker also tried to give the music a panoramic view that showed Africa, Asia, Australia, Europe, and the Americas all somewhere in the music, as well as unknown, unnameable places woven into it.[30] Parker wrote that "the music that we play comes out of the tradition of life and living things. It is inspired by anything that lives or has lived. The music is planet music; it uses music elementals from all over the world."[31] The theme of universalism would carry through much of his music and later grow to be a central feature of his work. Added to that was the political content with the goal of waking people up: "It's about revolution. It's about coming to grips with the past and the now and what we will have to deal with in the future." With Parker situated at the center of the music with his bass, he used the metaphor of creating the music "like rolling out pie dough to the edges, making it as wide as possible without thinning out."[32]

In Order to Survive blew onto the scene with a series of concerts, first at Roulette in Tribeca and later at the Knitting Factory on East Houston Street in April and June 1993.[33] Recording sessions in those months produced the material that would eventually be featured on the band's self-titled debut record, released on Black Saint in 1995. One painting by MusicWitness artist Jeff Schlanger from the Knitting Factory concerts was featured on the record cover.[34] At a special concert on June 28 at the Knitting Factory, Parker's mother attended, which was the only time she ever saw him play publicly.[35]

By 1994, Parker was experimenting with different lineups that could accommodate his growing range of compositions and ideas for improvisation. In June he hired drummer Jackson Krall and trumpeter Roy Campbell Jr. to join Cooper-Moore and himself for a double bill with the Charles Gayle–Sunny Murray Duo at St. Stephen's Church in Philadelphia.[36] Parker had been playing with Campbell since 1978 and Krall since 1984 in various formations. Later that same month, Parker organized a concert at Context Studios for the group to play "a piece for piano, strings, and voice" that included regulars Rob Brown and Cooper-Moore, this time joined by Billy Bang on violin, Susie Ibarra (b. 1970) on drums, and Evelyn Blakey on vocals.[37] Bang was a longtime collaborator, but Parker's musical associations with Ibarra had only recently begun with her involvement in the Little Huey Creative Music Orchestra in April 1994.[38] Ibarra had studied with Milford Graves, and Parker regarded Ibarra as a drummer "who could play time and who could play textures."[39] Then, in October 1995, Parker took a slimmed-down trio version of the band to Europe for the first time, playing at the Zuid-Nederlands Jazz Festival at the Effenaar club in Eindhoven, following a longer European tour with the David S. Ware Quartet.[40]

After returning to New York in December 1995, the band met at Tedesco Studios in Paramus, New Jersey, to record tracks for its second record, *Compassion Seizes Bed-Stuy*.[41] Like much of Parker's music, the songs of this record told a personal story, this one connected to his childhood. As the story goes, every time young Parker and his brother, Thomas, went to Bed-Stuy to visit their cousin Larry in the projects there, "Something crazy happened." One time, in the early 1960s when Parker was about ten years old, some boys a few years older intimidated Parker and his brother, telling them to give them money for cigarettes. The two brothers responded that they did not have any money. The older boys searched their pockets and took the fifteen or twenty cents that they had between the two of them and added, "Don't you two ever lie to us again. We're going to see you all tomorrow." After going back home to the Bronx, Parker and his brother lurked about their apartment for two weeks, refusing to go outside for fear that they might run into the same older boys and have to deal with them again. Eventually, their mother got to the bottom of it and explained that they were safe there, that there was no possibility that those other boys knew where they lived.[42]

Parker imagined the same thing happening, but around the corner, on the next block, where saxophonists Don Byas (1912–1972) and Albert Ayler (1936–1970) were sitting on the stoop of a brownstone. The two boys who had taken the Parker boys' money heard the music and were moved so much that they turned around and returned the money, saying, "We're sorry we shouldn't have done that. We're not going to bother you anymore."[43] The opening piece, "Compassion," begins with Parker's strong arco bass playing, to which Cooper-Moore and Ibarra eventually join in to open things up and further develop the sense of urgency. When Brown contributes his saxophone lines, he lifts the entire piece up with wavering, ascendant lines that set the stage for the entire record.

The record included "Malcolm's Smile" in honor of Malcolm X. Parker's opening arco playing over Ibarra's rhythms creates a buzzing buoyancy into which Cooper-Moore shoots flashes of light. Brown then emerges from that sonic landscape with optimistic lines lifting upward. "The thing I notice about Malcolm X is his smile, and that smile represented hope for me. It represented searching and strength," Parker stated.[44] The record also contained a tribute to actor and singer Paul Robeson (1898–1976), whom Parker admired as an artist as well as for his involvement in the Council on African Affairs and other anti-imperialist and anticapitalist political stances. The piece opens with Cooper-Moore's ominous and deliberate keystrokes setting the stage, across which Parker cuts with quick-handed arco, and later Brown adds considerable color. Beyond Parker's own experiences, the ideas behind the record were inspired by Bruce Baillie's film *Mass for the Dakota Sioux* (1964).[45] "The record was for the people in the housing projects. I wanted to play in the housing projects, I wanted to give this music back to them," Parker explained.[46]

The release of *Compassion Seizes Bed-Stuy* is also significant in that it was the first record Parker had as a leader working with label manager Steven Joerg. At the time, Joerg was at Homestead Records, an underground guitar-based rock label that was owned by the distributor Dutch East India. Joerg had developed a deepening interest in the jazz avant-garde and had already worked with saxophonist David S. Ware and pianist Matthew Shipp. Eventually, Joerg approached Parker about recording one of his groups, and the bassist decided to record the band's second record for the label. Joerg would soon leave Homestead Records to found his own label, AUM Fidelity, a move inspired by the work of Ware and Parker, who would be the label's most featured artists since its first release in 1998.[47]

In 1996 Parker continued to workshop material with the band with performances on the East Coast. The lineup had now solidified in the form of a quartet composed of Rob Brown, Cooper-Moore, Susie Ibarra, and Parker. "Because William and I pushed the music in that lineup, Susie's drumming was freed up for her to do what she does—play colors and swing things sometimes. Rob went straight to the essence," Cooper-Moore recalled. "William would ask us to do things we had never done before, like I remember him asking Susie to do a bass drum solo with just her feet. Or he asked me to play a solo with just one note. The thing is, it all worked. I think it was like a chamber ensemble in how the pieces fit very well together. Everybody in the band could push it in their own way." As for the improvisations, Cooper-Moore remarked, "It was often indistinguishable whose ideas were which. Inside the improvisation, there was a lot of giving, taking, and sharing. It was a band where everyone was a leader."[48]

In Order to Survive played at the First Unitarian Meeting House in Amherst, Massachusetts, in February 1996, and then showcased its work at

Figure 7.1 In Order to
Survive, New York, early 1996.
Left to right: Rob Brown, Susie
Ibarra, Cooper-Moore, Parker.
Credit: Clare O'Dea.

the inaugural Vision Festival in June at the Learning Alliance in Manhattan.[49] Vision Festival was organized by Parker's wife, Patricia Nicholson, and she has continued to organize, produce, and curate the festival in the years since. In that setting, In Order to Survive shared an evening with John Zorn's Masada group. In between the two main performances, dancers and poets performed, and Peter Kowald offered a solo piece. In Order to Survive presented two pieces, the first of which, "The Extermination," according to Peter Watrous of the *New York Times*, "sounded freely improvised. . . . Susie Ibarra kept things going with an interactive, coloristic style."[50] The band also performed its self-titled song.

Occasionally, the band would also feature an expanded lineup like the one that performed excerpts of *Mass for the Healing of the World* on June 24, 1996, at South Street Seaport, adding Assif Tsahar (tenor saxophone), Chris Jonas (soprano saxophone), Roy Campbell (trumpet), Matt Moran (vibraphone), and Denis Charles and Michael Wimberley (drums, percussion), in addition to the standard quartet performers.[51] It was an extended exploration of their latest musical concepts in an ecstatic three-drummer lineup over the course of one hour-long piece. Another performance at the Cooler in October of 1996 on a double bill with Sun Ra's Intergalactic Lounge was piano-less but added Tsahar and trombonist Alex Lodico with a piece called "Dedicated to the Aborigines of Hunt's Point," a reference to a neighborhood near where Parker grew up in the South Bronx.[52]

After workshopping new material at the Knitting Factory in August 1996 and February 1997, and at the Music Gallery in Toronto in June 1997, as well as showcasing their work at the Victoriaville festival in May 1997, they began to record for the band's third record, *The Peach Orchard*.[53] Material was gathered from live recordings at sessions at the Knitting Factory in February and July, as well as two sessions at Context Studios in March 1998.[54] The band also did its first U.S. tour, through Washington, Pittsburgh, Cleveland, and the Detroit area.[55] The two-CD release remains the band's most extensive recorded documentation, with eight tracks, each of which exceeds ten minutes in length, featuring extended improvisations and thoroughly developed compositional ideas. Of the record, Parker wrote that "the substructure of all music that is beautiful on a profound level is vision (the act of seeing and hearing beyond what our eyes and ears can take in). Vision allows us to experience and live within that endless periphery called poetry. Vision is also the catalyst for human revolution. The response to the cry and the cry itself."[56]

As Parker rooted his music deep within this concept of vision, he added, "The music of In Order to Survive is deeply rooted in the concept of vision. In this music I hear the history, the mystery and the now. All existing and vanishing at the same time. Everything is kept together by the undertow of this luminous lyricism that is ever present." Parker's vision brought particular ideas to mind, something internal and essential: "Music for me often begins with a visualization of something inside. Usually a dream, or vision about the past, or future. Memories from my childhood, filled with repeated images of the sun rising and setting. Images of light covering the world in a wash of color. A world where flowers walk and talk. Trees are mountains, and mountains are clouds." Parker connected the music to the condition of the world, its setting and its inhabitants and how all of existence is bound together. Again, compassion was central to his artistic vision. As he further elaborated, "The main force in playing this music is having the ability to feel the pain of all who suffer. To feel it as if it were happening to us; not resting until it ceases to be. Feeling for others and believing that the only way to survive is through love of God (Self) <humanity>. Making sure that each sound that comes from your instrument is directed and filled with the strongest truth that exists."[57]

Each of the eight tracks had an explicit story behind it that connected with Parker's overall artistic vision, many of which were dedicated to figures or entities that Parker admired. "Thot" (Thoth) was named for the Egyptian god of the same name who was regarded as a healer, the one who maintained the universe, and as the master of law was an arbiter between good and evil. Thoth was regarded as self-created and, as an autodidact, had invented science, mathematics, art, and other methods that humans employed to make sense of the world around them. "Thot" is a full-bodied piece that featured a magnificent solo by Cooper-Moore that set the stage for the record. "Three Clay Pots" has a melody that came to Parker when he was young, during one of the many walks he took while he lived in the Bronx. He dedicated it to Jeff Schlanger, the MusicWitness who became well-known for his live, motion painting of Parker and many other musicians in the scene in which Parker played: at the Vision Festival and many other New York concerts.

"Moholo" is a song that Parker dedicated to Louis Moholo (b. 1940), the South African drummer and percussionist whom Parker had first met and played with in 1981.[58] Moholo had left his native Cape Town in the early 1960s to escape the horrific indignities of apartheid for better artistic prospects in Europe. Nevertheless, Parker observed that Moholo always retained a sense of feeling "displaced and uprooted due to the politics of South Africa. Any joy was always tinged with a poignant sadness." Parker notes that "the freedom in South Africa has a bitter aftertaste. I tried to reflect melancholy, hope and struggle with this composition."[59]

"Theme for Pelikan" was dedicated to Dr. E. Pelikan Chalto, "musician, theoretician, philosopher, painter, poet. Pelikan was always one of the more advanced players and thinkers in the music."[60] He was an alto saxophone and clarinet player who met with Parker, Billy Bang, and Henry Warner at Nathan's Restaurant on 8th Street and 6th Avenue in Greenwich Village. Pelikan was known for giving lectures on Egyptology and the Hopi Indians or talking about Duke Ellington, Thelonious Monk, Cecil Taylor, and Eric Dolphy, coming away from which Parker would feel "invigorated and inspired."[61] The music possessed a playful beat and melody that evolved into a racing escapade of ideas and images.

The song "Leaf Dance" is the most lighthearted track on the record, intended as a hymn for autumn, "the time when leaves change color and eventually fall to the ground."[62] In this seasonal transition Parker saw the movement of dance. "Posium Pendasem #3" came from a series of compositions with sixteen parts that together formed a cycle called *The Bronx Mysteries*. This part developed a resolute theme from the opening piano lines over Ibarra rubbing shells. Gradually, Parker's arco bass reinforces the swaying piano in a dark, moody melody illustrating shimmering savannas of memory. "Posium" was a word that Parker made up, inspired by Latin, indicating a kind of special meeting.[63] The song that bears the band's name includes the vocal line in repetition, "In order to survive, we must keep hope alive," which had become the theme song for the band.

The title track, "The Peach Orchard," which closes the first disc, drew its inspiration from the history of the Navaho. As Parker explained it,

> The great Navaho chief Manuelito and his people were fighting against being pushed out of their homelands by the United States army. Out of all of the things that the Navaho cultivated, they loved their peach orchards the most. In the end of this struggle, they, like all Native Americans, lost everything, including their cherished peach orchard, which was destroyed. In reading about this, I immediately felt a deep sadness. I can only imagine the sadness they must have felt. It was the beginning of the end. In this composition you can hear the massive blanketing of America by Europe; you can also hear the voice not only of Manuelito, but of Nana, Geronimo, Wovoka, Sitting Bull, Kicking Bird, Kicking Bear, and all of the others.[64]

The rhythm section builds considerable tension, elevating Brown to practically cry through his horn, eventually reaching deep into the sound of human anguish.

The band recorded its fourth and final record, *Posium Pendasem*, practically concurrently with *The Peach Orchard*, over the course of two sessions on April 9 and 11, 1998, at the 30th Workshop Freie Musik at the Akademie Der Künste in Berlin.[65] This record featured a quintet lineup, adding Assif Tsahar on tenor saxophone and bass clarinet. As Cooper-Moore later commented, "With Susie [Ibarra] as the drummer, I can't think of a better band."[66] The record extended the series of songs that lent their name to the title of the album that Parker had begun on the previous record. The heart of the record is the fifty-minute "Posium Pendasem #7," which was accompanied by Parker's poem:

> It is the area to the left of silence
> The spot center of the sun
> Like a swelling harp string
> Pulled, tugged . . . and blurred
> The mists around the dark lake
> Reflects the blue sky that vibrates
> Around the tall buildings
> How come it is I who feels the pain
> That laces itself around this
> Inconsistent world
> The silence creeps up the wall
> Trying to escape that old southern
> Rope justice (hangin)
> Called on to testify in the murder trial
> Of the big square sound called swing
> The tall smallness of green grass the
> Smell of soil in prayer at the church
> Catfish grease left in the pan
> Feeling deeply for those who are not
> Here and those who don't hear

Workshop Freie Musik was an annual festival founded in 1969 and produced by the Free Music Productions (FMP) label. It served as the annual focal point for the Berlin free jazz scene for many years.[67] Parker had first worked at the Workshop Freie Musik as part of the Peter Brötzmann Trio and Brötzmann's Alarm Orchestra in 1985 and had returned the following year as part of two Cecil Taylor bands.[68] From that point forward, Parker returned every few years, playing again with Taylor, with bassist Joëlle Léandre (b. 1951), and with others over the years, before finally leading In Order to Survive there in 1998.[69]

By early 1999, Ibarra became disillusioned with her place as the drummer in the David S. Ware Quartet. Journalist David Yaffe wrote an extensive article in the *New York Times* that chronicled Ibarra's experience as one of the few female drummers working the music scene and the many examples of misogynistic behavior she had experienced from teachers, bandmates, and collaborators through the years. She stated, "Sometimes, professional musicians have either vibed me out or made passes at me. I tried to shrug it off, but it can be discouraging whether you have a teacher or a famous musician hitting on you."[70] Although she did not name anybody specifically, the article drew a reaction. A subsequent letter penned by Steven Joerg argued that Ibarra's opportunities had come quickly in comparison to Ware and his contemporaries, who had been laboring since the 1970s and in the 1990s were just starting to receive credit for their work.[71] The clash in the *Times* caused a rift in the community. Tsahar, who was married to Ibarra at the time, became upset, and Cooper-Moore thought that more could have been done to heal the fissure.[72] As this conflict ended up cutting right through In Order to Survive, Parker decided to vary the lineups for the concerts he had booked through the remainder of 1999. For a few concerts the band became a trio, with Rob Brown on saxophone and Cooper-Moore on percussion, although Ibarra did return for their performance at Guelph Jazz Festival, which was the final performance of that lineup of the band.[73] By this time, Parker was interested in developing music with new bands and formations and took the opportunity to shift his focus. It would be eleven years before Parker returned his attention to In Order to Survive.

In June 2010 Parker finally brought the band back together for the Vision Festival with the new lineup, which has evolved only slightly up to the present. Retaining Rob Brown and Cooper-Moore, Parker brought back Lewis Barnes on trumpet and added Hamid Drake on drums and percussion. When the band returned to play Vision Festival in 2012, it recorded the live set, which was released as the final disc in the eight-CD box set *Wood Flute Songs*.[74]

The material that Parker composed and developed for the Vision Festival in 2012 was dedicated to tenor saxophonist Kalaparusha Maurice McIntyre (1936–2013), who had temporarily lost his sight because of cataracts.[75] Parker wrote that "a vision came to me of Kalaparusha on the edge of an empty horizon, blind but dancing on the outer rim of the abyss sometimes called survival. The music on this CD is dedicated to him and all those who live on the edge of the abyss." Parker's well-crafted liner notes describe the music eloquently, both technically and figuratively: "The first group statement is followed by the trumpet of Lewis 'Flip' Barnes stepping right out with Cooper-Moore's piano making things a duet, maybe two duets with the added drive and pulse of the bass and the accents of the drums. There is always on some level a four-part call and response, a conversation, a communication of spirits." With the second statement, Parker added of Rob Brown's entrance, "The color changes, the shift moves to the accents creating pyramidal blocks . . . the music is pushing the stones so they can float and knit rainbows."[76] As with much of his other music, references to Native American history appear: "Images of Tiwanaku, Dos Pilas, Tenochtitlan, are conjured up."[77] As the music continues, "You hear the trio of piano, bass and drums creating another kind of trilogy rolling down the hills to the clusters and tremolos against the thick bass sound while every second Cooper-Moore and Hamid are at the table with the Harvest. And now strings, which are also drums, place images against the just turned purple Dawn. Hands on the skins of drums and smoke the prayer is what really motivates us. The bass is also a drum and the drum is also people who need compassion."[78]

The quintet version that appeared on the record then played the Umbrella Music Festival at the Hideout in Chicago in November 2012. Then back at the Stone in New York City, eleven months later, Parker added trombonist Steve Swell to make it a sextet.[79] Inspired by the larger band and wanting to continue exploring that sound, Parker added tenor saxophonist Kidd Jordan and pianist Dave Burrell sat in for Cooper-Moore as the band embarked for a short U.S. tour through Ann Arbor, Buffalo, and Hartford in October and November 2014.[80]

Parker went on a European tour in August and September 2016, performing mostly with saxophonist Peter Brötzmann's Die Like a Dog Trio, but booked In Order to Survive at the Sant'Anna Arresi Jazz Festival at Piazza del Nuraghe in Sardinia, Italy.[81] This iteration of the band included Brown, Cooper-Moore, Swell, Drake, and multi-instrumentalist Mixashawn Rozie. Upon his return to New York, Parker and the band were ready to record, and he elected to bring a quartet of Brown, Cooper-Moore, and Drake to Systems Two in Brooklyn to lay down five tracks for the second disc of a two-CD release, *Meditation/Resurrection*.[82] As with many of his records, Parker accompanied the disc with a poem:

"MEDITATION"

1

May those in darkness seek enlightenment
And be filled with hope
May fear of truth vanish
Love all no matter what
Seek peace
With all who live
Give to the poor
Believe in the unknown essence
Let it fill your soul
Let it dance like the wind
Each gesture healing the broken world
Seek peace over understanding
Let all feel the warm light of birth
Each sound is the voice of rain
May the day bring bright song
May all human beings be filled with the Holy Spirit
May all be emptied of duality
May oneness reside
Peace to all
Peace to all
Lift the curtain of woe
Let compassion flow through all
May green valleys welcome us all
Sing to lighten the heavy heart
Sing praise
Lift the cup
Offer your resonance
To the children
May light flow through your soul

2

Child of god
Child of sound
Walking near the horizon
Then the light came out of nowhere
The room filled with peace
May this peace touch

All those who live in the darkness
In the world of greed and evil
May this peace reach
All those who live in the world of ego and hate
Who think life is only about making money
Let us go to the desert to find the spirit
that will allow us to become ourselves
When we open the door of song
We will hear all the birds
Sing in adoration of this moment
We are the trees on the side of the mountain
We are the leaves floating on the river
We are the river
May the brothers and sisters share with those
who are less fortunate
Give to the poor as if they were family
not from the bottom
Give from the top
Feel the vibration of sound
The earth is a drum skin

3
There are tears under the eyelids of flowers
May the day be filled with forgiveness
May we all fly towards heaven with unceasing joy

4
Dream (the clue)
I had a dream
In the dream I saw my father
He revealed to me that he was a composer
He had this score, which was not like anything
I had ever seen
There were numbers and shapes
Drawings of pyramids
Over hieroglyphs
The date on the score was 1952[83]

The opening track, "Sunrise in East Harlem," was "inspired by the sounds one hears while sitting in front of apartment buildings. Talking about music and black people living in cities all over America." The track fittingly opens with the twinkling chords of Cooper-Moore, a resident of the neighborhood for over three decades and to whom the piece is dedicated. Parker then adds broad rays of light with some of the most inspired arco playing on record. The penultimate track, "Urban Disruption," continues with related themes. The piece illustrates "a landscape of tension between despair and hope. Urban disruption is global disruption."[84] Parker's thumping bass infuses a certain dynamism into the piece that pushes forward against mounting tension from piano and saxophone, each in turn advancing the narrative with color and light. The second track, "Some Lake Oliver," was dedicated to multi-instrumentalist Oliver Lake (b. 1942).[85] Parker explained that "I had this image in my mind of a body of water that could talk, sing, and dance. Every morning it would be filled with shimmering light. Arthur Blythe the saxophonist was sitting by the shore and as Oliver walks by he says to him, 'Some lake, Oliver.'"[86] Light flutters of piano tumble over percussion and bass, ushering in the scene that gives rise to Brown's soaring saxophone lines arching over the top of the subtle yet active rhythms.

Writing about his bandmates at the time, Parker noted, "If my music has had any success in the last 20 years it is because Cooper-Moore has been a major inspiration and contributor." About Brown, he noted that "he is a master improviser who is constantly inside the music, flowing with it and letting it vibrate with a purposeful tone. He speaks through his horn and says things that are beautiful, wonderful and thought-provoking. Things that make you feel and want to change the world." Parker reserved his greatest praise for Drake: "The connecting force behind all this music is Hamid Drake. His drumming is the foundation upon which trees and grass grow. He dances through the markers of numbered and measured handcuffed time and rhythm and opens up the cage so that all the languages the drum speaks can be heard. He shows us that rhythm is a melody that dances down the drumstick or through the hands and fingers onto drumheads, acknowledging that the body is also a drum called heartbeat as is the earth, realizing that the value of the mystery is reverence for that mystery."[87]

In the past few years, In Order to Survive has continued to evolve, playing Winter Jazz Festival in January 2017, Vision Festival later that year, and international dates in France, Canada, and elsewhere since that time.[88] A live date from 2018 will appear on a forthcoming record, *Live at Shapeshifter*, set to be released in 2019.[89] The band remains Parker's longest-standing small to midsize unit, and one that he continues to refresh with new ideas and personnel.

Eight

Into the Tone World:
Little Huey Creative Music Orchestra

If you look at nature, who's the soloist?
 Is it the tree?
Is it the maple? Is it the oak? Is it the sun?
Who's the bandleader? Is it the river?
Is it the mountains?

—— **William Parker**

At the same time that Parker developed In Order to Survive through the 1990s, he was also working on his big-band project, Little Huey Creative Music Orchestra. At the center of the concepts for this band was the character Little Huey, who was "going back to childhood, back to the Bronx, back to the housing projects." Little Huey Parker could also morph into other people from his neighborhood while he was growing up: Little Huey Jackson, Little Huey Johnson, Little Huey Brown, and so forth. The character "wants to be a poet because all he has is a pen and paper. He begins to write and he begins to retell what he's seen, whether through music, film, ideas, or just what he sees looking out the project windows," Parker explained. "I retell these stories and make them work in a way where they become larger than themselves."[1] In Little Huey, Parker's storytelling nature is given voice, especially for personal tales, experiences, and observations that in many cases he had waited decades to bring to full fruition.

As Parker further explained, "The Little Huey Creative Music Orchestra is committed to all those who are told not to dream. We exist for those who had the flame of hope put out in their lives. All those torn apart by war, poverty, madness, loneliness and hate." Parker introduced the character Huey Jackson in the narrative, "an aspiring poet who grew up in the housing projects of the South Bronx. Influenced by the work of Samuel Beckett, he began to write poems, short plays and essays. Huey envisioned a world where anything was possible. Talking flowers, bright blue trees, green snowflakes against a yellow sky. Everyone around Huey discouraged him from being a poet. To Huey the word 'poet' was synonymous with the words 'human being.'"[2]

What is at stake in Little Huey is self-expression and personal dignity. Parker developed it for every child who had been told to "shut up and sit down" when they asked a question or raised their voice "and are taught to be subservient to the system. It's for the kids given more instruction on how just to avoid jail than to be themselves." Parker was responding to the prevailing message he felt he received when growing up: "You can get by, but you can't be yourself. Don't rock the boat and you will stay on course, you won't get arrested, you will be a good citizen."[3]

On another level, some of these concepts behind Little Huey had materialized earlier with a piece that Parker had done with Patricia Nicholson and the Centering Dance Music Ensemble. The piece contained the line "I thought being a good citizen would guarantee a crust of bread," but then the character finds out that the bread is day-old stale bread. As Parker elaborated,

> The people in power think so little of us that they give us stale bread and try to convince us that it is fresh. Be quiet. Work your job. Be White-Black and do what White people do. They give you just enough to convince you that you are free, but you aren't. Meanwhile the powerbrokers are rigging the entire system, getting the big money, rigging politics, using a few Black superstars to convince the rest that they have it good. Meanwhile, overseas that government is starting wars, killing people, doing it to people like me and back home still giving us that stale bread which they say is fresh.

Little Huey was created to oppose that: "We made a big band to make a big sound to make a big change."[4]

Parker drew upon his many years of convening big bands. Parker had cut his teeth leading a few of his own big-band projects in the 1970s such as Aumic Orchestra and the Nascent Big Band, and even more so playing as part of the various expanded-unit and big-band projects led by Cecil Taylor

Figure 8.1 William Parker Mixed Orchestra (the original Little Huey Creative Music Orchestra) at Charlie Parker's former house, 151 Avenue B, New York, September 1985. *Left to right, front row*: Dave Hofstra, Parker, Will Connell Jr.; *middle row*: Dave Sewelson, Alex Ludico, Mave Suzuki; *back row*: Henry P. Warner, Charles "Bobo" Shaw, Denis Charles.

in the 1970s and 1980s.[5] However, Centering Big Band was the first really consistent big band that Parker led; it played from the late 1970s to the mid-1980s. It played at the Kool Jazz Festival at Soundscape in June 1984, and preparations for that performance were central to the development of Parker's big-band approach, which he described as "a coming together of individualists to see how they would respond to each other."[6] Centering Big Band had the familiar figures Jemeel Moondoc, Daniel Carter, David S. Ware, Roy Campbell, Raphe Malik, and vocalist Lisa Sokolov (b. 1954), among others, to fuel these potent interactions that were accidentally recorded at the time and later released.[7]

Parker described the creative process and public performance by Centering Big Band: "I didn't have to conduct the band; there was no conduction. Everyone knew when to come in and when to come out. The elements were there, I just gave a little guidance, just a little preconceived structure, maybe a melody here and there, and it just took off." Parker noted the music contained "elements maybe influenced by Duke Ellington." As for the internal dynamics, Parker noted, "We had very strong soloists and I had to let them go. The duos were pre-planned, and we mixed them up, trying to get a result with people who had never played together." Reflecting on that key moment in his career, Parker said in 2012, "It's all steps, leading to I still don't know what. It's led to developing a way of orchestrating, of putting music together, and knowing when you go to rehearsal, you are not sure of the exact result when you come out. It's just not that finite. It's really, really open. You have to hear things. That's why you can't put too much to ink for a while, because it takes time for these things to gel, so you have to stay open. I mean you know some things going in, but you have to stay open to the unknown."[8] Another precursor to Little Huey was the William Parker Orchestra, which played a few times in 1985–89; one participant, baritone saxophonist Dave Sewelson, remarked that it "formed one continuum" with Little Huey.[9]

Since issuing his manifesto in 1984, Parker had gradually emerged as a leader of the community of musicians on the Lower East Side. From that point on, he became the focal point of a new community that included some of his longtime cohort as well as a number of musicians from a half-generation younger who looked to him for inspiration. This community would include a number of key figures that he would turn to as he hired players for his new big-band projects in the 1990s. In many ways, Little Huey Creative Music Orchestra was a mix of the stalwart players who had managed to survive the money crunch of the 1980s and a number of people who were just emerging in the early 1990s to greater prominence.

The personnel in Little Huey Creative Music Orchestra has always fluctuated because of the necessities of staffing a large unit. For its first record, the band coalesced around a group that contained as many as twenty musicians in slightly varying lineups. The band included longtime associates Billy Bang, Roy Campbell, Will Connell, Jr., and saxophonists Dave Sewelson and Marco Eneidi. Parker had first played with Sewelson in a band led by pianist Wayne Horvitz in 1980, and Parker immediately included him in the Centering Dance Music Ensemble and the Thousand Cranes project. They played sporadically through the 1980s in a number of lesser-known bands led by Parker, including the 1992 recording of *The Olmec Series*, which was not released until 2006.[10] Of Sewelson, Parker later wrote, "deep, lyrical, at the center of the music anchoring, the light that guides us back to shore."[11] Parker had played with Eneidi since 1982, when he had been a part of the Thousand Cranes project, and they had worked together alongside each other in a number of sideperson situations throughout the 1980s, including several Bill Dixon–led ensembles and with Jackson Krall & the Secret Music Society, as well as Eneidi's own bands.[12] Parker described Eneidi as a "follower of the direct sound approach of altoness, he ignites things to happen with no shaded areas, an ecologist of sound and a lover of green plants and nature."[13]

Then there was another contingent of Little Huey Creative Music Orchestra that Parker had been building relationships with since about 1984. This included trombonists Alex Lodico and Masahiko Kono, and the tubist Dave Hofstra. All three had been drawn into Parker's circle since the momentous events at the Shuttle Theater in 1984 and had become collaborators with his various orchestra or big-band projects throughout the late 1980s and early 1990s.[14] Lodico and Kono also played alongside Parker in Jemeel Moondoc's Jus Grew Orchestra, which was very active in 1984–85.[15] A few years later, Parker referred to Lodico as "the house speaker, his robust sound is like a muezzin calling us to pray in the church of music, devoted to the continuation of the living traditions, tenured member of the orchestra."[16] Little Huey also included bandmates who Parker had hired for In Order to Survive, Rob Brown and Lewis Barnes. But many of the musicians were people Parker had begun to play with regularly only in the early 1990s, such as Assif Tsahar and Richard Keene (tenor saxophones), Chris Jonas (soprano saxophone), Joe Ruddick (baritone saxophone), Richard Rodriguez (trumpet), Steve Swell (trombone), Leopanar Witlarge and Akira Ando (cellos), Hal Onserud (bass), and Susie Ibarra, Gregg Bendian, and Shoji Hano (drums).[17] Parker's meeting with Rodriguez was entirely by chance. Rodriguez lived above a venue where they were playing and came downstairs to say, "This is very interesting music. Can I participate?" Thus, when taken together, Little Huey Creative Music Orchestra was an exposé of the community of musicians that Parker had built around himself over the previous decade.

According to Parker's approach, Little Huey Creative Music Orchestra was composed of seven stations: trombones, trumpets, baritone saxophones and tuba, soprano and tenor saxophones, alto saxophones, drums, and basses. As Parker wrote, "These sections can be compared to the branches of a tree, branches that lead back to a main body that is rooted in the soil called sound." In practice, this meant the following:

> Each station has the possibility to initiate the concept of self-conduction. Self-conduction is the concept of conducting oneself in and out of sections of a composition. It is the same concept one would use in a small group setting such as a trio or quartet. Each player in a section can play prearranged or composed material. There is also the option of creating parts or settings

at the moment, working individually or as a section. The rule is the moment always supersedes the preset compositional idea. Each player has the ability to create their own part if they feel the part they would create is better than the part at that moment.[18]

Put another way, "You have to be aware and train yourself not to wait for someone to tell you what to do, but to do it from the inside. People know their own melodies, harmonies, and rhythms. People just need to stop thinking and click into the intuitive." Parker admitted that the process is immediate for some people, but for others it might take four or more sessions until "something begins to release."[19]

Simpler riffs or lines, Rob Brown observed, "allow for very abstract things and pretty structured sounds to happen at the same time."[20] For Jason Kao Hwang, who joined the band in 1995, "The freedom William gives Little Huey elevates the music to fiery heights. Still, William does seem to steer us through it sometimes. Just a shout, riff, or rhythm at exactly the right moment can refocus the collective sound."[21] Dave Sewelson noted that "we make the music by trusting the moment, trusting each other. It's just like that deep trust that you have when you are going to sing 'Happy Birthday' with a group of people. You trust everyone will do it together and it will work, except that we do it with music we haven't encountered yet."[22] For Steve Swell, "It's a truly democratic system like no other. William's approach most times is to have a basic riff or melody and the rest of the band just goes from there. When you solo, you pick your own spot, which takes some courage on your part, and you determine how long you solo, stopping before it becomes more about you then it is about serving the greater whole."[23] It can be difficult, though, as saxophonist James Brandon Lewis, who joined the band in 2016, noted: "You have to be able to listen intently while you are in the lane of operation. It's all happening very quickly."[24]

Parker began rehearsing on a weekly basis with Little Huey Creative Music Orchestra at University of the Streets in January of 1994. No information survives from these earliest convenings of the band, other than that it played its first gig at the same venue, featuring a song titled "The Low Low Sky." This was dedicated to Sky Low Low, the Canadian professional wrestler who has the distinction of being the smallest in WWE history, standing at 3'6" and weighing 86 pounds.[25] From February to July of that year the band played as many as a dozen concerts, including a weekly May residency at CBGB's, one or more shows at University of the Streets, the Knitting Factory, twice at the Cooler, and a variety of other New York venues where it recorded material for the first album, *Flowers Grow in My Room*.[26] Parker asked each of the participants to chip in a hundred dollars, and they financed the record collectively. Parker also started the practice of sharing all royalty dividends with his bands, although often, in the early days, there was not much of a payout. Each performance included a new piece. At the center of the record and the live performances was a piece titled "We Cannot Put Off Being Human Another Day," which was the central narrative of the music on the record. Parker had thought of the composer Johannes Sebastian Bach writing new music for each liturgy, and he was aware that the audience was small and that listeners might come back again, so he wanted to make sure that each experience was unique.[27] This would become how Little Huey operated, never repeating pieces in the whole history of the band.

In 1995 Parker assembled the Little Huey Creative Music Orchestra for another prolific season of concerts. On Sunday evenings in January and February, the band had a residency at the Knitting Factory, where it work-shopped new material.[28] The 1995 lineup featured only slight changes to personnel, with tenor saxophonist Ben Koen joining and Mabo Suzuki playing both alto and baritone saxophones. Cooper-Moore joined on piano, further intensifying the interactive nature of the music. In reference to Cooper-Moore's contributions, Parker described him as "one of the quintessential masters of music in the twentieth century, piano, harp, ashimba flute, player and maker of these and other instruments, mentor, and mover of sound."[29] Sessions on January 29, February 19, and February 26 came to form the band's second record, *Sunrise in the Tone World*.[30]

Sunrise in the Tone World was a milestone for Parker as an artist. It bears his first explicit ideas concerning concepts of "the tone world." To Parker, the tone world is a spiritual sanctuary, one that can be reached only through music, a destination that can be attained only through the practice of the sound of the self.[31] In the rhythms, the melodies, and the sonic interactions with others, people can "leave themselves, step out into the music and go to their other self that they never before met. That self has wings that make you fly. And then, one discovers things." Or "when sound vibrates at a certain level we can see a corridor. At the end of this corridor there is a room where all the secrets of life are kept. This room is locked and can only be opened through sound. If we play the right combination of tones the door opens and we are allowed to enter the room. Once inside, a secret of life is revealed to us. Every time we play music we can enter the room."[32] In other words, it is a kind of transcendental meditative state brought on by the performance of musical self-expression.

Steve Swell's interpretation of the tone world was "Music can create a deeper sensibility and change the immediate environment we are in, change politics, change society. The more we enter the tone world, the more longer lasting changes we can make. If I do it right, I feel my soul and spirit taking flight, soaring through the music. When all of Little Huey is doing that, there is nothing like that on the planet."[33] Dave Sewelson placed the tone world as the last of the four states of human consciousness, preceded by sleep, wakefulness, and meditation.[34] In the tone world, Parker would see colors and shapes that bore meanings, and as he developed graphic scores for the music charts, he would sometimes include the symbols as features within the score. When playing concerts with the band, Parker would also generally use a special bass, one that he had painted red and black and that bore some of the symbols, each of which had a special meaning to him.

A self-titled poem accompanying *Sunrise in the Tone World* illustrates Parker's vision:

> *Dawn into Brightness into Mountain*
> *Illuminates. A (tear)ing shadow*
> *Clump of stones*
>
> *If we hung a saxophone*
> *From a tree and the wind blew through it*
> *What would it sound like?*
>
> *If the swaying branches*
> *From the same tree caressed a drum set*
> *What would it sound like?*
>
> *Sunrise prances into tone*

Sunrise in the Tone World is a two-CD set containing two hours of music, although there are many pieces from the Knitting Factory Sunday residency that do not appear on the release. The title piece was dedicated to "all the children of the present world. The tone world is the place where children live before they are born. It is the sphere we enter when music vibrates at an ultra-high level."[35] Each song on the record was a tribute to someone or something.[36] "The Bluest J" was written for bassist and composer Jay Oliver, a mostly unknown figure who left New York for Europe in 1980, hoping to find better opportunities there, and eventually died in Berlin in 1993. As Parker wrote of Oliver's passing, "Another (jazz) musician dies in poverty, unknown, unheralded. Life is not fair and death certainly is not fair. If we live in vision, that is as (poets/human beings), our lives are not easier but harder. There is no reward for shining brightly, only the brightness itself."[37]

"Voice Dancer Kidd" is a tribute to Parker's friend and collaborator, New Orleans saxophonist Kidd Jordan (b. 1935), whom Parker referred to as "one of the masters of Black Mystery Music."[38] He added, "Kidd is many things: teacher, organizer, catalyst and reed master. One of the few keeping the flame of human compassion burning." The third tribute was "Sunship for Dexter," for one of Parker's favorite tenor saxophonists, Dexter Gordon (1923–90). Gordon was an early bebop saxophonist who recorded a number of iconic albums for Blue Note, Prestige, and other labels in 1950–86.[39] Parker wrote that he considered being inspired by a musician to create music totally different from that musician's work to be the greatest tribute one could offer the inspirer: "It is about seeing the essence of life and feeding the creative seed in the music. It is never about copying the sound, it is about finding our own sound universe." Describing the piece, Parker noted that it was the only one on the record that had a present chord sequence: "Two tenor solos move across the piece playing in their own reality frame, as second and third layers of sound are created by the orchestra."[40]

"Huey Sees Light through a Leaf" is another autobiographical tale spun by Parker. In June 1968, at age sixteen, while living in the Claremont housing projects in the South Bronx, Parker had written this in his diary: "For the past year I have been fascinated by the beauty of sunlight. What a wonderful thing to discover in this landscape. I love how it changes colors in the sky from yellow, to orange, to red, to purple . . . today I was lying under a tree just about to die and I noticed light coming through a greenleaf. This instantly saved my life so I could go on another day."[41] The piece is a musical reflection of that event from Parker's childhood.

"And Again" was dedicated to the changing seasons. Parker wrote that "when we least expect it, out of despair hope arises. Winter turns into spring, spring turns into summer, and summer into fall." The piece "Mayan Space Station" was inspired by the thought "Don't worry about being avant garde, be human. Use all the colors . . . don't be afraid."[42] The closing piece, "The Poet and the Painter," was written for painter Yuko Otomo, whose work *#OB from Series Gogo and Digi* had appeared on the band's first record, *Flowers Grow in My Room*.

For the remainder of 1995 and 1996, Parker was busy with In Order to Survive, but he returned his attention to the big band in 1997 for the second Vision Festival, sponsored by the organization Arts for Art, which Patricia Nicholson had founded and led as artistic director. The performance, which included "Poeme—Coming to Get the Little Brother" (a tribute to "the Cambodian boat people") and "Hoang," was recorded, and "Hoang" was included in a two-CD compilation of the festival on AUM Fidelity the following year.[43]

The Little Huey Creative Music Orchestra returned to Vision Festival the following year, where Parker unveiled one of his masterpieces for the band, *Mass for the Healing of the World*.[44] The band was mostly intact from previous years, although Aleta Hayes was now the vocalist and the performance featured guests Kidd Jordan and Charles Waters on alto saxophones and Gunda Gottschalk on violin.[45] The performance at Vision Festival prepared the band to record again, this time at Teatro Nuovo in Verona, Italy, during the first international performance by the big band, on May 31, 1998. The recording was later released on Black Saint.[46]

In January 1999, Little Huey reconvened at Alice Tully Hall at Lincoln Center for the twentieth anniversary concert for Roulette, a venue that had emerged as one of the new institutions supporting the music.[47] The band performed "Elegy for Fred Hopkins." Hopkins (1947–99) was a Chicago-based bassist who had been a key figure in the Association for the Advancement of Creative Musicians and had passed away earlier that month.[48] Although Parker had played with Hopkins only a few times in the 1990s, he had admired him for many years and brought a touching tribute in the big-band setting. Two dates in France featured Little Huey at European festivals, first at Banlieues Bleues Festival in Paris on March 23 and then in Lyons the following evening.[49] On June 12 the band played at Tonic, a new venue that was beginning to draw the audience that had been going to the Knitting Factory by offering exciting and innovative bills. On that night the band played two tributes, one titled "Dramatic Blues," for swing-era bassist Walter "Hot Lips" Page (1900–57), and the other, "The Lowe Key," for tubist and trombonist Bill Lowe.[50] Page had been a key figure in the Count Basie Orchestra as well as the leader of his own group, called the Blue Devils.[51] But the main piece to come out of the year was "Assemblage of Spirits," which the band had presented at the French concerts and performed again at Context Studios in New York on July 1.[52]

For Little Huey, 1999 was its most active year since inception, and it built steadily toward another record that was captured over the course of four Tonic sessions from July to November.[53] The most significant personnel change was the replacement of Susie Ibarra with Andrew Barker, a drummer who had moved to Brooklyn from Atlanta the previous year.[54] Barker has held the drum chair in the ensemble ever since. Barker's close collaborator, alto saxophonist Charles Waters, became a long-term member of the band at that time as well.[55] Other new members at the time were alto saxophonist Ori Kaplan and vocalist Ellen Christi.[56] Parker had only met Kaplan a few months before, but Christi was a longtime collaborator, having been in the Parker big-band orbit since 1975.[57]

At each session during the Tonic residency Parker gave the band a new score. Andrew Barker described the process: "William would offer up skeletal lines, themes, and motifs—sometimes in graphic score form, and then encourage the performers to stray from them. Each section or musician could self-conduct and improvise within the ensemble as they saw fit. I never felt like I had to integrate myself into the orchestra, but rather I tried to listen and connect with the other musicians, and have the stamina to make it through a set!" Barker added, "There was always an arc that William was trying to get across. During the residency, the band just got stronger and stronger. Even though we were doing new material each time, the continuity of playing together on a regular basis developed a language and an instinctual ability to self-conduct."[58]

The concept for this new record, *Mayor of Punkville*, begins with a striking image from Parker:

There is a castle that is made entirely of light. In its windows we can see the many faces of tone. They await the arrival of the angel Gabriel who stands at the door of the spirit room. It holds a trumpet made of red ebony. This trumpet when sounded will be different from the previous one. You will be able to smell the soil, leaves and dust. You will be able to hear the oceans and the singing of doves. You will be able to see the reflections of all the forgotten ones. As you see them their memory will be implanted in your heart. It begins to rain music all over the world. Everyone is soaked in sound. What would happen if the world leaders along with the media decided to tell the truth? Would the axis of the earth shift? What would happen if we put the life of someone we don't know ahead of money, vanity and the value of property? What is that called? Is that the definition of ART?[59]

The record drew its name from a short story that Parker wrote. As Parker explained,

The story is about a city named Crescentville. Like many urban cities it was overrun by gangsters, politicians, and businessmen. Things eventually got so bad they began to put handcuffs on the flowers. People were shot for no reason except that they existed. Crescentville soon got to be known as Punkville. A musician named Bob Jefferson traveling to Chicago passes through during election time. He decides to campaign for Mayor. He runs for office and is elected Mayor of Punkville. He slowly begins to get an orchestra of musicians who play cosmic music. They go on to rid the city of corruption. The old Mayor, the CEOs, gangsters, politicians, television talk show hosts, movie stars, models, pro basketball, baseball, and football players are all put on a giant rocket ship and sent to another planet.[60]

The double record contains a number of new tributes to figures who had had an impact on Parker while he was growing up. Parker selected as the first piece a tribute to James Baldwin: "I can't imagine trying to make sense out of life without the inspiration of writers like James Baldwin, who when I was 16, told me it was all right for me to exist on my own terms."[61] The song was accompanied by a poem, "James Baldwin to the Rescue":

sound at the same time same time
truth caved in as i gave in, gave in
raw dry throat ready to sow
cactus dances to the radio . . . to the radio
first glimpse of spirit
mountain, river, tree
come on and follow me, tomorrow's song for the young ones
sun to sun . . . moon to moon
passing down resolve,
eloquent elusive winds

dusting feathers of a peacock, of a peacock, of a peacock   i know it
      must be hard to be named after God
i know it must be hard to be named after God
two grips dense thicket falls
rushing miracles through the stall
i wish i may i wish i might be anything i want tonight

homeboy, homeboy smoking slab working for the undertaker

what are the choices
throw ourselves over
needle in the toe
toe in the nose
nose in the mouth
mouth in the eye
throw ourselves over

sonorous angel
the norris jones, sirone drone angel
the very deep along zone angel, angel
ringing / singing / tossing / turning
like the 4 tops
throw ourselves over

James Baldwin to the rescue to the rescue
again and again and again and again

what do i see, what do i see
i see madness and sadness and superficial gladness

i know it must be hard to be named after God
your life is ending only to begin[62]

"Oglala Eclipse" is a monumental tribute to jazz musicians Lee Morgan, Andrew Hill, Jackie McLean, Alan Shorter, Charles Tolliver, Gary Bartz, Stafford James, Richard Davis, and Sam Rivers, as well as to Oglala Lakota leaders Red Cloud (1822–1909), Crazy Horse (ca. 1840–77), Kicking Bear (1846–1904), and Black Elk (1863–1950).[63] The jazz musicians mentioned in the tribute count among many of the key figures in Parker's coming-of-age period in the 1960s and 1970s, as well as a few innovative but less-heralded figures. The Oglala figures mentioned were the key political, religious, and military leaders during the period when the United States government subdued, conquered, and annihilated many of the members of the Lakota tribe. Parker explained, "The same sun has shone on all of them. They have all fed my sense of compassion and profundity for life."[64]

Parker added a special notice: "This piece is also for Tatanka Iyotanka also known as Sitting Bull (ca. 1831–90).[65] The renowned Hunkpapa Sioux—warrior and visionary. Sitting Bull was also a singer and composer—he wrote many songs for both secular and religious purposes. He would often times imitate the songs of birds in his improvisations." In terms of the music, Parker gave the orchestra "three or four" harmonic configurations and also gave them the freedom to change rhythms when needed. Another tribute, "Anthem," was for trumpeter Lester Bowie (1941–99), who was dying of liver cancer at the time that the recording was made and passed away two months later on November 8. It was written in the form of a canon and was "very simple like a frosted window melting in the sun."[66]

Parker developed "3 Steps to Nøh Mountain" for the Tibetan Buddhist leader Dalai Lama's visit to New York in the summer of 1999. The piece is a suite, containing three parts. The first part, "Departure," was intended to "set us on our journey up the mountain."[67] The second part, "Soft Wheel," sonically tells the story of how Parker acquired his first bass. Then, the closing part, "Laughing Eyes and Dancing Hearts," was based on a Central Asian melody strain, dedicated to the children of the world.

"Soft Wheel" was part of a myth that Parker told about how he acquired his first bass:

I was visiting my grandmother in South Carolina, well she's actually my great aunt but everyone calls her grandma. One day my feet were hurting so bad. I mean really, really bad all day and all night. I couldn't figure out what the problem was, until grandma told me to soak my feet in the big metal tub that was sitting on the porch. I filled the tub with hot water and Epsom salt. I got a good book and began to soak. After about 15 minutes or so my feet involuntarily began to move, splashing and twisting, I jumped out of the water and begin to dance. I had been dancing in the front yard for at least an hour when a door to door shoe salesman walks up carrying 2 suitcases of shoes. "Shoes for sale I've got shoes for sale, walking, talking, dancing, prancing shoes for sale. I've got wedding shoes, funeral shoes, party shoes all kinds of shoes, shoes for sale, shoes for sale." Grandma lets the salesman in. I continue to dance, she tries on shoes in the kitchen. In the middle of all this another guy wearing two left shoes pulls up in a horse drawn wagon. He has a bass fiddle in the back of the wagon resting on a bed of hay. I am still dancing, grandma buys 4 pairs of shoes one green, one blue, one yellow, and one red. Out of nowhere the guy with the 2 left feet says the strangest thing to me, "Parker if you want a soft ride you better get a soft wheel, if you have a hard wheel you're going to have a hard ride." He repeats this three times. I continue to dance way past supper time until all the excess dance is out of my body. Grandma has been cooking supper since six in the morning so it's definitely ready. We all sit down to eat, the shoe salesman, the guy with two left feet, grandma and myself. All in all things worked out perfectly. The guy with two left feet complained how buying shoes was a nightmare, so the salesman sold him a pair with left feet only. It seems there was a man in the next town who had two right feet. The most surprising thing was the man with two left feet gave me the bass fiddle that was in the wagon. And that was how I got started.[68]

For Parker, stories, histories, myths, and spirituality are all located in one continuum. Weaving these elements into songs has been the labor of his life.

Little Huey Creative Music Orchestra continued to play occasional concerts at Tonic through the fall of 1999, sometimes doing Saturday matinee performances with guests such as poet Steve Dalachinsky (1946–2019). Dalachinsky was a "downtown poet" and had been frequently presenting his work in avant-garde jazz contexts since at least the mid-1980s.[69] At a fourth recording session for *Mayor of Punkville* in November, the group rounded out the record with three interlude pieces and also recorded a long suite, "4 Views from the Window," but this final piece does not appear on the record.[70]

Little Huey played a number of concerts in 2000, beginning at Merkin Hall on March 9. With a piece titled "Songs for Mary Lou, Thomas and Bessie," Parker delivered his most personal tribute yet, this one for his mother, father, and most beloved aunt, Bessie Smith. As critic Ben Ratliff wrote in the *New York Times*, "The suite is a set of sincere songs about love of family and religion and nature, with highly poetic lyrics." Ratliff described the set as "pastoral music, but for a Lower East Side community garden instead of a wheat field. Brief hyper-romantic expanses—thick piano chords, unison melodies—emanated from the 19-piece band." Ratliff added, "Dean Bowman sang lines like 'the greatest revolutionary is a rose' and Leena Conquest sang, 'all I ever want is a sunny day.'" For Ratliff, a highlight was a part called "Corot's Pool," written and read by the late poet David Budbill (1940–2016), where Dave Hofstra's tuba and one of the baritone saxophones "created long, shifting chords, and saxophones chattered over unison trumpet lines. . . . Pious sincerity finally won out, especially in the last song, with a refrain of the word 'happiness' and a vamp that could have come from a 1960's soul-rock musical."[71]

Little Huey also had a notable marching-band performance from 6th Street and Avenue A to the New Age Café on St. Mark's Place as the opening of the fifth Vision Festival in May 2000. The festival program described the event as "Mardi Gras in the Tone World."[72] Parker referred to it as his attempt at being a pied piper to gather an audience for the festival.[73] They also played a concert performance on the closing night that included a rare appearance by Alan Silva (b. 1939) on keyboard.[74] Silva had been a source of inspiration for Parker, and the two had developed a friendship in the 1990s after first meeting in 1972. Having been impressed by the possibilities of the marching big band, Little Huey did it again in August, this time from Martin Luther King Boulevard and Lenox Avenue to Marcus Garvey Park in Harlem.[75] The goal was to bring this music of liberation out to the people.

In late February 2001, Little Huey Creative Music Orchestra played two dates in Massachusetts. The first was at the Bezanson Recital Hall at the University of Massachusetts-Amherst, which was recorded and broadcast in the Magical Triangle Jazz Series on WMUA radio.[76] The following day the band played in the Boston Creative Music Alliance concert series at ICA Theater at the Institute of Contemporary Art. New additions to the band included cellist Shia-Shu Yu and drummer Guillermo E. Brown (b. 1974).[77] In addition to playing bass, Parker also played marimba, shakuhachi, and bombard. The marimba, a common kind of xylophone, had its origins in West and Central Africa, but attained its modern stand-up and chromatic scale form after Mexican innovations in the mid- to late nineteenth century.[78] The shakuhachi is an ancient Japanese bamboo flute that has also been used as a part of Zen Buddhist meditation and has gained a slight yet growing presence in American and European music since the 1960s.[79] Bombards are a double-reed woodwind instrument commonly featured in traditional Breton music that produces a powerful sound often thought to resemble a trumpet. Parker also played a zintir, "a bass from Morocco," at the concert, which he had been playing privately for about three or four years, but that track was not included on the recording that was made of the event.[80]

The session at ICA Theater was recorded and later released as *Raincoat in the River* on Eremite Records.[81] It was dedicated to a street musician named Marvin Nuñez, "Uncle Marvin," whom Parker had known in the 1970s. Parker had sketched out ideas for the piece as early as 1973 but had had no opportunity to perform or record it in the interim. Nuñez is otherwise unknown and left no known recordings. According to Parker, Nuñez was one of the few tenor saxophone players to explore what he called "sub-tone music." Parker describes this as "a world of whispers heralded by vibrations so low and subtle they could not be heard by the naked ear. We don't hear the bass, we feel it through the soul of the ear. Through our feet, fingers, and the intuitive now."[82] These early sounds had had a distinct imprint on Parker in how he thought about the sound of the bass.

The title of the record came from the fact that "Marvin Nuñez wore a black raincoat with a fur lining all year round. He seemed to appear and disappear at will, coming out of the shadows and returning there after he visited." Parker had often met Nuñez at Nathan's Restaurant on 8th Street and 6th Avenue in the Greenwich Village. They were often joined by violinist Billy Bang and Henry P. Warner, and eventually Carl Lombard, also known as Pelikan.[83] One day while Parker was having a conversation on the street with drummer Steve McCall (1933–89), he was drawn by the sound of a saxophone. He followed it to Avenue D near the East River: "I looked over the railing and there was a black raincoat in the water. After that day, Uncle Marvin was never seen again."[84]

The record features one extended suite, separated into five sections. "Meditation for Two Voices" explores some of the possibilities of the sub-tone world.[85] In part II Parker returns to the common imagery of mountains in his work. He describes their presence in his imagination: "Mountains are one of the essential things in the world for me, even though I don't see them very often. Whether tall, small, brown, green, blue, black, purple, yellow, or orange, they have maintained all these years, while still remaining a mystery." Parker played a marimba on the track, which he used to illustrate the evaporation of the morning mist that covers the mountains. For Parker, these mysterious mountains are an alluring fantasy of sorts: "However, I believe we must stay in this world and work desperately to make the necessary changes. Death and war will never defeat the power of compassion and love."[86] Music critic Bob Blumenthal commented that this piece "mixed vamps and the dramatic colors of Masahiko Kono's electronically altered trombone and Yu's rich cello."[87]

With the final three sections, the suite takes a personal turn. "Anast Crossing the Lake of Light" imagines "a lake of light where all those who are in need gather to become one with 'song.'" In this case, Anast is the mother of music and makes her journey on a raft. Then, on the shore, she is met by Uncle Marvin, Albert Ayler, Mahatma Gandhi, and Parker's grandmother whom he never met, "all together at the edge of the water."[88]

The title piece is vibrant and visual in its scope, and it is about a day that a rainbow appeared without rain in an urban ghetto. The lyrics, sung by Leena Conquest, tell the transformational tale:

> There's a rainbow in the ghetto
> And it's changing everybody into poets
> Guns into trumpet bells of freedom
> Ringing ringing
> Chimes of justice
> Singing singing
> Raincoat in the river
> The end and the beginning
> Inverted flowers turning into children
> A Painters dream all the loved ones are gathered
> The sunsets again
> And the day begins to end
> Raincoat in the river
> At long last the color of the sky[89]

"Painters Celebration" is a tribute to saxophonist Marion Brown, who had made such an impression upon Parker when he was first listening to the music and had continued to be a source of inspiration.[90]

Critic Larry Blumenfeld wrote in the *New York Times* that Little Huey Creative Music Orchestra was the "fullest expression of Mr. Parker's aesthetic" and that the music drew from the legacies of Ellington (by creating personalized roles for each player) and Mingus (through vamps and bluesy refrains that build into colorful explosions of sound). The ensemble is as notable for its group dynamic as for the music it produces." In terms of conduction, Blumenfeld observed that "Mr. Parker held up colored papers to signal a change from one rhythm to another or a dynamic shift from soft to loud. The music created by the orchestra can be both unpredictable and profoundly beautiful, unlike anything else being made downtown." Speaking directly about *Raincoat in the River*, Blumenfeld stated that "the music blurs the line between free jazz, indigenous folk songs and contemporary classical, moving gracefully from gentle passages for one or two instruments to furious, fully orchestrated swells. Melodies are carried by a cello in one section, a Middle Eastern double-reeded horn in another."[91]

A performance at Roulette in May 2001 and a residency at CUANDO in August 2001 prepared the band to record its next record on May 29, 2002, at CBGB's during Vision Festival 7.[92] The band now included Sabir Mateen (b. 1951) on reeds, Dick Griffin (b. 1939) on trombone, and Matt Lavelle (b. 1970) on trumpet.[93] Parker had first crossed paths with Mateen in 1993, when he hired Parker to play in his own big band, Darkness, Light, and Beyond, and they had played together in many different bands over the years.[94] Parker and Griffin had met as early as 1995 but played together for the first time at a memorial concert for vocalist Jeanne Lee (1939–2000) in 2000. Parker had met Lavelle briefly in 1994, but they had not played together in any substantive way until he hired Lavelle for Little Huey.[95]

Spontaneous contains two interrelated pieces, "Spontaneous Flowers" and "Spontaneous Mingus." That night, Parker recalled standing outside of CBGB's "waiting to go over the sketch for the evening concert possibly an extension of the 1979 composition called 'Desert Flower,' possibly its own entity. The musicians arrive[d] one by one. Each section is a city within the nation of sound." The drive behind the record was a lifelong quest, as Parker put it, "to empty my mind when it comes to music so I can concentrate on the moment, on the spontaneous millionth of a second that occurs before each sound is born. It sounds like this or that, I don't know. Dance of sound within the dream."[96] For the evening, they used six bars of preset music;

the rest was entirely improvised.[97] In reference to the piece on Mingus, Parker stated, "There is this riff that comes out of nowhere. Well, it isn't out of nowhere, it is our history which lingers in the corridors of Blood, one part of Black Music: Gospel/Folk/Jazz/Blues/Cosmic space/Evolution of time and motion/Future forward. NOW!"[98] Parker considered the music to be the apex of the band at the time.[99]

Parker next summoned Little Huey Creative Music Orchestra to play on April 4–6, 2003, in protest of the American invasion of Iraq under the administration of President George W. Bush.[100] The group presented the extended *World Peace Suite*, which was composed of three parts: "Landscapes of Disharmony," "Blues for the People," and "Uprising." It was performed over the course of three nights, with one part being presented each night. The performances were a call to action against an unjust war orchestrated by the U.S. government.

The next major performance for Little Huey occurred at Tonic on July 5, 2003, during a memorial concert for Irving Stone (1922–2003), a major supporter of the music and the person for whom John Zorn's club, the Stone, was later named. It was a daylong event featuring numerous jazz and avant-garde luminaries. Little Huey's performance was one for the ages, captured eloquently by music critic Steve Smith:

> William Parker marshalled the considerable forces of his Little Huey Creative Orchestra. Following the extended string of small ensembles that had dominated the day, the massive sound that poured forth was a sanctified yawp, a jolt not just of volume but of sheer mass and density. Trumpeter Matt Lavelle's opening solo drew holy-roller shouts from audience members; the saxophones, by contrast, backed him with lush, buttery chords. The winds grew darker behind Charles Waters' squawk; backing Rob Brown, the saxes resumed their lushness but the brasses were argumentative. The band hushed to a subdued, minor key Mingus riff behind Roy Campbell's muted solo; the winds caressed, the brasses chortled. Andrew Barker dropped out momentarily, allowing Parker to assert the rhythmic lead under Sabir Mateen's brawling tenor utterances. Re-entering a moment later, Barker played fractals across Parker's granitic pulse; as the reeds played at one angle, the brasses at another, the music was simultaneously as brainy as Anthony Braxton and as earthy as James Brown. At the risk of Preacher-like hyperbole, at that moment there was no greater energy source on the face of the planet.[101]

One short piece, "Inscription," was recorded and then included on the compilation CD that appeared on the Tzadik record label.[102]

By 2003, it was clear that Parker's attention was being pulled ever more strongly into his quartet and quintet, which were getting considerable work both domestically and in Europe. Although he maintained a strong interest in Little Huey, his schedule did not allow him to assemble the band nearly as often as he had in the latter half of the 1990s or the early 2000s. The band celebrated its tenth anniversary at Vision Festival 9 on February 28, 2004, at St. Nicholas of Myra Church.[103] The set included an invocation for bassist Malachi Favors (1927–2004), an integral and founding member of the Art Ensemble of Chicago, who had succumbed to pancreatic cancer about a month before.[104] This version of the band included Parker's longtime friend David Budbill reciting poetry.[105]

Little Huey did not play in New York again until January 2005, which set it up to play in May at the 22nd Festival International de Musique Actuelle de Victoriaville in Quebec, one of the premier Canadian annual music festivals.[106] The centerpiece of the performance was a tribute to bassist Percy Heath (1923–2005), who passed away about a month before the Victoriaville concert. Parker had first met Heath in San Francisco in 1983 when he was there on tour with Cecil Taylor. Coming off stage, Heath had greeted Parker with a hug and called him "Iron Fingers." Parker responded by thanking him "for his powerful bass playing. When we spoke about the importance of space, timing, and playing the right thing at the right time in a musical situation. I saw Percy one other time at the North Sea Jazz Festival in Holland. He was in his seventies and I asked him if I could get anything for him. He replied, 'No, just keep playing your music.'"[107]

Returning to New York, Little Huey Creative Music Orchestra played Vision Festival 10 on June 19, 2005, with Parker's old friend Alan "Juice" Glover on tenor saxophone.[108] The band played a tribute to John Gilmore (1931–1995), the longtime member and eventual leader of the Sun Ra Arkestra, titled "Gilmore's Hat," with Leena Conquest weaving beautiful lyrical lines in his honor.[109] The band also featured an augmented percussion section that included Parker's twenty-year-old son Isaiah and three of his friends. Parker, for his part, was "resplendent in a gleaming orange suit with a yellow tie, which drew marveling shouts from the band."[110] Later that summer, Little Huey returned to Italy to play two nights at Sant' Anna Arresi in Sardinia, where it performed two medleys of tunes, the final song concluding with Parker singing and the band playing "In Order to Survive."[111] Then, in September, the band assembled at Angel Orensanz Center in New York for a benefit concert to raise money for Hurricane Katrina victims in New Orleans. It had a personal touch, too, for Parker's collaborator, saxophonist

Kidd Jordan, was a New Orleans resident and had been briefly unaccounted for after evacuating his home near the 17th Street Canal the night before the breach of the levees.[112]

After a nearly two-year hiatus, Little Huey Creative Music Orchestra gathered for a performance at Vision Festival 12 in June 2007. The live performance was marred by sound problems, so the band met the next day and recorded in the space before the festival resumed.[113] This iteration of the band included new members, both old associates and younger emerging players. Veterans Bill Cole (double reeds) and Joe Morris (guitar, banjo) both added instrumental elements not included in Little Huey before that time.[114] Brahim Frigbane on oud and vocalist Sangeeta Bandyopadhyay did much to add the international flavor that was also central to the concept and vision. This version also included three up-and-coming string players, Mazz Swift (violin), Jessica Pavone (viola), and Shayna Dulberger (bass).[115]

For this performance, they did one four-part suite. The concept behind the record was Parker's concept of "universal tonality," the idea that "all sounds, like human beings, come from the same place. They have different bodies and faces, but the soul of each sound comes from the same parent 'creation.'" Parker added, "All sounds have a heartbeat and breathe the same as each human being. Some sounds are born in Africa; others are born in Asia, Europe, Australia, or America. These sounds pass through certain human beings. We don't invent sounds, we are allowed to encounter them; we don't own them, they existed before we were born and will be here after we are gone."[116]

In terms of the music, the suite of songs aimed to blend sound "with intent and message." Each part of the music is intricately multilayered. In poetic terms, Parker describes it: "The soil is silence, the root coming out of the soil is called the bass line, and the rhythms are called branches. Motifs, scales and melodies are the leaves. Improvisations are the fruit which ripens as we listen. The initial seed is anything that is beautiful."[117] Parker frames the suite with the following poetic prose:

> we are all facing the wind may we be filled with light let it blow across
> my face let it illuminate the night let us live for the absence of hate may
> all fear vanish from the heart may all our eyes see the light may our
> hearts open up to all in need may those in need look out for the signs of
> the double sunrise may the silent light fill our souls may the serene rain
> dampen the earth filled with compassion we seek understanding of
> sound that lives around the tops of mountains may we love those we call

family and those we call strangers in the same way do not kill another human being we can not bring them back to life[118]

In a sort of summary, Parker said, "One day a double sunrise will appear in the sky. We have until that time to become One with music." At the center of the vocalist parts of the music are *tarana*, Persian devotional syllables.[119] Although these take on a kind of romantic poeticism, they are intended to convey the love between a devotee and the divine through desire for wisdom.

Since 2007, performances by Little Huey Creative Music Orchestra have been even more sporadic. The group appeared at an AUM Fidelity mini-festival in October 2009, where it played an extended piece in honor of composer and pianist George Russell (1923–2009), who had passed away the previous summer.[120] A seven-year hiatus followed until Little Huey reassembled in 2016 and 2017 with very different lineups that included a number of younger players such as James Brandon Lewis and Yoni Kretzmer (tenor saxophones), Heru Shabaka-ra and Waldorn Ricks (trumpets), and Darius Jones (alto saxophone).[121] In these late versions of the band, Parker has turned to more instruments, such as shakuhachi, shenai, hunting horn, doussn'gouni, pocket trumpet, and a number of double reeds that he acquired while touring around the world.[122] In another big-band performance, albeit with a different lineup that was billed as the William Parker Essential Orchestra, Parker presented a composition titled "Inscription" at Roulette on February 16, 2013, as a tribute to Cecil Taylor, with Taylor in attendance.[123] Parker is planning a ten-CD box set of previously unreleased music by Little Huey to be released in 2020.[124]

Nine

Toward a Universal Sound: William Parker Quartet and Raining on the Moon

Art is the blood of the people

whether they are aware of it or not.

It is still the role of the musician to incite revolution,

spiritual and human change.

. . . if your art is doing what it is supposed to do

you should be on the most-wanted list. —— **William Parker**

When In Order to Survive came to an end in 1999, Parker began thinking about what kind of small-group work he would like to do and who he would hire for his new band. The most propitious encounter was with percussionist Hamid Drake (b. 1955). Parker had first played with Drake in 1993 as the two composed the rhythm section for Peter Brötzmann's Die Like a Dog Trio and Quartet.[1] Drake recalled that in their very first sound check together, "Something immediately happened, something clicked. There was a resonance in how we played, an ease in how we communicated musically, in how we shared ideas."[2] Although the bulk of the band's recordings from the period were not released until 2007 and later, Die Like a Dog was quite active throughout the mid-1990s, playing primarily in Europe at many of

Figure 9.1 Parker and Peter Brötzmann outside Clemente Soto Velez Cultural Center, New York, April 18, 2010. *Credit*: ©Peter Gannushkin/downtownmusic.net.

the premier festivals and clubs.[3] The band shifted between trio and quartet versions, sometimes including Toshinori Kondo on trumpet and electronics. Parker saw Brötzmann as "a very unique player, not coming out of church or the blues, but rather coming from out of the self-tradition of art poetry post–World War II. Underneath he has a love for the entire tradition of saxophone with a cathartic urgency and all art that is serious and uncompromising."[4] In addition to Parker's own bands, Die Like a Dog was one of the substantial ways in which Parker connected with European audiences throughout the 1990s.

As critic David Keenan wrote of a performance by the band in Lisbon in 2000, "With Peter Brötzmann's Die Like a Dog Quartet, Parker had been part of some of the most internally luminescent fireworks on the main stage. Especially when drummer Hamid Drake moved to hand drum and Parker took up percussion, there were some truly exquisite hushed moments."[5] Having seen this trio perform many years later at Vision Festival 19 in 2014, I would echo these comments. The audience was transfixed by every sound, whether large or small, bellowed or presented at a whisper. It is with Drake that Parker, perhaps, has achieved his deepest musical understanding, implicitly interconnected to such a degree rarely seen in improvised music.

Born in Monroe, Louisiana, Drake grew up in Chicago, where he originally emerged as an in-demand R&B and reggae drummer, and where he has lived most of his life. As poet David Budbill wrote, "The propulsive force of Hamid's drumming means that no matter how far out a solo may go, it always swings. When a drummer who is as great a time keeper as Hamid is gets in a situation where he is free to go outside time you get the best of both measured and free playing."[6]

In 1997–2000, Parker and Drake's work together intensified with a tour and recording as part of the Frode Gjerstad Trio as well as work with multi-instrumentalist Kali Z. Fasteau and reeds player Fred Anderson.[7] As they spent more time together "off-stage, eating together, talking, traveling," a deep friendship formed between Parker and Drake "that basically hasn't changed since, except getting even deeper. We've become like family," Drake related more than twenty years later.[8] Based on their experience together and their implicit deep understanding of each other, Parker and Drake decided to make their own music together. This began as a "proposal on the front steps of a church in June 1999."[9] Drake flew out to New York in 2000, and their first concert took place on Saturday, April 1, at AUM HQ, which was the name for a series of concerts that AUM Fidelity manager Steven Joerg organized at his apartment in Park Slope, Brooklyn.[10] A crowd assembled of approximately eighty people such that the room was packed to the brim to hear the two play live. "It was our first true duet together," Drake remarked, "though even when we play in larger groups, it always feels like we are in a duet dialogue with one another."[11]

Two days after the live duo performance, Parker and Drake entered the studio. The session was released soon after, but it was later reissued with the live set accompanying it in a two-CD set on AUM Fidelity.[12] In addition to playing bass, Parker also employed balafon, bombard, shakuhachi, slit drum, and dumbek, while Drake met him with various drums, tabla, frame drum, and bells. As a result of their inherent understanding of each other, they immediately began working regularly together and building a well-developed repertoire. Parker and Drake's bass-drum duo recordings were certainly a landmark in this rare combination, extending the vocabulary and possibilities of the instruments. In 2005 they recorded a second studio session that would also be released to considerable acclaim.[13]

Figure 9.2 Parker and Hamid Drake with Patricia Nicholson (not pictured), Judson Memorial Church, New York, May 29, 2017. *Credit*: ©Luciano Rosetti.

William Parker Quartet

After the first duo session, however, Parker hired Drake for his new quartet. As the story goes, Parker had originally written the tunes with drummer Billy Higgins in mind because they had played duo together many times before Higgins had moved to California, but the two had never recorded together.[14] But in 2000, Higgins was undergoing a liver transplant and was unavailable, so Parker chose Drake instead. The band also included long-time collaborators Lewis Barnes and Rob Brown.

On May 26, 2000, not even two months after Parker and Drake had recorded their duo record, the quartet entered the studio and recorded tracks for its first record, *O'Neal's Porch*, and it was on this record that Parker and Drake's uniquely identifiable sound really came into being.[15] As bandmate Barnes stated at the time, "William and Hamid play together like twins separated at birth! No two guys can better anticipate each other's musical moves than these two men, and on top of it all they play in and out better than anyone and at the same time!"[16] Drake recalled Barnes stating that he and Parker were "brothers from another mother."[17] Rob Brown observed that the quartet constituted a new period for William: "The music is free, tuneful,

Figure 9.3 O'Neal Williams (1917–1999) and Ethel Williams (1924–2014), Parker's uncle and aunt, Orangeburg, South Carolina, December 1964.

rhythmically grooving, it is sound, soft, harsh. The whole spectrum."[18] For Drake, the interwoven solos from Brown and Barnes were one of the singular accomplishments of the debut record, an element that they would build on through the years that followed.[19]

The record was written in memory of Parker's uncle, O'Neal Clay Williams (1917–1999), who had married his mother's sister, Ethel Jefferson (1924–2014). Williams had lived in Orangeburg, South Carolina, and it was on his porch that the family often gathered during summer visits when everyone got together. The title piece is littered with grooves and "dancing bass and drums."[20] As Budbill notes, it's as if all four of them "go out there in the front yard of O'Neal's porch and dance in the yard" because there are so many dance rhythms in the music.

The opening track, "Purple," a color that Parker often associates with the sky in his poetry, features ensemble improvisation with the different players passing the melody and the energy of the music back and forth between them. The deep melodies are never lost as they improvise: "No matter how far out they go, they always carry with them fragments of the head."[21] After horn solos that improvise off the theme, Parker and Drake demonstrate their deep understanding of one another in a brief duet, "Rise," which also features a beautiful moment with Parker playing arco bass while Drake solos quietly over the top before the horns join back in.

"Leaf" is a personal tale about a day in the life of Parker. It opens with a robust, walking bass line, charting the course in a determined manner. Brown and Barnes provide the sounds of the city, "the energy, excitement, and distraction. Yet plowing through all that hustle and chaos, is the determined William Parker intent on going somewhere with that steady, focused walk and his calm, undistracted manner," Budbill notes. He adds, "While the sounds of the city crash and bang all around him, William moves steadily on, not oblivious to the life around him, but rather totally within that life, yet always focused on his own life also, always listening to the music coming from the Tone World. As he moves through the weltering swirl, he is the point of reference, the inner eye, the stillness at the center of the storm."[22]

The William Parker Quartet played only sporadically in its first few years, appearing in New England and New York, followed by its first European date in Stirling, Scotland, in April 2002, where Parker also played with the David S. Ware Quartet and a duo with Hamid Drake as part of a residency. A U.S. West Coast tour through San Francisco, Portland, and Seattle in April 2004 set the band up to do a live recording for its next album. The opportunity came during a Canadian tour in June and July of that year that began at the Suoni per il Popolo festival in Montreal, followed by appearances at annual jazz festivals in Ottawa, Calgary, Edmonton, and Vancouver.[23] Material for the record was drawn from the bookend performances of the tour.[24]

Parker praised his bandmates' performances on the record: "They have a unique way of interlacing lines and phrases: taking them up or down a step, super-imposing harmonies, rhythms and inflections. Sometimes the head is disintegrated altogether or altered to become a living entity. Notes, phrases and sounds are invented as we go along. Hamid Drake has a very special way of doing everything on drums. His sound is filled with life-affirming energy and concern for others."[25]

The record, *Sound Unity*, contains six tracks. The title track was taken from a phrase coined by artist Marilyn Sontag that Parker saw as "a cry for the unity between all human beings and sound." In this instance, by sound, Parker meant "light, color, movement and silence." He defined unity as "brotherhood among all men and women and children." It was a call "to all those who can hear to unite—unite, but not give up your individuality."[26]

The record contains three tributes. The opening track, "Hawaii," was for saxophonist Frank Lowe, whose album *Black Beings* was Parker's first appearance on a record. Explaining the dedication, Parker wrote that "I visited Frank before he entered the hospital with lung cancer. He instinctively knew he was dying and spoke about going to Hawaii where it is warm. Frank liked tunes with bounce and joy. He was one of the kindest human beings I ever met. He is a member of a particular tribe of people called angels." The second track, "Wood Flute Song," was written for trumpeter Don Cherry, whom Parker considered to be "one of the greatest musicians who ever lived. He loved music and people so deeply that one could not help but to feel this when around him." At the time, Parker indicated that he would dedicate future songs to him and would go on to name his most extensive release, the eight-CD box set *Wood Flute Songs* (2015), in his honor. Parker would later write that "Don was always a source of light for me and many others." The song "Poem for June Jordan" was for "the unsung writer" who had always had an influence on Parker, for "her words were always insightful and very honest and again, filled with compassion."[27] The liner notes indicate that Parker had written lyrics for this piece that were not incorporated into the recorded version that he hoped to record later. In 2007, with the Raining on the Moon Quintet, he recorded the version with lyrics released on *Corn Meal Dance*.[28]

"Harlem" represents a memory from Parker's childhood, "a medium tempo impression I had of sitting on the steps of my Aunt Millie's apartment building on 145th Street and Saint Nicholas Avenue when I was a kid. I used to sit there and watch people walk by. The stories of Minton's Playhouse or the Savoy Ballroom and places like the Baby Grand or Wells Waffle House still dance in my head." The final piece, "Groove," is exactly that, "a dance that circles around itself, touching on the shores of Jamaica, waving goodbye at the same time it is saying hello."[29]

In fall 2004 the quartet played a date at the annual festival at Sant' Anna Arresi in Sardinia.[30] At that concert it debuted another tribute, one that Parker had written for the songwriter eden ahbez (1908–95), the ascetic who had famously lived camping beneath the first "L" of the Hollywood sign in Los Angeles and studied Asian mysticism. He wrote "Nature Boy," which topped the billboards when Nat Cole recorded it, and was an early antiestablishment figure who ate only raw vegetables, fruits, and nuts, and claimed to survive on three dollars per week.[31] He typically adorned himself in sandals and a white robe with shoulder-length hair and a beard. Perhaps ahbez's most famous statement was "I look crazy but I'm not. And the funny thing is that other people don't look crazy but they are."[32]

The quartet continued to build its audience in Italy, returning to Turin the following March.[33] Then, after a brief return to New York, the band returned for a longer tour in April, landing initially in Sweden for a radio recording and television broadcast, and then seven dates in Rome and northern Italy, followed by one performance in Hungary, where Parker was beginning to have a presence. A second 2005 European tour, in July and August, had the quartet for two more concerts in southern Italy and a performance at Rantajatsit (Jazz on the Beach) in Raahe, Finland. The group returned to do a release show at the Blue Note jazz club in New York for *Sound Unity*.[34]

The band's next opportunities came in the form of a U.S. West Coast tour in May 2006 at the Penofin Jazz Festival in Ukiah, California, and then in clubs in Portland, Oakland, and Santa Cruz. It was the third of these, in the historic jazz club Yoshi's, that yielded another live recording. Yoshi's had been originally opened in Berkeley in 1972 and had moved locations several times before settling in its current location in 1997, a 330-seat concert hall with an attached Japanese restaurant.[35] The quartet played two sets. This was a period when Parker abandoned his original idea of never playing the same composition twice in performance because he was aiming for the unit to get tighter and build a repertoire.[36]

The opening piece, "Tears for the Children of Rwanda," was dedicated to the victims of the genocide. The song is "filled with Joy, Hope, moving forward and having a future." Musically, the piece is structured so that the melody also doubles as the rhythm, and Rob Brown's solo reminded Parker of the color of "purple jade."[37] The bass and drum duet in the piece references the tune "Wood Flute Song." From there, the band played "Petit Oiseau" (Little Bird) and "Groove #7," both of which were later recorded in the studio and appeared on *Petit Oiseau*, which was released the following year.[38] "Corn Meal Dance," which was rapidly becoming one of Parker's classics, and "Hopi Spirits" rounded out the first set.

The quartet opened the second set with its Don Cherry tribute "Wood Flute Song," which Parker described as "the kind of piece that takes you to the middle of the action immediately."[39] The key moment in the piece had the drums unveil Parker doing fingertip strums and playing stops before the band returned to the head. Another tribute included with the second set was "The Golden Bell," written for his early collaborator, trumpeter Arthur Williams, whom Parker had worked with regularly in 1973–80, primarily within Jemeel Moondoc's Ensemble Muntu.[40] Williams had passed away quite young, but Parker had always been enamored with his compositions, which he described as "very colorful" and which "would cover a very wide dynamic range." In fact, in 2016 Parker would help with the release of Williams's only record—a posthumous release on NoBusiness Records titled *Forgiveness Suite* that was taken from a December 19, 1978, live session at WKCR radio with Parker, Toshinori Kondo (trumpet), Peter Kuhn (bass clarinet), and Denis Charles (drums).[41]

Parker claimed that Cherry had described Williams's sound on trumpet as "silver bullets" and that Dizzy Gillespie had "[sung] praises for Arthur's playing with the Milford Graves unit at the 1967 Newport jazz festival."[42] The title of the piece, "The Golden Bell, is a kingdom where all the trumpet players live in harmony without critics polls," Parker mused. "It is only about the sound of life, the sky, the rain, and the gentle wind called breath. In the Golden Bell, I was thinking about ascension of the spirit into another place where the only tears cried were tears of happiness."[43]

In January 2007, Parker recorded a new project with the quartet named *Alphaville Suite: Music Inspired by the Jean Luc Godard Film* of the same title. It had been more than forty years since Parker had first watched Godard's films, but his dream of writing music inspired by Godard had finally become reality. Parker wrote of the film, which had originally been released in 1965, "It didn't take long for me to realize that Alphaville wasn't just another science fiction spy thriller. It was a wake-up call for modern society to be vigilant. Much like George Orwell's *1984*, it was prophetic in its prediction of the idea man invents machine; machine controls man and as a result our humanity is diminished." Parker added, "The next thirty years would give birth to a new age of technology placing computer chips in every appliance from toasters to automobiles. The business of computer science was moving so fast that the real concept of human progress would eventually vanish. The only remnant of that progress is poetry. The poetry that exists in all that is beautiful. It is the musicians, painters, writers, dancers, filmmakers and actors, who would keep the flame of compassion burning in the years to follow."[44]

For Parker, Alphaville Suite was an opportunity to explore the similarity in dialogues that happen in film and in musical improvisation/composition. As he wrote, "Just as a film has a storyline, musical improvisation/composition has a melodic and rhythmic line. In both forms there is dialogue, call and response; things happen that have to do with the texture, timbre, color and shape of the story." For this project, he designed it to be a double quartet, one being the regular quartet and the second a string quartet. Parker described the process as "eight musicians blending as one yet not giving up their individuality."[45]

For the recording, Parker hired a number of emerging figures, all of whom were beginning to establish themselves in their own right: Mazz Swift (violin), Jessica Pavone (viola), Julia Kent (cello), and Shiau-Shu Yu (cello). Vocalist Leena Conquest, whom Parker was working with in his Raining on the Moon Quintet at the time, joined as a special guest, laying down her vocal tracks the day after the band had recorded the entire work. Music critic Ed Hazell, who was present in the studio for the recording session, observed the following:

> It all unfolded in Leon Dorsey's 27th-floor penthouse studio overlooking Lincoln Center, which commands quite a view. William mixed things up quite a bit, they recorded as an octet a couple times, and one piece, originally scored for the entire ensemble, ended up as a string quartet setting for Hamid. There was a devastating piece for a trio improvisation by Flip Barnes, William doing his most bone-chilling arco work, and Hamid on cymbals with scored string quartet parts cued in and out by William. William and the strings recorded a backing track for a song that Leena Conquest recorded the next day.[46]

In Bologna in 2010, the biggest thrill for Parker was that he had an opportunity to reedit parts of the *Alphaville* film, adding color to one scene and shortening the film so that it could fit with the live performance. Parker still to this day has ambitions to further the project.

In March 2007 the regular quartet played the Bergamo Jazz festival in Italy. A Midwest U.S. tour followed in April, visiting Grinnell College in Iowa, playing a matinee date at the Empty Bottle in Chicago, and then concerts in Texas in Houston and Austin.[47] The Houston concert, at Diverse Works, was recorded, thus capturing another important phase in the band's development at the time. The band was incredibly tight by that time, and it performed seamlessly. Parker considered what the band was doing as "folk dance music" of a certain kind, adding that "the music is full of color and always tells a story, instead of words we use sound, melody and rhythm."[48] Four-part rhythmic harmony was particularly important to Parker, with each member of the band laying different things out simultaneously. The audience received the music enthusiastically.

The band played two sets. Parker referred to "Hamid's Groove" as "one of the themes for the new century that is sure to change your mood." As he suggested, "See if you can imagine a stadium of people that are grooving to music that is laced with freedom and allows you to be yourself." "Hamid's Groove" was the second part of the "Groove Sweet," a pun because the piece is a suite. The first set closed with "Malachi's Mode," for bassist Malachi Favors, which was written in a way to emulate Favors's style of playing "strong and powerful with a singing resonance."[49] When saxophonist Roscoe Mitchell heard the piece in Sardinia, he asked for the sheet music to use with one of his own bands.[50] Parker explained his play on time in the piece with "three quarter time in six eight time has always conjured up joy for me. There must be a mystical formation inside the number 3 and its multiples."[51]

The second set opened with "O'Neal's Porch," filled with danceable grooves: "If you really get inside you can hear that the back beat has never left this music, it's the center of everything, invisible and visible at the same time." On "Red Desert," Parker further explored double reeds by playing a Catalan instrument called the gralla. "Ojibway Song" is a piece that Parker never notated but that he says "always spontaneously appears when needed to raise the level of the music even further, it has a celebratory and ceremonial feel at the same time." The band transitioned into "Sunrise in the Tone World," a piece that it rarely played, showcasing Parker on a bass solo and exploration with shakuhachi. Then the band closed with "Ascent of the Big Spirit," dedicated to the violinist Leroy Jenkins (1932–2007), who had died earlier that year.[52]

A European tour through France, Italy, and Switzerland followed immediately in mid-April 2007.[53] Then, in July, the group appeared at the Pitchfork Music Festival in Chicago for the first time.[54] By December, it was ready to enter the studio to lay down tracks for the third record, *Petit Oiseau*. Many of the tracks previously recorded live appeared on the record, such as "The Golden Bell," "Malachi's Mode," and the title track. "Groove #7," "Hamid's Groove," and "Daughter's Joy," from previous live sets, constituted "Groove Sweet," which also appeared on the record.[55] "Grooves are one of the core elements that contribute to life and its continued legacy," Parker explained. "There was a groove since day one; if you listen, start with your own heartbeat, it all dances."[56]

The title track was Parker's attempt to compose a post-bop song. Its English translation, "Little Bird," was a character in Parker's tone poem "Music and the Shadow People." In the poem, Little Bird is born without wings, but his mother instructs him to fly "from the inside," and soon he is soaring higher than all of the other birds. The title is also a double allusion to saxophonist Charlie Parker. Given the meaning of the song, Parker decided to structure it so that only the melody was preset, allowing the soloists to play off of "the rhythmic flow of the sound."[57] Lewis Barnes, who took the first solo, noted that "I used two mutes for this date. Each mute adds a different color to the trumpet. A cup mute was used for Little Bird. The sound of Rob's alto and the cup mute reminded me of the sound I felt when Bird and Miles played together in the 40s."[58]

Two songs on the record were written to address the theme of change in some way. "Four for Tommy" was a kind of challenge issued for "Tommy Flanagan or Tommy Turrentine," who Parker imagines giving him what he calls "the bebop look, which is the stare given by the senior members of the musical family when they question your choice of notes or when they feel you are not playing the changes. The changes do not have to be preset, and they can be what you want them to be, changing each moment." The piece is a declaration of independence from conservative jazz. "Dust from a Mountain" is a piece about personal and communal transformation, "based off of a dream that one day people will wake up and realize that life is precious; so precious that we should drop all the petty things that divide us and seek unity with each other."[59] Almost as a metaphor for the challenge of personal transformation, each musician played an instrument for which he is not necessarily known. Brown played a B-flat clarinet, Parker played an Ojibwa cedar flute, and Drake played a frame drum and a balafon.

And finally, as in all of Parker's work, the record contains tributes. The closing piece, "Shorter for Alan," was for the trumpeter Alan Shorter (1932–88), whom Parker had met in the early 1970s. Parker felt that many false stories had been promulgated about Shorter and had kept in contact with him up until a few years before his death. "Talaps Theme" was a different sort of dedication, this one for the Sami, the Finno-Ugric people who were once indigenous to a large swath of Scandinavia and Russia. As in his many songs for America's indigenous peoples, Parker situated this tribute both as an act of solidarity as well as a way of preserving a memory of the past.

A short January 2008 tour had the band return to Italy and Switzerland as well as play its first concert in Russia, at the DOM Cultural Center in Moscow.[60] A U.S. West Coast tour followed in May, which had the band return to Yoshi's in a reprise of its visit the previous year. The quartet's April 2009 European tour was more extensive. It played in Spain, Austria, three concerts in Italy, and finally two nights in Paris.[61] The first Paris gig, at the Sunset Jazz Club, also included an interview that, together with the performance, was broadcast live on the Radio/Internet France Musique station.

The quartet played its first Vision Festival in June 2009, where Parker added three guests to make the band a septet. On this occasion, cornetist Bobby Bradford, alto saxophonist James Spaulding, and violinist Billy Bang joined them, dipping into the band's repertoire while also playing new pieces. Nothing was said beforehand. For Parker, this was a test of his theory of universal tonality, that they would be able to meet and play together without anything set in advance. The idea was that the working quartet would establish the framework of the music and the guests would then find their place in it. Of the performance, Parker remarked, "Africa [was] always there and maybe some kind of Blue mountain music and some reverse Reggae. Flexibility of time and rhythm changing all the time with no particular pattern. Listen and dance to the music within."[62]

They began with "O'Neal's Porch," with Bradford taking the first solo, which allowed his language to shape the piece in a medium, danceable tempo. Later in the piece, Bang would do what Parker called "sing and speak that Alabama magic." On "Daughter's Joy," Parker explored the possibilities of double alto and double brass, "all with individual voices on their instruments all writing a different paragraph contributing to the larger story." "Gilmore's Hat" began with Parker's bass lines and Bang playing counter, with the rest of the band playing the theme as Barnes shot in doses of the Blues. "Deep Flower" was a tribute for pianist Andrew Hill, who had been integral to Parker early in his musical life and had drawn him into a broader community of artists.[63]

The expanded version of the band would play again on January 30, 2010, at the Festival Sons d'hiver in France, again with Spaulding and Bang, though with Nasheet Waits replacing Drake on drums.[64] On February 4, in Bologna, Italy, Parker led a double-quartet performance with Waits that included Italian musicians Emanuele Parrini (violin), Paolo Botti (viola), Stefano Amato and Francesco Guerri (cello), and vocalist Cristina Zavalloni.[65] They debuted Parker's "Alphaville Suite," the live score for French filmmaker Jean-Luc Godard's film *Alphaville*, which Parker had recorded three years prior.[66] Parker remained in Italy for the week following, leading a workshop at the Nino Rota Conservatory in Monopoli.[67] In October and November 2010, the quartet played in Washington, DC, and then embarked for a U.S. West Coast tour, which would be the last work for the band for more than a year, as Parker began to give his eye to other projects.

In 2011 Parker was commissioned to compose music for the AMR Ensemble in Geneva for four saxophones, trumpet, bass clarinet, voice, additional bass, and his own quartet, which together he called the Creation Ensemble.

At the time, his longtime friend violinist Billy Bang was dying of lung cancer, so his aim was to write a piece of music that would be healing, including "Psalm for Billy Bang." As Parker wrote not long after, "Both jazz life and jazz death can be very heavy." For the performance, he also arranged two existing tributes, "Wood Flute Song" for Don Cherry and "Deep Flower" for Andrew Hill. Part of the adaptation of the pieces involved him writing lyrics for both songs that had not previously existed.[68] The mantra throughout this concert was "Help me find a love that's meant for me that's all I want." Bang died five days after the concert, at his home in Harlem, and was buried in Woodlawn Cemetery in the Bronx, the cemetery that also holds Parker's father and brother.[69]

In 2012 and 2013 the quartet revisited some venues and festivals it had performed at previously, including a return to Suoni per il Popolo in Montreal in June 2012 and a U.S. West Coast tour in May 2013 that had it returning triumphantly to Yoshi's and to the Penofin Jazz Festival. In October the quartet played two nights during Parker's residency at the Stone, where it celebrated the release of the eight-CD box set *Wood Flute Songs*, half of which contained music from the quartet.[70] On the second night, poet David Budbill accompanied the music with his own compositions as well as playing flute and percussion. Parker liked how that set went well enough to bring Budbill to Milano, Italy, for a performance in November, where on a Sunday morning more than a thousand people crowded a theater to hear them. As Budbill wrote later, "They asked for an encore and furthermore, when we came out of the stage door there were dozens of people waiting to ask us for autographs. As an American poet, I am most certainly not used to such treatment!"[71] Parker's profile in Italy had been on the rise since being named musician of the year by *Musica Jazz* in 2005.[72] By 2013, Parker had become a household name in Italy and drew enthusiastic crowds wherever he went.

Again the band took a hiatus for over a year, before reconvening for its first performance in South America at the Festival Internacional de Jazz de Provincia in a town just outside of Santiago, Chile, in January 2015. This came at the conclusion of a workshop that Parker led at the Cultural Foundacion de Providencia. The quartet returned to South America to play two nights in the Festival Jazz na Fábrica in São Paulo on August 15–16, 2015.[73] The performance on the second night was recorded and released by the Brazilian label Selo Sesc.[74] The quartet opened with "Deep Flower." Parker's slow, ascendant bass lines open with Drake's crisp cymbal and drum strikes. Mournful horn lines follow, floating over the deep, open resonance of the bass in a fitting tribute. "Harlem" turns to memories of Parker's youth and all the history and community of Harlem, a place with music and poetry in its streets. The band closed with a classic from their songbook, "Corn Meal Dance," which Parker had first developed in 2006 and had played with the band through the years as well as with a vocal version for "Raining on the Moon."

In October 2016, Parker reassembled the band, but for the first time in all the years of the group changed personnel, adding Jalalu-Kalvert Nelson on trumpet. Nelson was from Oklahoma City and had established himself as a composer commissioned by orchestras, chamber groups, and dance companies, including Kronos Quartet, the Brooklyn Philharmonic, and the Oklahoma Symphony. Parker regarded him as someone who "was always able to transform any music situation into a magical experience."[75]

The record opens with "Criminals in the White House," a piece of biting political critique that Parker had written in 2001 during the administration of President George W. Bush and had been developing with the quartet since 2010.[76] Parker quipped that "the White House since its inception has been filled with a plethora of gangsters passing themselves off as good guys. And after the 2016 election, we are in crisis mode once again."[77] "Leaves/Rain" is an agile and contemplative stutter-time waltz. It is a window into the playful mind of Parker: "Imagine a leaf falling from a branch going on a journey before being taken by the wind on an excursion in space running into some renegade raindrops looking for some fun." Another water-themed piece, "Handsome Lake," was written for Seneca religious leader Hadawa'ko (Shaking Snow), who was also known as Handsome Lake. Parker was impressed both by Hadawa'ko's reputation for overcoming alcoholism and calling his people to return to the longhouse religious traditions as well as telling the story "How America Was Discovered," which tells the history of America through indigenous eyes. "The goal of this music," Parker explains, "is to never forget the grooves and funk that is very close to the heart of all indigenous people wherever they come from."[78] Parker had originally written the piece, which came to him in a kind of vision, in no more than five minutes.

"Rodney's Resurrection" was written for Rodney Diverlus, a dancer whom Parker had met while taking part in the residency for "Decidedly Jazz Danceworks," under the direction of choreographer Kimberley Cooper in Calgary, Canada. The dancer had made such an impression on Parker that he had an image of Diverlus "coming up from the ashes back to life and landing on his feet." The two-part piece "Horace Silver" is a memorial piece for the jazz pianist that Parker had written after Silver's passing in 2014; he was one of Parker's favorite musicians. For the second part of the piece, Parker played a double-reed instrument called a tarota. The record's closing piece is another tribute, "Give Me Back My Drum," one of a ten-part suite written for civil rights leader Dr. Martin Luther King Jr. Parker had been workshopping the piece in various settings with different groups, first in Berlin with Jalalu-Kalvert Nelson and Ernie Odom; then with the Transformational Music Ensemble, directed by saxophonist Keir Neuringer in Philadelphia; and finally a large-scale version at Roulette in Brooklyn, with Muhammad Ali, Marshall Allen, Dave Burrell, Odean Pope, and Bobby Zankel, along with dancers and actors.[79]

The William Parker Quartet is one of the premier bands of the past two decades as evidenced by its appearances at some of the world's great festivals and by its prolific output of recordings. In an age in which it is common for a band to break up after one or two records, it is a singular accomplishment that the band has stayed together for nearly two decades. This long period of playing together has managed to deepen the music even further as the bandmates have gained an implicit understanding of one another. As Hamid Drake remarked, "This extended period of working together has allowed us to work as a group should, like a family."[80] The William Parker Quartet continues to perform and create.

Raining on the Moon
Quintet and Sextet

Aside from Hamid Drake, Parker's other key encounter in the late 1990s was with vocalist Leena Conquest. Conquest was from Dallas, Texas, and had first become aware of Parker through her work with drummer Sunny Murray in a group called the Reform Art Unit, which was based in Vienna, Austria. Prior to that time, she had mainly been a standards vocalist working in straight-ahead jazz settings, but around 1994–95 she began to build a reputation as someone with a wider range of vocal abilities appealing to those in the free jazz community.[81] After moving to New York in 1995, Conquest worked with French American sculptor Alain Kirili and happened to perform at some loft events that included Cecil Taylor. Kirili admired the recording that Conquest had done with the Reform Art Unit, and he introduced her to Parker.

Parker recalled their first encounter differently. According to him, they first worked together in a Latin ensemble that performed music dedicated to the great Cuban bassist Israel "Cachao" Lopez (1918–2008). In that setting, Parker recalled that Conquest "sang a very lovely ballad and showed a huge emotional range that was direct." He also admired her outlook on life: "She was not afraid of the word revolution and she was not afraid of the word prayer. I needed someone to contrast the music and clearly state the words and the message."[82]

Conquest was the first vocalist that Parker recorded with and included in one of his active, touring groups on a regular basis. He explained the allure: "All my life I had been drawn to words, first through poetry and later I discovered that poetry was very close to lyrics. If you sing a poem it is a song. I had also long been intrigued by words and music as a form of protest."[83] Composing lyrics for the group allowed Parker to engage in an entirely new layer of imagery with words that had previously been unavailable to him. Through this process, Parker managed to bring audiences into the world of his imagination, whether conveyed via the personal, fantastical, or political.

In November 1999 Parker invited Conquest to join Little Huey for one of the final performances of the season at Tonic.[84] Although Parker had worked intermittently with vocalists throughout his entire career, they had never been central to his musical vision. Conquest would do much to change that. In 2000 she became a regular performer in Little Huey Creative Music Orchestra, alongside vocalists Aleta Hayes and Dean Bowman.[85] Her first recording with Parker was on *Raincoat in the River*.[86] Conquest recalled being immediately drawn to his "grace, freedom, community, and poetry. He would give us some guidelines, but I always felt that he wanted us to bring what we carried to the table. It's like I was coming to share as opposed to being told what to do."[87]

In 2001 Parker decided to expand his quartet to include Conquest in what was to become known as the Raining on the Moon Quintet, taking its name from the group's first record. The idea came to Parker as a kind of spiritual statement about spiritual liberation. He wrote that "those without vision cannot enter the internal world where it does rain on the moon."[88] The band gathered at the basement home studio of drummer Andrei Strobert (1959–2006), Strobe Light Sound Studio, to lay down the tracks. Parker included a poem in the liner notes for the record:

> *When I was 8 years old*
> *I saw an orange mountain,*
> *At second glance I could clearly see*
> *it was a concrete building*

full of black and brown children
Then I saw the sun,
it was flat like a pancake
In the reflection of my shadow
I could see the Moon,
It was surrounded by trees
Tears waltzed upward past my cheeks
into my eyes[89]

Parker later wrote that "*Raining on the Moon* is the voice of protest wrapped in rhythm, ballads, hymns and melody."[90] The track "Song of Hope" begins with bass and drums, but Conquest quickly comes in with her rich vocals. "My name is Hope" opens Parker's poetic, optimistic ballad. Then Conquest improvises off of those general themes.

"I would call it soundscape singing, which is a kind of nouveau scatting," Conquest said, "because it wasn't rigid. Rather than following chordal progression, I sang free. It could be a holler or a shout, which for me connected better with the tradition of ritual singing. I felt the old field hollers coming through me, and elements from even before that, before slavery, all the way back to Africa. Just the voice. I was unrestrained and I could sing what I felt."[91] With some of the songs being brought in from the quartet and now adding vocals, the band became even more groove-based.[92] In 2010, when the quintet worked with Amiri Baraka and performed at the University of Massachusetts, they were joined by a choir. Conquest felt that this historical reckoning had never been stronger than in that moment, as the vocals were augmented and overpowering. Putting the music together and integrating the lyrics into the rest of the music was an organic process. Chorus lines were often set because they paired so well with Parker's bass lines, but her placement of the words in relation to the sounds was based on intense listening and improvising.[93]

Raining on the Moon gradually began to play regularly, limited only by Parker's busy schedule. After playing at Vision Festival 7 in 2002, the band played its first European date at Temporada 2004 in Barcelona, Spain, in March.[94] The Barcelona concert is significant in that it opened with "Despues de la Guerra [After the War]," which was the first piece that Parker ever composed, having penned his earliest ideas for the piece in 1971.[95] He followed that piece with "Soledad (Dedicated to the late Black Panther activist George Jackson)," which he had also first worked on around the same time. George Jackson (1941–71) had been the cofounder of the revolutionary Maoist-Marxist organization Black Guerrilla Family while he was held in

Figure 9.4 Parker with the Raining on the Moon Sextet, the Stone, New York, October 10, 2013. *Credit:* ©Peter Gannushkin/downtownmusic.net.

San Quentin Prison for an indeterminate sentence.[96] Jackson's book *Soledad Brother*, published a year before his death, was a collection of writings he did while in prison as well as a manifesto addressing Black liberation.[97] In a letter to his mother that was included in the book, Jackson stated:

> I have a plan, I will give, and give, and give of myself until it proves our making or my end. The men of our group have developed as a result of living under a ruthless system a set of mannerisms that numb the soul. We have been made the floor mat of the world, but the world has yet to see what can be done by men of our nature, by men who have walked the path of disparity, of regression, of abortion, and yet come out whole. There will be a special page in the book of life for the men who have crawled back from the grave. This page will tell of utter defeat, ruin, passivity, and subjection in one breath, and in the next, overwhelming victory and fulfillment.[98]

Jackson's imprisonment for one year to life for the robbery of seventy dollars from a gas station and subsequently spending eight-and-a-half of his eleven years of imprisonment in solitary confinement exemplified the injustices faced by Black America.[99] Parker's tribute to Jackson fits within a broad range of related works that portray Jackson as an icon of the Black struggle and followed earlier dedications like Archie Shepp's *Attica Blues*, a reference to the prison uprising at the Attica Correctional Facility in New York that occurred in the wake of Jackson's death in 1971.[100]

The Raining on the Moon Quintet's appearance at the New York Is Now! Festival in Rome in 2004 helped set up a more extensive European tour the following year, with four dates in Italy as well as a residency at the International Improvised Music Workshop in Györ, Hungary. Some of Parker's work in Hungary was broadcast on live television, and footage was also featured at the Mosoly Festival in Budapest later that year.[101] One critic wrote glowingly that "the workshop might own the title of the most sensational and vivid performance conducted by William Parker, the creative jazz leader. He (as his elder, Charles Mingus) is said to have a unique talent in 'harnessing an orchestra' even if they are from different background creating an extravagant big-band-sounding music. The 'music drawings' of Bicskei Zoltán from Vajdaság will be part of the closing concert commemorating the lately deceased double-bass players Peter Kowald and Malachi Favors Maghostut."[102]

Parker's most dedicated European audience was certainly in Italy, and the concerts there received an enthusiastic reception. From there, the group stopped in Brussels before flying to Norrköping, Sweden, and then for a date in Kerava, Finland. It returned for two additional concerts in Italy in July. With the growing popularity that the band had there, Raining on the Moon scheduled additional Italian concerts for the summer of 2006.[103]

By the time of the August 24, 2006, concert in Roccella Jonica, Italy, the group had expanded to a sextet, including pianist Eri Yamamoto. Yamamoto had first been brought into the ensemble in January of that year at a performance without Conquest during Parker's residency at the Stone.[104] Once the sextet assembled, Conquest observed that "the addition of Eri added a whole new color to the music that had not been there before, an entire layer to the ensemble sound."[105] Drake noted the "lyrical dynamic of Yamamoto's piano-playing that opened up a whole new range of possibilities for the entire group and each of the individual players had an additional person to dialogue with."[106] Parker apparently agreed and made Yamamoto a permanent member of the band as it went into the studio to record in January 2007. As he later wrote of Yamamoto, "She has anchored our sonic excursions as we travel over many different musical landscapes and textures."[107]

Parker's creative powers had never been more potent, and from this came two full records, *Corn Meal Dance* and *Great Spirit*, as well as some outtakes released later.[108] It was a marathon session, beginning the tracking around noon and working for seven hours before they broke to have a meal together. In all, they recorded fourteen tracks, most requiring only one take to get right. As the producer and label owner Steven Joerg noted, "The whole ensemble was evidently ready, and the joy of creation they all felt performing these pieces is well palpable on listening."[109]

Corn Meal Dance is an extension of the continuum of "collaboration between vocalists and instrumentalists in our beloved and road-tested tradition of creative, self-determination music," referencing such vocalists as Abbey Lincoln, June Tyson, Jeanne Lee, Asha Puthli, Jean Carne, Jayne Cortez, and Dee Dee Bridgewater.[110] The record contains nine pieces, many of which had been first developed with the William Parker Quartet and were eventually given lyrics. For example, Parker crafted a vocal version of "Tears for the Children of Rwanda" that he titled "Tutsi Orphans." The vocal version is a dramatic plea to end the killing, Conquest spinning these lyrics:

> *I am your brother please don't cut my throat*
> *I am your sister please don't cut my throat*
> *Let me live to see the sunrise*
> *If you kill me you have killed yourself*
> *We truly are one*
> *Let us live in peace*
> *Let me live to see tomorrow*
>
> *I saw a black angel, angel*
> *standing by*
> *writing poems on the sky*
>
> *The black angel has come to tell us to set ourselves free*
> *That was the only way it was going to be*
> *That each one of us was the savior if we wanted to be*
>
> *The black angel looked into the sun*
> *the sun turned blue*
> *there was thunder*
> *there was rain*
> *lightning danced across the horizon*
> *logs and flowers jumped up and down*
> *the people danced in the streets*
> *they had set themselves free*
>
> *I saw a black angel standing by*
> *Writings poems on the sky*[111]

"Poem for June Jordan" had also evolved from a quartet piece. Other pieces, such as "Soledad," dedicated to George Jackson, and "Gilmore's Hat," dedicated to John Gilmore, had been developed with Raining on the Moon as early as 2004 and 2005, respectively, and had already been performed internationally.

However, the title piece, situated as the middle track, is in many ways the heart of the record. Conquest made these soulful lyrics come alive:

> *Beautiful flower covered by the sun mother*
> *ascending north to the forever mountains*
> *where it rains eternally*
>
> *My sister sails across the lake that calls the people to drop their anger*
> *May all ill thoughts towards other human beings vanish*
> *may all ill thoughts towards other human beings vanish*
>
> *Entering the grace of yesterday*
> *picking up a Ju-Ju stick on the way*
> *Calling out to all painters of autumn*
> *painters of autumn*
> *The mountain is dancing*
> *dancing in the reflection that echoes over the light that bounces between*
> *   the stars*
>
> *The face of the stream in the middle of the forest*
> *Oh little green frog pulling all the stops out*
> *Hi sound! . . . hi silence!*
>
> *All the world's a dream to me except you*
> *except your sweet soul*
> *The mountain is dancing*
> *dancing in the reflection that echoes over the light that bounces between*
> *   the stars*
> *between the stars*
>
> *Hi sound*
> *Hi silence*[112]

Before ever meeting Parker, saxophonist James Brandon Lewis had been drawn to the record, especially the melodies and the lyrics: "You can feel the humanity in it. William has a lot of joy in his compositions. He doesn't shy away from emotion. But it's not even the notes or the chords that he plays; he's a vessel for the music."[113]

Originally, Parker had discussed the possibility of releasing the entire session as a two-CD set in 2007, but at the time he ultimately decided to distill the work into *Corn Meal Dance*. It was not until 2015 that the rest of the session, *Great Spirit*, saw the light of day. The later release was spurred by an invitation to perform at the Joy of Jazz Festival in Johannesburg, South Africa, in 2015.[114] Parker's records, and Raining on the Moon's releases in particular, had been sold at Miro's House of Music store in Pretoria, and the growing popularity resulted in a demand for Parker at the annual festival.

In 2007 Raining on the Moon's European tour began at the Alhambra Concert Hall in Geneva, followed with three dates in Italy, and concluded at the Bimhuis in Amsterdam.[115] The group appeared at Vision Festival 13 in New York on Parker's birthday in January 2008 and then embarked for its first performance in Africa at the Jazz in Carthage festival in Tunisia.[116] Some European dates followed through the summer and autumn in Italy, at the Bergen International Jazz Festival in Norway, and at the Angra Jazz festival in the Azores.[117] The group received such a positive reception in Bergen that it was invited back the following year and returned to Italy again in 2010.[118]

In 2012 Raining on the Moon recorded a live set at the Suoni per il Popolo festival in Montreal that featured six previously unreleased compositions, including material Parker had been developing since the 1970s, such as "Late Man of This Planet" and a tribute to vocalist and actress Abbey Lincoln (1930–2010).[119] In his notes about the recording, Parker stated, "Whenever there is truth there is something beautiful waiting in the wings. Often times we find ourselves. We have been very fortunate to tour the world and develop the idea of words, sound and music."[120]

Since 2012, Raining on the Moon has had only sporadic performances in New York and elsewhere, with its most significant concert taking place at the Joy of Jazz festival in Johannesburg in September 2015.[121] Raining on the Moon continues to be an active band, although Parker has also given his attention to new projects.

Ten

Honoring the Elders:
Tribute Projects and Other Bands

Once upon a time, the music called jazz
was considered the music of the future.
——**William Parker**

Inside Songs of
Curtis Mayfield

Since 2000, the William Parker Quartet and Raining on the Moon have
served as springboards for Parker to develop other bands. The greatest
example of this was the Inside Songs of Curtis Mayfield. Parker had been
deeply inspired by Mayfield's music since first listening to him in the early
1970s. As opportunities to compose and perform his own music ballooned
from the mid-1990s onward, Parker eventually turned to a Mayfield-focused
project. The earliest direct reference to Mayfield was in the song "Sitting by
the Window," which Parker presented with the band In Order to Survive at
Context Studios on March 19, 1998.[1] But in 2001, as Parker was first thinking
about the possibilities of expanding beyond the William Parker Quartet, he
assembled this new band and presented its music at the Banlieues Bleues
Festival in Paris in March 2001.[2]

As was common with the festival, artists were invited to do some kind of
work with the community. Parker elected to lead a workshop in high schools

around Paris. He sent a cassette tape of the music for "People Get Ready/ The Inside Song," and the teenagers learned the music in advance.[3] Parker then arrived about two weeks prior to the concert and rehearsed with the kids, who eventually made up a chorus of ninety children who took part in the performance.[4] Many of the children were from Mali, Senegal, or other parts of West Africa; French was their second language, and most did not know English, so they had to learn the English words in addition to the music. Parker insisted that the young performers all get cake and ice cream immediately following the show, and someone videotaped them dancing to "New World Order." An unknown audience member taped the performance itself and was selling copies of it in France. Parker eventually acquired a copy, and he included two tracks from the bootleg on the official release when it finally came out in 2010.[5]

The band included the personnel that would form Raining on the Moon, with the exception of Rob Brown. Vocalist Leena Conquest in particular was excited to work with Parker on the project because "Curtis Mayfield was my soundtrack growing up. I listened to him on the Black radio station in Dallas as a teenager."[6] Drake, too, considered the project nostalgic as one who "grew up on the Impressions." To that, Parker added another of his great inspirations, poet Amiri Baraka, on most of the pieces he wrote for the band, the "inside" part of the project. Having Baraka deliver his recitations was certainly one way to directly tap into the era when Mayfield was active, and even in what turned out to be the final years of his life, Baraka still brought his impressive skills as an orator and historian to the work.[7] The band is the most extensive work that Parker has ever done with a poet.

Another key figure that Parker hired for the band was pianist Dave Burrell (b. 1940). Burrell had established himself by recording dozens of records since his first one had appeared in 1969.[8] He had a reputation as a fearless avant-gardist, although he played a variety of styles of music. Despite the fact that Burrell and Parker had frequented many of the same circles, they had not performed together until 1988 and never regularly in any group until Parker hired him for the Curtis Mayfield project.[9] Parker also hired saxophonists Darryl Foster and Sabir Mateen, both of whom had done stints in Little Huey Creative Music Orchestra. Other musicians appeared as guests on select tracks.

The concept of the record lay in the idea that "every song written or improvised has an inside song which lives in the shadows, in-between the sounds and silences and behind the words, pulsating, waiting to be reborn as a new song," Parker wrote. In Parker's view, Mayfield had emerged from the

1960s civil rights era, a time hallmarked by an array of musicians, including drummer Max Roach, Charles Mingus, Archie Shepp, Jackie McLean, and John Coltrane, to name but a few. "Curtis Mayfield was right in the middle directing his music to the cry of freedom," Parker notes. This all happened through the process of field holler into spiritual into blues into swing into bebop into post-bop into avant-garde back into ritual, which Parker called "a circle, and all part of the bigger tune called Peoples' Music."[10]

Parker saw this as revolutionary music aimed at tearing down unjust structures: "reclamation of land, self-determination, and right to change existing structure rather than assimilation into a quagmire misnamed progress, *Inside Songs* are time into rhythm, rhythm into pulse into chant." Parker saw Mayfield as having come out of the same cultural continuum as many of the radical Black poets that he had grown up reading: "Long live the revolutionary poets and musicians of the past and present, who continue to protest through their art, not resting until all things are as they should be. Underneath the pulse and crust are shouts for liberation and respect, to the left of the melody ready to surface from the gaps in the cement that covers the grass in the South Bronx inhabited by the low baggy pants clan that later signed contracts with Madison Avenue."[11]

Still, Parker was explicit that he did not see this project as a cover band: "We can never play Curtis Mayfield better than Curtis Mayfield did. So, we built another house out of the same wood they build basses and violins with, wood struck by purple lightning bolts. Then we find our center within his music so that we have become ourselves. Hopefully to present a full spectrum story that would be in tune with the original political and social message laid out by Curtis." *Inside Songs of Curtis Mayfield* was a call to action and a new consciousness for Parker: "We need thinkers, movers who can dance on the beat, ahead of the beat and around the beat. Those who can self-ignite and keep the fire of compassion glowing, who will never forget the despair on the faces of the people who think their only hope is 'basketball.' Let's play all night for them until the volcano of justice erupts, stretching the sentiments of each lyric as a way of responding to the call to get ready; get ready to prepare for a new world. The music, the poetry, the dance and theatre once stolen will be returned."[12]

Conquest recalled the creative process involving different layers of song. First and foremost, the band worked with a wide range of Mayfield's originals, such as the tune "People Get Ready." Then Amiri Baraka added his poetry. Then the band added its improvisations. Together, these created "something more than a pop song; it became a different kind of symphony."[13]

Audience members often recognized the songs, and the band interpreted them using improvisation in a way that retained their soulfulness. If any aesthetic remained from the original, it was the feature of very strong bass lines.

Burrell and Conquest often posed suggestions about how to bring the music away from the originals. For example, in the piece "Freddie's Dead," the opening is quite similar to the original, but then improvisation begins to allow it to be reshaped, while Conquest's vocals, though quite different in pitch and tone, are nevertheless "the spitting image of the spirit of Mayfield."[14] Conquest's vocal work remains some of the rare female-voiced interpretations of Mayfield's compositions. Rather than aim to duplicate the original, Burrell noted that the focus was always to match the level of passion, funk, and sincerity that Mayfield had instilled in the originals.

At one concert in southern Italy, a montage of film cuts of police attacking protesters and brutalizing civil rights demonstrators demanding voting rights in the 1960s and 1970s was projected onto a massive screen behind the band. As Burrell recalled, "All around us the sound was so great. And I realized we were representing the reality of what we had to do in the 1960s to change America and to get the attention of the world."[15] Following the performance, audience members who had been deeply affected by the experience asked the band members to autograph books that they had brought with them about all kinds of aspects of the American civil rights movement. At other live performances, Baraka would speak of the current political situation in the United States, especially of the potential that existed within the presidency of Barack Obama.[16]

The band's debut record was composed of a number of other live performances after the Banlieues Festival in 2001. These concerts occurred in Italy, Switzerland, and the United States, often accompanied by local choirs, such as Brooklyn's New Life Tabernacle Generation of Praise choir, which was brought together at the Clemente Soto Vélez cultural center for Vision Festival 13.[17] The band also toured in Spain, France, Portugal, Poland, Croatia, Canada, and extensively in Italy, and it later released a live record taken entirely from a performance at the 2004 New York Is Now! Festival in Rome.[18] One of the strongest performances occurred at Jazz à La Villette in Paris, where Drake recalled that the acoustics were perfect for what the band was doing.[19] The band's heaviest period of touring was 2007–09, with its final performances as part of a residency at Bohemian Caverns in Washington, DC, in February 2011.[20] These final performances were important because the music was, finally, performed before a primarily Black audience, reviving

Figure 10.1 Amiri Baraka and Parker performing with the Inside Songs of Curtis Mayfield at Teatro Manzoni, Milan, Italy, January 20, 2008. *Credit*: ©Luciano Rosetti.

the Black cultural icon of Mayfield for his intended audience, together with the force of Baraka's words, Conquest's voice, and Parker's compositions and arrangements.[21] Drake considered his time with the band some of the most precious years of his long career.[22]

Essence of Ellington

Parker's other great tribute project of the period honored the figure he had grown up listening to most: Duke Ellington. Ellington's accomplishments as a pianist, composer, and bandleader stand high in the jazz tradition. Parker's father's dream had been for his son to one day play in the Ellington orchestra, and in some ways his father had looked to Ellington as a role model for his sons when they were just aspiring musicians. Appropriately, Parker included a portrait of his own father in the record booklet.[23] Although Ellington's career ended just as Parker's began, Parker had developed his own big band with inspiration from Ellington.

Just as the Curtis Mayfield project was coming to an end in early 2011, Parker turned his attention to the Essence of Ellington. He drew together people with whom he had played extensively, such as Sabir Mateen (tenor saxophone), Rob Brown (alto saxophone), Dave Sewelson (baritone saxophone), Steve Swell (trombone), Matt Lavelle (trumpet), and Dave Burrell (piano). Parker also hired two relative newcomers: Darius Jones (alto saxophone) and Willie Applewhite (trombone). Parker had played only once before with Jones, hiring him for a big-band performance in 2008. Applewhite had played once with Little Huey Creative Music Orchestra in 2009 but had not become a regular member.

The inaugural performance of Essence of Ellington was at University of the Streets on June 12, 2011, where it was joined by members of the York College big band. Parker's group returned there the following month for two performances at the University of the Streets festival.[24] This gave the group enough material to capture its first European date, in November at the Vila Flor Cultural Center in Guimarães, Portugal.

Then, in February 2012, the band played at the Teatro Manzoni in Milan before a rapt crowd. Parker was even able to expand the band, adding Kidd Jordan and Ras Moshe on saxophones, Roy Campbell on trumpet, Ernie Odoom on voice, and Hamid Drake on drums. The live concert was recorded and released on Parker's own label, Centering Records.[25] The band played interpretations of well-known Ellington pieces and, like the Mayfield project, attempted to use the essence of the pieces as the point of departure. The concert featured "Sophisticated Lady," "In a Sentimental Mood," "Take the A Train," and "Caravan." In addition, Parker showcased two of his own compositions, "Portrait of Louisiana," dedicated to the jazz educator and historian Clyde Kerr Jr. (1943–2010), and "Essence of Ellington." The latter piece, played as an encore at the concert, brought the sensational performance to a close. It was to be the band's major moment, for it performed only once more, at the Suoni per il Popolo festival in Montreal in June.[26]

The Essence of Ellington project was significant in that, as Dave Burrell noted, "for so many decades, no one had dared take a different approach to playing Ellington until this particular record came about." For example, Parker's concept in adapting Ellington's song "Sophisticated Lady" was imagining that she had retired and was on Social Security, a kind of radical approach in the tune's evolution. As Burrell stated, "Parker wanted to jolt the music out of its normalcy. Ellington had never gone very far into the jazz avant-garde; I thought being able to find the doors to go through and have

Ellington liberated in so many ways was extraordinary. It was a contribution to something that is a central corpus of Americana."[27]

Trios

Beyond the quartet and its related projects, the early 2000s was a period of considerable experimentation for Parker trying out a number of different ensembles, the bulk of which were short-lived trios. He intended them as a series, each with bass, drums, and another instrument. He had worked in quite a few formations in the early 1990s with figures such as Rob Brown, Assif Tsahar, Billy Bang, Cooper-Moore, Matthew Shipp, and Whit Dickey, but he finally settled into a trio with Daniel Carter and Hamid Drake in early 2000. Carter, a longtime collaborator and close friend, was a quintessential multi-instrumentalist, by this point playing alto, tenor, and soprano saxophones; flute; and clarinet. Drake was relatively new to the Parker circle but was involved in nearly every Parker project at that time, including the quartet, the Raining on the Moon Quintet, and the Inside Songs of Curtis Mayfield, all of which were taking off in 2000 or 2001.

Andrei Strobert engineered the recording, like much of Parker's work around that time, and recorded a session at his Strobe Light Sound Studio in Greenwich Village on April 2, 2000.[28] For the session, Parker selected Duke Ellington's standard "Come Sunday" as well as the spiritual "There Is a Balm in Gilead," which he also was working on as a solo piece. The rest were his own compositions, including the piece "Blues for Percy," for bassist Percy Heath. The most extensive work was the three-part "Foundation," which featured rhythmic explorations. Parker accompanied the record with a poem that bore the record title "Painter's Spring":

> spring morning into green sky smoked mountain
> sun peering through the efflorescent eye of an
> owl as three fisherman gaze into the water
> the ear blinks as it steps out of the water
> the painted left turn signals waves and turns into
> music I sit on the porch turning my bass fiddle[29]

The band never played again. This seems not a result of the music itself as much as other Parker projects taking precedence at the time. With his quartet getting significant attention and plenty of work, this trio fell by the

Figure 10.2 Painter's Spring, the Stone, New York, January 26, 2006. *Left to right*: Daniel Carter, Hamid Drake, Parker. *Credit*: ©Peter Gannushkin/downtownmusic.net.

wayside. But it remains an interesting document of Parker's early work with Drake in a pared-down setting, with Carter navigating the rhythms adeptly with his expert improviser's ear.

Parker also worked with Perry Robinson and Walter Perkins in a short-lived clarinet trio in 2001 and 2002. Robinson played clarinet and ocarina, a vessel or shell-like instrument with a mouthpiece and number of finger holes. Perkins played drums. The William Parker Clarinet Trio also laid down tracks at Strobe Light Sound Studio in January 2001 and released the record *Bob's Pink Cadillac* on Eremite Records.[30] Parker used the setting to experiment with a number of instruments he had not previously recorded on elsewhere. He played the gralla, a Catalan double-reed instrument, that he would later use with his quartet.[31] Parker also played a jogibaba and orchestra bells, as well as providing vocals for the trio. Among other songs, the band worked on "Overcoat in the River," a variation of "Raincoat in the River," which he had developed for Little Huey Creative Music Orchestra. Tracks from a live session at Tonic, the five-part "Ebony Fantasy," on August 1, 2001, were also included on the release.[32] The band played only three other live performances: in February 2002 at the Unitarian Meeting House in Amherst, Massachusetts; a one-year anniversary show at Tonic on August 1, 2002; and an event for the Boston Creative Music Alliance in September.

In 2002 Parker formed another trio with Drake, this time with longtime friend and collaborator violinist Billy Bang. Bang had been off the scene for quite a few years but had reemerged as he worked on his soul-searching Vietnam projects. At Strobe Light Sound Studios, the William Parker Violin Trio recorded six tracks to be released as *Scrapbook* on Thirsty Ear Recordings.[33] The music was made to come alive by the deep blues tradition and plenty of Black church sound and feeling. "Sunday Morning Church" established these connections explicitly, as did "Dust on a White Shirt." But the band never took off and never performed live.

In 2004 the trio Luc's Lantern had more life. The band marked the first extensive work that Parker did with pianist Eri Yamamoto (b. 1970). She was beginning to emerge with significant work aimed at fusing New York jazz and Japanese folk traditions. Yamamoto had originally worked in straight-ahead settings until forming a friendship with fellow pianist Matthew Shipp in 1997, after which she edged into free-music circles and eventually met Parker. The other member of the trio was Michael T. A. Thompson, whom Parker had first played with only the previous year in Matt Lavelle's New York Trumpet Nemesis.[34] The band recorded ten tracks at Park West Studios in Brooklyn.[35]

The songs on *Luc's Lantern* carry a noticeably somber character, somehow reflective of New York in the years after 9/11. Many of them are mournful or yearn for the past or envision a brighter future. Parker accompanied each piece with a poem. The opening piece, "Mourning Sunset," set the tone:

> *Mourning was over*
> *The darkness of this world ends*
> *Unable to see the shape of hope as it fades down in the eastern sky*
> *I wish things were just things again like the old*
> *days when there were*
> *only flowers and memories.*
> *Before progress was born*[36]

The next track, "Evening Star Song," carries this feeling forward with the poem "Carry the lost pieces of yesterday, in the promise of melody and in the pastoral roots, keep them close to your heart."[37] "Jacki," a piece for Jacki Byard, is a sentimental piece, again returning to his youth:

How I wish for those days when nothing existed
except Booker Ervin and
that happy fellow who played the big piano on the
side of Manhattan.[38]

The song "Bud in Alphaville" represents Parker's first time approaching the Jean-Luc Godard film that had had such an impact upon him in his youth, a prelude to his *Alphaville Suite*, which appeared in 2007. The title track is the most powerful piece, which Parker accompanied with this poem:

A dream lifts my center eye
It is raining rose petals so the ground is soft and fragrant
I see a forest where only black trees with yellow and purple teeth grow
Trees that play violins and write poems
This is a recurring dream but each night
A small lantern is left on the porch so I can make my way back home[39]

Luc's Lantern had one European tour, performing one night in Rotterdam and a subsequent week in north Italian jazz clubs from Arezzo and Milan to Florence and Marostica in October 2007.[40]

Parker's major trio of recent years is Farmers by Nature, a collective trio originally formed by drummer Gerald Cleaver (b. 1963) that also includes pianist Craig Taborn (b. 1970). The fusion of musical ideas in this band has resulted in one of the great freely improvised bands of the new century. Cleaver, a native of Detroit, had first emerged in Chicago before moving to New York. Parker had played with Cleaver and Taborn as early as 1996–97, when they were both hired for Roscoe Mitchell's Note Factory project, and then Parker subsequently played with Cleaver in the Matthew Shipp Trio.[41] In August 2006, two months after the three were by chance reunited as the three sidepeople of the Rob Brown Quartet, they arranged a concert at the Stone, where they first explored their improvisational possibilities together as a trio.[42] The potential for the three was immediately obvious, but because of their mutually busy schedules with other bands, they were not able to play again until December of 2007, for two concerts.[43]

On June 19, 2008, the band finally recorded live tracks captured during a performance at the Stone.[44] The band featured a certain kind of energy music, with Taborn and Parker leading the way and with Cleaver as an aesthetic counter in his minimalist yet ever-effective rhythmic undercurrents. The band characteristically allows one of the musicians to begin and set the tone with the others joining in as they see fit. Then, often passing ideas back and forth rather freely, the band hashes through ideas in a succinct fashion, going in one direction for as long as is fitting, then, sometimes abruptly, setting course in an entirely new direction. The band might then return to ideas that had been spelled out earlier and explore a bit further, while continuing to challenge one another.

Farmers by Nature played at the Penofin Jazz Festival in Potter Valley, California, in May 2010, then was back for a date at the Stone in New York in June.[45] A week after the Stone gig, the band entered Scrootable Labs in Brooklyn to record the band's second record, *Out of This World's Distortions*.[46] As Cleaver wrote of this record, "We are always seeking a connection to that which is and always has been," cutting to the "root of things." Indeed, the ease of their improvising connections, along with the incredible depth they are able to achieve, is one of the most remarkable characteristics of the trio. The title for the record had come to Cleaver one night in the mental zone in between wakefulness and sleep and referred to what he called "the clear indomitableness of Earth. I think of us humans as the World. I'm often saddened by how out of touch I, and the World, can be with the Earth. But even in my short years on the planet, I'm happily baffled by how resourceful Earth is at taking care of itself and its willing subjects, all while realigning us, the World, whether we're willing or not." In the face of all "the gross, horrific dreadful evil that the World can perpetrate against Earth and itself," Cleaver envisions "rising from the morass unscathed, winsome beauty, uncorrupted power; magnificent, graceful, elegant. That is Earth, rising out of this World's distortions."[47] On the eve of the recording, the saxophonist Fred Anderson passed away in Chicago, and the news was heavy on all of them as they recorded. The opening track was performed in his honor, and the entire record is a tribute to Anderson's memory.

In 2011 Farmers by Nature celebrated the release of its second record at the Suoni per il Popolo festival in Montreal on June 21.[48] Then the band embarked for its first European tour with an appearance at the Bimhuis in Amsterdam and a concert in the Bleu Indigo Series in Paris.[49] Recordings from two subsequent concerts in France, at the Cite de la Musique in Marseille and the 30eme Festival Jazz Musique Imrovisee in Besançon, came to form the band's third record, *Love and Ghosts*.[50] The tour concluded at Club CD in Ljubljana, Slovenia.[51]

Farmers by Nature has performed a little less in recent years because of the busy schedules of all three members, but continued to extend its explorations at Vision Festival 17 in 2012, at its third record release at Shapeshifter

Figure 10.3 Farmers by Nature with Craig Taborn, Parker, and Gerald Cleaver, Roulette, Brooklyn, June 12, 2012. *Credit*: ©Peter Gannushkin/ downtownmusic.net.

in Brooklyn in 2014, and two nights during Taborn's residency at the Stone in January 2016. Witnessing the January 29 concert, I wrote the following:

> For the first set, the band played one long improvised piece. Throughout the set, the music possessed a sort of collaborative sentience—each player contributed to its evolution, while bringing their own truth to the collective. Within moments, the three felt fully calibrated—having reintroduced themselves to each other, the three masterful players settled down for a deep and intense musical conversation. Taborn, Parker, and Cleaver each took turns in leading that interaction in the kind of tight association that is built on trust and intimacy in sound. The music had a strong and robust center—even as it shifted as each transformed it, the piece itself felt very grounded, whether by the presence of constant propulsion, or by patient evolution. Some of Taborn's most exciting playing came as he led the group towards the peaks of the piece. Cleaver's direct, yet unobtrusive style provided constant forward-motion outlined in flashes of light. Parker exhibited some very inventive playing—even taking a solo played with two bows, one on each side of the bridge that seemed to illustrate the dual-nature of the music. Together the

music they produced hung in the air like shimmering curtains of sound that form the threshold between the reality that we can touch, hear, and see, and that which lies beyond. In sonic gestures of profound and honest beauty, they moved along that precipice, drawing the audience along for the journey, allowing all who witnessed it a chance to glimpse through the veil.[52]

Organ Quartet

In 2010 Parker began a very personal project with a group that became known as the William Parker Organ Quartet. It was in honor of his Uncle Joe, Joseph Edwards (b. 1918), the husband of his mother's sister Carrie Lee Jefferson, who was in his 101st year at the time of this writing.[53] Parker considered Uncle Joe to be "a seer, a self-healer of the deepest sense, sitting at the table with Chief Joseph of the Nez Perce Indian tribe or the boxer Jack Johnson."[54] The record includes songs for his family, tunes that he thought they would like. Having forged a deep connection with Gerald Cleaver working together in Farmers by Nature, he hired him for the band. He also added longtime collaborators Darryl Foster (tenor saxophone) and Cooper-Moore (organ).

On January 22, 2010, the Organ Quartet recorded at Gallery Recording Studio in Brooklyn and released the record on Centering Records.[55] The record is a tribute to those who had toiled before to improve his life, and those of his cousins, and by extension other African Americans. As Parker stated, "The spirit house is sacrificing for the children and never letting them know. It is where weary workers rest their heads and rejuvenate from working a 60-hour week." "The Struggle" brings sound to images of the civil rights struggle "that occurred and is still occurring in America and Africa. It is for Kwame Nkrumah, Patrice Lumumba, Sojourner Truth, and all people who have to struggle day to day to survive." There are also references to spirituals imprinted deeply in the music, with tunes such as "Let's Go Down to the River," which Parker referred to as a "modern day hymn with ties to the past." "Ennio's Tag" was written for Parker's son Isaiah Ennio Parker, whose middle name came from Ennio Morricone, who had been one of Parker's favorite composers when he was a teenager. The song "Oasis" employs the word that Uncle Joe used to refer to his backyard. To sum up his feelings about the record, Parker states that "the most important thing I hear is this indefatigable love for life that resonates throughout. In the end, this is all we really have."[56]

The title track is an ode to family and history, bearing tons of energy or, as Parker described it, "a head-bobbing shuffle that shifts like a boxer in training, jabbing, dancing with shifting footwork. Changing tempos and colorations while keeping the feeling of 140th Street and Lenox Avenue in Harlem with a distant Savoy Ballroom in the background. The spirit house can be the gym, the church or the gatherings at the kitchen table." Parker imagined performing the music as a gathering, stating, "Aunts, uncles, and cousins who are also musicians gather on the front steps."[57] Parker still plans to do a house concert at his uncle's house to celebrate the music with his relations.[58]

Subsequent performances saw the band occasionally expand to form a quintet, with the addition of Lewis Barnes on trumpet, such as two sets that it played at Bohemian Caverns in Washington, DC, where it presented an array of Parker tunes, some of which were drawn from other projects, such as "Wood Flute Song," "Criminals in the White House," and "Tears for the Children of Rwanda."[59] The band never got a lot of attention, but it did manage a rebirth of sorts in March 2017, when it embarked on a European tour through Switzerland, Italy, and France.[60] By then, the band had reverted to a quartet, with James Brandon Lewis replacing Foster on tenor saxophone. The year 2018 witnessed two subsequent dates for the band in Europe.[61] Lewis recalled being struck by Parker's incredible melodic sense and the spiritual elements of his music before previously hiring him to record on his own album in 2011, and he eagerly joined the Organ Quartet for the tour. As Lewis stated, "On tour, the music had a constant flow. Some of the charts had chords on them, some didn't, each piece had a beautiful melody that was a launchpad for improvisation. When we weren't performing, William was always working, composing, watching documentaries, always focused."[62]

Work with Milford Graves and Charles Gayle

In the second half of the 1980s, despite being busy with the Cecil Taylor Unit, Parker managed to find time to develop connections with drummer Milford Graves and tenor saxophonist Charles Gayle. Back as a teenager, Parker had first listened to Graves's early work with the Lowell Davidson Trio and the Giuseppi Logan Quartet, and later found Graves's record *Bäbi* to be ear-opening.[63] In working in Jemeel Moondoc's band Ensemble Muntu in the mid-1970s, Parker took part in a tribute piece titled "Theme for Milford (Mr. Body and Soul)," which appeared on *First Feeding*.[64] Parker found Graves to reveal "several layers of drumming that at first glance might be cells of broken rhythm, dampening of sounds, that create tones of speech-like quality plus melodies and rhythms. In his period as a leader, one could hear the link to African drumming and links to Latin variations of that."[65]

Parker did not play with Graves until 1985, at which time they played in a collective trio with Peter Brötzmann that continued to perform intermittently until 2002.[66] Parker and Graves soon after played more regularly together in a number of formations, including a trio with saxophonist Charles Gayle that also began playing in 1985 and was particularly active in 1991–96.[67] Parker and Gayle had begun working together in 1984, around the time of the Sound Unity Festival, and had recorded with drummer Rashied Ali in Berlin as part of the Total Music Meeting at the Haus der jungen Talente in Berlin in 1991. That encounter had come as the result of FMP Records inviting three saxophonists, Gayle, Brötzmann, and Evan Parker; three bassists, Parker, Peter Kowald, and Fred Hopkins; and three drummers, Ali, Tony Oxley, and Andrew Cyrille for a week-long residency. The nine figures had spent a week playing in different formations, and several records resulted from the encounter, including the masterpiece by Gayle, Parker, and Ali, *Touchin' on Trane*.[68] Parker described Gayle's contributions as "streams of sound coming out of what one could call the cosmic church loaded blues-laced beautiful sound. His improvisations danced on waves of electric energy."[69]

In 2004 Graves and Parker began playing a duo together, debuting their work at the Vision Saturday Night Series at St. Nicholas of Myra Church in New York.[70] A subsequent performance in February 2005 cemented the relationship, with Parker expanding the possibilities on shenai, wood flute, and doussn'gouni through six improvisations. The duo eventually expanded to include multi-instrumentalist Anthony Braxton (b. 1945) when the three were invited to play in Rome.[71] The following May, Parker and Braxton returned to Italy, this time in Vicenza, to play a duo at the Festival New Conversations in May 2007 that was later included in a national broadcast there.[72] They had originally planned to release the Vicenza recording, but the drums were under-recorded, so they opted instead to go into the studio about a year later to lay down tracks for *Beyond Quantum*, although that was their last meeting.[73] Around the same time, in July 2007, Parker and Braxton joined Cecil Taylor and Tony Oxley in a group called the Classic Quartet for a concert at the Royal Festival Hall in London.[74] It was a reunion of Parker back in the Cecil Taylor Unit, in a certain sense, plus Braxton's expansive

Figure 10.4 Milford Graves and Parker, St. Nicholas of Myra Church, New York, February 21, 2004. *Credit*: ©Peter Gannushkin/downtownmusic.net.

way of playing, and spawned a subsequent tour in October through Germany and Italy.[75]

One other band to emerge from Parker's work with Graves was a trio with alto saxophonist Kidd Jordan. They first performed as a quartet with Charles Gayle at Vision Festival 3 in 1998.[76] By 2002, the band was a trio with just Jordan, Parker, and Graves when they returned to Vision Festival.[77] Kidd had previously played on Motown Records with many great R&B and blues figures such as Nancy Wilson, Aretha Franklin, Stevie Wonder, and Big Joe Turner, but "Kidd's true love is free improvisation and had developed his own unique system that is filled with the blues, gospel, and his own new thing."[78] The band eventually toured internationally at Festival Sons d'hiver in France in 2008 and again in Paris the following year.[79]

Parker and Graves had long shared a musical connection, but they developed a shared spiritual sensibility in relation to the music as well. Graves was the first person Parker talked to who also spoke about healing through sound, which confirmed some of his own ideas. Graves had been a practicing herbalist and acupuncturist for many years. Eventually, Graves recorded Parker's heartbeat, determining that the sound that Parker's heart

CHAPTER TEN

254

produced was D flat, which provided Parker a deeper, even more personal understanding of his own sound. In 2013 they presented a piece titled "Heart Sound Music with Organic Graphics" based on this experience at Roulette in Brooklyn, with Graves on percussion and with his recording of the heartbeat, Parker playing doussn'gouni, and Patricia Nicholson dancing.

Solo

Throughout his career, Parker has performed in solo settings. His earliest known live solo performance was at St. Mark's Church-in-the-Bowery on March 11, 1977.[80] It was not until 1987–92 that he began to perform solo on a regular basis.[81] In 1993 he made his first surviving solo recordings, which were not released until 2006 as part of *Long Hidden: The Olmec Series*.[82] There are two solo works on the record, along with pieces by a sextet. The first is the spiritual "There Is a Balm in Gilead," bearing these lyrics:

> *There is a balm in Gilead to make the wounded whole*
> *There is a balm in Gilead to heal the soul*
> *Sometimes I feel discouraged and think my work's in vain*
> *but then the Holy Spirit revives my soul again*

Parker dedicated the piece to all victims of calamities, both natural and caused by humans.

The other solo piece on the record is the three-part title track, on which Parker plays donso ngoni (ngoni), a hunter's harp from the Wasulu people of Mali, made from calabash, a kind of gourd, covered by a dried animal skin with a rattle affixed to the top. Parker's fascination with instruments that reached beyond the standard jazz corpus had begun back in 1973, when he had witnessed Rafael Garrett, Kali Z. Fasteau, and Frank Lowe play as a trio. The group had played "all kinds of beautiful flutes, cello, and various other string instruments." Parker had acquired a kora, a twenty-one-string West African lute, "but it was the ngoni that made my heart sing." Parker's first ngoni was the traditional six-string version, but he had also commissioned an eight-string version from an instrument builder in Paris. It was the latter instrument that he played on *Long Hidden*, one that he considered to be more akin to the banjo or guitar. He considered the title track to be "daily music, music that is listened to as we go about our daily chores. Perhaps they are meditations on things we see as we are driving home from gigs or sitting in a laundry in Muscogee, Oklahoma, waiting for our clothes to dry. It is connected to the people sitting on the porch after supper, playing that old guitar, a suspending time of tuning and detuning dreams."[83]

Parker continued to perform on solo bass, on ngoni, and on other instruments throughout the 1990s and 2000s in New York and while on tour throughout the world. In January 1996 he played solo in a series of concerts to raise money to restore his old Dudek bass.[84] The head of the instrument had been "crushed by airline handlers whose corporate bosses took no responsibility."[85] Then, in a January 1997 live session at Beanbenders in Berkeley, California, Parker recorded two additional tracks that were later included on *Long Hidden*. The first was "Cathedral of Light," a piece that he had been working on since 1975 and had played with various ensembles.[86] As he wrote, "Inside this piece is my entire theory of music—sound is light and light is sound. Can you imagine a cathedral of light and what would happen if sun poured through that cathedral? How life would change. How every flower, plant, tree and living creature would advance then dance in the color created by the slicing of light through a prism called a bow." The second piece was a solo version of "Compassion Seizes Bed-Stuy," this one with a cry throughout that states, "Lord have mercy fill these young black men with your spirit, before they fill another prison with young black men."[87]

In May 2006 Parker played a solo memorial tribute to British guitarist Derek Bailey; in 2009 he did a solo performance dedicated to saxophonist Joseph Jarman (1937–2019) that was followed by a healing ceremony because Jarman was gravely ill at the time; and in 2013 he dedicated a solo performance to Earl Freeman, among more than a dozen New York performance dates.[88] In 2015 Parker played solo as well as in ensemble format with child drum prodigy Kojo Roney at JACK in Brooklyn as part of Roney's residency there.[89] Since 2007, Parker has performed in solo format in the United Kingdom, Croatia, Belgium, Slovenia, Portugal, France, Poland, Switzerland, and a number of times in Italy.[90] In October 2018 he was finally able to bring his solo work to Shenzhen, China.[91]

In July 2008, while on tour in Canada, he did a solo performance at the club Somewhere There in Toronto. Parker had been invited in tandem with painter Jeff Schlanger for a collaboration at the opening of a permanent collection of a series of paintings that Schlanger produced of Parker's 2007 interactions with Toronto's Association of Improvising Musicians. Jean Martin of Barnyard Records recorded the performance.[92] Parker performed a nearly fifty-minute variation of "Cathedral of Light" that he titled "Cathedral Wisdom Light."[93] He also included tributes to Don Cherry and Ella Parker,

Figure 10.5 *Cathedral Wisdom Light,* live painting of Parker performing solo at Somewhere There, Toronto, July 26, 2008. *Credit:* ©Jeff Schlanger, music witness®.

the former in honor of one of his great inspirations, the latter a lighthearted honoring of the Parker family parakeet.

Scott Thomson, also of Barnyard Records, described the setting on the night of the recording: "William Parker made this music for forty rapt listeners on a hot July night in Toronto. It's a music where the form unfolded in the playing, literally a new music. His signature synaesthetic philosophy invites color-drenched metaphors: Prismic refraction, gardens blooming, a harvest feast being prepared. This music is playful, as seriously playful as your life."[94] Thomson was loosely quoting Rashied Ali's statement on the music that had become the title of Valerie Wilmer's book about the loft scene in the 1970s.[95] But Thomson went on to describe the synthesis of sensory experiences at Somewhere There on July 26, 2008:

> Jeff Schlanger, the co-conspirator in this sightsound music, swirled a serious dance of paint, making the sounds tangible in color. As a place for informal music, Somewhere There invited its forty guests to get inside the mysterious space where these men played. The experience was so enveloping for me that I could see the sounds William played, first in a billowing cloud and then shooting out like light-tendrils that circled my head. As this magic unfolded, though I was sitting in the back with only a wall behind me, I swear that from over my shoulder I could hear children laughing. Seriously.[96]

Parker played solo at the Guelph Jazz Festival in 2011 on the tenth anniversary of 9/11. For the final day the festival organized music for twenty-four hours straight, so Parker went on stage at 6:15 AM. Bassist Joshua Abrams had played the night before at 1 AM with his band Natural Information Society, and then he elected to stay up all night to see Parker's performance. At daybreak, as Parker went on stage, the MacDonald Stewart Art Centre was packed. Parker played a riveting improvisation that was "music for the restoration of the soul" as a preparation for Heaven.[97] Parker included storytelling both during and after his playing, and then took great joy in teaching the crowd to sing a Don Cherry song.[98] Abrams described the experience as "entering a magic space of being."[99] When they departed the concert hall, there was a double rainbow in the sky.

In 2011 Parker released his other major solo bass recordings, a three-CD set on his own Centering Records titled *Crumbling in the Shadows Is Fraulein Miller's Stale Cake*.[100] The record contains two discs of music recorded in 2010 and the reissue of *Testimony*, a record originally released in a small pressing on Zero In Records in 1995. Joshua Abrams recalled his first encounter with Parker's music was with *Testimony* when he was a disc jockey at

WNUR, Northwestern University's radio station. "I was struck immediately by how open and expansive his music was," Abrams recalled, "but at the same time it comes from the spirit of the tradition. There was a dance to it, it was not an avant-garde that was strictly cold and cerebral, so it really appealed to me."[101]

The narrative of the record centers on the figure Fraulein Miller, who owned "about 200 slaves in South Carolina." According to Parker,

> Legend has it she was a benevolent master who would save pieces of cake for the slaves from time to time. This was something she was very proud of. Then one day several slaves made their way into the kitchen stealing large knives. They had made the decision to cut the throats of the overseers and escape. At the crucial moment just before bloodshed was to occur, they heard the sound of a low string instrument, it was a bass being bowed and the music was like a dance, but you couldn't dance to it without listening and you couldn't listen without feeling it. These displaced and tortured Africans held out their arms, they intertwined them like branches from a tree. Becoming unified as one voice they looked in the slave master's eyes turning and walked off the plantation into the horizon never to be seen again.

In a more succinct introduction, Parker wrote that the music is "an anti-war tone poem; an anti-oppression tale in praise of the creative spirit."[102]

The forty-eight-page booklet that accompanies the record is one of the most extensive writings by Parker. In the course of it, Parker discusses his sociopolitical outlook, touching on issues of warfare, nonviolent resistance, and the concept of freedom, embedded in the African American experience. Here he echoed other writings: "Freedom is one of the biggest myths that has been perpetrated on the American people. Freedom cannot really exist unless every person in the world is free. What they really mean in America when words like democracy and freedom are used is the businessmen and politicians who rule America are free to follow one agenda, make as much money as they can. Not caring about who dies along the way." Parker went on to argue that "in order to do this, the American people had to be medicated. Medicated through distortion of history, the dangling of the great dream." After additional descriptions of other social doping, Parker pointed at the culprits pulling the strings behind the scenes: "The moneymakers never lose their focus because they have sold their souls to the dark side, they have made pacts with the devil, they no longer feel guilty, they no longer have any conscience." In all of this, Parker saw that he had a role to play in undoing the carnage: "Cosmic music . . . breaks down their lies and exposes hypocrisy."[103] Parker's solo works are his deepest and most personal, and it is in that format that he defines himself as healer, guide, and revolutionary most brilliantly. His hopes rest in his unfettered belief in art as the antidote to all of the social disruptions he identifies and free musical expression as the most poignant of art forms. Like his Igbo ancestors bore staves of peace to purify the world of human crimes, so has Parker wielded his bass to speak beauty and truth to power and injustice.

Eleven

All People Need Truth to Survive:
Recent Work and Legacy

We are improvisers,
our entire life is a rehearsal for heaven. —— **William Parker**

As prolific as Parker has been and as active as he has been in recording and performing, he still has many hundreds of compositions that he has never had the opportunity to record or even perform. Parker's recent records have become even more expansive in scope in his pursuance of universal tonality. *For Those Who Are, Still*, released in 2015, combines a number of live performances with one studio session.[1] Each of the separate recordings within the box set breaks new ground for Parker and represents some of his most ambitious work to date. Most of the sessions involve relatively new work, but the collection opens with an older session titled *For Fannie Lou Hamer*, named for the civil rights activist (1917–1977). In 1962–71, Hamer had been one of the leaders of the civil rights movement, organized Mississippi's Freedom Summer, and ran for public office, surviving several assassination attempts in the process. Reflecting back on her work, she once stated, "I guess if I'd had any sense, I'd have been a little scared—but what was the point of being scared? The only thing they could do was kill me, and it kinda seemed like they'd been trying to do that a little bit at a time since I could remember."[2]

For Fannie Lou Hamer, recorded live in 2000, was commissioned by the Kitchen, a nonprofit organization that had been founded in 1971 and aimed to be a place where "experimental artists and composers share progressive ideas with like-minded colleagues."[3] The commission was for the Kitchen House Blend project, which required Parker to compose a score for performance by the Kitchen House Band. Drawing together the talents with whom Parker was just then surrounding himself, such as vocalist Leena Conquest and cellist Shiau-Shu Yu, as well as longtime collaborator trombonist Masahiko Kono, Parker's compositions in honor of the civil rights icon represented a bold step forward in ways that foreshadowed much of his work with the Raining on the Moon Quintet and the Inside Songs of Curtis Mayfield, among other projects.

The twenty-eight-minute piece is a stunning compositional work opening with the shimmering strings and lower brass of Todd Reynolds (violin), Shiau-Shu Yu (cello), Nicki Parrot (bass), and Masahiko Kono (trombone), forming a grounding of the music with occasional accents from percussion. But then a soulful reed lead voice rises from the intricate, dark tension, eventually joined by trumpet weaving its way up and then taking the torch and pushing higher. Once that eventually dissipates, the voice of Leena Conquest emerges warm, resonant, and incisive:

> *When you smile the big orange mountain cries*
> *And its tears fall down like rain*
> *When you smile the big orange mountain cries*
> *And its tears fall down like rain*
> *There is enough compassion in you*
> *To illuminate the sun eternally*
>
> *She was carrying the people*
> *Carrying them on her back*
> *Through the deep blue-purple cotton fields*
> *Not eating or sleeping for days*
> *She would take two sometimes three people across the long corridor*
> *This small woman did not know the word enemy*
> *She was carrying the people on her back*
> *The cotton sack on her waist was always filled with sunshine*
> *Sunshine*

One day the cracker police
Beat her with clubs and leather straps
They beat her on her legs
Until they groped like Okra
Blood poured from these wounds
Blood mixed with tears of compassion
They beat her until she fell to her knees
But she would not let them win
She stood up
They looked in her eyes
She stood up as thunder gathered
In the left side of the sky
They beat her again
And again and again

Rising up
One more time
Rising rising up
One more time
She hops on one foot and tips her hat
Vanishing like a swift wind
And the people begin to float
Across the blue-purple fields
Float with the power
All the mountains in the world begin to move in ¾ time
I can see the face of god in the beautiful sky

There is enough compassion in you
To illuminate the sky
Eternally[4]

After the lyrical lines conclude, the lead reed voice returns over a chorus-like undercurrent of strings, vocals, and percussion. The piece, in many ways, anticipates Parker's work with Raining on the Moon, the Inside Songs of Curtis Mayfield, and his later vocal works.

Red Giraffe with Dreadlocks, recorded live in Paris twelve years later, is a realization of many of Parker's principles of universal tonality. The band included the William Parker Quartet with Cooper-Moore instead of Lewis Barnes, as well as Sangeeta Bandyopadhyay (voice), Mola Sylla (b. 1956, voice, mbira, ngoni), Bill Cole (double reeds), and Klaas Hekman (bass saxophone, flute). As a kind of test of the ideas behind Parker's theory of universality, these musicians brought their own individual sounds, "each musician retaining their own identity within the developing web of association." Illustrating this beautifully was Parker's decision to have vocals from Senegal and India coexist, alongside Parker's bass and shakuhachi, made buoyant by Drake's jazz kit and frame drum, and Cole's wide variety of hypnotic double reeds. The suite opens with the low rumble of Bill Cole's double reeds and Parker's bass forming a backdrop for the vocal duet of Bandyopadhyay and Sylla to rise and soar. Parker did not even ask the vocalists to perform in English, allowing the diction and inflections of Bandyopadhyay in Hindi and Sylla in Wolof languages to contribute to the complexity of the piece. As one critic put it, *Red Giraffe with Dreadlocks* generates a new ensemble that can only uncover the music it wants to play through the experience of playing it."[5]

Parker asks the question "What is the system for unlocking sound so that music can be elevated to magic?" He follows with his own explanation: "The first thing that the composer must accept is that music does not need human beings to exist, it is a natural force like the wind and rain. Music can be whatever you want it to be at the same time it has its own universe that we are just beginning to understand. When certain sounds are put together at the right moment, magic occurs." He adds, "It is the musician's role to tap into this magic every time they play or compose music. It is the listener's job to open their souls and spirits so they can be reunited with the family they call sound. Let the music in without any interference from education or intelligence. Rebuild the intuitive; mix that with compassion for all who live and the music has a better chance. No one system of music should dominate the world. Every human being should have a personal relationship with sound."[6]

The other major recording within the box is *Ceremonies for Those Who Are Still*, Parker's most eloquent tribute to date, in honor of Rustam "Roost" Abdullaev, whom Parker had met while on tour in Moscow. Parker was immediately struck by the bassist: "Roost had the qualities that I like best in musicians. He was open to everything and anything that would bring enlightenment to the world."[7] Parker added that Roost was "one of those people who could see the beautiful in life; every flower, blade of grass, butterfly was noticed and acknowledged."[8] Abdullaev was killed in an auto accident on April 21, 2013. For the tribute, Parker brought his trio of tenor saxophonist Charles Gayle and Chicago-based drummer Mike Reed to play with the National Forum of Music symphony orchestra and choir in Poland, which commissioned the work, conducted by Jan Jakub Bokun. The extended suite bore mournful elements but also exhibited considerable energy as a triumphant way to celebrate a life.

As one might expect, Parker's work with the symphony was aimed at freedom in the music. Writer Philip Clark noted that "music notation must also exist as provocation: a route map that points musicians along pathways they would not necessarily walk themselves, another way of listening and responding."[9] But Parker's approach certainly did not subvert the symphony to a position of mere support within rigid strictures; it aimed to coordinate the various elements together as they sought free expression through the music. Still, as Parker noted explicitly, "This is not about notation meeting improvisation, it is about music."[10] The notation allowed for individual interpretation of shape, articulation, and punctuation, and it rarely regulated volume. It sent a message to the participants: "Don't just scan the notes. Use your ears to turn this notation into music. Draw yourself into the performative act by listening."[11] Creation has to happen in the moment with the tools and the instincts of the performers. The piece was performed at Jazztopad Festival in Warsaw on November 15, 2013, and also featured a tribute to Sonny Rollins, among others.

Another box set, *Voices Fall from the Sky*, is an ambitious project that allows Parker to feature voice with lyrical poems. For Parker, "The first instrument of communication that human beings use is the voice," growing from a newborn baby's cry to complex language. For it is also the storytelling capacity of the voice—in particular, folktales and myths—that helped inspire Parker in this project with what he refers to as "mystery systems." "What is song?" Parker asks in the liner notes to the record. "Song is a flying poem using sounds and words."[12] He was inspired by the image of voices coming from the sky that turned into leaves or birds floating to the ground and then taking back off or evaporating into the sky.[13] The original concept came with the idea of seven separate records, each one with music written for a different vocalist, but he later decided to do fewer recordings and put the project out together as a box set. When considered together, the box set featured many new recordings as well as lesser-known pieces from his catalogue.

In some ways the record speaks to all of the vocalists and poets that Parker had worked with throughout his career, from his first gigs in the Bronx with Maxine Sullivan to encounters with George Edward Tait and Louis Reyes Rivera at the Poetry Theater in the 1970s and with Yusef Waliyaya at the Afrikan Poetry Theater in Jamaica, Queens. By 1973, Parker had met Jeanne Lee and worked with her in a variety of projects and hired her for the Thousand Cranes project. Parker met Ellen Christi in 1973, when she first arrived in New York, and by 1976, he met Lisa Sokolov through Lee, who would become a lifelong collaborator. Many other encounters with vocalists would follow. Parker also thought of the project as a way of paying homage to great arrangers that he admired, such as Lalo Schifrin, Quincy Jones, Duke Ellington, and Claus Ogerman.[14]

Voices Fall from the Sky features some of these key figures in Parker's earlier development and a number of the premier vocalists of the early twenty-first-century New York music scene as well as people from all over the world. The record includes Christi and Sokolov as well as frequent collaborators Leena Conquest, Sangeeta Bandyopadhyay, and Ernie Odoom. It also includes Timna Comedi, Morley Kamen, Amirtha Kidambi, Kyoko Kitamura, Bernardo Palombo, Omar Payano, Jean Carla Rodea, AnnMarie Sandy, Raina Sokolov-Gonzalez, Mola Sylla, Fay Victor, and Andrea Wolper.

The first volume of the box set opens with a chanted invocation by Payano intended to "call together spirits who heal to gather and to conjure, to work their magic." At the center of the record are statements against war. "Despues de la Guerra" is one of the first pieces Parker ever composed, back in 1971, but is presented here with a new melody and lyrics. Rodea and Palombo combine for a powerful duet of timeless music. Rodea, Parker states, "has one foot in the folk music which to me means the people and the other foot in the now sound which also means the people." Another piece, "So, Important," features Kitamura in duet with pianist Eri Yamamoto, considering that in war, "the real Hero is the soldier who refuses to kill."[15] "Revolution" follows these in its call for resistance, featuring the Brazilian vocalist Comedi with the following lyrics:

> I am a shadow in the window
> Lighting up the night
> So, don't give up the fight for life
> It is your birth right
> To break the chains of oppression
> And rise up rise up revolution
> Whenever I look into your eyes
> I see the sun set sunrise[16]

With "City of Flowers," Parker returns to *One Thousand Cranes*, featuring Wolper in an adaptation of the original "City of Death." As Parker explained, the original title was "any modern city that attempts to mechanize people using drugs, and prisons to sedate minorities, while the rulers step on anyone that gets in the way of corporate profits and their own fascist tendencies." "We Often Danced" features Fay Victor, moving within and extending the tradition of the music. The piece "is a memory about the act of the inside survival of slaves coming from Africa to the Americas and how the dream of dancing is a station of hope for all oppressed people in the world."[17] The first volume also contains a tribute to pianist Borah Bergman (1926–2012) and a piece for a 2015 public park installation in New Orleans for the Airlift Music Box project. The title piece, which brought Amirtha Kidambi together with trombonist Steve Swell and violinist Jason Kao Hwang, forms one of the peaks of the record in terms of its vitality.

The second volume contains a series of tributes. Parker had written the opening piece, "All I Want," for violinist Billy Bang shortly after his death in 2011. The title refers to Bang's many decades' struggle with the aftereffects of his involvement as a soldier in the Vietnam War. According to Parker, "All he wanted was to be at peace with himself and the world."[18] "Baldwin's Interlude" was one of the first pieces that Parker wrote dedicated to writer James Baldwin, who had served as a great inspiration to Parker ever since first encountering his writings in the 1960s. "For Julius Eastman" is a reissued recording originally laid down in the early 1990s, released in 2001, and written for Eastman, whom Parker had first encountered at the Third Street Music School on the Lower East Side in the 1980s. The piece features Sokolov with pianist Yuko Fujiyama. The fourth track, "Aborigine Song," was dedicated to saxophonist Don Byas and was based on a dream that Parker had of him. "Poem for June Jordan," which Parker had developed and recorded with his quartet first in 2004, and to which he added lyrics for Raining on the Moon in 2007, again honors the activist whom Parker admired deeply, with the song here given a reinterpretation and new life.

"Tour of the Flying Poem" is one of the most explicit exercises in Parker's theory of universal tonality on the record, with Cooper-Moore and Mola Sylla making this piece come alive as an operetta for small children. "Prayer" also has universalist aspirations. "Sweet Breeze" is a look back at Parker's childhood in the Bronx. "If you stand on the corner and close your eyes and the wind blows right you can see and feel things called memories," Parker quipped about the piece.[19] It bears the following lyrics in its first verse:

> Sweet breeze on the corner
> brings me back to the place I was born
> Sweet breeze on the corner
> brings me back to the place I was born
> I see Friday afternoon sun

Fading into evening that has not come
We listen to Antiques by Ornette Coleman
Cod fish and rolls[20]

The third volume of the box set, subtitled "Essence," features vocal pieces for larger ensembles. It includes familiar pieces such as "The Essence of Ellington," the title piece of the project of the same name. "For Fannie Lou Hamer" is a new interpretation of the piece that Parker had written for his Kitchen commission in 2000 and had released on *For Those Who Are, Still*, with Conquest taking center stage, bass playing by Nicky Parrott, and Parker supporting with marimba, glockenspiel, and double reeds. "The Blinking of the Ear" was originally composed in 2015 for solo piano, but it soon evolved to include an ensemble of cello, saxophones, trumpet, trombone, and voice, featuring mezzo-soprano AnnMarie Sandy. After the recording was completed, the piece was further developed and expanded on a later record, one which Parker considered to be one of the most vibrant examples of universal tonality. Parker dedicated the piece to filmmaker Hollis Frampton (1936–84), who was an inspiration during his youth, and the music bears images of the civil rights movement: "You can hear the cry of freedom in the background and the conflict of art versus reality—whether one wants to follow the spirit or be avant-garde in a world where people are still recovering from reservations, plantations, and prisons."[21] "Lights of Lake George" is a masterpiece of universal tonal synthesis, bringing together Bandyopadhyay with Hamid Drake and Gerald Cleaver on percussion, and Brahim Frigbane playing oud, almost as another voice with music that positively dances. "Natasha's Theme," taken from the *Alphaville Suite*, closes the album, relaying the message "Let the poets live, do not kill them. It is for you that the sun rises, only for you. . . ."[22]

In May 2014 Parker debuted a new project, *Flower in a Stained-Glass Window*, which he dedicated to Rev. Dr. Martin Luther King Jr. Ars Nova Workshop in Philadelphia commissioned the work, which was written for chamber ensemble with four soloists, one performing each night over the course of a four-night series. Muhammad Ali, brother of Rashied Ali, played drums, and Parker invited Marshall Allen, Dave Burrell, Odean Pope, and Bobby Zankel as soloists, with Keir Neuringer as concert master. Then, in January 2015, Parker presented the fifth installment of the work, "Yes I Dream of Freedom," at Roulette in New York, which expanded to include a twenty-five member troupe with additional instrumentalists, vocalists, actors, and dancers. This bigger iteration was called William Parker's Tone Motion Theater.

The starting point for the work was the image of King as a young seminary student looking through a stained-glass window and hearing words about nonviolence "as inspired by Mahatma Gandhi and perhaps Henry Salt and Henry David Thoreau. The message being: social and political justice and equality for all human beings." After laying down his initial compositional ideas in 2014, "The inspiration of Bañuel, Fernando Arrabal, and Jerzy Grotowski kicked in. And black surrealism and vision that has come to me most of my life," Parker wrote. In particular, this vision struck Parker: "Imagine it is April 4, 1968. A dying Doctor King's spirit leaves his body. On the way home it encounters Tasunke Witko the Lakota Sioux who was rushing to the scene to bring him back to life through music, sounds and movement. Instead of reminiscing of the past they talk about how the revolution must come from within. Freedom cannot be handed out. It is already inside of us. And most importantly it is in improvisational music."[23]

The record was finally recorded at Park West Studios in Brooklyn in the spring of 2017 with a band that included Abraham Faure Mennen (tenor and soprano saxophones), Steve Swell (trombone), Parker's son, Isaiah (piano), Kesivan Naidoo (drums), and Parker on bass. Tracks were laid down over the course of three sessions, with Conquest doing her vocal tracks at the final session in May. The music was a combination of composed sections and fully improvised parts. One of the musicians, South African drummer Kesivan Naidoo, had met Parker through a mutual friend, the late saxophonist Zim Ngqwana, "so when Mr. Parker called me to do the session, I felt like the ancestors had a hand in it," Naidoo said. He further observed of the session, "When I arrived at the studio, the vintage drums were perfectly in tune and ready for action. Mr. Parker had a few ideas written down but he mainly explained the vibe that he wanted for the record. We did a first take of one of the tunes that had a quick listen back. Mr. Parker was very happy with the sound and the approach. Then we just got into the music and did first takes of every piece."[24]

The tracks on the record each explore aspects of King's legacy and the long struggle for freedom of Black America. Parker explains that the opening track, "Fallen Flower," is his "description of Martin Luther King as I saw him, as part of a stained-glass window looking into the future. Reflecting on the murderers who killed him and the absence of the future and the past and how fleeting the present is." Parker followed that with "Gone," a powerful statement of Parker's own denunciation of war and violence, especially violence in the service of profit: "This situation will continue unless we can truly embrace the concept of why we live." "Emmett Till" is a memorial for the teenager brutally slain in Mississippi in 1955: "Echoes of this murder culture unfortunately live today in the deaths of young Black men who are killed by the police." "Give Me Back My Drum," Parker declares, "is the cry of the African whose drum has been declared illegal by those who own and run the plantations."[25]

Some of the pieces included on the record widen the scope even further. "Broken Earth" is an anticapitalist exposé that mourns the violence committed against the Earth in the name of money; it leaves the listener nevertheless energized to take part in the coming changes that must happen for human survival. "'Children,'" Parker notes, "is a medium tempo statement based off of my definition of Democracy from my High School days, when I discovered that Patriotism is the love of injustice." Parker, whose work has often been inspired by dreams, wrote "I Had a Dream Last Night" based on a vision that he had in 2012 in which Jesus Christ returned, materializing as a woman and arriving via bus to bring changes to the world.[26]

Parker has a number of other projects recently recorded or soon to be recorded, most of them included in a new "William Parker Vocal Series" for Centering Records. This time, each individual vocalist will get their own record with music written specifically for them. These include a project titled Blue Lime Light with vocalist Raina Sokolov-Gonzalez and featuring soloist Jason Kao Hwang on violin, other strings, oboe, bass, piano, and drums. Parker plans to pair vocalist Fay Victor with Hamid Drake and himself for a project titled "Harlem Speaks," a solo vocalist record with Lisa Sokolov, and another one with vocalist Ellen Christi and trumpeter Jalalu Kalvert Nelson called "The Majesty of Jah." Two solo projects, one for vocalist Lisa Sokolov and one for pianist Eri Yamamoto, are also in preparation. In larger projects, Parker will feature Kyoko Kitamura with a small chamber ensemble of tuba, vibraphone, saxophone, bass, and drums, and another one with Andrea Wolper and a small jazz ensemble.[27] Parker is also planning a record for overtone flute and shakuhachi.

Contributions and Innovations

Over nearly fifty years, Parker has built a body of work that is varied in form and monumental in scope such that he has created a whole part of jazz that is his own. Parker brings together elements of the tradition and has maintained a hungry, innovative edge throughout his years on the bandstand.

Much of his music has served as a kind of cultural repository for the Black revolutionary spiritual school of music from which he first emerged. But Parker chose not to pursue the possibilities of that music in an attempted isolation, but rather has striven through his career to draw it into what he calls "universal tonality," the idea that master musicians from any part of the world should be able to meet and play together, to speak to one another through their musical languages. In many ways, Parker has confronted the problem that cinematographer Arthur Jafa faced when he said, "The question is how come we can't be as black as we are and still be universal?"[28] Or as Amiri Baraka prophetically stated in the 1960s, the "use of Indian music, old spirituals, even heavily rhythmic blues licks (and soon electronic devices) by new music musicians point toward the final close in the spectrum of the sound that will come. A really new, all-inclusive music. The whole people."[29] Parker's music is the full embodiment of this movement toward universalism, stretching far beyond what Baraka had originally envisioned. Parker's claim to universalism is his boldest artistic statement, and through this he has demanded a place for revolutionary Black music on the world stage.

"William Parker is the walking embodiment of the spirit of free jazz," Matthew Shipp said. "He is its foremost bassist, yet he completely transcends it. But at the same time, he also embodies every aspect of 1960s idealism, though he is very much a player of this time period. By some force of alchemy or magic, he transcends it."[30] Violinist Jason Kao Hwang put it a different way: "William's vision of music is inseparable from his life. He lives his music and the music lives within him at a high level. He is unconcerned about pleasing authority because his focus is upon the celebration of life. To do good free improvisation, you have to live it, connecting music within each breath. William's originality is a powerful contribution to this music. His life practice is a roadmap to self-discovery."[31]

Parker's rich, full, deep sound on bass draws some parallels with Jimmy Garrison, Wilbur Ware, Malachi Favors, and Charlie Haden. "Despite having done some measure of apprenticeship with Jimmy Garrison, Wilbur Ware, and Richard Davis," Shipp pointed out, "his own playing is home-made, an autodidactic, self-made reality. He somehow manages to be studied in his approach, while never being engulfed by the pitfalls of jazz education. He is an endless reservoir. Even after years of playing, he will suddenly come up with something new. He seems to have no limits."[32] "William is a groover, but he loves odd time signatures," James Brandon Lewis noted. "He has a unique ability to mix the groove in with the free."[33] These comments were echoed by bassist Joshua Abrams, who perceived Parker's ability to "translate swing to freer music" such that "it always retains a heartbeat and momentum pushing forward."[34]

Some of Parker's unique approach begins with composition. Once the initial spark of an idea manifests itself, he composes a piece. But he never feels that the ideas need to be set in stone: "You want to let it breathe and grow; if you try to control it, you will suppress it or kill it." Music making is an act of faith for Parker, a practice of trust in the music and the musicians: "The spontaneous composition in the moment is what you're trying to have happen with any present composition. It's about having faith and letting the moment happen." This focus on the moment means that each time Parker plays a piece, even if he has played it before, the goal is "to play like it is our first time. Listen for the moment. What worked yesterday may not work today."[35]

Parker pushes back against external structure: "We only feel we need to have a one, a two, a three, an upbeat and a downbeat because we have been trained to need those things. We only feel we need a key because we have been trained to need one. But what if you're playing music that doesn't have a key? What do you do?" For Parker the codification of music into genres, styles, or systems drains it of its vitality. It also enforces structures of power and value placed upon music that is created to challenge prevailing expectations: "It pits us against the world of tactile imperialism and capitalism. We are told, we don't fit into the world and that to fit into this world, we must change things about ourselves. So it's about resisting that pull and following your heart."[36]

Throughout his career, Parker has also been dedicated to maintaining an independence from forces that would compromise his decisions as an artist. After many years of work he found a way to make a living with his music through a combination of touring, commissions, grants, self-production, and records. There were no easy doors open to him. But he also did not look at well-funded venues like Jazz at Lincoln Center with envy, but rather referred to that institution as "Uncle Tom's Cabin" because he felt that it dressed up jazz to appeal to a conservative, primarily white audience.[37] Parker is currently working on a piece titled "Marshmallow Nigger" about jazz presented in that context.

Parker has taught at Bennington College, New York University, the New England Conservatory of Music, California Institute of the Arts, New School University, and Rotterdam Conservatory of Music. He has also taught music workshops in places such as Paris, Berlin, Tokyo, South Africa, and New

York. Wherever he has engaged with students, he has encouraged them to break the "rules" that had been enforced on them by their jazz teachers or by traditional pedagogy or notation. At the New School, which has a reputation as a conservative jazz program aimed and training its students to play standards, Parker was something of an iconoclast, challenging students to see beyond chord changes by getting them to listen to music from Senegal, Mali, Thailand, and a variety of other places. Or, in another instance, he told students that swing has nothing to do with syncopated beat in 4/4 time. Most of the students had come to him because they were seeking something distinctly different from what the mainstream could offer.[38] Parker encouraged his students to find their own structure, sound, and aesthetic, not to copy the great figures of the past as is so common in music education.

In 2013 he was the recipient of the Doris Duke Performing Artist Award, which enabled him to record and produce many of his recent works. "[William Parker] is something of a father figure, dispensing life lessons as well as wisdom about musical technique," stated critic Larry Blumenfeld.[39] Saxophonist James Brandon Lewis, who moved to New York in 2012, said that Parker has always been an encouraging force for him: "I felt immediately accepted by him, both personally and musically. He shows the same humanity on the bandstand that he does in his day to day life. He makes me feel like music is the deepest thing and the lightest thing at the same time. I hope to get to that place, that centeredness that he has."[40] For many young, emerging, or recently established Black musicians in particular, Parker is synonymous with the term *elder*, a figure in the community passing down knowledge, traditions, and cultural values to the next generation.

Community,
Solidarity,
Compassion

Community is everything for Parker. It is the reason he breathes, creates music. He has expressed this in the narratives of his work, in his many tributes to the living and the dead, and in his own efforts to invigorate the community of artists. Despite his many accomplishments and opportunities, Parker never abandoned the community that nurtured him. His people. Parker's deep commitment to justice and his trust in the role of art and music as a revolutionary force to better society have been the guiding light throughout his life. As Parker's wife, Patricia Nicholson, said, "Music is the through line

Figure 11.1 Cooper-Moore, Christian McBride, Parker, Jason Kao Hwang, Charles Gayle, and Hamiet Bluiett, Angel Orensanz Foundation, December 4, 2012. *Credit*: ©Peter Gannushkin/downtownmusic.net.

for William. It holds everything together, his spirituality, life, community."[41] "Parker understands that being creative is part of human life play, just like we need to eat and breathe," Joshua Abrams commented.[42] "Music has always been his motivator, never eyeing some careerist tangent," Steve Swell observed of Parker. "He's been the bedrock of the Lower East Side community for decades."[43] Drummer Andrew Cyrille referred to Parker as the "mayor of the Lower East Side" because of his long involvement and dedication to the furthering of the musicians' community there.[44]

Over the course of nearly fifty years, Parker's body of work is itself a record of the living memory of Black revolutionary music and the broader form of music that he defines as universal tonality. Parker's emergence in the "Black revolutionary spiritual school" and his gradual move toward universalism without betraying his roots stakes a powerful claim for the place of Black music at the international table of human sound. Parker drew some inspiration from Hazrat Inayat Khan (1882–1927), a Sufi from India who came to the United States in the 1910s and wrote considerably about the universality of music, aspects of which Parker commonly discussed with Hamid Drake.[45] Khan's theories of the universal sacred as well as the healing power of music, rhythm, and harmony were quite powerful for Parker in forming his own ideas about universal tonality.[46] The musical act of creation, as orchestrated by Parker in recent years, drawing together performers from places as far-flung as India, Senegal, Japan, and Brazil, to name but a few, constitutes an ambitious act of community building that transcends all manner of traditional boundaries. The global reach of Parker's work is the manifestation of universal tonality in practice.

As Swell observed, "Parker's music is so much bigger than one ensemble or region or genre. The general public and many critics think they understand what he is about as an artist but have only been exposed to a small fraction of his work."[47] Amazingly, Parker maintains his fierce dedication to the sanctity of individual expression while delving into common humanity and seeking profound "mysteries" of existence, spirituality, and what makes humanity whole. It is in these aspects of his work that the true power of his art has been fully realized.

Parker's music is itself a road map of those artists who came before him and his contemporaries who passed away before their time was due. His many dozens of tributes pay homage to the dead, revive their memories, and instill new potency in their legacies. His songs written for many of the great avant-garde artists from the Black Arts movement era and beyond are themselves a living memory of the whole history of free jazz and its descendant musics. As Parker wrote, "So many musicians gone, one could spend a lifetime paying homage to all of them. It is part of documenting the history so that all of the names are mentioned, not just the ones who are better known. We try to do this musical life justice; as much as we can. The survivors must look out for each other whenever we can."[48] Parker's music has kept alive the collective memory of the music and the community that has produced it, as if placing those now existing only in memory alongside the living practitioners of the music today. This monumental legacy has few equivalents, if any, in the period since the so-called golden age of free jazz in the 1960s. Even more so, Parker's work shatters the image of the so-called decline of the music, self-evident in the potency of his body of work. Parker's genius has been not only in extending the tradition of free jazz but also in creating a living music that looks forward with the confidence of innovation. To him, jazz never declined; it is as vibrant as ever, as evidenced through his own notes.

Parker sometimes played a role in drawing out figures from an earlier generation who had not received proper attention or who had not played in front of New York audiences enough in previous times. Kidd Jordan and

Fred Anderson are two examples of figures who had fallen off the radar of many critics, and Parker made sure to invite them to play with him at Vision Festival and recorded with them.[49] The record *Two Days in April* showcases the talents of Jordan and Anderson in the live setting, revealing indomitable energy and intensity even in the later stages of their careers.

Parker's acts of honoring the ancestors of the music share similarities with his other acts of solidarity through music. One of the centerpieces of Parker's artistic vision is the solidarity he expressed with indigenous people, especially Native Americans. Although this had been a lifelong part of his artistic vision, this focus further intensified after beginning to work with Hamid Drake, for the two would often read and discuss the history of indigenous peoples of the United States. Drake noted that they had a shared respect for indigenous peoples who had experienced, in some ways, "a similar experience of oppression as our people have in this country. But also because of the longstanding relationship between African Americans and Native Americans."[50] Dozens of his pieces are dedicated to eminent Indian figures, the Lakota Sioux especially, whom Parker sometimes honors in the same breath as key Black jazz luminaries. "Oglala Eclipse" is perhaps the greatest example of this, although it is one of the foremost themes running through much of his work. Parker expresses profound empathy for the destruction of indigenous populations, decries the colonialist and capitalist forces that laid waste to them, and has demanded greater dignity for them through these memorials. Setting the Lakota Sioux's struggles right alongside the five-hundred-year struggle by African-descended peoples in the Americas pinpoints the common humanity of these peoples as they face related challenges. Parker is also quick to remind listeners that the great Hunkpapa Sioux warrior Sitting Bull was also a composer, singer, and improviser—additional points of shared humanity and life purpose.

Parker's core influences came out of the Black Arts movement, although he also had profound influences from many artists from white America, Europe, Latin America, and elsewhere. Nevertheless, as Matthew Shipp notes, "William's music embodies Black universal consciousness, a major custodian of it in the post–Amiri Baraka period." Parker has gathered ideas and aesthetics from anything that he encountered that interested him, but still operated, according to Shipp, "as an African American composer capable of summoning spirits, of conjuring such force and speaking to the whole history of the African-descended community. In a certain sense, he is a prophet. Like the prophets of the Old Testament that lived alone in the desert. They weren't part of the establishment, they would get divine proclamations and just put them out there. The music that William does just comes through him like that, it's not manufactured."[51]

Rage might erupt from Parker, however, if the things sacred to him—the music and the community—were threatened. Parker took particular issue with critic Howard Mandel. In 2014, after Mandel had written a negative review about the Evolving Series, a regular improvised music series put on by Arts for Art, Parker penned an open letter. He wrote that the review was, "as usual, a display of marginalizing the music, the musicians and taking stabs at the non-profit producer, Arts for Art."[52] Parker went on to discredit Mandel for his lack of understanding of improvised music and to forbid him from attending future events sponsored by Arts for Art. When Mandel ignored this and came to Vision Festival two months later, Parker exploded.

Parker's position as community leader now stretches back decades. This has manifested itself in many forms. As drummer Andrew Barker said, "I think the legacy of William Parker is really one of community and humanity. Of course, William is a virtuoso player and he will have the 'legendary bassist' status, but I think William really believes the Albert Ayler quote that 'Music is the healing force of the universe.' I think he does his best to live that every day."[53] Through the years, Parker has often been regarded as a healer, and he sometimes refers to himself as a kind of shaman. When bassist Peter Kowald became mortally ill after a heart attack in New York City in 2002, he asked to be taken to see Parker at his apartment before he was taken to the hospital, stating, "I just need to see William."[54] Steve Swell observes that Parker is always at the center of the community; he always knows who is sick and who is struggling to make ends meet, and is always willing to lend a helping hand. For Dave Burrell, Parker's "humanitarian gestures," such as getting fellow bassist Henry Grimes a new instrument, were the kind of acts that made Parker the incontrovertible leader of the artist community.[55] Hamid Drake, who studied Buddhism among other religions, regarded Parker as having a bodhisattva-like quality, referring to the concept of a person who has attained enlightenment but who remains in that state of awakening not only for himself but in service of enlightening the entire community.[56]

In Parker's conception, healing can take many forms. Parker often talks of it on a cosmological scale: that the fate of the entire world may hinge on the playing of the next note. For Parker, music has a spiritual role in not only maintaining existence but also in filling it with meaning and for improving the world. Without music, the world might be thrown into disarray or might collapse entirely.

In 2004 Parker wrote the following:

At this point in time many things have come together as a result of listening to the silence that exists before sound is made. This silence is also present before every action that we initiate in life. It is at these moments that we can see the movements and inner workings of the flow. Flow is the spontaneously created map that leads us to the center of sound, the essential house where all beauty resides. Through silence, ancient griots have left signposts for the modern griot to learn from, formulas that change according to who is bowing the violin or sarangi, and who is blowing the flute, trumpet or saxophone. There are an infinite number of combinations that coincide with the makeup and nature of the universe.[57]

This is the music of William Parker: "If one foot dips into the black mud of the Mississippi blues while the other foot is in Nepal, it does so on its own because it wants to at that particular moment. It is still the same universe and the same lake of sound. All people in the world need the language of truth to survive."[58]

William Parker continues to compose, perform, and build community around the world and at home on New York's Lower East Side.

William Parker Discography

Records as a Leader

In Order to Survive. *Compassion Seizes Bed-Stuy*. Homestead Records, HM–2 (1997).

In Order to Survive. *In Order to Survive*. Black Saint, 120159–2 (1995).

In Order To Survive. *Live/Shapeshifter*. AUM Fidelity, AUM110/111 (2019).

In Order to Survive. *The Peach Orchard*. AUM Fidelity, AUM010/011 (1998).

In Order to Survive. *Posium Pendasem*. Free Music Productions, FMP CD 105 (1999).

Little Huey Creative Music Orchestra. *Flowers Grow in My Room*. Centering Records, CD1002 (1994).

Little Huey Creative Music Orchestra. *For Percy Heath*. Les Disques Victo, Victo CD 102 (2006).

Little Huey Creative Music Orchestra. *Mass for the Healing of the World*. Black Saint, 120179–2 (2003).

Little Huey Creative Music Orchestra. *Mayor of Punkville*. AUM Fidelity, AUM015/16 (2000).

Little Huey Creative Music Orchestra. *Raincoat in the River*, vol. 1/ICA Concert. Eremite Records, MTE036 (2001).

Little Huey Creative Music Orchestra. *Spontaneous*. Splasc(h) Records, CDH 855.2 (2003).

Little Huey Creative Music Orchestra. *Sunrise in the Tone World*. AUM Fidelity, AUM002/3 (1997).

Raining on the Moon. *Corn Meal Dance*. AUM Fidelity, AUM043 (2007).

Raining on the Moon. *Great Spirit*. AUM Fidelity, AUM098 (2015).

William Parker. *At Somewhere There*. Barnyard Records, BR–0313 (2010).

William Parker. *Centering: Unreleased Early Recordings 1976–1987*. No Business Records, NBCD 42–47 (2012).

William Parker. *Crumbling in the Shadows Is Fraulein Miller's Stale Cake*. Centering Records, CENT1005/6/7 (2011).

William Parker. *Flower in a Stained-Glass Window -&- The Blinking of the Ear*. Centering Records, CENT1018/1019 (2018).

William Parker. *For Those Who Are, Still*. AUM Fidelity, AUM092/093/094 (2015).

William Parker. *The Inside Songs of Curtis Mayfield (Live in Rome-2004)*. Rai Trade/Radio 3 (2007).

William Parker. *I Plan to Stay a Believer: The Inside Songs of Curtis Mayfield*. AUM Fidelity, AUM062/063 (2010).

William Parker. *Lake of Light: Compositions for Aquasonics*. Gotta Let It Out, GLI019CD (2018).

William Parker. *Lifting the Sanctions*. No More Records, No. 6 (1998).

William Parker. *Long Hidden: The Olmec Series*. AUM Fidelity, AUM036 (2006).

William Parker. *Luc's Lantern*. The Blue Series. Thirsty Ear, THI 57158.2 (2005).

William Parker. *Migration of Silence Into and Out of The Tone World*. Centering Records, CENT1020-1029 (2021).

William Parker. *Song Cycle*. Boxholder Records, BHX 017 (2001).

William Parker. *Stan's Hat Flapping in the Wind*. Centering Records, CENT1012 (2016).

William Parker. *Testimony*. Zero In Records, Zero In 1 (1995).

William Parker. *Through Acceptance of the Mystery Peace*. Centering Records (1980).

William Parker. *Voices Fall from the Sky*. Centering Records, CENT1015/16/17 (2018).

William Parker Bass Quartet Featuring Charles Gayle. *Requiem*. Splasc(h) Records, CDH 885.2 (2006).

William Parker Clarinet Trio. *Bob's Pink Cadillac*. Eremite Records, MTE032/33 (2001).

William Parker Creation Ensemble. *Wood Flute Songs: Anthology/Live 2006–2012*. AUM Fidelity, AUM080–87 (2013).

William Parker Double Quartet. *Alphaville Suite: Music Inspired by the Jean Luc Godard Film*. Rogueart, Rog–0010 (2007).

William Parker Orchestra. *Double Sunrise over Neptune*. AUM Fidelity, AUM047 (2008).

William Parker Orchestra with Special Guest Kidd Jordan. *Essence of Ellington*. Centering Records, Centering 1008/1009 (2012).

William Parker Orchestra with Special Guest Kidd Jordan. *Live in Milano*. Centering Records, CENT1008/9 (2012).

William Parker Organ Quartet. *Uncle Joe's Spirit House*. Centering Records, CENT 1004 (2010).

William Parker Quartet. *Ao Vivo Jazz Na Fábrica*. Selo SESC SP, CDSS 0076/16 (2016).

William Parker Quartet. *Live in Wroclove*. For Tune, 0002 02 (2013).

William Parker Quartet. *Meditation/Resurrection*. AUM Fidelity, AUM104/105 (2017).

William Parker Quartet. *O'Neal's Porch*. Centering Records, CD1003 (2001).

William Parker Quartet. *Petit Oiseau*. AUM Fidelity, AUM050 (2008).

William Parker Quartet. *Raining on the Moon*. The Blue Series. Thirsty Ear, THI 57119.2 (2002).

William Parker Quartet. *Sound Unity*. AUM Fidelity, AUM034 (2005).

William Parker Trio. *. . . . And William Danced*. Ayler Records, aylCD–044 (2002).

William Parker Trio. *Painter's Spring*. The Blue Series. Thirsty Ear, THI 57088.2 (2000).

William Parker Violin Trio. *Scrapbook*. The Blue Series. Thirsty Ear, THI 57133.2 (2003).

Records as a Coleader/Collaborator

Agustí Fernández and William Parker. *Second Set*. Radical Records, MPE 047 (2001).

Alan Silva, Kidd Jordan, William Parker. *Emancipation Suite #1*. Boxholder Records, BXH 023 (2002).

Anthony Braxton, Milford Graves, William Parker. *Beyond Quantum*. Tzadik Key Series, 7626 (2008).

Associated Big Band. *Associated Big Band*. Stork Records, Stork 1001 (1991).

Barre Phillips, Joëlle Leandre, William Parker, Tetsu Saitoh. *After You Gone*. Les Disques VICTO, CD 091 (2004).

Billy Bang and William Parker. *Medicine Buddha*. No Business Records, NBCD 71 (2014).

Blue Series Continuum. *GoodandEvil Sessions*. The Blue Series. Thirsty Ear, THI 57134.2 (2003).

Blue Series Continuum. *High Water*. The Blue Series. Thirsty Ear, THI 57143.2 (2004).

Blue Series Continuum. *Masses*. The Blue Series. Thirsty Ear, THI 57103.2 (2001).

Blue Series Continuum. *Sorcerer Sessions (Featuring the Music of Matthew Shipp)*. The Blue Series. Thirsty Ear, THI 57141.2 (2003).

Borah Bergman, Kidd Jordan, William Parker, Michael Wimberly. *vita brevis*. SomeRealMusic, 03 (2013).

Charles Gayle, William Parker, Rashied Ali. *Live at Crescendo*. Ayler Records, aylCD–077/78 (2008).

Charles Gayle, William Parker, Rashied Ali. *Touchin' on Trane*. Free Music Productions, FMP CD 48 (1993).

Collective 4tet. *Bindu*. Stork Music, STORK1015 (1993).

Collective 4tet. *Dreamcatcher*. Stork Music, STORK1007 (1992).

Collective 4tet. *In Transition*. Leo Records, 2009.

Collective 4tet. *Live at Crescent*. Leo Lab, 1997.

Collective 4tet. *Moving Along*. Leo Records, 2005.

Collective 4tet. *Orca*. Leo Lab, 1997.

Collective 4tet. *The Ropedancer*. Leo Lab, 1996.

Collective 4tet. *Synopsis*. Leo Records, 2003.

Commitment. *Commitment*. Flying Panda Records, 1980.

Commitment. *The Complete Recordings 1981/1983*. No Business Records, NBLP 14/15 (2010).

Commitment. *Live in Germany, 1983*. No Business Records, 2010.

The Cosmosamatics. *The Cosmosamatics*. Boxholder Records, BXH 022 (2001).

Creative Collective. *Live at the Guelph Jazz Festival 2011*. Creative Collective, 01 (2011).

Daniel Carter, William Parker, Matthew Shipp. *Seraphic Light*. AUM Fidelity, AUM106 (2017).

David Budbill and William Parker. *What I Saw This Morning*. Judevine Mountain Productions, (no issue number) (2017).

David Budbill and William Parker. *Zen Mountains Zen Streets: A Duet for Poet and Improvised Bass*. Boxholder Records, BX001/002 (1999).

David Budbill, William Parker, Hamid Drake. *Songs for a Suffering World*. Boxholder Records, BXH 044 (2003).

Derek Bailey, John Zorn, William Parker. *Harras*. Avant, AVAN 056 (1995).

Echoes Quintet. *Echoes*. Terre Sommerse, 2007.

The Element Choir and William Parker. *At Christ Church Deer Park*. Barnyard Records, Barnyard 326 (2011).

Eloping with the Sun. *Counteract This Turmoil like Trees and Birds*. Rogeuart, 2016.

Eloping with the Sun. *Eloping with the Sun*. Riti Records, RITI CD 007 (2002).

Farmers by Nature. *Farmers by Nature*. AUM Fidelity, AUM053 (2009).

Farmers by Nature. *Love and Ghosts*. AUM Fidelity, AUM089/90 (2014).

Farmers by Nature. *Out of This World's Distortions*. AUM Fidelity, AUM067 (2011).

Fred Anderson, Hamid Drake, Kidd Jordan, William Parker. *2 Days in April*. Eremite, MTE023/024 (2000).

Fred Anderson, William Parker, Hamid Drake. *Blue Winter*. Eremite Records, MTE047/048 (2005).

Free Zen Society. *Free Zen Society*. The Blue Series. Thirsty Ear, THI 57177.2 (2007).

Freedomland. *Amusement Park*. Rent Control Records, 2002.

Freedomland. *Yia's Song*. Rent Control Records, 2004.

Intermission. *Song of Low Songs*. BV Haast Records, 1996.

Intermission. *Unanswered Questions*. BV Haast Records, 1999.

Ivo Perelman, Matthew Shipp, William Parker, Bobby Kapp. *Heptagon*. Leo Records, CD LR 807 (2017).

Ivo Perelman, Matthew Shipp, William Parker, Gerald Cleaver. *Serendipity*. Leo Records, CD–LR 668 (2013).

Ivo Perelman, William Parker, Gerald Cleaver. *The Art of the Improv Trio*, vol. 4. Leo Records, CD–LR 774 (2016).

Jemeel Moondoc and William Parker. *New World Pygmies*. Eremite, MTE020 (1999).

Joe Morris and William Parker. *Invisible Weave*. No More Records, No. 4 (1997).

Joe Morris, William Parker, Gerald Cleaver. AUM Fidelity, AUM073 (2012).

Joëlle Leandre and William Parker. *Contrabasses*. Leo Records, CD LR 261 (1998).

Joëlle Leandre and William Parker. *Live at Dunois*. Leo Records, CD LR 535 (2009).

Ken Aldcroft and William Parker. *Live at the Tranzac*, vol. 1. Trio Records, TRP–DS04–023 (2016).

Kidd Jordan, Hamid Drake, William Parker. *Palm of Soul*. AUM Fidelity, AUM038 (2006).

Marco Eneidi, Glenn Spearman, William Parker, Jackson Krall. *Live at Radio Valencia*. Botticelli Records, 1014 (2000).

Marco Eneidi, William Parker, Denis Charles. *Vermont Spring 1986*. Botticelli Records (1986).

Marco Eneidi, William Parker, Donald Robinson. *Cherry Box*. Eremite Records, MTE025 (2000).

Matthew Shipp, Rob Brown, William Parker. *Magnetism*. Bleu Regard, CT 1957 (1999).

Matthew Shipp and William Parker. *DNA*. Thirsty Ear, THI 57067.2 (1999).

Matthew Shipp, William Parker, Beans, HPRIZM. *Knives from Heaven*. Thirsty Ear, THI 57198.2 (2011).

Melodic Art-Tet. *Melodic Art-Tet*. No Business Records, NBLP 62/63 (2013).

The Music Ensemble. *The Music Ensemble*. Roaratorio, ROAR 103 (2001).

New York 3. *Give*. Extraplatte, EX383–2 (1999).

Ninni Morgia and William Parker. *Prism*. Ultramarine Records, UM007 (2010).

Oliver Lake and William Parker. *To Roy*. Intakt Records, CD 243 (2014).

Other Dimensions in Music. *Live at the Sunset*. Marge, MARGE38 (2007).

Other Dimensions in Music. *Now!* AUM Fidelity, AUM006 (1998).

Other Dimensions in Music. *Other Dimensions in Music*. Silkheart, SHCD 120 (1990).

Other Dimensions in Music Featuring Fay Victor. *Kaiso Stories*. Silkheart, SHCD158 (2011).

Other Dimensions in Music with Matthew Shipp. *Time Is of the Essence; The Essence Is Beyond Time*. AUM Fidelity, AUM013 (2002).

Patricia Nicholson and William Parker. *Hope Cries for Justice*. Centering Records, CENT1014 (2017).

Peter Brötzmann, William Parker, Hamid Drake. *Song Sentimentale*. Otoroku Records, ROKU016LP (2016).

Peter Brötzmann, William Parker, Michael Wertmüller. *NOTHUNG*. In Tone Music, in Tone CD 5 (2002).

Peter Kowald and William Parker. *The Victoriaville Tape*. Les Disques VICTO, CD 088 (2003).

Raoul Bjorkenheim, William Parker, Hamid Drake. DMG @ *The Stone*, vol. 2: *December 26, 2006*. DMG, ARC 0722 (2008).

Rashid Bakr, Frode Gjerstad, William Parker. *Seeing New York from the Ear*. Cadence Jazz Records, CJR 1069 (1996).

Sacred Scrape. *Secret Response/Live in the U.S. 1992*. Rastacan Records, BRD–015 (1994).

Sprawl. *Sprawl*. Trost Records, TR 070 (1997).

Thomas Borgmann, Peter Brötzmann, William Parker, Rashid Bakr. *The Cooler Suite*. GROB 539 (2003).

Trio Hurricane. *Live at Fire in the Valley*. Eremite Records, MTE010 (1997).

Trio Hurricane. *Suite of Winds*. Black Saint, 120102–2 (1994).

Udu Calls Trio. *The Vancouver Tapes*. Long Song Records, LSRCD135/2013 (2014).

Wayne Horvitz, Butch Morris, William Parker. *Some Order, Long Understood*. Black Saint, BSR 0059 (1983).

William Parker and Ad Peijnenburg. *Brooklyn Calling*. Dino, CD 32004 (2004).

William Parker, Gianni Lenoci, Vittorino Curci, Marcello Magliocchi. *Serving an Evolving Humanity*. Silta Records, SR1003 (2010).

William Parker and Giorgio Dini. *Temporary*. Silta Records, SR0903 (2009).

William Parker and Hamid Drake. *First Communion + Piercing the Veil*. AUM Fidelity, AUM039/40 (2007).

William Parker and Hamid Drake. *Summer Snow*. AUM Fidelity, AUM041 (2007).

William Parker and ICI Ensemble. *Winter Sun Crying*. Neos Jazz, NEOS 41008 (2011).

William Parker, Konrad Bauer, Hamid Drake. *Tender Exploration*. Jazzwerkstatt, JWL121 (2013).

William Parker and Oluyemi Thomas with Lisa Sokolov + Joe McPhee. *Spiritworld*. Straw2Gold, S2G–004 (2006).

William Parker and Stefano Scodanibbio. *Bass Duo*. Centering Records, CENT1013 (2017).

Records as a Sideperson

Agustí Fernández Trio. *One Night at the Joan Miró Foundation*. Synergy Records,
    SRCD55301 (1999).

Alan Silva and the Celestial Communication Orchestra. *H.Con. Res.57/Treasure Box*.
    Eremite Records, MTE039–MTE042 (2003).

Alan Silva and William Parker. *A Hero's Welcome: Pieces for Rare Occasions*. Eremite,
    MTE017 (1999).

Albert Beger. *Evolving Silence*, 2 vols. Earsay's Jazz, ES097/091 (2006).

Alexandre Pierrepont and Mike Ladd. *Maison Hantee*. Rogue Art, Rog–0017 (2008).

Amy Sheffer. *We'um*. I Am Shee Records (no issue number) (1987).

Arthur Williams. *Forgiveness Suite*. No Business Records, NBLP97 (2016).

Assif Tsahar Trio. *Ein Sof*. Silkheart, SHCD 148 (1997).

Assif Tsahar Trio. *Shekhina*. Eremite Records, MTE04 (1996).

Bill Cole Untempered Ensemble. *Duets and Solos*, 2 vols. Boxholder Records, BXH 011/015
    (2000–2001).

Bill Cole Untempered Ensemble. *Live in Greenfield, Massachusetts, November 20, 1999*.
    Boxholder Records, BXH 008/009 (2000).

Bill Cole Untempered Ensemble. *Proverbs for Sam*. Boxholder Records, BXH 056 (2008).

Bill Cole Untempered Ensemble. *Seasoning the Greens*. Boxholder Records, BXH 031 (2002).

Bill Cole and William Parker. *Two Masters: Live at the Prism*. Boxholder Records, BXH 047
    (2005).

Bill Dixon. *Thoughts*. Soul Note, SN 1111 (1987).

Bill Dixon. *Vade Mecum I*. Soul Note, 121208–2 (1994).

Bill Dixon. *Vade Mecum II*. Soul Note, 121211–2 (1996).

Billy Bang. *Changing Seasons*. Bellows, Bellows 004 (1981).

Billy Bang Sextet. *The Fire from Within*. Soul Note, SN 1086 (1985).

Billy Bang Sextet. *Live at Carlos 1*. Soul Note, 121136–1 (1987).

Billy Bang's Survival Ensemble. *Black Man's Blues*. No Business Records, NBLP 38 (2011).

Billy Bang's Survival Ensemble. *New York Collage*. Anima Records, AN 1002 (1978).

Bobby Zankel and the Wonderful Sound 6. *Celebrating William Parker @ 65*. Not Two
    Records, MW962–2 (2017).

Carlos Ward. *Live at the Bug and Other Sweets*. Peull Music, PM0002 (1995).

Cecil Taylor. *Burning Poles*. Mystic Fire Video, 76240 (1991).

Cecil Taylor. *The Dance Project*. Free Music Productions, FMP 130 (2008).

Cecil Taylor. *In Florescence*. A&M Records, A&M SP 5286 (1990).

Cecil Taylor European Orchestra. *Alms/Tiergarten (Spree)*. Free Music Productions, FMP
    CD 8/9 (1989).

Cecil Taylor Segments II: Orchestra of Two Continents. *Winged Serpent (Sliding
    Quadrants)*. Soul Note, SN 1089 (1985).

Cecil Taylor Unit. *Calling It the Eighth*. Hat Hut, HAT Musics 3508 (1981).

Cecil Taylor Unit. *Live in Bologna*. Leo Records, LR 404/405 (1988).

Cecil Taylor Unit. *Live in Vienna*. Leo Records, LR 408/409 (1988).

Cecil Taylor Unit. *Nicaragua: No Parasan/Willisau '83 Live.* Nica (no issue number) (1984).

Cecil Taylor Unit. *Tzotzil Mummers Tzotzil.* Leo Records, LR 162 (1988).

Charles Gayle. *Consecration.* Black Saint, 120138–2 (1993).

Charles Gayle Quartet. *Blue Shadows.* Silkheart, SHCD 157 (2007).

Charles Gayle Quartet. *Daily Bread.* Black Saint, 120 158–2 (1998).

Charles Gayle Quartet. *More Live at the Knitting Factory February, 1993.* Knitting Factory Works, KFWCD 137 (1993).

Charles Gayle Quartet. *Raining Fire.* Silkheart, SHCD 137 (n.d.).

Charles Gayle Quartet. *Translation.* Silkheart, SHCD 134 (1994).

Christoph Gallio. *À Gertrude Stein.* Percaso Productions, 16 (1996).

Christopher Cauley. *FINland.* Eremite, MTE06 (1996).

Daniel Carter, William Parker, Federico Ughi. *The Dream.* 577 Records, 577–6 (2006).

Daniel Carter, William Parker, Watson Jennison, Federico Ughi. *LIVE!* 577 Records, 5797 (2017).

Dave Burrell Full-Blown Trio. *Expansion.* High Two, HT001 (2004).

Dave Capello and Jeff Albert with William Parker. *New Normal.* Breakfast for Dinner Records, (no issue number) (2016).

David S. Ware. *Onecept.* AUM Fidelity, AUM064 (2010).

David S. Ware. *Shakti.* AUM Fidelity, AUM052 (2008).

David S. Ware Quartet. *BalladWare.* The Blue Series. Thirsty Ear, THI 57173.2 (2006).

David S. Ware Quartet. *Corridors and Parallels.* AUM Fidelity, AUM019 (2001).

David S. Ware Quartet. *Cryptology.* Homestead Records, HMS220–2 (1995).

David S. Ware Quartet. *Dao.* Homestead Records, HMS230–2 (1996).

David S. Ware Quartet. *Earthquation.* DIW Records, DIW–892 (1994).

David S. Ware Quartet. *Flight of I.* DIW Records, DIW–856 (1992).

David S. Ware Quartet. *Freedom Suite.* AUM Fidelity, AUM023 (2002).

David S. Ware Quartet. *Godspelized.* DIW Records, DIW–916 (1996).

David S. Ware Quartet. *Great Bliss,* 2 vols. Silkheart, SHCD 127–128 (n.d.).

David S. Ware Quartet. *Live in the World.* The Blue Series. Thirsty Ear, THI 57153.2 (2005).

David S. Ware Quartet. *Live in Vilnius.* No Business Records, NBLP 4/5 (2009).

David S. Ware Quartet. *Oblations and Blessings.* Silkheart, SHCD 145 (1996).

David S. Ware Quartet. *Renunciation.* AUM Fidelity, AUM042 (2007).

David S. Ware Quartet. *Surrendered.* Sony/Columbia Records, CK63816 (2000).

David S. Ware Quartet. *Third Ear Recitation.* DIW Records, DIW–870 (1993).

David S. Ware Quartet. *Wisdom of Uncertainty.* AUM Fidelity, AUM001 (1997).

David S. Ware String Ensemble. *Threads.* The Blue Series. Thirsty Ear, THI 57137.2 (2003).

David S. Ware Trio. *Live in New York, 2010.* AUM Fidelity, AUM 102/103 (2017).

David S. Ware Trio. *Passage to Music.* Silkheart, SHLP/SHCD 113 (1988).

David S. Ware's Planetary Unknown. *David S. Ware's Planetary Unknown.* AUM Fidelity, AUM068 (2011).

David S. Ware's Planetary Unknown. *Live at Jazzfestival Saalfelden 2011.* AUM Fidelity, AUM074 (2012).

Declared Enemy. *Our Lady of the Flowers.* Rogueart, Rog–0057 (2015).

Declared Enemy. *Salute to 100001 Stars: A Tribute to Jean Genet.* Rogueart, 2006.

Die Like a Dog. *Aoyama Crows.* Free Music Productions, FMP CD 118 (2002).

Die Like a Dog. *Close Up.* Free Music Productions, FMP CD 144 (2011).

Die Like a Dog. *Fragments of Music; Life and Death of Albert Ayler.* Free Music Productions, FMP CD 64 (1994).

Die Like a Dog. *From Valley to Valley.* Eremite, MTE018 (1999).

Die Like a Dog. *Little Birds Have Fast Hearts,* 2 vols. Free Music Productions, FMP CD 97, 101 (1998–99).

Die Like a Dog. *Never Too Late but Always Too Early (Dedicated to Peter Kowald).* Eremite Records, MTE 037/038 (2003).

Dorgon + William Parker. *9.* Jumbo Recordings, Jumbo 1 (1998).

Dorgon + William Parker. *Broken/Circle.* Jumbo Recordings (1998).

Douglas Ewart Quintet. *Crepuscule IV in Powderham Park.* CD4 in *Visionfest/Visionlive.* The Blue Series. Thirsty Ear (2003).

Earl Freeman. *The Universal Jazz Symphonette Presents Soundcraft '75/Fantasy for Orchestra.* Anima Record Co., AN 1001 (1975).

Eddie Gale. *Bach Dancing and Dynamite Society Presents.* Creative View, (no issue number) (2008).

Eddie Gale and the All-Star Band. *Tribute to Coltrane, Live at the San Jose Jazz Festival.* Creative View, 1002006 (2007).

Ellen Christi. *Instant Reality.* NYCAC Records, (no issue number) (1992).

Ellen Christi. *Star of Destiny.* NYCAC Records, NYCAC 504 (1986).

Ellen Christi with Menage. *Live at Irving Plaza.* Soul Note, SN 1097 (1984).

Ellen Christi Quartet. *Synchronicity.* CD7 in *Visionfest/Visionlive.* The Blue Series. Thirsty Ear, THI 57131.2 (2003).

Eri Yamamoto. *Duologue.* AUM Fidelity, AUM048 (2008).

Evan Parker Trio and Peter Brötzmann Trio. *The Bishop's Move.* Victo, 093 (2004).

The Feel Trio. *2 Ts for a Lovely T.* Codanza Records, Codanza One (2002).

The Feel Trio. *Celebrated Blazons.* Free Music Productions, FMP CD 58 (1994).

The Feel Trio. *Looking* (Berlin Version). Free Music Productions, FMP CD 25 (1990).

Frank Lowe. *Black Beings.* ESP-Disk, ESP 3013 (1973).

Frank Lowe Quartet. *Out Loud.* Triple Point Records, TPR209 (2014).

Frode Gjerstad Trio. *Frode Gjerstad with Hamid Drake and William Parker.* Cadence Jazz Records, CJR 1108 (1999).

Frode Gjerstad Trio. *On Reade Street.* FMR, CD256–0208 (2008).

Frode Gjerstad Trio. *The Other Side.* Ayler Records, aylDL–019 (2006).

Frode Gjerstad Trio. *Remember to Forget.* Circulasione Totale, CT 199710 (1998).

Frode Gjerstad Trio. *Ultima.* Cadence Jazz Records, CJR 1108 (1999).

Gianni Lenoci 4tet Featuring William Parker. *Secret Garden.* Silta Records, SR1103 (2011).

Hamid Drake and Bindu. *Blissful.* Rogue Art, Rog–0011 (2008).

Henrik Walsdorff Trio. *Henrik Walsdorff Trio.* Jazzwerkstatt, JW 10135 (2013).

Hocus Pocus Lab Orchestra with William Parker. *What Shall We Do (Without You).* Silta Records, DL001 (2011).

Hugh Ragin. *Revelation*. Justin Time, JTR 8502–2 (2004).

Ivo Perelman. *Book of Sound*. Leo Records, CD LR 697 (2014).

Ivo Perelman. *LIVE*. Zero In Records, Zero In 2 (1997).

Ivo Perelman. *Sad Life*. Leo Records, Leo Lab CD 027 (1996).

Ivo Perelman Quartet. *En Adir (Traditional Jewish Songs)*. Music and Arts, CD–996 (1997).

Ivo Perelman Quartet. *Sound Hierarchy*. Music and Arts, CD–997 (1997).

Ivo Perelman and Matthew Shipp. *The Art of Perelman–Shipp*, vol. 1: *Titan*. Leo Records, CD–LR 794 (2017).

Ivo Perelman and Matthew Shipp. *The Art of Perelman–Shipp*, vol. 3: *Pandora*. Leo Records, CD–LR 796 (2017).

Jack Wright. *Sample Tape 1979–1985*. Spring Garden Music [download] (2015).

Jackson Krall. *Jackson Krall and the Free Music Society*. Stork Music, Stork1003 (1984).

James Brandon Lewis. *Divine Travels*. Sony/OKeh Masterworks, 76664 (2014).

Jeff Cosgrove. *Alternating Current*. Grizzley Music, (no issue number) (2014).

Jemeel Moondoc All-Stars. *Live in Paris*. Cadence Jazz Records, CJR 1151 (2002).

Jemeel Moondoc and Ensemble Muntu. *The Evening of the Blue Men*. Muntu Records, 1002 (1979).

Jemeel Moondoc and Ensemble Muntu. *First Feeding*. Muntu Records, 1001 (1977).

Jemeel Moondoc and Ensemble Muntu. *The Intrepid Live in Poland*. PolJazz, PSJ–106 (1981).

Jemeel Moondoc and Ensemble Muntu. *New York Live!* Cadence Jazz Records, CJR 1006 (1981).

Jemeel Moondoc Quintet. *Nostalgia in Times Square*. Soul Note, SN 1141 (1986).

Jemeel Moondoc Sextet. *Konstanze's Delight*. Soul Note, SN 1041 (1983).

Jemeel Moondoc Trio. *Judy's Bounce*. Soul Note, SN 1051 (1982).

Jemeel Moondoc Trio. *Live at the Glenn Miller Café*, vol. 1. Ayler Records, aylCD–026 (2002).

Jeremy Danneman. *Help*. Ropeadope Records, 32696 (2015).

Jeremy Danneman. *Honey Wine*. Ropeadope Records, (no issue number) (2017).

Jeremy Danneman. *Lady Boom Boom*. Ropeadope Records, (no issue number) (2015).

Jerome Cooper Quintet. *Outer and Interactions*. About Time Records, AT–1008 (1988).

Jim Staley with William Parker and Joey Baron. *Scattered Thoughts: Duets at Roulette*. Einstein Records, EIN020 (2010).

Jimmy Lyons. *Wee Sneezawee*. Black Saint, BSR 0067 (1984).

Jimmy Lyons Quartet. *The Box Set*. Ayler Records, aylCD–036–040 (2003).

Joe Morris Ensemble. *Elsewhere*. Homestead Records, HMS233–2 (1996).

Joe Morris–Rob Brown Quartet. *Illuminate*. Leo Lab, CD 008 (1995).

Joel Futterman, William Parker, Jimmy Williams. *Authenticity*. Kali Records, 0109 (1999).

Joëlle Leandre. *Europa Dgaz: At the Le Mans Jazz Festival*. Leo Records, Leo 458/459 (2006).

John Blum Astrogeny Quartet. *John Blum Astrogeny Quartet*. Eremite Records, MTE049 (2006).

John Blum with Sunny Murray and William Parker. *In the Shade of Sun*. Ecstatic Peace, E#5D (2009).

Kali Z. Fasteau. *An Alternative Universe*. Flying Note Records, Flying Note 9015 (2011).

Kali Z. Fasteau. *VIVID*. Flying Note Records, FNCD 9007 (2001).

Kazutoki "Kappo" Umezu. *Seikatsu Kojyo Iinkai*. SKI No. 1 (1975).

Ken Vandermark. *Momentum 1: Stone*. Catalytic-Sound, KV–112017–009–AGR (2016).

Khan Jamal. *Speak Easy*. Gazell, GJCD 4001 (1989).

Kidd Jordan Quartet. *New Orleans Festival Suite*. Silkheart, SHCD 152 (n.d.).

Konstrukt and William Parker. *Live at NHKM*. Holidays Records, HOL–081 (2015).

Marco Eneidi Coalition. *Marco Eneidi Coalition*. Botticelli Records, 1010 (1994).

Marco Eneidi Quintet. *Final Disconnect Notice*. Botticelli Records, 1011 (1994).

Mat Maneri Featuring Joe McPhee. *Sustain*. The Blue Series. Thirsty Ear, THI 57122.2 (2002).

Mat Maneri Quartet. *Blue Decco*. The Blue Series. Thirsty Ear, THI 57092.2 (2000).

Matthew Shipp. *Nu Bop Live*. RAI Trade, RTPJ 0016 (2009).

Matthew Shipp Horn Quartet. *Strata*. Hatology, 522 (1998).

Matthew Shipp Quartet. *Critical Mass*. 2.13.61 Records, 213CD003 (1995).

Matthew Shipp Quartet. *The Flow of X*. 2.13.61 Records, THI21326.2 (1997).

Matthew Shipp Quartet. *Pastoral Composure*. The Blue Series. Thirsty Ear, THI57084.2 (2000).

Matthew Shipp Quartet. *Points*. Silkheart, SHCD 129 (1990).

Matthew Shipp String Trio. *By the Law of Music*. Hat Hut, HAT ART CD 6200 (1997).

Matthew Shipp String Trio. *Expansion, Power, Release*. Hatology, 558 (2001).

Matthew Shipp Trio. *Circular Temple*. Quinton Records, QTN1 (1992).

Matthew Shipp Trio. *Harmony and Abyss*. The Blue Series. Thirsty Ear, THI 57152.2 (2004).

Matthew Shipp Trio. *The Multiplication Table*. Hatology, 516 (1998).

Matthew Shipp Trio. *Prism*. Brinkman Records, BRCD 058 (1996).

Matthew Shipp Trio. *The Trio Plays Ware*. Splasc(h) Records, CDH 862.2 (2004).

Matthew Shipp's New Orbit. *Matthew Shipp's New Orbit*. Thirsty Ear, THI 57095.2 (2001).

Michael Marcus. *Here At!* Soul Note, 121243–2 (1994).

Michael Marcus. *Under the Wire*. Enja Records, ENJA 6064 (1991).

Michael Marcus Trio. *Ithem*. Ayler Records, aylCD–006 (2004).

Mike Pride. *Mike Pride's Scrambler*. Not Two, MW–766–2 (2005).

Mikko Innanen with William Parker and Andrew Cyrille. *Song for a New Decade*. TUM Records, TUM CD 042–2 (2015).

Morley. *Undivided*. Creative Collective, 01 (2011).

Pasquale Innarella. *Live in the Ghetto*. Terre Sommerse, TSJEI010 (2009).

Paul Dunmall. *Blown Away*. Duns, 053 (2007).

Paula Shocron, William Parker, Pablo Diaz. *Emptying the Self*. Nendo Dango Records, (no issue number) (2017).

Peter Brötzmann Chicago Tentet. *American Landscapes*, 2 vols. Okka Disk, OD12067/12068 (2007).

Peter Brötzmann Chicago Tentet. *Stone/Water*. Okkadisk, OD12032 (2000).

Peter Brötzmann Chicago Tentet Plus Two. *Broken English*. Okka Disk, OD12043 (2002).

Peter Brötzmann Chicago Tentet Plus Two. *Short Visit to Nowhere*. Okka Disk, OD12044 (2002).

Peter Brötzmann Clarinet Project. *Berlin Djungle*. Free Music Productions, FMP 1120 (1987).

Peter Brötzmann Tentet. *The März Combo*. Free Music Productions, CD 47 (1993).

Peter Kuhn Quartet. *The Kill*. Soul Note, SN 1043 (1982).

Peter Kuhn Quintet. *Livin' Right*. Big City Records, LPK 225 (1979).

Peter Kuhn Quintet. *No Coming, No Going: The Music of Peter Kuhn, 1978–79*. No Business Records, NBCD 89–90 (2016).

Peter Kuhn Trio. *Ghost of a Trance*. Hat Hut Records, IR09 (1981).

Philip Wilson. *The Philip Wilson Project*. Jazzdoor, JD 1243 (1991).

Ralphé Malik Quartet. *Companions*. Eremite Records, MTE034 (2002).

Ralphé Malik Quartet. *Last Set: Live at the 1369 Jazz Club*. Boxholder Records, BXH042 (2004).

Rob Brown Ensemble. *Crown Trunk Root Funk*. AUM Fidelity, AUM044 (2008).

Rob Brown Quartet. *The Big Picture*. Marge Records, Marge 31 (2004).

Rob Brown Trio. *Breath Rhyme*. Silkheart, SHLP 122 (1989).

Rob Brown Trio. *High Wire*. Soul Note, 121266 (1996).

Rob Brown Trio. *Round the Bend*. Bleu Regard, CT 1962 (2002).

Roscoe Mitchell and the Note Factory. *Nine to Get Ready*. ECM Records, ECM 1651 (1999).

Roscoe Mitchell and the Note Factory. *This Dance Is for Steve McCall*. Black Saint, 120150–2 (1993).

Roy Campbell. *New Kingdom*. Delmark Records, DE–456 (1992).

Roy Campbell Pyramid. *Ancestral Homeland*. No More Records, No. 7 (1998).

Roy Campbell Pyramid. *Communion*. Silkheart, SHCD 139 (1994).

Roy Campbell Pyramid. *Ethnic Stew and Brew*. Delmark Records, DE–528 (2001).

Roy Campbell and Joe McPhee Tribute to Albert Ayler. *Live at the Dynamo*. Marge, 45 (2009).

Sonny Simmons 25th Century Orchestra. *Sonny Simmons 25th Century Orchestra*. Zing Magazine (no issue number) (2012).

Sonoluminescence Trio. *Cleaning the Mirror*. Otoroku Records, DS004 (2015).

Sonoluminescence Trio. *Live at La Resistenza*. El Negocito Records, eNR041 (2015).

Sonoluminescence Trio. *Live at the Record Centre*. Record Centre Records, RCR–003 (2017).

Sonoluminescence Trio. *Telling Stories*. Art Stew Records, ASR–003 (2015).

Sophia Domancich. *Washed Away*. Marge, 43 (2009).

Stephen Haynes and Pomegranate. *New Music for Bill Dixon*. New Atlantis Records, NA–CD–015 (2015).

Steve Cohn Trio. *WE*. Unseen Rain Records, UR–9997 (2011).

Steve Dalachinsky. *Incomplete Directions*. Knitting Factory Records, KFR–235 (1999).

Steve Swell Quintet. *Soul Travelers*. Rogueart, Rog–0067 (2016).

Steve Swell's Fire into Music. *Steve Swell's Fire into Music*. Ballroom, (no issue number) (2006).

Steve Swell's Fire into Music. *Swimming in a Galaxy of Goodwill and Sorrow*. Rogueart, ROG–0009 (2007).

Steve Swell's Kende Dreams. *Hommage à Bartók*. Silkheart, SHCD 160 (2015).

Takashi Tazamaki. *Eikou no Hata/Live in New York, 1987*. Ombasha Records, OMBA 004 (1988).

Takashi Tazamaki and Kalle Laar. *Floating Flames*. Ear-Rational Records, ECD–1038 (1994).

Thollem McDonas, William Parker, Nels Cline. *The Gowanus Session*. Porter Records, PRCD–4068 (2012).

Tiziano Tononi and Daniele Cavallanti. *Spirits Up Above*. World Series. Splasc(h) Records, CDH 877.2 (2007).

Todd Capp and the Improvising Orchestra. *Volume I: Quintessence*. Lucky Tiger, LT 10013 (1999).

Tony Malaby's Tamarindo. *Somos Agua*. Clean Feed, CF304CD (2014).

Tony Malaby's Tamarindo. *Tamarindo Live*. Clean Feed, CF200CD (2010).

Tony Malaby's Tamarindo. *Tony Malaby's Tamarindo*. Clean Feed, CF 099 (2007).

Toxic. *This Is Beautiful Because We Are Beautiful People*. ESP-Disk, ESP–5011 (2017).

The Turbine! *Entropy/Enthalpy*. Rogue Art, ROG–0058 (2015).

Wayne Horvitz. *Simple Facts*. Theater for Your Mother, TFYM 004 (1980).

Werner Ludi. *Ki*. Intakt, CD 051 (1998).

William Hooker Quartet. *Lifeline*. Silkheart, SHCD 119 (n.d.).

Ye Ren Trio. *Another Shining Path*. Drimala Records, DR 99–347–01 (1999).

Zusaan Kali Fasteau. *Prophecy*. Flying Note Records, FNCD 9003 (1993).

Zusaan Kali Fasteau. *Sensual Hearing*. Flying Note Records, FNCD 9005 (1997).

Introduction: "Flowers Grow in My Room"

Epigraph: William Parker, liner notes, *Through the Acceptance of the Mystery Peace* (Centering Records, 1980).

1. William Parker, liner notes, *Mass for the Healing of the World* (Black Saint, 2003), [1].

2. William Parker, email to author, December 31, 2018.

3. William Parker, liner notes, *Flowers Grow in My Room* (Centering Records, 1994), [3].

4. William Parker, *Who Owns Music? Notes from a Spiritual Journey*, 2nd ed. (Köln: Herausgeberin, 2013), 92.

5. Take, for example, the work of abstract expressionist Jackson Pollock (1912–56), one of whose works graced the cover of the Ornette Coleman record that served as the namesake for the genre.

6. Amiri Baraka [LeRoi Jones], "The Changing Same (R&B and New Black Music)," in *The Black Aesthetic*, ed. Addison Gayle Jr. (Garden City, NY: Doubleday, 1971), 126.

7. Saidiya Hartman examines the erasure of histories of enslaved peoples in devastating detail and insight. Saidiya Hartman, *Lose Your Mother: A Journey along the Atlantic Slave Route* (New York: Farrar, Straus and Giroux, 2007).

8. Christina Sharpe, *In the Wake: On Blackness and Being* (Durham, NC: Duke University Press, 2016), 7.

9. Sharpe, *In the Wake*, 7–8.

10. Hartman, *Lose Your Mother*, 6.

11. William Parker, "Introduction," *Bill Collector*, August 1984, n.p.

Chapter 1: Enslavement and Resistance

Epigraph: Sun Ra, "'The Visitation,'" in *Black Fire! An Anthology of Afro-American Writing*, ed. Larry Neal and LeRoi Jones (New York: William Morrow, 1968), 213.

1. Estimates of the number of people involved in the Great Migration in these years vary. U.S. Bureau of the Census, *Historical Statistics of the United States: Colonial Times to 1970* (Washington, DC: U.S. Government Printing Office, 1975), 95; Robert H. Zieger, *For Jobs and Freedom: Race and Labor in America since 1865* (Lexington: University of Kentucky Press, 2007), 70–71; Sarah-Jane Mathieu, "The African American Great Migration Reconsidered," in "North American Migrations," special issue, *OAH Magazine of History* 23, no. 4 (2009): 20.

2. As late as 1950, Jefferson family letters discuss the cotton harvest. Ethel Williams, Cope, SC, to Mary L. Parker, Bronx, NY, September 5, 1950, William Parker private archive.

3. An estimated 90 percent of enslaved people from the Bight of Biafra were Igbo. The Kingdom of Nri translates as *Ọ̀ràézè Ǹrì*. David Hackett Fischer and James C. Kelly, *Bound Away: Virginia and the Westward Movement* (Charlottesville: University Press of Virginia, 1994), 60, 62; A. E. Afigbo, "Traditions of Igbo Origins: A Comment," *History in Africa* 10 (1983): 1–10; J. Akuma-Kalu Njoku, "Establishing Igbo Community Tradition in the United States: Lessons from Folkloristics," *Journal of American Folklore* 125, no. 497 (2012): 330.

4. Nancy C. Neaher, "Igbo Metalsmiths among the Southern Edo," *African Arts* 9, no. 4 (1976): 46–49; Paul T. Craddock et al., "Metal Sources and the Bronzes from Igbo-Ukwu, Nigeria," *Journal of Field Archaeology* 24, no. 4 (1997): 405–29.

5. Igbo-Ukwu translates as Great Igbo. David Northrup, "The Growth of Trade among the Igbo before 1800," *Journal of African History* 13, no. 2 (1972): 217–21.

6. Northrup, "The Growth of Trade," 221; J. E. G. Sutton, "The International Factor at Igbo-Ukwu," *African Archaeological Review* 9 (1991): 146–57; Elizabeth Isichei, *A History of African Societies to 1870* (Cambridge: Cambridge University Press, 1997), 247. For a broad overview of historical and anthropological research done on Igbo-Ukwu and the region, see A. E. Afigbo, "Anthropology and Historiography of Central-South Nigeria before and since Igbo-Ukwu," *History in Africa* 23 (1996): 1–15.

7. Northrup, "Growth of Trade among the Igbo," 218, 220, 227–30.

8. J. N. Lo-Bamijoko, "Classification of Igbo Musical Instruments, Nigeria," *African Music* 6, no. 4 (1987): 26.

9. Meki Nzewi, "Ancestral Polyphony," *African Arts* 11, no. 4 (1978): 74.

10. By guitar, Equiano refers to some form of xalam, the precursor of the American banjo. Stickado refers to a xylophone. Olaudah Equiano, *The Interesting Narrative and Other Writings*, ed. Vincent Carretta (New York: Penguin, 2003), 34, 242nn45–46.

11. *Eadas* is an Igbo word for an edible tuber. By Indian corn, he refers to maize, which had been transplanted from the Americas to West Africa by that time and was distinguished from millet, which was also grown there. Equiano, *The Interesting Narrative*, 35, 242nn52–53.

12. Equiano, *The Interesting Narrative*, 37, 35–36.

13. Northrup, "Growth of Trade," 231, 247–48.

14. Chukwuma Azuonye, "Ìgbò ènwē ézè: Monarchical Power versus Democratic Values in Igbo Oral Narratives," in *Power, Marginality and African Oral Literature*, ed. Graham Furniss

and Liz Gunner (Cambridge: Cambridge University Press, 2008), 65; Axel Harneit-Sievers, *Constructions of Belonging: Igbo Communities and the Nigerian State in the Twentieth Century* (Rochester, NY: Boydell and Brewer, 2006), 48.

15. P. A. Oguagha, "The Impact of European Trade on Igbo-Igala Commercial Relations in the Lower Niger, c. 1650–1850 AD," *Journal of the Historical Society of Nigeria* 11, no. 3/4 (1982–1983): 14.

16. It has been estimated that the Igbo accounted for approximately 80 percent of the 20,000 people who were sold into slavery via Bonny on an annual basis in the late eighteenth century. J. Adams, *Sketches Taken during Ten Voyages to Africa, between the Years 1786 and 1800; Including Observation on the Country between Cape Palmas and the River Congo; and Cursory Remarks on the Physical and Moral Character of the Inhabitants* (London: Hurst, Robinson, 1832), 38–40; G. Ugo Nwokeji, "The Atlantic Slave Trade and Population Density: A Historical Demography of the Biafran Hinterland," in "On Slavery and Islam in African History: A Tribute to Martin Klein," special issue, *Canadian Journal of African Studies* 34, no. 3 (2000): 618.

17. Douglas B. Chambers, "'My Own Nation': Igbo Exiles in the Diaspora," *Slavery and Abolition* 18, no. 1 (1997): 72–97; Paul E. Lovejoy, "Ethnic Designations of the Slave Trade and the Reconstruction of the History of Trans-Atlantic Slavery," in *Trans-Atlantic Dimensions of Ethnicity in the African Diaspora*, eds. Paul E. Lovejoy and David V. Trotman (London: Continuum, 2003), 31; Michael A. Gomez, "A Quality of Anguish: The Igbo Response to Enslavement in North America," in *Trans-Atlantic Dimensions of Ethnicity in the African Diaspora*, ed. Paul E. Lovejoy and David V. Trotman (London: Continuum, 2003), 83–85; Renee Soulodre-La France, "'I, Francisco Castañeda, Negro Esclavo Caravali': Caravali Ethnicity in Colonial New Granada," in *Trans-Atlantic Dimensions of Ethnicity in the African Diaspora*, ed. Paul E. Lovejoy and David V. Trotman (London: Continuum, 2003), 101–3; Verene A. Shepherd, "Ethnicity, Colour and Gender in the Experiences of Enslaved Women on Non-Sugar Properties in Jamaica," in *Trans-Atlantic Dimensions of Ethnicity in the African Diaspora*, ed. Paul E. Lovejoy and David V. Trotman (London: Continuum, 2003), 198; Njoku, "Establishing Igbo Community Tradition," 330.

18. Whydah is the anglicized version of *Xwéda* from the Yoruba language and gave name to the present-day coastal city of Ouidah in Benin. Robin Law, "Ideologies of Royal Power: The Dissolution and Reconstruction of Political Authority on the 'Slave Coast,' 1680–1750," *Africa: Journal of the International African Institute* 57, no. 3 (1987): 321; Robin Law, "The Slave Trade in Seventeenth-Century Allada: A Revision," *African Economic History*, no. 22 (1994): 59–92.

19. David Ross, "Robert Norris, Agaja, and the Dahomean Conquest of Allada and Whydah," *History in Africa* 16 (1989); Robin Law, "'The Common People Were Divided': Monarchy, Aristocracy and Political Factionalism in the Kingdom of Whydah, 1671–1727," *International Journal of African Historical Studies* 23, no. 2 (1990): 201–29.

20. Catherine Hutton, *The Tour of Africa: Containing a Concise Account of All the Countries in That Quarter of the Globe, Hitherto Visited by Europeans; with the Manners and Customs of the Inhabitants* (London: Baldwin, Cradock and Joy, 1821), 2:322–34.

21. Robin Law, "Dahomey and the Slave Trade: Reflections on the Historiography of the Rise of Dahomey," in "Special Issue in Honour of J. D. Fage," *Journal of African History* 27, no. 2 (1986): 237–67; Robin Law, "Slave-Raiders and Middlemen, Monopolists and Free-Traders: The Supply of Slaves for the Atlantic Trade in Dahomey c. 1715–1850," *Journal of African History* 30, no. 1 (1989): 45–68; Robert S. Smith, *Warfare and Diplomacy in Pre-colonial West Africa*, 2nd ed. (Madison: University of Wisconsin Press, 1989), 48, 122; Stanley B. Alpern, *Amazons of Black Sparta: The Women Warriors of Dahomey* (New York: New York University Press, 1998), 165; John K. Thornton, *Warfare in Atlantic Africa 1500–1800* (London: Routledge, 1999), 79, 82, 86.

22. Gomez, "A Quality of Anguish," 84; Gregory E. O'Malley, "Diversity in the Slave Trade to the Colonial Carolinas," in *Creating and Contesting Carolinas: Proprietary Era Histories*, ed. Michelle LeMaster and Bradford J. Wood (Columbia: University of South Carolina Press, 2013), 241–46.

23. Mali has been anglicized from Nyeni or Niani (Manding languages).

24. D. T. Niane, *Sundiata: An Epic of Old Mali*, rev. ed. (London: Pearson, 2006).

25. Roderick J. McIntosh and Susan Keech McIntosh, "The Inland Niger Delta before the Empire of Mali: Evidence from Jenne-Jeno," *Journal of African History* 22, no. 1 (1981): 1, 7–8; Timothy A. Insoll, "The Road to Timbuktu: Trade and Empire," *Archaeology* 53, no. 6 (2000): 48–52; Sophie Sarin, "In the Shadow of Timbuktu: The Manuscripts of Djenné," in *From Dust to Digital: Ten Years of the Endangered Archives Programme*, ed. Maja Kominko (New York: Open Book, 2015), 173–87.

26. Jan Jansen, "The Representation of Status in Mande: Did the Mali Empire Still Exist in the Nineteenth Century?" *History in Africa* 23 (1996): 87–89.

27. O'Malley, "Diversity in the Slave Trade," 241–46.

28. Jansen, "The Representation of Status in Mande," 83.

29. Daniel Kloza, "African Origins of Igbo Slave Resistance in the Americas," in *Olaudah Equiano and the Igbo World: History, Society and Atlantic Diaspora Connections*, ed. Chima J. Korieh (Trenton: Africa World Press, 2009), 351.

30. Fischer and Kelly, *Bound Away*, 63, 64.

31. Gomez, "A Quality of Anguish," 89–92.

32. Chima J. Korieh, "Igbo Identity in Africa and the Atlantic Diaspora," in *Olaudah Equiano and the Igbo World: History, Society and Atlantic Diaspora Connections*, ed. Chima J. Korieh (Trenton: Africa World Press, 2009), 301–2; Gomez, "A Quality of Anguish," 84–89.

33. Quoted in Gomez, "A Quality of Anguish," 89.

34. Cited in Gwendolyn M. Hall, *Slavery and African Ethnicities in the Americas: Restoring the Links* (Chapel Hill: University of North Carolina Press, 2005), 126.

35. Douglas B. Chambers, *Murder at Montpelier: Igbo Africans in Virginia* (Jackson: University Press of Mississippi, 2005), 159.

36. Chambers, "'My Own Nation,'" 85.

37. David Evans, "The Reinterpretation of African Musical Instruments in the United States," in *The African Diaspora: African Origins and New World Identities*, ed. Isidore Okpewho et al. (Bloomington: Indiana University Press, 2001), 382–86.

38. LeRoi Jones, *Blues People: Negro Music in White America and the Music That Developed from It* (New York: Morrow Quill, 1963), 17.

39. By 1810–20, Virginians of African descent were being mostly sold and forcibly relocated to other parts of the South. See Fischer and Kelly, *Bound Away*, 230–31.

40. Jefferson family letters discuss attending church revivals. Ethel Jefferson and Lemuel Jefferson Jr., Orangeburg, SC, to Mary Louise Jefferson et al., New York, NY, August 16, 1939, William Parker private archive.

41. Jayne Morris-Crowther, "An Economic Study of the Substantial Slaveholders of Orangeburg County, 1860–1880," *South Carolina Historical Magazine* 86, no. 4 (1985): 296–98.

42. 1880 U.S. Census, township of Orange, Orangeburg County, South Carolina, population schedule, p. 58, enumeration district 149, dwelling 577, family 481, Thomas Glover (NARA microfilm publication T9, roll 1237); 1900 U.S. Census, township of Orange, Orangeburg County, South Carolina, population schedule, sheet 17, enumeration district 65, dwelling 319, family 321, Thomas Glover (NARA microfilm publication T623, roll 1241); 1920 U.S. Census, township of Orangeburg, Orangeburg County, South Carolina, population schedule, enumeration district 70, sheet 11B, dwelling 216, family 217, Thomas M. Glover (NARA microfilm publication T625, roll 1705); 1930 U.S. Census, township of Orange, Orangeburg County, South Carolina, population schedule, enumeration district 38–7, sheet 15A, dwelling 308, family 354, Thomas Glover (NARA microfilm publication T626, roll 2341).

43. 1900 U.S. Census, township of Orange, Orangeburg County, South Carolina, population schedule, sheet 17, enumeration district 65, dwelling 319, family 321, Thomas Glover (NARA microfilm publication T623, roll 1241).

44. Lemuel Jefferson Jr., Fort Bragg, NC, to Mary Louise Jefferson, New York, NY, December 4, 1940, William Parker private archive.

45. The word *buckra* is derived from *mbakara* in either the Efik or Ibibio language in what is now Nigeria. William Parker, interview by author, digital recording, February 2, 2016.

46. Ethel Jefferson and Lemuel Jefferson Jr., Orangeburg, SC, to Mary Louise Jefferson et al., New York, NY, August 16, 1939, William Parker private archive; Lemuel Jefferson Sr. (scribed by Lemuel Jefferson Jr.) Orangeburg, SC, to Mary Louise Jefferson et al., New York, NY, August 30, 1939, William Parker private archive; Lemuel Jefferson Jr., Fort Bragg, NC, to Mary Louise Jefferson, New York, NY, December 4, 1940, William Parker private archive; Lemuel Jefferson Jr., Fort Bragg, NC, to Mary Louise Jefferson, New York, NY, December 18, 1940, William Parker private archive.

47. Cornelius O. Cathey, *Agriculture in North Carolina before the Civil War* (Raleigh, NC: State Department of Archives and History, 1966), 10–12, 42–44.

48. Duncan P. Randall, "Wilmington, North Carolina: The Historical Development of a Port City," *Annals of the Association of American Geographers* 58, no. 3 (1968): 445.

49. Lisa Y. Henderson, "The Involuntary Apprenticeship of Free People of Color in Wayne County, North Carolina, 1830–1860" (master's thesis, Columbia University, 1990), 8.

50. By contrast, the population of enslaved people increased 8 percent and the white population only by 1.5 percent during the same period.

51. The 1860 census records 737 free Black people in Wayne County (out of a total free Black population in the state of 30,463); Robert P. Stuckert, "Free Black Populations of the Southern Appalachian Mountains: 1860," *Journal of Black Studies* 23, no. 3 (1993): 359.

52. Deed Book 16, Register of Deeds Office, Wayne County Courthouse, Goldsboro, NC, 16, 360.

53. Henderson, "The Involuntary Apprenticeship of Free People of Color," 8–10.

54. *Cape Fear Recorder*, September 14, 1831; John Hope Franklin, *The Free Negro in North Carolina, 1790–1860* (New York: W. W. Norton, [1943] 1971), 71, 74, 211–21; Henderson, "The Involuntary Apprenticeship of Free People of Color," 10–11.

55. Henderson, "The Involuntary Apprenticeship of Free People of Color."

56. 1850 U.S. Census, Duplin County, North Carolina, population schedule, North Division, p. 10A (printed, 19 handwritten), dwelling 143, family 143, Elizabeth Parker (NARA microfilm publication M432, roll 629).

57. 1850 U.S. Census; 1860 U.S. Census, Cumberland County, North Carolina, population schedule, Cumberland East, p. 47, dwelling 318, family 322, Betsey Parker (NARA microfilm publication M653, roll 894); 1870 U.S. Census, Wayne County, North Carolina, population schedule, township of Brogden, p. 55, dwelling 436, family 436, Betsey Parker (NARA microfilm publication M593, roll 1165); 1880 U.S. Census, Wayne County, North Carolina, population schedule, township of Brogden, enumeration district 295, p. 44, dwelling 400, family 400, Betsey Parker (NARA microfilm publication T9, roll 986).

58. "Our Heritage," *Mount Olive Tribune*, July 9, 1993.

59. James H. Merrell, *The Indians' New World: Catawbas and Their Neighbors from European Contact through the Era of Removal* (Chapel Hill: University of North Carolina Press, 1989), 95–97, 102, 106, 110–13, 129.

60. Rebecca S. Seib, *Settlement Pattern Study of the Indians of Robeson County, N.C., 1735–1787* (Pembroke, NC: Lumbee Regional Development Association, 1983), 3, 8–13, 54, 62, 79; Julian T. Pierce et al., *The Lumbee Petition* (Pembroke, NC: Lumbee River Legal Services, 1987), 1:11–16; Malinda Maynor Lowery, *Lumbee Indians in the Jim Crow South: Race, Identity and the Making of a Nation*, First Peoples: New Directions in Indigenous Studies (Chapel Hill: University of North Carolina Press, 2010), 5–6.

61. Malinda Maynor Lowery, *The Lumbee Indians: An American Struggle* (Chapel Hill: University of North Carolina, 2018), 32. Theda Perdue and Michael D. Green, *The Columbia Guide to American Indians of the Southeast* (New York: Columbia University Press, 2001),

132. Drowning Creek's strategic placement was not lost on European settlers. In 1781, for example, a group of Scottish loyalists to the British crown gathered there in a late, desperate attempt to thwart the American rebels. See Gregory De Van Massey, "The British Expedition to Wilmington, January–November, 1781," *North Carolina Historical Review* 66, no. 4 (1989): 387.

62. Karen I. Blu, *The Lumbee Problem: The Making of an American Indian People* (New York: Cambridge University Press, 1980), 43–44.

63. Lowery, *Lumbee Indians in the Jim Crow South*, xi; see also 23, 43. Burnt Swamp contained some of the oldest Native American settlements and the highest concentrations of Native American and African American populations after the Civil War. Later generations of the Winn family moved back to Burnt Swamp Township, and many married Lumbee Indians who also dwelled there or in neighboring areas of Robeson County, despite the increasingly racialized politics that unfolded after the collapse of Reconstruction and the renewal of white supremacy. The most prominent were the brothers John (b. 1859) and Joe Winn (1865–1911), but many other descendants also gravitated to the Robeson area. 1900 U.S. Census, Robeson County, North Carolina, Indian population schedule, enumeration district 104, sheet 17, dwelling 66, family 67, Joe Winn (NARA microfilm publication T623, roll 1241); 1910 U.S. Census, Robeson County, North Carolina, population schedule, enumeration district 102, sheet 11B, dwelling 197, family 197, John Winn (NARA microfilm publication T624, roll 1129); 1920 U.S. Census, Robeson County, North Carolina, population schedule, enumeration district 120, sheet 5B, dwelling 91, family 91, John Winn (NARA microfilm publication T625, roll 1319); Robert C. Lawrence, *The State of Robeson* (New York: J. Little and Ives, 1939), 94–96; Lowery, *The Lumbee Indians: An American Struggle*, 33.

64. Sylviane A. Diouf, *Slavery's Exiles: The Story of the American Maroons* (New York: New York University Press, 2014), 131, 132.

65. Native Americans of Robeson County joined together with free people of African descent in the uprising of 1773, for example. Racial classifications imposed in the late nineteenth century would fracture the community by causing tension between groups. Mark D. Groover, "Creolization and the Archaeology of Multiethnic Households in the American South," in "Evidence of Creolization in the Consumer Goods of an Enslaved Bahamian Family," special issue, *Historical Archaeology* 34, no. 3 (2000): 102–4; Lowery, *The Lumbee Indians: An American Struggle*, 42.

66. "The Dismal Swamp," *Inter Ocean*, September 21, 1878; Diouf, *Slavery's Exiles*, 209, 226. The swamp's reputation as a site of maroon communities is underscored in that it is the setting of Harriet Beecher Stowe's second novel, *Dred: A Tale of the Great Dismal Swamp* (Boston: Phillips, Sampson, 1856).

67. Frederick Douglass, *My Bondage and My Freedom* (New York: Miller, Orton and Mulligan, 1855), 436; "The South," *Niles' Register*, September 17, 1831; "Somewhat Alarming," *Norwich Courier*, September 21, 1831; "The Insurrection," *New Hampshire Gazette*, September 6, 1831; Edmund Jackson, "The Virginia Maroons," *Liberty Bell*, January 1, 1852.

68. John Ferdinand Smyth Stuart, *A Tour in the United States of America* (London: G. Robinson, J. Robson, and J. Sewel, 1784), 2:102; "The Great Dismal," *Daily Advertiser*, August 13, 1790;

James Redpath, *The Roving Editor, or Talks with Slaves in the Southern States* (New York: A. B. Burdick, 1859), 293; Frederick Law Olmstead, *A Journey in the Back Country* (New York: Mason Brothers, 1860), 159; Johann David Schoepf, *Travels in the Confederation, 1783–1784*, trans. and ed. Alfred J. Morrison (Philadelphia: William Campbell, 1911), 2:100; "The Dismal Swamp," *Sun*, April 17, 1845; Robert Arnold, *The Dismal Swamp and Lake Drummond: Early Recollections* (Norfolk, VA: Green, Burke and Gregory, 1888), 38–41; Robert C. McLean, ed., "A Yankee Tutor in the Old South," *North Carolina Historical Review* 48, no. 1 (1970): 62.

69. Redpath, *The Roving Editor*, 292; Diouf, *Slavery's Exiles*, 216.

70. "Peat in the Dismal Swamp," *DeBow's Review* 4, no. 4 (1867): 371; Alexander Hunter, "Through the Dismal Swamp," *Potter's American Monthly* 17, no. 115 (1881): 7; Alexander Hunter, "The Great Dismal Swamp," *Outing* 27, no. 1 (1895): 70; Frederick Street, "In the Dismal Swamp," *Frank Leslie's Popular Monthly*, March 1903, 530; Henry Clapp Jr., *The Pioneer or Leaves from an Editor's Portfolio* (Lynn, MA: J. B. Tolman, 1846), 77; Roy F. Johnson, *Tales from Old Carolina: Traditional and Historical Sketches of the Area between and about the Chowan River and the Great Dismal Swamps* (Murfreesboro, NC: Johnson Publishing, 1965), 162–63.

71. Street, "In the Dismal Swamp," 530.

72. Isaac Weld, *Travels through the States of North America* (London: John Stockdale, 1799), 1:179; "The Game of the Dismal Swamp," *Forest and Stream* 38, no. 21 (1892): 420; Hunter, "The Great Dismal Swamp," 70; "The Dismal Swamp and Its Occupants," *Natural Science News* 1, no. 37 (1895): 146; Johnson, *Tales from Old Carolina*, 162–63; Diouf, *Slavery's Exiles*, 223; Stuart, *A Tour in the United States*, 102; Alfred Trumble, "Through the Dismal Swamp," *Frank Leslie's Popular Monthly*, April 1881, 409; Schoepf, *Travels*, 100.

73. Bruce A. Sorrie et al., "Noteworthy Plants from Fort Bragg and Camp McKall, North Carolina," *Castanea* 62, no. 4 (1997): 241.

74. E. J. Crossman, "The Redfin Pickerel, Esox a. americanus in North Carolina," *Copeia*, no. 1 (1962): 118.

75. Lowery, *The Lumbee Indians: An American Struggle*, 32.

76. Cedar trees also afforded knowledgeable healers some remedies. Thomas E. Ross, *One Land, Three Peoples: An Atlas of Robeson County, North Carolina* (private printing, 1992), 34; Arvis Locklear Boughman and Loretta Oxendine, *Herbal Remedies of the Lumbee Indians* (Jefferson, NC: McFarland, 2003), 101–2; Lowery, *The Lumbee Indians: An American Struggle*, 32.

77. Hunter, "The Great Dismal Swamp," 71; Street, "In the Dismal Swamp," 530; Diouf, *Slavery's Exiles*, 225.

78. "Our Heritage," *Mount Olive Tribune*, July 9, 1993.

79. Winn Family Marker, Center Street, Mount Olive, NC.

80. Some of the early property acquisitions were made by Adam Winn Sr., but these were inherited at some point by Adam Winn Jr. It is not always clear which Adam is indicated in individual records, but certainly by the 1830s, the Adam Winn appearing in the records

was the younger. Grantee Book 7A, p. 97, Duplin County Register of Deeds Office; Grantee Book 8A, p. 239, DCRD; Grantee Book 1–5–10–14–15, p. 155, DCRD; Grantee Book 8B, p. 128, DCRD; Duplin County Tax Records, North Carolina State Archive; Grantee Book 1–5–10–14–15, p. 155, DCRD; Grantee Book 12, pp. 70–72, DCRD.

81. The 1850 agricultural schedule for Duplin County lists Winn as owning 400 improved acres and 1,500 unimproved acres with a total value of $3,800. He also possessed farm implements valued at $100, 6 horses, 6 milch cows, 30 other cattle, 6 asses and mules, 2 oxen, 20 sheep, and 60 swine, with the total livestock value at $715. Also, he had in his stores 350 bushels of Indian corn, 10 bushels of oats, 70 pounds of wool, 100 bushels of peas and beans, 3 bushels of Irish potatoes, 1,000 bushels of sweet potatoes, and 450 pounds of butter, with the total of homemade manufactures valued at $42. See https://ncfpc.net/tag/winn.

82. One brief overview of African American slaveholders is Thomas J. Pressly, "The Known World of Free Black Slaveholders: A Research Note on the Scholarship of Carter G. Woodson," in "The African American Experience in the Western States," special issue, *Journal of African American History* 91, no. 1 (2006): 81–87.

83. "Adam Wynne" sold four of his enslaved children in 1852 to Dr. Dortch of Stantonsburg, Mr. John Davis of Lenoir, and Mr. Fornifold "Fourney" Jernigan of Wayne (the last of these figures being a notorious kidnapper and enslaver of free Black children in the area). At the death of Jernigan in 1858, Adam sued to recover six of his children (indicating that additional ones had either been sold to Jernigan or kidnapped). *North-Carolina State*, March 17, 1852, https://ncfpc.net/tag/winn; *William K. Lane v. Jane Bennett et al.*, 56 NC 371 (1858), https://ncfpc.net/2013/04/28/not-so-fast-those-slaves-are-mine.

84. 1850 U.S. Census, Duplin County, North Carolina, population schedule, North Division, p. 10A (printed, 19 handwritten), dwelling 143, family 143, Elizabeth Parker (NARA microfilm publication M432, roll 629). Free Black people being descended from free white mothers was one of the more common origins of such families in North Carolina; the law indicated that children born of free mothers were also free. Warren Milteer, "The Complications of Liberty: Free People of Color in North Carolina from the Colonial Period through Reconstruction" (PhD diss., University of North Carolina, 2013), 25–33.

85. 1870 U.S. Census, Wayne County, North Carolina, population schedule, township of Brogden, p. 55, dwelling 436, family 436, Betsey Parker (NARA microfilm publication M593, roll 1165); 1850 U.S. Census, Duplin County, North Carolina, population schedule, North Division, p. 10A (printed, 19 handwritten), dwelling 143, family 143, Elizabeth Parker (NARA microfilm publication M432, roll 629).

86. 1860 U.S. Census, Cumberland County, North Carolina, population schedule, Cumberland East, p. 47, dwelling 318, family 322, Betsey Parker (NARA microfilm publication M653, roll 894); 1870 U.S. Census, Wayne County, North Carolina, population schedule, township of Brogden, p. 55, dwelling 436, family 436, Betsey Parker (NARA microfilm publication M593, roll 1165); 1880 U.S. Census, Wayne County, North Carolina, population schedule, township of Brogden, enumeration district 295, p. 44, dwelling 400, family 400, Betsey Parker (NARA microfilm publication T9, roll 986).

87. Eric Anderson, *Race and Politics in North Carolina 1872–1901: The Black Second* (Baton Rouge: Louisiana State University Press, 1981), 9; Judkin Browning, "Visions of Freedom and Civilization Opening before Them: African Americans Search for Autonomy during Military Occupation in North Carolina," in *North Carolinians in the Era of the Civil War and Reconstruction*, ed. Paul D. Escott (Chapel Hill: University of North Carolina Press, 2008), 71.

88. H. Nutt, letter to Z. B. Vance, December 12, 1864, reprinted in W. Buck Yearns and John G. Barrett, eds., *North Carolina Civil War Documentary* (Chapel Hill, NC: University of North Carolina Press, 1980, reprinted 2002), 257–58.

89. Lowry's band included Lumbees, free and enslaved Black people, and poor white people from Robeson County and nearby areas. William McKee Evans, *To Die Game: The Story of the Lowry Band, Indian Guerrillas of Reconstruction* (Syracuse, NY: Syracuse University Press, 1995).

90. *Goldsboro Star*, May 28, 1881.

91. And challenging the prevailing narrative that the Ku Klux Klan's activities diminished rapidly after its initial popularity among some white North Carolina communities in the early 1870s, the *Goldsboro Star* wrote about the threat that the organization posed to the African American community there. *Goldsboro Star*, July 9, 1881.

92. Anderson, *Race and Politics in North Carolina*, 329–30.

93. The paper ran from the mid- to late 1880s until 1913.

94. 1880 U.S. Census, Wayne County, North Carolina, population schedule, township of Brogden, enumeration district 295, p. 44, dwelling 400, family 400, Betsey Parker (NARA microfilm publication T9, roll 986).

95. As late as 1962, Willie Parker maintained a correspondence with Parker's father, Thomas. Willie Tyson Parker, Death Certificate, North Carolina State Board of Health, Bureau of Vital Statistics; Willie T. Parker, Goldsboro, NC, to Thomas Bill Parker, Bronx, NY, October 3 1962, William Parker private archive.

96. 1910 U.S. Census, Wayne County, North Carolina, population schedule, enumeration district 103, sheet 19B, dwelling 381, family 381, Dortch Parker (NARA microfilm publication T674, roll 1137); Leonard Rogoff, *Down Home: Jewish Life in North Carolina* (Chapel Hill: University of North Carolina Press, 2010), 46; Mark Bauman, "Southern Jewish Women and Their Social Service Organizations," *Journal of American Ethnic History* 22, no. 3 (2003): 54.

97. 1930 U.S. Census, Wayne County, North Carolina, population schedule, city of Goldsboro, enumeration district, 96–17, sheet 7A, dwelling 132, family 151, Dortch Parker (NARA microfilm publication T626, roll 2341).

98. 1870 U.S. Census, Wayne County, North Carolina, population schedule, township of Brogden, p. 55, dwelling 436, family 436, Betsey Parker (NARA microfilm publication M593, roll 1165); 1880 U.S. Census, Wayne County, North Carolina, population schedule, township of Brogden, enumeration district 295, p. 44, dwelling 400, family 400, Betsey Parker (NARA microfilm publication T9, roll 986).

99. Map Collection, University of North Carolina, http://dc.lib.unc.edu/cdm/ref/collection/ncmaps/id/506.

100. 1900 U.S. Census, Wayne County, North Carolina, population schedule, township of Goldsboro, enumeration district 101, sheet 20, dwelling 450, family 457, Dallas Dickson (NARA microfilm publication T623, roll 1241); 1910 U.S. Census, Wayne County, North Carolina, population schedule, enumeration district 103, sheet 19B, dwelling 373, family 373, Dallas Dixon (NARA microfilm publication T674, roll 1137).

101. Sarah Bryan and Beverly Patterson, *African American Music Trails of Eastern North Carolina* (Raleigh: North Carolina Arts Council, 2013), 47–55.

102. Bryan and Patterson, *African American Music Trails*, 51–52.

103. Alando Mitchell, quoted in Bryan and Patterson, *African American Music Trails*, 51.

104. Mitchell, quoted in Bryan and Patterson, *African American Music Trails*, 52.

105. Bryan and Patterson, *African American Music Trails*, 51.

106. Bryan and Patterson, *African American Music Trails*, 53.

107. Jurden "Chick" Wooten, quoted in Bryan and Patterson, *African American Music Trails*, 62–63.

108. "Harlemites," *Goldsboro News-Argus*, July 3, 1937, 3.

109. Bryan and Patterson, *African American Music Trails*, 4.

110. Rory McVeigh, *The Rise of the Ku Klux Klan: Right-Wing Movements and National Politics*, Social Movements, Protest, and Contention 32 (Minneapolis: University of Minnesota Press, 2009), 152, 158–59.

111. William Parker, interview by author, digital recording, July 29, 2016.

112. Joyce Hansen, "A Place for Everyone," *Bronx County Historical Society Journal* 42, no. 2 (2005): 73.

113. Gilbert Osofsky, "Harlem: The Making of a Ghetto," in *Harlem: A Community in Transition*, ed. John Henrik Clarke (New York: Citadel, 1969), 378.

114. 1940 U.S. Census, New York County, New York, population schedule, Manhattan, enumeration district 31–1940, sheet 62B, household 212, Dortch Parker (NARA microfilm publication T627, roll 2671).

115. Mary Louise Jefferson filed for divorce from Pratt in 1944. Mary L. Pratt, New York, NY, to Hester and Clark, Attorneys and Counsellors at Law, Savannah, GA, June 16, 1944, William Parker private archive.

116. Lemuel Jefferson Jr., Fort Bragg, NC, to Mary Louise Jefferson, New York, NY, December 18, 1940, William Parker private archive.

117. See the Harlem map in this chapter. Steven Watson, *The Harlem Renaissance: Hub of African-American Culture, 1920–1930*, Circles of the Twentieth Century (New York: Pantheon, 1995), 2.

118. Watson, *The Harlem Renaissance*, 131–32.

119. Christopher Gray, "Tracing Scott Joplin's Life through His Addresses," *New York Times*, February 4, 2007.

120. Watson, *The Harlem Renaissance*, 131–32.

121. Watson, *The Harlem Renaissance*, 131–32.

122. Watson, *The Harlem Renaissance*, 131–32.

123. Watson, *The Harlem Renaissance*, 86, 106, 125–28, 131–32, 158.

124. Lynne Fauley Emery, *Black Dance from 1619 to Today*, 2nd ed. (Hightstown, NJ: Princeton Book Co., 1988), 220–21.

125. Emery, *Black Dance from 1619 to Today*, 221, 234–35.

126. A letter from Mary Louise Jefferson's aunt Caroline "Carrie" Jefferson refers to the former as "Mrs. Mary L. Parker" and refers to her "hubbie" in the body of the letter, although the couple were not legally married until October 14, 1958. Caroline Jefferson, Orangeburg, SC, to Mary L. Parker, Bronx, NY, January 15, 1945, William Parker private archive.

Chapter 2: Struggle, Beauty, and Survival

Epigraph: Sonia Sanchez, "poem at thirty," in *Black Fire! Anthology of Afro-American Writing*, ed. Larry Neal and LeRoi Jones (New York: William Morrow, 1968), 250.

1. Walter Laidlaw, ed., *Statistical Sources for Demographic Studies of Greater New York, 1910* (New York: New York Federation of Churches, 1910); Walter Laidlaw, ed., *Statistical Sources for Demographic Studies of Greater New York, 1920* (New York: Cities Census Committee, 1922); Walter Laidlaw, ed., *Population of the City of New York, 1890–1930* (New York: Cities Census Committee, 1932), 54–56; *Record and Guide*, November 4, 1911, November 18, 1911, January 2, 1915; Ada H. Muller, "A Study of a Bronx Community" (master's thesis, Columbia University, 1915).

2. Laidlaw, ed., *Statistical Sources for Demographic Studies, 1920*, 139–86; Laidlaw, ed., *Population of the City of New York*, 102–5; Bureau of the Census, *Census Tract Data on Population and Housing, New York City: 1940* (New York: Bureau of the Census, 1942), 6–14; Richard William Giordano, "A History of the Morrisania Section of the Bronx in Three Periods: 1875, 1925, 1975" (master's thesis, Columbia University, 1981), 105–7.

3. Katherine Jeannette Meyer, "A Study of Tenant Associations in New York City with Particular Reference to the Bronx, 1920–1927" (master's thesis, Columbia University, 1928), 205–6.

4. Mark Naison, "Introduction," in *Before the Fires: An Oral History of African American Life in the Bronx from the 1930s to the 1960s*, ed. Mark Naison and Bob Gumbs (New York: Fordham University Press, 2016), xi; Caroline Zachry Institute of Human Development

and the Common Council for American Unity, *Around the World in New York: A Guide to the City's Nationality Groups* (New York: Common Council for American Unity, 1950), 55–56; Donald G. Sullivan, "1940–1965: Population Mobility in the South Bronx," in *Devastation/Resurrection: The South Bronx*, ed. Robert Jensen (Bronx, NY: Bronx Museum of Art, 1979), 40.

5. Rodney Lewis, "Growing Up in Morrisania: A Recollection," *Bronx County Historical Society Journal* 42, no. 1 (2005): 19; Gilbert Osofsky, *The Making of a Ghetto* (New York: Harper and Row, 1963); Dominic J. Capeci, *The Harlem Riot of 1943* (Philadelphia: Temple University Press, 1977); Jervis Anderson, *This Was Harlem* (New York: Farrar, Straus and Giroux, 1982); Mark Naison, *Communists in Harlem during the Depression* (Urbana: University of Illinois Press, 1983); James De Jongh, *Vicious Modernism: Black Harlem and the Literary Imagination* (Cambridge: Cambridge University Press, 1990), 73–81.

6. Samuel Lubell, "The Boiling Bronx: Henry Wallace Stronghold," *Saturday Evening Post*, October 23, 1948, 18–19, 63–64; New York City Housing Authority, *City-Wide Public Housing*, September 30, 1962; Joel Schwartz, *The New York Approach: Robert Moses, Urban Liberals, and Redevelopment of the Inner City* (Columbus: Ohio University Press, 1993), 89, 115–17.

7. Mark Naison, "Memories of Morrisania: Introduction," *Bronx County Historical Society Journal* 42, no. 1 (2005): 5, 6.

8. Andrea Butler Ramsey, "Growing Up 'Bronx' 1943–1960: Poor but Privileged," *Bronx County Historical Society Journal* 42, no. 1 (2005): 11.

9. Joyce Hansen, "A Place for Everyone," *Bronx County Historical Society Journal* 42, no. 2 (2005): 76.

10. Parker's parents moved to the Washington Avenue apartment when they first came to the Bronx. Caroline Jefferson, Orangeburg, SC, to Mary L. Parker, Bronx, NY, January 15, 1945, William Parker private archive.

11. John McMahon, "The Melrose-Morrisania Community and Junior High School 120," ca. 1959. Folder Morrisania, Bronx County Historical Society, [2].

12. William Parker, liner notes, *Flowers Grow in My Room* (Centering Records, 1994), [3].

13. "Intergroup Relations in New York City: Progress and Problems, A Survey Summary," National Council of Christians and Jews, Manhattan-Westchester Region, February 1954, 7–11, box 59, folder 685, Mayor Wagner Papers, NYC Municipal Archives; New York City Housing Authority, Project Data, December 31, 1977; Evelyn Gonzalez, *The Bronx,* the Columbia History of Urban Life (New York: Columbia University Press, 2004), 122.

14. Reverend Ernest Davies and Gertrude Solomon, The Claremont Area Housing Committee, to Mayor Robert Wagner, April 14, 1954, box 137, folder 1990, Mayor Wagner Papers, NYC Municipal Archives.

15. William Parker, interview by author, digital recording, August 16, 2018.

16. Thomas Parker, U.S. Individual Tax Return, 1948, William Parker private archive.

17. William Parker, email to author, February 4, 2019.

18. Mary Louise worked at Arnel Co., 1944–45, and perhaps later. She briefly worked at the Lane Curtain Co. in 1949. Mary L. Parker, W-2 Withholding Receipts, 1944, 1945, 1949, William Parker private archive.

19. Patricia Nicholson, interview by author, digital recording, October 30, 2016.

20. Mary L. Parker, U.S. Individual Income Tax Returns, 1958, 1975, William Parker private archive.

21. Thomas Parker, U.S. Individual Income Tax Returns, 1950–61, William Parker private archive.

22. Mary L. Parker, U.S. Individual Income Tax Returns, 1962–63, 1965–69, William Parker private archive; Thomas Parker, U.S. Individual Income Tax Returns, 1962–63, 1965–69, William Parker private archive.

23. Parker interview, August 16, 2018.

24. The strong family bonds are evident in surviving letters. Ethel Jefferson and Lemuel Jefferson Jr., Orangeburg, SC, to Mary Louise Jefferson et al., New York, NY, August 16, 1939, William Parker private archive; Lemuel Jefferson Sr. (scribed by Lemuel Jefferson Jr.), Orangeburg, SC, to Mary Louise Jefferson et al., New York, NY, August 30, 1939, William Parker private archive; Lemuel Jefferson Jr., Fort Bragg, NC, to Mary Louise Jefferson, New York, NY, December 4, 1940, William Parker private archive; Lemuel Jefferson Jr., Fort Bragg, NC, to Mary Louise Jefferson, New York, NY, December 18, 1940, William Parker private archive; Carrie Lee Edwards et al., New York, NY, to Mary Parker, Orangeburg, SC, September 8, 1948, William Parker private archive; Ethel Williams, Cope, SC, to Mary L. Parker, Bronx, NY, February 11, 1949, William Parker private archive; Ethel Williams, Cope, SC, to Mary L. Parker, Bronx, NY, September 5, 1950, William Parker private archive.

25. William Parker, interview by author, digital recording, February 2, 2016.

26. William Parker, *Who Owns Music? Notes from a Spiritual Journey*, 2nd ed. (Köln: Herausgeberin, 2013), 129.

27. Parker interview, February 2, 2016.

28. Carolyn Smith and Jack Smith, interview with the Bronx African American History Project, BAAHP Digital Archive at Fordham University, September 16, 2015, 2; Gonzalez, *The Bronx*, 116.

29. Marshall Berman, *All That Is Solid Melts into Thin Air* (New York: Simon and Schuster, 1982), 282.

30. Helen Bailey, interview with the Bronx African American History Project, BAAHP Digital Archive at Fordham University, October 13, 2015, 24.

31. Dana Driskell, interview with the Bronx African American History Project, BAAHP Digital Archive at Fordham University, October 19, 2015, 11.

32. Edgar M. Hoover and Raymond Vernon, *Anatomy of a Metropolis: The Changing Distribution of People and Jobs within the New York Metropolitan Region* (Cambridge, MA: Harvard University Press, 1959), 229–60; Jill Jonnes, *South Bronx Rising: The Rise, Fall, and Resurrec-*

tion of an American City (New York: Fordham University Press, 2002), 152; Gonzalez, The Bronx, 118; Herbert E. Meyer, "How Government Helped Ruin the South Bronx," Fortune, November 1975, 144–45; Joseph P. Fried, "Is South Bronx Revival Plan Simply Folly?" New York Times, June 19, 1978.

33. Hetty Fox, interview with the Bronx African American History Project, BAAHP Digital Archive at Fordham University, October 1, 2015, 23.

34. John Braithwaite, interview with the Bronx African American History Project, BAAHP Digital Archive at Fordham University, December 4, 2015, 5; Fox interview, October 1, 2015, 21–23.

35. William Parker, interview by author, digital recording, January 27, 2017.

36. Duke Ellington and His Orchestra, Ellington at Newport (Columbia, 1957).

37. Parker interview, February 2, 2016.

38. Ella Fitzgerald and Duke Ellington, Ella at Duke's Place (Verve Records, 1966); Duke Ellington, Soul Call (Verve Records, 1967); Duke Ellington and His Orchestra, Duke Ellington's Far East Suite (RCA Victor, 1967); Willis Jackson and Brother Jack McDuff, Together Again, Again (Prestige, 1967).

39. William Parker, interview by author, digital recording, July 15, 2016.

40. Parker, Who Owns Music?, 22.

41. Parker interview, February 2, 2016.

42. Another South Bronx resident echoed these remarks. Hansen, "A Place for Everyone," 76.

43. William Parker, interview by author, digital recording, February 10, 2017.

44. William Parker, interview by author, digital recording, July 15, 2016.

45. Parker's poem appeared in liner notes published many years later. See William Parker, Sunrise in the Tone World (AUM Fidelity, 1998), [15].

46. William Parker, interview by author, digital recording, January 27, 2019.

47. Kenny's was an early club to feature singer Nancy Wilson (1937–2018). See interview with Howie Evans in Naison and Gumbs, eds., Before the Fires, 16–17.

48. Club 845 (845 Prospect Avenue) was a major cultural center from the 1930s to the 1960s that featured renowned artists such as Dizzy Gillespie and Thelonious Monk. Club 845 closed during the time of the fires in the late 1960s as the area's population was pushed out. Hunts Point Palace was perhaps the most important club, featuring a blend of Latin, calypso, R&B groups, and jazz from World War II until the 1970s, featuring Charlie Parker, Gillespie, Dexter Gordon, and many others. Naison, "Introduction," xiv–xv, 164–65, 167.

49. Evans interview, Before the Fires, ed. Naison and Gumbs, 16–17.

50. The clippings were still in William Parker's possession in 2016. Another Black resident recalled having similar heroes. Lewis, "Growing Up in Morrisania," 19–20.

51. Eugene Chadbourne, "Floyd Brady," Allmusic.com, accessed January 30, 2019, www.allmusic.com/artist/floyd-brady-mn0001569697/biography.

52. Parker interview, February 2, 2016.

53. Parker interview, February 2, 2016.

54. Parker interview, January 27, 2019.

55. Parker interview, February 2, 2016.

56. Ornette Coleman, *Free Jazz* (Atlantic, 1961).

57. William Parker, interview by author, digital recording, April 20, 2018.

58. Jazz Composer's Orchestra, *Jazz Composer's Orchestra* (JCOA Records, 1968).

59. Parker interview, February 2, 2016.

60. Dan Morgenstern and Ira Gitler, "Newport '67," *DownBeat*, August 1967, 39.

61. Parker interview, February 2, 2016.

62. Parker interview, August 16, 2018.

63. Parker, liner notes, *Flowers Grow in My Room*, [3].

64. June Bernardin, "My Reflections: Growing Up in Morrisania," *Bronx County Historical Society Journal* 42, no. 1 (2005): 16–17; Hansen, "A Place for Everyone," 77.

65. Hansen, "A Place for Everyone," 77.

66. *People's Voice*, June 28, 1947; *Amsterdam News*, April 15, 1950; Edward S. Lewis, "The Urban League, a Dynamic Instrument in Social Change: A Study of the Changing Role of the New York Urban League, 1910–1960" (PhD diss., New York University, 1961), 185.

67. Bernardin, "My Reflections," 17.

68. Oral histories of the time period frequently note that students rarely had more than one Black teacher throughout their entire education. Hansen, "A Place for Everyone," 77.

69. Cooper-Moore, interview by author, digital recording, September 30, 2016.

70. William Parker, *In Order to Survive* (Black Saint, 1995), [2].

71. Parker interview, February 2, 2016.

72. Victor Marrero, director of the Bronx Model Cities program, quoted in Martin Tolchin, "Rage Permeates All Facets of Life in the South Bronx," *New York Times*, January 17, 1973.

73. Parker interview, February 2, 2016.

74. Parker interview, January 27, 2019.

75. Parker interview, February 2, 2016.

76. The Bronx lost 108,000 dwelling units in total. Naison, "Introduction," xv; Michael A. Stegman, *The Dynamics of Rental Housing in New York City* (Piscataway, NJ: Center for Urban Policy Research, 1982), 177–79; James L. Wunsch, "From Burning to Building: The Revival of the South Bronx 1970–1999," *Bronx County Historical Society Journal* 38, no. 1 (2001): 5.

77. Victor George Mair, quoted in Martia Goodson et al., eds., "South Bronx Narratives," in *Devastation/Resurrection: The South Bronx*, ed. Robert Jensen (Bronx, NY: Bronx Museum of Art, 1979), 56.

78. Fox interview, October 1, 2015, 24.

79. Parker interview, January 27, 2019.

80. William Parker, interview by author, digital recording, February 8, 2016.

81. Parker interview, February 8, 2016.

82. Parker interview, January 27, 2017.

83. Parker interview, February 8, 2016.

84. One historian dated the surge of heroin to 1965. Wunsch, "From Burning to Building," 8.

85. Mark Naison, "'It Takes a Village to Raise a Child'": Growing Up in the Patterson Houses in the 1950s and Early 1960s, An Interview with Victoria Archibald-Good," *Bronx County Historical Society Journal* 40, no. 1 (2003): 17.

86. Overdoses on heroin by children as young as thirteen were not uncommon. Eulalio Rodriguez, "Portrait of a Blighted Area: The South Bronx," *Sunday News*, September 26, 1971.

87. Naison, "'It Takes a Village to Raise a Child,'" 17–18.

88. Lewis, "Growing Up in Morrisania," 20–21.

89. Parker interview, February 2, 2016.

90. The Buddy Young Football League head office was located at 68 East 131st Street in Harlem.

91. Victor Mastro and John Hogrogian, "Bronx, Blacks, and the NFL," *Coffin Corner* 15, no. 1 (1993): 2, 4.

92. "Chuck Griffin Project to Rename 115th Street and Second Avenue," posted on Facebook by Un-common-sense.com, July 8, 2013.

93. "Football Team Seeks Help," *New York Times*, August 20, 1972, 6.

94. Brian D. Goldstein, *The Roots of Urban Renaissance: Gentrification and the Struggle over Harlem* (Cambridge, MA: Harvard University Press, 2017), 66; Al Harvin, "People in Sports: 3 Rangers Find Consolation on Trip with Team Canada," *New York Times*, March 30, 1977, A22.

95. Kris Needs, "Hendrix: The Gigs That Changed History—#9 The Harlem Street Fair," October 30, 2015, www.loudersound.com/features/hendrix-the-gigs-that-changed-history -9-the-harlem-street-fair.

96. Interestingly, this performance was not well received, and after one additional performance in downtown Manhattan, Hendrix would elect to dissolve the band and form the Band of Gypsies, in part because "he wanted a black band and a black drummer. He wanted to get together with the roots, going back to what he really loved—soul, R&B and blues."

Needs, "Hendrix"; "Jimi Hendrix Sings at Harlem Benefit," *New York Times*, September 6, 1969, 18.

97. "Jimi Hendrix Sings," 18.

98. "New York City," *Southern Courier*, October 12–13, 1968, 2.

99. Parker interview, August 16, 2018.

100. Parker interview, February 2, 2016.

101. Parker interview, January 27, 2017.

102. Parker interview, February 2, 2016.

103. William Parker, Liner Notes, *Flowers Grow in My Room*, [3].

104. William Parker, interview by author, July 15, 2016.

105. Parker, *Who Owns Music?*, 129.

106. Parker interview, July 15, 2016.

Chapter 3: Consciousness

Epigraphs: Ron Wellburn, "The Black Aesthetic Imperative," in *The Black Aesthetic*, ed. Gayle Addison Jr. (Garden City, NY: Doubleday, 1972), 132; Larry Neal, "The Black Arts Movement," in "Black Theatre," special issue, *Drama Review* 12, no. 4 (1968): 28.

1. William Parker, interview by author, digital recording, July 15, 2016.

2. William Parker, interview by author, digital recording, February 16, 2016.

3. From Amiri Baraka [LeRoi Jones], *The Dead Lecturer* (New York: Grove, 1964).

4. Miriam Parker, interview by author, digital recording, June 6, 2017.

5. Marion Brown, *Afternoon of a Georgia Faun* (ECM, 1970); William Parker, interview by author, digital recording, February 2, 2016.

6. Jeff Land, *Active Radio: Pacifica's Brash Experiment* (Minneapolis: University of Minnesota Press, 1999), 113, 117–18, 121.

7. It was the title track of a record Brown released in 1969. James Brown, *Say It Loud—I'm Black and I'm Proud* (King Records, 1969). Parker interview, February 2, 2016.

8. William Parker, interview by author, digital recording, February 8, 2016.

9. Parker interview, February 8, 2016.

10. Amiri Baraka [LeRoi Jones], "The Changing Same (R&B and New Black Music)," in *The Black Aesthetic*, ed. Addison Gayle Jr. (Garden City, NY: Doubleday, 1971), 122–23.

11. Neal, "The Black Arts Movement," 28. For a detailed study of the origins of the movement, see Larry Neal, "The Social Background of the Black Arts Movement," in "Black American Culture in the Second Renaissance—1954–1970," special issue, *Black Scholar* 18, no. 1 (1987):

11–22. For an overview of the political context, see Darwin T. Turner, "Retrospective of a Renaissance," in "Black American Culture in the Second Renaissance—1954–1970," special issue, *Black Scholar* 18, no. 1 (1987): 2–10. James Smethurst examines some threads linking the Black Arts movement to earlier phases of Black radicalism. James Smethurst, "'Don't Say Goodbye to the Porkpie Hat': Langston Hughes, the Left, and the Black Arts Movement," *Callaloo* 25, no. 4 (2002): 1224–37.

12. Amiri Baraka [LeRoi Jones], "Black Art," in "Black American Culture in the Second Renaissance—1954–1970," special issue, *Black Scholar* 18, no. 1 (1987): 23.

13. Others include *Ebony Journal* (Atlanta), *Say Brother* (Boston), *Right On!* (Cincinnati), *Colored People's Time* and *Profiles in Black* (Detroit), *From the Inside Out* (Los Angeles), *Kaleidoscope* (Omaha), *New Mood, New Breed* (Philadelphia), *Black Chronicle* (Pittsburgh), *Vibrations for a New People* and *Black Dignity* (San Francisco), and *For the People* (South Carolina), as well as national programs such as *Black Journal* and *Soul!*

14. Devorah Heitner, *Black Power TV* (Durham, NC: Duke University Press, 2013), 4.

15. George Gent, "Television: *Black Journal* Premiere," *New York Times*, June 13, 1968.

16. Gayle Wald, *It's Been Beautiful:* Soul! *and Black Power Television* (Durham, NC: Duke University Press, 2015), 1.

17. Fred Ferretti, "Harris Polls Weigh Effects of Ethnic Programming," *New York Times*, July 4, 1969.

18. Heitner, *Black Power TV*, 125.

19. Laurie Ouellette, *Viewers Like You: How Public TV Failed the People* (New York: Columbia University Press, 2002), 148; Wald, *It's Been Beautiful*, 8.

20. Wald, *It's Been Beautiful*, 1–2.

21. Lisa Jones, quoted in Wald, *It's Been Beautiful*, 8.

22. Wald, *It's Been Beautiful*, 8.

23. Gayle Wald, "Black Music and Black Freedom in Sound and Space," in "Sound Clash: Listening to American Studies," special issue, *American Quarterly* 63, no. 3 (2011): 677.

24. Heitner, *Black Power TV*, 4. The Black Arts movement had avant-garde elements from the very beginning, especially in the literary figures LeRoi Jones and A. B. Spellman. See Lorenzo Thomas, "The Shadow World: New York's Umbra Workshop and Origins of the Black Arts Movement," *Callaloo*, no. 4 (1978): 54.

25. Amiri Baraka [LeRoi Jones], quoted in Heitner, *Black Power TV*, 134.

26. Komozi Woodard, "It's Nation Time in NewArk: Amiri Baraka and the Black Power Experiment in Newark, New Jersey," in *Freedom North: Black Freedom Struggles outside the South, 1940–1980*, ed. Jeanne Theoharis and Komozi Woodard (New York: Palgrave Macmillan, 2003), 287–311.

27. Heitner, *Black Power TV*, 152.

28. Parker interview, July 15, 2016.

29. Chinua Achebe's novel was one of the first African novels to garner critical international acclaim. Chinua Achebe, *Things Fall Apart* (New York: Anchor, [1958] 1994).

30. Wellburn, "The Black Aesthetic Imperative," 140–41.

31. A. B. Spellman, "Not Just Whistling Dixie," in *Black Fire! An Anthology of Afro-American Writing*, ed. Larry Neal and LeRoi Jones (New York: William Morrow, 1968), 159–60.

32. Philippe Carles and Jean-Louis Comolli, *Free Jazz/Black Power*, nouvelle edition (Paris: Gallimard, [1971] 2000), 36.

33. Ornette Coleman Double Quartet, *Free Jazz* (Atlantic, 1961).

34. Wellburn, "The Black Aesthetic Imperative," 143.

35. Leslie B. Rout Jr., "Reflections on the Evolution of Post-War Jazz," in *The Black Aesthetic*, ed. Addison Gayle Jr. (Garden City, NY: Doubleday, 1971), 158.

36. Ornette Coleman Trio, *At the "Golden Circle" Stockholm*, 2 albums (Blue Note, 1965).

37. Jones [Baraka], "The Changing Same," 125, 126.

38. Spellman, "Not Just Whistling Dixie," 159–60; Jones [Baraka], "The Changing Same," 118–31; Wellburn, "The Black Aesthetic Imperative," 132–33, 136–46; Rout, "Reflections on the Evolution of Post-war Jazz," 150–60; Larry Neal, "The Black Arts Movement," 37; Werner Sollors, *Amiri Baraka/LeRoi Jones: The Quest for a "Populist Modernism"* (New York: Columbia University Press, 1978), 47–48; Lorenzo Thomas, "Neon Griot: The Functional Role of Poetry Readings in the Black Arts Movement," in *Close Listening: Poetry and the Performed Word*, ed. Charles Bernstein (New York: Oxford University Press, 1998), 312–13; Kalamu Ya Salaam, *The Magic of Juju: An Appreciation of the Black Arts Movement* (Chicago: Third World Press Foundation, 2016), 126–34.

39. Lorenzo Thomas examines the relationships among jazz, poetry, and literary circles, arguing that they were intermingling well before the 1960s. See Lorenzo Thomas, "'Communicating by Horns': Jazz and Redemption in the Poetry of the Beats and the Black Arts Movement," in "Poetry and Theatre Issue," *African American Review* 26, no. 2 (1992): 291–98; Lorenzo Thomas, "'Classical Jazz' and the Black Arts Movement," in "Special Issues on the Music," *African American Review* 29, no. 2 (1995): 237–40.

40. New York Art Quartet, *New York Art Quartet* (ESP-Disk, 1965).

41. Eldridge Cleaver, *Soul on Ice* (New York: Dell, 1968), 26.

42. M. L. Rosenthal, "Some Thoughts on American Poetry Today," in "Contemporary Poetry in America," special issue, *Salmagundi*, no. 22/23 (1973): 61–63.

43. W. D. E. Andrews, "'All Is Permitted': The Poetry of LeRoi Jones/Amiri Baraka," *Southwest Review* 67, no. 2 (1982): 215. Also see Patrick Roney, "The Paradox of Experience: Black Art and Black Idiom in the Work of Amiri Baraka," in "Amiri Baraka Issue," *African American Review* 37, no. 2/3 (2003): 417.

44. Joseph Jarman, *Song For* (Delmark, 1967).

45. Archie Shepp, *Fire Music* (Impulse!, 1965); John Coltrane, *Meditations* (Impulse!, 1966); John Coltrane, *Om* (Impulse!, 1967); John Coltrane, *Live in Seattle* (Impulse!, 1971).

46. Archie Shepp, liner notes, *Fire Music* (Impulse!, 1965).

47. Eric Porter, *What Is This Thing Called Jazz? African American Musicians as Artists, Critics, and Activists*, Music of the African Diaspora, series ed. Samuel A. Floyd Jr. (Berkeley: University of California Press, 2002), 205.

48. Porter, *What Is This Thing Called Jazz?*, 205.

49. William Parker, *Who Owns Music? Notes from a Spiritual Journey*, 2nd ed. (Köln: Herausgeberin, 2013), 33–34.

50. Translation by author. French original: "Il faut plus que de la colére pure et simple pour pouvoir composer l'emouvante thrène que Shepp fir pour Malcolm X . . . une oeuvre de tendresse et de furie, d'amour et de haine, de passion et de vision politique. . . ." E. Boundzéki Dongala, "Le 'New Jazz': Une Interprétation," *Présence Africaine*, Nouvelle Série, no. 68 (1968): 147.

51. Translation by author. French original: "Shepp est en train de donner une dimension explicitement sociale au jazz là où elle n'existait qu'implicitement. Son saxophone n'est plus un simple instrument de musique, c'est une arme à laquelle il croit, et ce n'est pas la seule arme qu'il ait." Dongala, "Le 'New Jazz,'" 147.

52. Parker interview, February 8, 2016.

53. William Parker email to author, September 7, 2018.

54. William Parker email to author, September 1, 2018.

55. From Ernesto Cardenal, *La Hora Cero y Otros Poemas* (Barcelona: Ediciones Saturno, 1971).

56. Parker email, September 1, 2018.

57. Jerzy Grotowski, *Towards a Poor Theatre*, ed. Eugenio Barba, A Theatre Arts Book (New York: Routledge, [1968] 2002): 255–56.

58. Parker email, September 7, 2018.

59. Parker email, September 1, 2018.

60. William Parker, *Music and the Shadow People* (New York: Centering Music, 1995); William Parker and the Little Huey Creative Music Orchestra, *Mayor of Punkville* (AUM Fidelity, 2000).

61. François Truffaut, "A Certain Tendency in French Cinema," *Cahiers du Cinéma*, no. 31 (1954), reprinted in *The French New Wave: Critical Landmarks*, eds. Peter Graham and Ginette Vincendeau (London: Palgrave Macmillan, 2009), 39–63; Jean-Luc Godard, "Review of Alexandre Astruc's *Une Vie*," *Cahiers du Cinéma*, no. 89 (1958), reprinted in *The French New Wave: Critical Landmarks*, ed. Peter Graham and Ginette Vincendeau (London: Palgrave Macmillan, 2009), 155–61.

62. Mark Cousins, quoted in *The Story of Film: An Odyssey*, episode 7: *European New Wave* (2011).

63. Parker interview, February 8, 2016.

64. Ingmar Bergman, interviewed by Lars-Olaf Löthwall, in *The Ingmar Bergman Archives,* eds. Paul Duncan and Bengt Wanselius (Köln: Taschen, 2008), 276.

65. Parker interview, February 2, 2016.

66. Richardson, along with figures such as Lorenza Mazetti, Lindsay Anderson, Karel Reisz, John Fletcher, and Walter Lassally, played a key role in the movement, which aimed to challenge film orthodoxy. Tony Richardson, quoted in Scott MacKenzie, *Film Manifestos and Global Cinema Cultures: A Critical Anthology* (Berkeley: University of California Press, 2014), 149.

67. Sillitoe's original was the title story of a collection that won the Hawthornden Prize for Literature in 1959. Saul Maloff, "The Eccentricity of Alan Sillitoe," in *Contemporary British Novelists,* ed. Charles Shapiro (Carbondale: Southern Illinois Press, 1965), 95–113; Stanley S. Atherton, "Alan Sillitoe's Battleground," *Dalhousie Review* 10 (autumn 1968): 324–31; Eugene F. Quirk, "Social Class as Audience: Sillitoe's Story and Screenplay 'The Loneliness of the Long-Distance Runner,'" *Literature/Film Quarterly* 9, no. 3 (1981): 162.

68. Parker interview, February 2, 2016.

69. Allen R. Penner and Alan Sillitoe, "Human Dignity and Social Anarchy: Sillitoe's 'The Loneliness of the Long-Distance Runner,'" *Contemporary Literature* 10, no. 2 (1969): 254.

70. Anthology Film Archives was cofounded in 1970 by filmmakers Jonas Mekas, Stan Brakhage, Peter Kubelka, Ken Kelman, James Broughton, and Jerome Hill, along with historian P. Adams Sitney. Kristen Alfaro, "Access and the Experimental Film: New Technologies and Anthology Film Archives' Institutionalization of the Avant-Garde," *Moving Image* 12, no. 1 (2012): 45.

71. Stan Brakhage, *Essential Brakhage: Selected Writings on Filmmaking,* Documentext series (Kingston, NY: McPherson, 2001), 12.

72. Brakhage, *Essential Brakhage,* 25.

73. Gareth Evans, "The Eye and the Hand: Brakhage's Challenge to Ocularcentrism," in *Stan Brakhage: The Realm Buster,* ed. Marco Lori and Esther Leslie (East Barnet, UK: John Libbey, 2018), 63.

74. William Parker, liner notes, *Wood Flute Songs* (AUM Fidelity, 2013), [1].

75. Jonas Mekas, "Brakhage Buys 8 mm. Camera," *Village Voice,* May 14, 1964.

76. Mekas, "Brakhage Buys"; Jonas Mekas, "On 'People's Movies,' or the Difference between Melodrama and Art," *Village Voice,* August 20, 1964.

77. Jonas Mekas and Gerald R. Barrett, "Jonas Mekas Interview October 10, 1972," *Literature/Film Quarterly* 1, no. 2 (1973): 104. *Dog Star Man* was included as one of the first ten films in the Library of Congress National Film Registry. Steve Anker, "Obituary: Stan Brakhage," *Film Comment* 39, no. 3 (2003): 11.

78. Camille J. Cook and Anne Rorimer, "Contemporary Film Art," *Bulletin of the Art Institute of Chicago* 67, no. 5 (1973): 14.

79. Allen S. Weiss, "An Eye for an I: On the Art of Fascination," in "Recent Film Theory in Europe," special issue, *SubStance* 15, no. 3 (1986): 89.

80. Jerry White, "Brakhage's Tarkovsky and Tarkovsky's Brakhage: Collectivity, Subjectivity, and the Dream of Cinema," in "A Sense of Sight: Special Issue Devoted to Stan Brakhage," *Revue Canadienne d'Études Cinématographiques/Canadian Journal of Film Studies* 14, no. 1 (2005): 71.

81. Jonas Mekas, "On Dreyer's *Gertrud*," *Village Voice*, September 23, 1965; Abigail Child, "Notes on Sincerity and Irony," in *Stan Brakhage: Filmmaker*, ed. David E. James (Philadelphia: Temple University Press, 2005), 198–99; William Parker, interview by author, digital recording, January 27, 2019.

82. Jonas Mekas, "On Bill Vehr and the Ornamental Cinema," *Village Voice*, February 17, 1966.

83. Jonas Mekas, "On the Degeneration of Film Festivals," *Village Voice*, July 1, 1965.

84. Fred Camper, "Brakhage's Contradictions," *Chicago Review* 47, no. 4/48, no. 1 (winter 2001/spring 2002): 84.

85. Robert Kelly, "On the Art of Vision," *Film Culture* 37 (1965): 14.

86. Parker interview, January 27, 2019.

87. Paul Arthur, "The Chimeric Cinema of Ken Jacobs," *Film Comment* 33, no. 2 (1997): 58.

88. Jonas Mekas, "On the Baudelairean Cinema," *Village Voice*, May 2, 1963.

89. Arthur, "The Chimeric Cinema of Ken Jacobs," 58; Stan Brakhage, *Film at Wit's End: Eight Avant-Garde Filmmakers*, Documentext series (Kingston, NY: McPherson, 1989), 149–53.

90. Critic Jonas Mekas considered the film one of the best of 1964. Jonas Mekas, "The Year 1964," *Village Voice*, January 7, 1965.

91. Jonas Mekas, "Bruce Baillie, External Traveler," *Village Voice*, April 1, 1971.

92. Bruce Baillie, quoted in Harriet Polt, "The Films of Bruce Baillie," *Film Comment* 2, no. 4 (1965): 52.

93. Polt, "The Films of Bruce Baillie," 51.

94. Parker, liner notes, *Wood Flute Songs*, [1].

95. Parker email, September 7, 2018; Carlos Kase, "On the Importance of Anthology Film Archives: A Historical Overview and Endorsement," in *Captured: A Film/Video History of the Lower East Side*, ed. Clayton Patterson et al. (New York: Seven Stories Press, 1998), 86–87.

96. Parker email, September 1, 2018; Carel Rowe, "Myth and Symbolism: Blue Velvet," in *Black Leather Lucifer*, ed. Jack Hunter (Glitter Books, 2012), 31; Anna Powell, "The Occult: A Torch for Lucifer," in *Black Leather Lucifer*, ed. Jack Hunter (Glitter Books, 2012), 60, 73–77.

97. Kenneth Anger, quoted in Clay Smith, "Kustom Film Kommando: Interview with Filmmaker Kenneth Anger," *Austin Chronicle*, October 31, 1997, www.austinchronicle.com/screens/1997-10-31/518703/print.

98. Parker interview, February 2, 2016.

99. Parker, liner notes, *Wood Flute Songs*, [2].

100. Parker interview, February 2, 2016.

101. William Parker, interview by author, digital recording, February 23, 2016.

102. Cecil Taylor, *Conquistador!* (Blue Note, 1966).

103. Parker interview, February 2, 2016.

104. Parker interview, February 2, 2016.

105. Charles Mingus, *Mingus Ah Um* (Columbia, 1959).

106. Todd Mayfield and Travis Astria, *Traveling Soul: The Life of Curtis Mayfield* (Chicago: Chicago Review Press, 2017), 223–27.

107. Parker interview, April 20, 2018.

108. The liner notes written by Ornette Coleman for the record *Ornette at 12* were one of Parker's inspirations. Coleman referred to various kinds of art as the forerunners of a process that would forge greater equality. It was one of the sparks for Parker's idea of "the art form of living" as a day-to-day practice. Ornette Coleman, liner notes, *Ornette at 12* (Impulse!, 1969); Parker interview, February 23, 2016; William Parker, interview by author, digital recording, January 27, 2017.

109. Parker interview, February 2, 2016.

110. Mercè Mur Effing, "The Origin and Development of Self-Help Literature in the United States: The Concept of Success and Happiness, an Overview," *Atlantis* 31, no. 2 (2009): 135.

111. Parker interview, February 2, 2016.

112. Parker interview, January 27, 2017.

113. John Coltrane, *A Love Supreme* (Impulse!, 1964).

114. Jones [Baraka], "The Changing Same," 130.

115. Jones [Baraka], "The Changing Same," 130–31.

116. Like some of his contemporaries, Ayler found some of his earliest and greatest support in Europe. Albert Ayler, *Spirits* (Debut Records, 1964); Albert Ayler, *Bells* (ESP-Disk, 1965); Albert Ayler Trio, *Spiritual Unity* (ESP-Disk, 1965); Albert Ayler, *Love Cry* (Impulse!, 1968).

117. Albert Ayler, *Music Is the Healing Force of the Universe* (Impulse!, 1970).

118. For a study of some artists who viewed music as a force for liberation or healing, see Gayle Wald, "Soul Vibrations: Black Music and Black Freedom in Sound and Space," in "Sound Clash: Listening to American Studies," special issue, *American Quarterly* 63, no. 3 (2011): 673–96.

119. From Parker, *Who Owns Music?*, 91–92.

120. William Parker, interview by author, digital recording, August 9, 2018.

121. William Parker, interview by author, digital recording, February 10, 2017.

122. Parker interview, February 2, 2016.

123. Ornette Coleman, *The Shape of Jazz to Come* (Atlantic, 1959).

124. Archie Shepp, *Attica Blues* (Impulse!, 1972). Archie Shepp and other figures from the new music addressed issues of concern to the Black communities of the time, much like their contemporaries in other musical genres such as James Brown and Roberta Flack. William L. Van Deburg, *New Day in Babylon: The Black Power Movement and American Culture, 1965–1975* (Chicago: University of Chicago Press, 1992), 212.

125. Some Black nationalists and key figures in the Black Arts movement remained frustrated with the inability of Black popular music to be a vehicle for cultural nationalism. Michael Hanson, "Suppose James Brown Read Fanon: The Black Arts Movement, Cultural Nationalism, and the Failure of Popular Music Praxis," *Popular Music* 27, no. 3 (2008): 341–65.

126. Although Stuart Hobbs wrote specifically about visual art, many of his observations provide commentary on the fate of avant-garde music as well. Stuart D. Hobbs, *The End of the American Avant Garde*, the American Social Experience Series (New York: New York University Press, 1997), 184–86.

127. Parker interview, February 10, 2017.

128. Parker interview, February 2, 2016.

Chapter 4: The Loft Scene

Epigraphs: William Parker, *Who Owns Music? Notes from a Spiritual Journey*, 2nd ed. (Köln: Herausgeberin, 2013), 33; Cooper-Moore, interview by author, digital recording, September 30, 2016.

1. Bronen's Music Store had several locations. The store that exists at 2462 Webster Avenue today is across the street from the location where Parker purchased his bass. The earlier store was consumed by one of the fires in the South Bronx around 1971–72. Subsequently, during the blackout of July 13, 1977, the store was further damaged and forced to close. After moving temporarily to a home office and then to Fordham Road, Bronen's eventually returned to the neighborhood and opened the current location. Andrew Bronen, phone interview by author, digital recording, September 5, 2018.

2. Curtis Stephen, "New York 1977: The Night the Lights Went Out," Curtisstephen.com, July 12, 2017, http://curtisstephen.com/new-york-1977-the-night-the-lights-went-out.

3. "Violins by Juzek," *Etude* 71 (1953): 52; Karel Jalovec, *The Violin Makers of Bohemia: Including Craftsmen of Moravia and Slovakia* (London: Anglo-Italian, 1959), 116, 149; Roy Ehrhardt, *Violin Identification and Price Guide* (Kansas City: Heart of America Press, 1977), 1:24; "William Juzek," *New York Times*, July 7, 1942; "Czechoslovak Musical Instruments Co.," *Music Supervisors' Journal* 17, no. 5 (1931): 75.

4. Bronen interview, September 5, 2018.

5. Peter Kowald, liner notes, trans. Isabel Seeberg and Paul Lytton, *Posium Pendasem* (Free Music Production, 1999), [7].

6. Jazzmobile, Jazzmobile.org, accessed September 5, 2018.

7. John Gennari, *Blowin' Hot and Cool: Jazz and Its Critics* (Chicago: University of Chicago Press, 2006), 287.

8. Richard Davis's noted early records as a leader include *The Philosophy of the Spiritual* (Cobblestone, 1972) and *Epistrophy & Now's the Time* (Muse Records, 1972). Some of Davis's key work in the avant-garde includes Eric Dolphy, *Out to Lunch!* (Blue Note, 1964); Andrew Hill, *Point of Departure* (Blue Note, 1964); Andrew Hill, *Andrew!!* (Blue Note, 1964); Sam Rivers, *Hues* (Impulse!, 1973); Pharaoh Sanders, *Karma* (Impulse!, 1969); and Robin D. G. Kelley, "New Monastery: Monk and the Jazz Avant-Garde," in "New Perspectives on Thelonious Monk," special issue, *Black Music Research Journal* 19, no. 2 (1999): 160–62.

9. Richard Davis later taught at the University of Wisconsin for more than two decades, leading courses in jazz and Black music, beginning in 1978. "The Changing Scene," *Music Educators Journal* 65, no. 1 (1978): 85; Leslie Gourse, "In the Heyday of the Studio Musician: Thad Jones and Mel Lewis Start a Big Band at the Village Vanguard," *Massachusetts Review* 39, no. 4 (1998/1999): 586.

10. Hassan Dawkins's birth name was William Dawkins. Dawkins played in the loft scene in the mid-1970s but has only one recording (as a sideperson) to his name, which was recorded at Studio We in April and May 1975 but not released until many years later: Ted Daniel, *In the Beginning* (Altura Music, 1997).

11. William Parker, email to author, September 6, 2018.

12. Parker first outlined his ideas for a music school in the 1980s. William Parker, email to author, June 18, 2019.

13. Parker, *Who Owns Music?*, 66.

14. William Parker, interview by author, digital recording, February 8, 2016.

15. Cooper-Moore interview, September 30, 2016.

16. Parker played a few gigs at Club 845 in 1971 or 1972. William Parker, interview by author, digital recording, January 27, 2019.

17. The original movie was part of a broad movement in 1920s film that explored the "jazz life." Charles Merrell Berg, "Cinema Sings the Blues," *Cinema Journal* 17, no. 2 (1978): 2.

18. Sullivan's recorded work includes twenty records as a leader as well as many film, theater, and television credits. There was a period in the 1950s when she was among the most sought-after vocalists on the circuit. Laurence A. Glasco, *The WPA History of the Negro in Pittsburgh* (Pittsburgh: University of Pittsburgh Press, 2004), 329–30; Linda Dahl, *Stormy Weather: The Music and Lives of a Century of Jazz Women* (New York: Limelight Editions, 2004), 133; Arnold Shaw, *The Street That Never Slept: New York's Fabled 52nd Street* (New York: Coward, McCann and Geoghegan, 1971), 93; Barney Josephson and Terry Trilling-Josephson, *Café Society: The*

Wrong Place for the Right People (Champaign-Urbana: University of Illinois Press, 2009), 52; Britain Scott and Christiane Harrassowitz, "Beyond Beethoven and the Boyz: Women's Music in Relation to History and Culture," *Music Educators Journal* 90, no. 4 (2004): 54; Katharine Cartwright, "'Guess These People Wonder What I'm Singing': Quotation and Reference in Ella Fitzgerald's 'St. Louis Blues,'" in *Ramblin' on My Mind: New Perspectives on the Blues*, ed. David Evans (Champaign-Urbana: University of Illinois Press, 2008), 287.

19. Sullivan's immense work was finally recognized in her final years, and she was given the Humanitarian Award by the Harlem School of the Arts in 1985. "Commentary," *Black Perspective in Music* 13, no. 1 (1985): 127.

20. The upturn in Bertha Hope's career is marked by a series of concerts she led at Bradley's and other notable clubs in New York City in the early 1990s. Leslie Gourse, *Madame Jazz: Contemporary Women Instrumentalists* (New York: Oxford University Press, 1995), 165–67; Owen McNally, "Many Colors of Woman Concert Features Bertha Hope," *Hartford Courant*, August 28, 1997.

21. Parker interview, February 8, 2016; Rick Lopez, *The William Parker Sessionography: Attempting a Complete Historical Arc* (New York: Centering, 2014), 9, 21.

22. Parker's mother made a travel case for his bass out of a mattress that he used for several years in the 1970s before it disintegrated. Parker interview, February 8, 2016.

23. William Parker, interview by author, digital recording, January 27, 2017.

24. Parker email, September 6, 2018.

25. Ed Hazell, liner notes, *Centering: Unreleased Early Recordings 1976–1987* (NoBusiness, 2012), [14]; Will Hermes, *Love Goes to Buildings on Fire: Five Years in New York That Changed Music Forever* (New York: Farrar, Straus and Giroux, 2012), 22; Andrzej Ceynowa, "Black Theaters and Theater Organizations in America, 1961–1982: A Research List," in "Black Theatre Issue," *Black American Literature Forum* 17, no. 2 (1983): 93.

26. Nathan L. Grant, "Ben Caldwell," in *The Concise Oxford Companion to African American Literature*, ed. William L. Andrews et al. (New York: Oxford University Press, 2001), 64; Mel Gussow, "Federal Offers 'World of Ben Caldwell,'" *New York Times*, April 10, 1982.

27. Grant, "Ben Caldwell," 64; see also Charles D. Peavy, "Satire and Contemporary Black Drama," *Satire Newsletter* 7 (fall 1969): 40–49; Ronald V. Ladwing, "The Black Comedy of Ben Caldwell," *Players* 51, no. 3 (1976): 88–91.

28. In the 1980s Caldwell began painting, although much of his life work was destroyed in a fire in 1991, after which he returned to writing monologues and sketches that gained some notoriety when performed by comedian Dick Gregory, or for his casting of Morgan Freeman doing an impression of Richard Pryor. Grant, "Ben Caldwell," 65; Gussow, "Federal Offers 'World of Ben Caldwell.'"

29. Ben Caldwell had been arrested in 1971 for illegal gun possession, a charge that many community members believed was in fact the result of a police plant. The Ben Caldwell Defense Committee was formed and made the statement that the arrest "symbolizes the new direction the police are moving that is aimed at new purges of outspoken Black creative

artists" and "to justify and cover up their political motives to squash Black dissent." He was later acquitted. See "About Books and Authors," *Black World* (January 1972): 75.

30. Grant, "Ben Caldwell," 65.

31. *Magnet* 34 (May/June 1998): 41; William Parker, interview for *Opprobrium* magazine, reprinted in Lopez, *William Parker Sessionography*, 7.

32. Lopez, *William Parker Sessionography*, 4.

33. Taylor Ho Bynum, "Guest Post: Taylor Ho Bynum on Bill Lowe," *Destination: Out*, February 1, 2012, http://destination-out.com/?p=3384.

34. Ron Libscombe was supposed to play cello on this date but did not show up. Wade Barnes has appeared on a handful of lesser-known records over the years: the Universal Jazz Symphonette, *Sound Craft '75 Fantasy for Orchestra* (Anima Records, 1975); Abdullah Sami, *Peace of Time* (Abdullah Sami Records, 1978); Brooklyn Conservatory Faculty Jazz Ensemble, *Bridging the Gap* (360 Records, 1983); Pucci Amanda Jones, *Wild Is the Wind* (CIMP, 1998). The other figures involved have no known recordings.

35. Parker email, September 6, 2018.

36. Jazz Composer's Orchestra releases: *Communication* (Fontana, 1966); *The Jazz Composer's Orchestra* (JCOA Records, 1968); Don Cherry and the Jazz Composer's Orchestra, *Relativity Suite* (JCOA Records, 1973); Carla Bley, Paul Haines, and the Jazz Composer's Orchestra, *Escalator over the Hill* (JCOA Records, 1974); Roswell Rudd and the Jazz Composer's Orchestra, *Numatik Swing Band* (JCOA Records, 1973); Grachan Moncur III and the Jazz Composer's Orchestra, *Echoes of Prayer* (JCOA Records, 1975); Leroy Jenkins and the Jazz Composer's Orchestra, *For Players Only* (JCOA Records, 1975); Clifford Thornton and the Jazz Composer's Orchestra, *The Gardens of Harlem* (JCOA Records, 1975).

37. Alan Silva's band continued to perform and record until 1989. Parker email, September 6, 2018; Alan Silva and His Celestial Communication Orchestra, *Luna Surface* (BYG Records, 1969); Alan Silva and the Celestial Communication Orchestra (BYG Records, 1971).

38. Parker interview, January 27, 2019.

39. Ed Hazell, "A Place to Play What We Want: A Short History of the New York Lofts," in liner notes, *Muntu Recordings* (NoBusiness, 2009), 20.

40. Ron Wellburn, "The Black Aesthetic Imperative," in *The Black Aesthetic*, ed. Addison Gayle Jr. (Garden City, NY: Doubleday, 1971), 132–33.

41. Michael C. Heller, *Loft Jazz: Improvising New York in the 1970s* (Berkeley: University of California Press, 2017), 8, 40–42.

42. Parker would later look back to Dixon and others for inspiration when attempting to establish his own autonomy and self-sufficiency as an artist in the mid-1980s, and their work would form the starting point for his essay "In Order to Survive," in which he articulated the struggles of artists at that time. See chapter 8. Amy Abugo Ongiri, *Spectacular Blackness: The Cultural Politics of the Black Power Movement and the Search for a Black Aesthetic* (Charlottesville: University of Virginia Press, 2010), 129.

43. Robert Levin, "The Jazz Composers' Guild: An Assertion of Dignity," *Down Beat*, May 6, 1965, 17–18; Daniel Walden, "Black Music and Cultural Nationalism: The Maturation of Archie Shepp," *Negro American Literature Forum* 5, no. 4 (1971): 150.

44. Bill Dixon quoted in Ben Young, *Dixonia: A Bio-discography of Bill Dixon*, Discographies no. 77, ed. Michael Gray (Westport, CT: Greenwood, 1998), 344.

45. Heller, *Loft Jazz*, 43.

46. Hermes, *Love Goes to Buildings on Fire*, 22–23.

47. Hazell, "A Place to Play What We Want," 21–22; Hermes, *Love Goes to Buildings on Fire*, 22.

48. Heller, *Loft Jazz*, 40–49.

49. Hermes, *Love Goes to Buildings on Fire*, 22–23.

50. Hazell, "A Place to Play What We Want," 22–23.

51. Fly, "Squatting on the Lower East Side," in *Resistance: A Radical Political and Social History of the Lower East Side*, ed. Clayton Patterson et al. (New York: Seven Stories Press, 2007), 213; Sarah Ferguson, "The Struggle for Space: 10 Years of Turf Battling on the Lower East Side," in *Resistance: A Radical Political and Social History of the Lower East Side*, ed. Clayton Patterson et al. (New York: Seven Stories Press, 2007), 142–43; Daniel Edelman, "DLA Statement: Squatting on East Seventh Street," in *Resistance: A Radical Political and Social History of the Lower East Side*, ed. Clayton Patterson et al. (New York: Seven Stories Press, 2007), 187–88; Aaron Jaffe, "Frank Morales Interviewed by Aaron Jaffee in the Odessa Coffee Shop, Avenue A, Lower East Side," in *Resistance: A Radical Political and Social History of the Lower East Side*, ed. Clayton Patterson et al. (New York: Seven Stories Press, 2007), 193–212.

52. Roger Baird, liner notes, *The Music Ensemble* (Roaratorio, 2001), [2].

53. Billy Bang, liner notes, *The Music Ensemble* (Roaratorio, 2001), [1].

54. William Parker, interview by author, digital recording, February 16, 2016.

55. William Parker, email to author, September 10, 2018.

56. Doug Bradley and Craig Werner, *We Gotta Get Out of This Place: The Soundtrack of the Vietnam War* (Amherst: University of Massachusetts Press, 2015), 210.

57. William Parker, interview by author, digital recording, February 2, 2016.

58. Bradley and Werner, *We Gotta Get Out of This Place*, 210.

59. Parker email, September 10, 2018.

60. Parker, *Who Owns Music?*, 47.

61. Amiri Baraka [LeRoi Jones], quoted in Parker, *Who Owns Music?*, 47.

62. Bang, liner notes, *The Music Ensemble*, [2, 1].

63. Art Ensemble of Chicago's music is widely known and has been incredibly influential. Oregon was founded in 1971 by multi-instrumentalist Ralph Towner (b. 1940), woodwind

player Paul McCandless (b. 1947), bassist Glen Moore (b. 1941), and sitarist and percussionist Collin Walcott (1945–1984). It has released twenty-nine records since 1972.

64. Association for the Advancement of Creative Musicians is a community arts organization founded by working class Black artists on the south side of Chicago in 1965. It remains one of the most important and influential Black arts organizations in the U.S. Bang, liner notes, *The Music Ensemble*, [1].

65. James Lindbloom, quoted in Lopez, *The William Parker Sessionography*, 8. Other Dimensions in Music put out six records between 1990 and 2011. William Parker was not in the band Test, but these other two groups certainly influenced it. Test released five records between 1998 and 2016.

66. Baird, liner notes, *The Music Ensemble*, [2–3].

67. The Music Ensemble performed the following day at the Department of Music at SUNY-Stonybrook. William Parker, ed., *Bill Collector*, no. 1 (1984): n.p.

68. The Columbia students famously used the radio station as a way of broadcasting their messages, covering the protests, and providing live coverage during the uprising. The issues they addressed ranged from civil rights to the Vietnam War. Louis Lusky and Mary H. Lusky, "Columbia 1968: The Wound Unhealed," *Political Science Quarterly* 84, no. 2 (1969): 229–30, 233, 241–43, 245–46, 256–57, 268.

69. The Music Ensemble, *The Music Ensemble* (Roaratorio, 2001).

70. Bang, liner notes, *The Music Ensemble*, [1].

71. Anita Weschler (1903–2000) was an American artist known especially for her sculptures.

72. These performances included the core quintet plus Dewey Johnson and Earl Freeman. Lopez, *William Parker Sessionography*, 9, 21. The building later became Yaffa Café, a Middle Eastern restaurant that survives to this day.

73. William Parker, email to author, September 11, 2018.

74. Parker interview, February 8, 2016; Baird, liner notes, *The Music Ensemble*, [3].

75. Billy Bang, *Vietnam: The Aftermath* (Justin Time, 2001); Billy Bang, *Vietnam: Reflections* (Justin Time, 2005).

76. Parker appeared on Billy Bang's Survival Ensemble, *New York Collage* (Anima Records, 1978); Billy Bang's Survival Ensemble, *Black Man's Blues* (NoBusiness Records, 2011); Billy Bang Sextet, *The Fire from Within* (Soul Note, 1985); Billy Bang Sextet, *Live at Carlos 1* (Soul Note, 1987).

77. Baird, liner notes, *The Music Ensemble*, [2].

78. Parker, *Who Owns Music?*, 46.

79. William Parker, interview by author, digital recording, December 21, 2018.

80. Sultan played bass, congas, and other percussion instruments. Parker also played in Sultan's band Aboriginal Music Society. Parker interview, February 8, 2016.

81. Cooper-Moore interview, September 30, 2016.

82. Lopez, *William Parker Sessionography*, 4.

83. Claudine Isé, "Considering the Art World Alternatives: LACE and Community Formation in Los Angeles," in *Sons and Daughters of Los: Culture and Community in L.A.*, ed. David E. James (Philadelphia: Temple University Press, 2003), 88–90.

84. Parker interview, February 8, 2016; "Back Matter," in "Robert Creeley, A Gathering," special issue, *Boundary 2* 6, no. 3–7, no. 1 (1978): 566; "Action Exchange," *American Libraries* 10, no. 7 (1979): 400; Leonard Levy, "The ABCs of Media," *Threepenny Review*, no. 2 (summer 1980): 7–8; Felix Stefanile, letter to the editor, *Georgia Review* 35, no. 4 (1981): 901.

85. Concert flyer, quoted in Lopez, *William Parker Sessionography*, 25.

86. Lopez, *William Parker Sessionography*, 25, 26.

87. Alan Glover, quoted in Lopez, *William Parker Sessionography*, 28.

88. Lopez, *William Parker Sessionography*, 35, 325, 327.

89. Parker interview, February 8, 2016.

90. William Parker, email to author, September 14, 2018.

91. Kowald, liner notes, *Posium Pendasem*, [7].

92. Hermes, *Love Goes to Buildings on Fire*, 22; Heller, *Loft Jazz*, 35–36.

93. Heller, *Loft Jazz*, 38–39.

94. Hazell, "A Place to Play What We Want," 40.

95. William Parker, liner notes, *Mayor of Punkville* (AUM Fidelity, 2000), [3].

96. Kelley, "New Monastery," 145.

97. Hermes, *Love Goes to Buildings on Fire*, 23.

98. Bernard Gendron, "The Downtown Music Scene," in *The Downtown Book: The New York Art Scene 1974–1984*, ed. Marvin J. Taylor (Princeton, NJ: Princeton University Press, 2006), 44; Alex Stewart, *Making the Scene: Contemporary New York City Big Band Jazz* (Berkeley: University of California Press, 2007), 32.

99. Gendron, "The Downtown Music Scene," 49.

100. Gendron, "The Downtown Music Scene," 49; Gary Giddens, "Up from the Saloon: Lofts Celebrate Alternative Jazz," *Village Voice*, June 7, 1976; Robert Palmer, "Jazz in the New York Lofts—New Music in a New Setting," *New York Times*, October 10, 1976; Stanley Crouch, "Rashied Ali and the Lofts: Up from Slavery," *SoHo Weekly News*, June 24, 1976; Ron Wellburn, "The SoHo Loft Jazz," *Music Journal* (March 1977): 26–28; Chris Flicker and Thierry Trombert, "Qu'est-ce que la loft generation," *Jazz* (France), June 1977, 13–23; Werner Panke, "New York Loft Scene," *Jazz Forum* (United Kingdom), February 1978, 56–59; Christoph Wagner, "Im Maschinenraum der Avantgarde: Die New Yorker Loft-Szene," in "Neue Zeitschrift für Musik," *Artmix and Electronics* 168, no. 5 (2007): 66–67; Tamar Barzel, "The Praxis of Composition-Improvisation and the Poetics of Creative Kinship," in *Jazz/Not Jazz: The Music and Its Boundaries*, ed. David Ake et al. (Berkeley: University of California Press, 2012), 178–79.

101. Les Ledbetter, "Aficionados of Innovative Jazz Get Their Fill at Studio Rivbea," *New York Times*, July 10, 1974.

102. Alice Sparberg Alexiou, *Devil's Mile: The Rich, Gritty History of the Bowery* (New York: St. Martin's, 2018), 225.

103. Josh Rosenthal, "Hangin' on the Bowery: Observations on the Accomplishment of Authenticity at CBGB," *Ethnography* 9, no. 2 (2008): 149–50; Daniel Kane, "Richard Hell, 'Genesis: Grasp,' and the Blank Generation: From Poetry to Punk in New York's Lower East Side," *Contemporary Literature* 52, no. 2 (2011): 337–38; Richard E. Ocejo, *Upscaling Downtown: From Bowery Saloons to Cocktail Bars in New York City* (Princeton, NJ: Princeton University Press, 2014), 30.

104. Heller, *Loft Jazz*, 84.

105. Hermes, *Love Goes to Buildings on Fire*, 123.

106. Heller, *Loft Jazz*, 50, 53, 138.

107. "Commentary," *Black Perspective in Music* 3, no. 3 (1975): 348.

108. Heller, *Loft Jazz*, 52.

109. William Parker recalled playing at the Brook on 17th Street and two places on Mercer Street, one named Inroads and the other known as the Kitchen. See the loft map in this chapter.

110. In addition to Lowe and Parker, *Black Beings* also featured Joseph Jarman on soprano and alto saxophones, Rashid Sinan on drums, and Raymond "the Wizard" Cheng on violin.

111. Jemeel Moondoc, "Muntu: The Essay," in liner notes, *Muntu Recordings* (NoBusiness, 2009), 47–49.

112. Moondoc, "Muntu: The Essay," 55.

113. Parker email, September 10, 2018.

114. Moondoc, "Muntu: The Essay," 54.

115. Ed Hazell, "Carved Out of the Hard Dark Ebony of Africa: The Story of Jemeel Moondoc and Muntu," in liner notes, *Muntu Recordings* (NoBusiness, 2009), 64.

116. The April 20, 1975, performance at Ali's Alley was not released until *Muntu Recordings* (NoBusiness, 2009).

117. Heller, *Loft Jazz*, 109.

118. Ed Hazell, "A Muntu Sessionography," in liner notes, *Muntu Recordings* (NoBusiness, 2009), 92–95.

119. Quoted in Hazell, "Carved Out of the Hard Dark Ebony of Africa," 68.

120. Hazell, "Carved Out of the Hard Dark Ebony of Africa," 68.

121. Parker interview, February 8, 2016.

122. Hazell, "A Muntu Sessionography," 95–99, 100–101.

123. Hazell, "Carved Out of the Hard Dark Ebony of Africa," 71.

124. Hazell, "A Muntu Sessionography," 101.

125. Hazell, "Carved Out of the Hard Dark Ebony of Africa," 73–74.

126. Jemeel Moondoc, quoted in Hazell, "Carved Out of the Hard Dark Ebony of Africa," 75.

127. Hazell, "Carved Out of the Hard Dark Ebony of Africa," 76.

128. Lopez, *William Parker Sessionography*, 14.

129. Parker interview, February 8, 2016.

130. Lopez, *William Parker Sessionography*, 26–27.

131. William Parker, interview by author, digital recording, July 15, 2016; Patricia Nicholson, interview by author, digital recording, October 30, 2016.

Chapter 5: "Music That Will Give People Hope"

Epigraph: William Parker, *Who Owns Music? Notes from a Spiritual Journey*, 2nd ed. (Köln: Herausgeberin, 2013), 34.

1. Parker revived this piece many decades later, performing it with vocalist Leena Conquest and pianist Eri Yamamoto on a tour in Italy in March 2009. Parker then recorded a version of this piece with his band Raining on the Moon, appearing on William Parker, *Wood Flute Songs: Anthology/Live 2006–2012*, CD 7, track 3 (AUM Fidelity, 2013). Rick Lopez, *William Parker Sessionography: Attempting a Complete Historical Arc* (New York: Centering, 2014), 371.

2. Patricia Nicholson, interview by author, digital recording, October 30, 2016.

3. Patricia Nicholson, quoted in Ed Hazell, "Centering: Art Is the Process of Living," in liner notes, *Centering: Unreleased Early Recordings 1976–1987* (NoBusiness, 2012), 15.

4. Nicholson interview, October 30, 2016.

5. Unfortunately, the notebook has since been lost.

6. William Parker, interview by author, digital recording, April 5, 2016.

7. Hazell, "Centering: Art Is the Process of Living," 16.

8. Nicholson interview, October 30, 2016.

9. Nicholson interview, October 30, 2016.

10. Hazell, "Centering: Art Is the Process of Living," 15–16.

11. Lopez, *William Parker Sessionography*, 73, 75.

12. Concert program cited in Lopez, *William Parker Sessionography*, 73.

13. Concert flyer, December 16, 1990, Centering Archive, New York.

14. William Parker, email to author, September 21, 2018.

15. Hazell, "Centering: Art Is the Process of Living," 14–15.

16. Nicholson interview, October 30, 2016.

17. William Parker, interview in Ed Hazell, "A Different Architectural Blueprint in Each Section," in liner notes, *Centering: Unreleased Early Recordings 1976–1987* (NoBusiness, 2012), 32–33.

18. Parker, *Who Owns Music?*, 26, 27, 34.

19. A live recording of this performance was broadcast during the 1994 "Loft Festival." Hazell, "Centering: Art Is the Process of Living," 17; Lopez, *William Parker Sessionography*, 12, 23.

20. Parker email, September 21, 2018.

21. Lopez, *William Parker Sessionography*, 22.

22. Released on William Parker, *Centering: Unreleased Early Recordings 1976–1987* (NoBusiness, 2012), disc 6, tracks 1–3.

23. Rozanne Levine appeared on a number of early recordings with Parker. Then, after falling into obscurity in the 1980s, she had a resurgence in the 1990s and 2000s, working with Anthony Braxton, Mark Whitecage, the Nu Band, and others.

24. Parker interview in Hazell, "A Different Architectural Blueprint," 62.

25. Parker interview in Hazell, "A Different Architectural Blueprint."

26. Patricia Nicholson, quoted in Hazell, "A Different Architectural Blueprint," 62.

27. Parker recorded another version of this piece with the same title on the record *Song Cycles*, which he dedicated to bassist Henry Grimes. Various artists, *Song Cycle* (Boxholder Records, 2001); Patricia Nicholson, quoted in Hazell, "Centering: Art Is the Process of Living," 20.

28. Rozanne Levine, quoted in Hazell, "Centering: Art Is the Process of Living," 20.

29. William Parker, *Centering: Unreleased Early Recordings 1976–1987* (NoBusiness Records, 2012), disc 6, track 1.

30. John Hagen played tenor saxophone, soprano saxophone, and bassoon. Parker had previously workshopped *Document Humanum* in Ensemble Muntu at the Loft Jazz Festival, live at WKCR-FM, February 29, 1976. Lopez, *William Parker Sessionography*, 17, 22.

31. Levine, quoted in Hazell, "Centering: Art Is the Process of Living," 17.

32. William Parker, *Long Hidden: The Olmec Series* (AUM Fidelity, 2006), track 6. The recording is just 3:46 in length, but in live performances it reached as long as 37:50 at the Guelph Jazz Festival in 1999 and 51:13 at Somewhere There in Toronto in 2008. Lopez, *William Parker Sessionography*, 218, 364.

33. Excerpts of this extended version appeared on William Parker, *At Somewhere There* (Barnyard Records, 2010), track 1.

34. William Parker interview in Hazell, "A Different Architectural Blueprint," 32.

35. "Commitment" provided the name to the collaborative quartet that Parker later joined with Jason Kao Hwang, Will Connell, and Zen Matsuura in 1979.

36. William Parker interview in Hazell, "A Different Architectural Blueprint," 34.

37. William Parker, email to author, September 27, 2018.

38. Roderic Knight, review of *Kora Melodies from the Republic of Gambia*, by Alhaji Bai Konte, *African Arts* 8, no. 1 (1974): 78–79, 88.

39. Parker email, September 27, 2018.

40. William Parker interview in Hazell, "A Different Architectural Blueprint," 34–35. Lewis Worrell gained his greatest visibility through his work with Albert Ayler, Sunny Murray, Archie Shepp, and Robin Kenyatta. Donald Garrett is better known as a saxophonist and bass clarinetist, but occasionally played the bass. Henry Grimes had a significant impact in the 1960s and early 1970s, but then fell into obscurity before having a resurgence and numerous recordings since 2004.

41. William Parker interview in Hazell, "A Different Architectural Blueprint," 35.

42. Lopez, *William Parker Sessionography*, 25, 39.

43. *Corn Meal Suite* was never released on record and has no relation to Parker's later work *Corn Meal Dance*, which he recorded in 2006. An interview that accompanied the 1993 radio airing erroneously stated that the piece had been performed and filmed in 1976, although flyers that survived from the time indicate that the piece was first developed between June 1977 and early 1978. Lopez, *William Parker Sessionography*, 25.

44. Parker learned about David Ware's music as a teenager from Cooper-Moore. William Parker, interview by author, digital recording, December 21, 2018.

45. William Parker interview in Hazell, "A Different Architectural Blueprint," 37.

46. David S. Ware's most high-profile early recording was on Cecil Taylor's record *Dark to Themselves* (Enja Records, 1976).

47. Drummer Sinan Tertemiz recorded the concert on a half-track Revox machine, but it is unknown whether a copy has survived. Hazell, "A Different Architectural Blueprint," 41; William Parker, email to author, September 25, 2018.

48. William Parker, quoted in Hazell, "A Different Architectural Blueprint," 41.

49. Hazell, "A Different Architectural Blueprint," 41.

50. Lopez, *William Parker Sessionography*, 39.

51. Hazell, "A Different Architectural Blueprint," 41.

52. Parker, *Centering*.

53. Ortiz Walton, *Music: Black, White, and Blue* (New York: Morrow, 1972), 144–46.

54. Valerie Wilmer, *As Serious as Your Life: The Story of the New Jazz* (Westport, CT: Lawrence Hill, 1977), 247.

55. Milton C. Cummings Jr., "Government and the Arts: An Overview," in *Public Money and the Muse*, ed. Stephen Benedict (New York: W. W. Norton, 1991), 57; National Endowment for the Arts, *A Brief Chronology of Federal Support for the Arts: 1965–2000* (Washington, DC: National Endowment for the Arts, 2000), 34.

56. Michael Brenson, *Visionaries and Outcasts* (New York: New Press, 2001); Jane Alexander, *Command Performance* (New York: Public Affairs, 2000); Gregory B. Lewis and

Michael Rushton, "Understanding State Spending on the Arts, 1976–99," *State and Local Government Review* 39, no. 2 (2007): 109–10.

57. Douglas P. Starr, "Private and Government Sources: Funding the Arts," *Music Educators Journal* 69, no. 8 (1983): 44.

58. Eric Porter, *What Is This Thing Called Jazz? African American Musicians as Artists, Critics, and Activists* (Berkeley: University of California Press, 2002), 214–16, 222–24.

59. Quoted in Homer A. Jack, "The Second U.N. Special Session on Disarmament," *Arms Control Today* (February 1982): 4.

60. John Simpson, "Global Non-proliferation Policies: Retrospect and Prospect," *Review of International Studies* 8, no. 2 (1982): 80; "North Atlantic Treaty Organization: Documents from the Bonn Summit," *International Legal Materials* 21, no. 4 (1982): 905–6.

61. Stefan Frölich, "Wider die nukleare Bedrohung: Die Amerikanische 'Nuclear Freeze Campaign' 1980–84," *Vierteljahrshefte für Zeitgeschichte* 38, no. 4 (1990): 647; Sharon Erickson Nepstad, "Disruptive Action and the Prophetic Tradition: War Resistance in the Plowshares Movement," in "War and Peace," special issue, *U.S. Catholic Historian* 27, no. 2 (2009): 98; Matt Meyer and Paul Magno, "Hard to Find: Building for Nonviolent Revolution and the Pacifist Underground," in *The Hidden 1970s: Histories of Radicalism*, ed. Dan Berger (New Brunswick, NJ: Rutgers University Press, 2010), 261.

62. See Christopher Harless, "Announcing the Impossible," in *Faith, Resistance, and the Future: Daniel Berrigan's Challenge to Catholic Social Thought*, ed. James L. Marsh and Anna J. Brown (New York: Fordham University Press, 2012), 240; Anna J. Brown, "The Language of the Incandescent Heart: Daniel Berrigan's and Etty Hillesum's Responses to a Culture of Death," in *Faith, Resistance, and the Future*, ed. James L. Marsh and Anna J. Brown (New York: Fordham University Press, 2012), 62–63.

63. Michele Naar-Obed, "Nonviolent Peace Activism," in "War, Dissent, and Justice: A Dialogue," special issue, *Social Justice* 30, no. 2 (2003): 121; Sharon Erickson Nepstad, "Persistent Resistance: Commitment and Community in the Plowshares Movement," *Social Problems* 51, no. 1 (2004): 48, 50, 52, 54–56; Sharon Erickson Nepstad and Stellan Vinthagen, "Strategic Changes and Cultural Adaptations: Explaining Differential Outcomes in the International Plowshares Movement," in "Special Issue: Antiwar Movements," *International Journal of Peace Studies* 13, no. 1 (2008): 16, 21.

64. "Pursuit of Peace," Atomic Bomb Museum, accessed June 19, 2017, www .atomicbombmuseum.org/5_timetable.shtml.

65. Arjun Makhijani and Michio Kaku, "Nuclear Disarmament and Its Verification," *Economic and Political Weekly* 17, no. 38 (1982): 1531; Tony Travers, "Cities and Conflict Resolution," in *The Quest for Security: Protection without Protectionism and the Challenge of Global Governance*, ed. Joseph E. Stiglitz (New York: Columbia University Press, 2013), 277.

66. Charles B. Strozier, *Until the Fires Stopped Burning: 9/11 and New York City in the Words and Experiences of Survivors and Witnesses* (New York: Columbia University Press, 2011),

213–14; Robert Jay Lifton, *Death in Life: Survivors of Hiroshima* (Chapel Hill: University of North Carolina Press, 1991), 104; Tony Delamothe, "Hiroshima: The Unforgettable Fire," *British Medical Journal* 299, no. 6706 (1989): 1023; Linda W. Rees, "A Thousand Cranes: A Curriculum of Peace," in "A Curriculum of Peace," special issue, *English Journal* 89, no. 5 (2000): 98; Mary F. Wright and Sandra Kowalczyk, "Peace by Piece: The Freeing Power of Language and Literacy through the Arts," in "A Curriculum of Peace," special issue, *English Journal* 89, no. 5 (2000): 61–62.

67. Sasaki Sadako, quoted in Christine Stewart-Nuñez, "Filaments of Prayer," *North American Review* 298, no. 1 (2013): 43.

68. Glenn D. Hook, "Evolution of the Anti-Nuclear Discourse in Japan," in "War, Peace and Culture," special issue, *Current Research on Peace and Violence* 10, no. 1 (1987): 38; Lindsley Cameron and Masao Miyoshi, "Hiroshima, Nagasaki, and the World Sixty Years Later," *Virginia Quarterly Review* 81, no. 4 (2005): 42.

69. Patricia Nicholson, email to author, September 27, 2018.

70. Peter Kornbluh, "Test Case for the Reagan Doctrine: The Covert Contra War," *Third World Quarterly* 9, no. 4 (1987): 1118–19.

71. "Reagan's Rag-Tag Mob," *Economic and Political Weekly* 22, no. 11 (1987): 429–30; Barry H. Barlow, "The Nicaraguan-Contra Negotiations of 1988: A Test of the Reagan Doctrine," *Canadian Journal of Latin American and Caribbean Studies* 18, no. 35 (1993): 68–70.

72. Cecil Taylor, liner notes, *Nicaragua: No Parasan* (Nica, 1984).

73. Peter Kowald, liner notes, trans. Isabel Seeberg and Paul Lytton, *Posium Pendasem* (Free Music Production, 1999), [6].

74. William Parker, interview in *Rising Tones Cross*, film by Ebba Jahn, 1985.

75. Charles Gayle, interview in *Rising Tones Cross*, film by Ebba Jahn, 1985.

76. Charles Gayle, poem recited in *Rising Tones Cross*, film by Ebba Jahn, 1985.

77. Peter Kowald, interview in *Rising Tones Cross*, film by Ebba Jahn, 1985.

78. Kowald interview in *Rising Tones Cross*.

79. Amy C. Beal, *Carla Bley* (Urbana-Champaign: University of Illinois Press, 2011), 27–28.

80. William Parker, interview in *Rising Tones Cross*, film by Ebba Jahn, 1985.

81. Patricia Nicholson, interview in *Rising Tones Cross*, film by Ebba Jahn, 1985.

82. Nicholson interview, October 30, 2016.

83. Kowald, liner notes, *Posium Pendasem*, [9].

84. Parker email, September 27, 2018.

85. Miriam Parker, interview by author, digital recording, June 6, 2017.

86. Miriam Parker interview, June 6, 2017.

87. Hazell, quoted in "Centering: Art Is the Process of Living," 17.

88. Matthew Shipp, interview by author, digital recording, July 29, 2016.

89. Cooper-Moore, interview by author, digital recording, September 30, 2016.

Chapter 6: "Music Is Supposed to Change People"

Epigraph: The title is from an article by Robert Palmer, "Cecil Taylor Group at New Village Club," *New York Times*, January 8, 1982. The epigraph is from Steve Lake, "Cecil Taylor in Berlin," in liner notes, *Cecil Taylor in Berlin '88* (FMP, 1989), 43.

1. Cecil Taylor, quoted in A. B. Spellman, *Four Lives in the Bebop Business* (New York: Limelight Editions, [1966] 1985), 6.

2. Cecil Taylor, quoted in Bert Noglik, "A Light Ignited in the Open: Cecil Taylor—Both Sides of the Wall," in liner notes, *Cecil Taylor in Berlin '88* (FMP, 1989), 65.

3. Taylor's concerts at the Five Spot are also what propelled the club onto the world stage as a serious place to hear jazz in New York. It brought such financial success to the owner, Joe Termini, that it allowed him to open a second club, the Jazz Gallery. Spellman, *Four Lives*, 6–7, 9–10; Steven Block, "Pitch-Class Transformation in Free Jazz," *Music Theory Spectrum* 12, no. 2 (1990): 181.

4. Cecil Taylor Quartet, *Looking Ahead!* (Contemporary Records, 1959); Iain Anderson, *This Is Our Music: Free Jazz, The Sixties, and American Culture* (Philadelphia: University of Pennsylvania Press, 2007), 59.

5. Cecil Taylor, quoted in Nat Hentoff, liner notes, *Looking Ahead!* (Contemporary Records, 1959).

6. Iain Anderson, "Jazz Outside the Marketplace: Free Improvisation and Nonprofit Sponsorship of the Arts, 1965–1980," *American Music* 20, no. 2 (2002): 138; Anderson, *This Is Our Music*, 114; Charles H. Rowell and Brent Hayes Edwards, "An Interview with Brent Hayes Edwards," *Callaloo* 22, no. 4 (1999): 787.

7. Cecil Taylor, liner notes, in Cecil Taylor, *Unit Structures* (Blue Note, 1966).

8. Andrew W. Bartlett, "Cecil Taylor, Identity Energy, and the Avant-Garde African American Body," *Perspectives of New Music* 33, no. 1/2 (1995): 276.

9. Ekkehard Jost, "Instant Composing as Body Language," in liner notes, *Cecil Taylor in Berlin '88* (FMP, 1989), 87.

10. Lynette Westendorf, "Cecil Taylor: Indent—'Second Layer,'" *Perspectives on New Music* 33, no. 1/2 (1995): 295.

11. Jost, "Instant Composing as Body Language," 87–88.

12. Kevin Lynch, "Cecil Taylor and the Poetics of Living," *DownBeat*, November 1986, 24.

13. Meinrad Buholzer, "Cecil Taylor (Interview)," *Cadence*, December 1984, 5.

14. Lopez, *The William Parker Sessionography*, 7–8.

15. Jemeel Moondoc had also been slated to play soprano saxophone at the concert, but he was hospitalized with sickle-cell anemia just before the concert and was not able to play. William Parker, email to author, January 30, 2019.

16. William Parker, interview by author, digital recording, February 23, 2016.

17. William Parker, interview by author, digital recording, January 27, 2017.

18. Cecil Taylor, quoted in Carl E. Baugher, *Turning Corners: The Life and Music of Leroy Jenkins* (Redwood, NY: Cadence Jazz Books, 2000), 147n4.

19. William Parker, email to author, October 3, 2018; Parker interview, January 27, 2017; Lopez, *William Parker Sessionography*, 33.

20. Bill Brower and Willard Jenkins, "Bill Brower: Notes from a Keen Observer," in "Jazz in Washington," special issue, *Washington History* 26 (2014): 61–62, 64, 70.

21. *Coda* 177 (December 1980): 33; Parker interview, February 23, 2016.

22. Parker email, January 30, 2019.

23. Perfect Sound Forever, accessed October 3, 2018, www.furious.com/perfect/soundscape .html.

24. Parker interview, February 23, 2016.

25. Parker interview, January 27, 2017.

26. Jost, "Instant Composing as Body Language," 93.

27. Cecil Taylor, interview in Spencer A. Richards, liner notes, Cecil Taylor Unit, *Live in Vienna* (Leo Records, 1988).

28. Jost, "Instant Composing as Body Language," 94.

29. "Cecil Taylor at the Public," *New York Times*, May 28, 1981; Eleanor Blau, "Weekender Guide, Friday: Cecil Taylor Unit at the Public Theater," *New York Times*, May 29, 1981; John Rockwell, "Cecil Taylor and Newest Unit Perform at Public," *New York Times*, June 1, 1981.

30. Lopez, *William Parker Sessionography*, 44–45.

31. Bill Dixon, *November 1981* (Soul Note, 1982).

32. Cecil Taylor, *Calling It the 8th* (Hat Hut, 1983).

33. Lopez, *William Parker Sessionography*, 45.

34. Parker interview, February 23, 2016.

35. Parker interview, January 27, 2017.

36. Palmer, "Cecil Taylor Group at New Village Club."

37. Parker interview, January 27, 2017.

38. Palmer, "Cecil Taylor Group at New Village Club."

39. Parker interview, January 27, 2017.

40. Vincent Zanetti, "Le Griot et le Pouvoir: Une Relation Ambiguë," *Cahiers de Musiques Traditionnelles* 3: *Musique et Pouvoirs* (1990): 161–72; Manthia Diawara, "The Song of the Griot," *Transition*, no. 74 (1997): 16–30.

41. Paul Oliver, *Savannah Syncopators: African Retentions in the Blues* (Worthing, UK: Littlehampton Book Services, 1970); Amiri Baraka, "Jazz Criticism and Its Effects on the Art Form," in *New Perspectives on Jazz*, ed. David Baker (Washington, DC: Smithsonian Institution, 1990), 57; Oriane Chambet-Werner, "Entre Jazz et 'Musique du Monde': Regards Croisés sur la Rencontre de l'Autre," *Cahiers de Musiques Traditionnelles* 13: *Métissages* (2000): 91–102; Jean-Philippe Marcoux, "Troping and Groupings: Jazz Artistry, Activism and Cultural Memory in Langston Hughes's 'Ask Your Mama,'" CLA *Journal* 53, no. 4 (June 2010): 387–409; Kathy Lou Schultz, "Amiri Baraka's *Wise Why's Y's*: Lineages of the Afro-Modernist Epic," *Journal of Modern Literature* 35, no. 3 (2012): 25–50.

42. Taylor used the multivolume work *A Book of the Beginnings*, by Gerald Massey, which was readily available in African bookstores in Harlem. The book was originally published in 1881 but was reprinted many times. Gerald Massey, *A Book of the Beginnings: Containing an Attempt to Recover and Reconstitute the Lost Origines of the Myths and Mysteries, Types and Symbols, Religion and Language, with Egypt for the Mouthpiece and Africa as the Birthplace* (London: Williams and Norgate, 1881).

43. Parker interview, February 23, 2016.

44. Spearman's frequent collaborators included saxophonist Marco Eneidi (1956–2016) and drummer Donald Robinson (b. 1953), among others. Glenn Spearman, *Night after Night* (Musa-Physics, 1981).

45. Borca appears on a number of recordings with Jimmy Lyons and Cecil Taylor but has never led a recording session of her own.

46. Malik's three records as a leader with his quartet are *Looking East: A Suite in Three Parts* (Boxholder Records, 2001); *Companions* (Eremite, 2002); and *Last Set: Live at the 1369 Jazz Club* (Boxholder Records, 2004).

47. Andre Martinez, cited in Lopez, *William Parker Sessionography*, 47.

48. Parker interview, February 23, 2016.

49. Other than his work with Taylor, Andre Martinez is best known for his contributions to the collective band Earth People, which released five records in 2001–7.

50. Martinez, quoted in Lopez, *William Parker Sessionography*, 48.

51. The collaborations of Cecil Taylor and Dianne McIntyre began with a performance at the Studio Museum in New York in 1978, before Parker had started playing in the Unit. They had met previously while Cecil was teaching at Antioch College in McIntyre's native Ohio.

52. Danielle Goldman, *I Want to Be Ready: Improvised Dance as a Practice of Freedom* (Ann Arbor: University of Michigan Press, 2010), 57, 75–87, 141, 144; Gia Kourlas, "Dianne McIntyre Talks about Her Love Affair with Dance," August 20, 2012, www.timeout

.com/newyork/dance/dianne-mcintyre-talks-about-her-love-affair-with-modern-dance; Ahmed Abdullah, *Life's Force* (About Time Records, 1979).

53. Goldman, *I Want to Be Ready*, 75; Kourlas, "Dianne McIntyre Talks about Her Love Affair with Dance."

54. Dianne McIntyre, "Home," accessed October 3, 2018, www.DianneMcIntyre.com. One scholar has argued that through her portrayal of the body, McIntyre was influential in shaping a sense of the "black female self." John Perpener III, "Dance, Difference, and Racial Dualism at the Turn of the Century," *Dance Research Journal* 32, no. 1 (2000): 67–68.

55. Dianne McIntyre, quoted in Rhett S. Jones, "Community and Commentators: Black Theatre and Its Critics," *Black American Literature Forum* 14, no. 2 (1980): 69.

56. Goldman, *I Want to Be Ready*, 79.

57. Parker interview, February 23, 2016.

58. Martinez, cited in Lopez, *William Parker Sessionography*, 51.

59. Agostino Mela, cited in Lopez, *William Parker Sessionography*, 51; Gautam Dasgupta, "Pinuccio Sciola: Sculptor in the Time of Stone," *Performing Arts Journal* 17, no. 1 (1995): 35–42.

60. Parker email, January 30, 2019.

61. *Coda* 192 (October 1983): 26.

62. Alex Ross, "Free Jazz by German Saxophonist," *New York Times*, November 25, 1992; William Parker, quoted in Lopez, *William Parker Sessionography*, 41.

63. Steve Swell, interview by author, email transcript, February 20, 2017.

64. Parker interview, February 23, 2016.

65. Lopez, *William Parker Sessionography*, 55–56.

66. Lopez, *William Parker Sessionography*, 56.

67. Stanley Crouch, "Cecil Taylor: Pitfalls of the Primitive," *Village Voice*, March 30, 1982, 59.

68. Parker interview, January 27, 2017.

69. Crouch, "Cecil Taylor," 59; Spellman, *Four Lives in the Bebop Business*, 28; Kelley, "New Monastery: Monk and the Jazz Avant-Garde," 153–54.

70. Crouch, "Cecil Taylor," 59.

71. Arun Nevader, "John Coltrane: Music and Metaphysics," *Threepenny Review*, no. 10 (1982): 26; Christoph Wagner and Nina Polaschegg, "C.T.—der Ausserirdische: Cecil Taylor, Wegbereiter des Freien Jazz, wird 75," *Neue Zeitschrift für Musik* 165, no. 2: *Soundscapes* (2004): 57; Gabriel Solis, *Monk's Music: Thelonious Monk and Jazz History in the Making* (Berkeley: University of California Press, 2008), 162.

72. William Parker, interview by author, digital recording, February 16, 2016. Critic Howard Mandel once referred to Parker as among the "wild bunch" in a review of his work. Howard Mandel, "Beneath the Underdog," *DownBeat*, July 1998.

73. Matthew Shipp, interview by author, digital recording, July 29, 2016.

74. Crouch, "Cecil Taylor," 59.

75. Martinez, quoted in Lopez, *William Parker Sessionography*, 47.

76. Gennari, *Blowin' Hot and Cool: Jazz and Its Critics*, 355.

77. Peter Watrous, "Cecil Taylor, Long a Rebel, Is Finding Steady Work," *New York Times*, May 10, 1991.

78. *Jazz*, directed by Ken Burns, 2001; "Jazz," pbs.org, accessed October 4, 2018, www.pbs .org/kenburns/jazz/home; Jan Stevens, "On Ken Burns *Jazz* Documentary and Bill Evans," accessed October 4, 2018, www.billevanswebpages.com/burns.html; Jeffrey St. Clair, "The Aesthetic Crimes of Ken Burns: Now That's Not Jazz," Counterpunch.org, accessed January 26, 2016.

79. Bartlett, "Cecil Taylor, Identity Energy, and the Avant-Garde African American Body," 286.

80. Brian Lamb, "The All-American Skin Game, or the Decoy of Race," *Booknotes*, C-SPAN, May 12, 1996; Stanley Crouch, "Tupac Shows Risk of Being Rapped Up in Stage Life," *New York Daily News*, September 11, 1996; Stanley Crouch, "The Root of Alex Haley's Fraud," *New York Daily News*, April 12, 1998; Stanley Crouch, "Nation in Love with Minstrelsy: Spike Lee, Tyler Perry, Snoop Dogg and the Struggle to Define Blackness," *New York Daily News*, April 25, 2011; Stanley Crouch, "Cornel West Is an Expert Showman but Nothing More: The Lead Huckster of the Ivy League's Takedown," *New York Daily News*, May 23, 2011; Jerry Gafio Watts, *Amiri Baraka: The Politics and Art of a Black Intellectual* (New York: New York University Press, 2001), 203.

81. Jost, *Free Jazz*, 90.

82. Tomasz Stańko, "Statements," in liner notes, *Cecil Taylor in Berlin '88* (FMP, 1989), 58.

83. Stańko, "Statements."

84. Imre Fabian, "Cologne," *The New Grove Dictionary of Opera*, ed. Stanley Sadie (London: Macmillan, 1998), 904–5.

85. Lopez, *William Parker Sessionography*, 67.

86. Martinez, quoted in Lopez, *William Parker Sessionography*, 67.

87. Cecil Taylor Segments II (Orchestra of Two Continents), *Winged Serpent (Sliding Quadrants)* (Soul Note, 1985).

88. Lopez, *William Parker Sessionography*, 68.

89. Nicole Wild, *Dictionnaire des Théâtres Parisiens au XIXe Siècle: Les Théâtres et la Musique* (Paris: Aux Amateurs de Livres, 1989), 76–77.

90. Lopez, *William Parker Sessionography*, 69.

91. Jon Pareles, "Jazz: Cecil Taylor Septet," *New York Times*, November 20, 1984; *Village Voice*, November 20, 1984, 128; concert poster, Cecil Taylor Unit, December 17, 1984; *Coda*, no. 199 (December 1984): 37.

92. Martinez, quoted in Lopez, *William Parker Sessionography*, 69.

93. Gary Giddens, center page, *Village Voice*, December 12, 1984.

94. Ras Moshe, quoted in Lopez, *William Parker Sessionography*, 69.

95. Lopez, *William Parker Sessionography*, 69.

96. Nele Hertling, "A Few Words of Introduction," trans. Barbara Fussmann, liner notes, *Cecil Taylor in Berlin '88* (FMP, 1989), 5.

97. The results of the Workshop Freie Musik constituted part of *Olu Iwa* (Soul Note, 1986).

98. Steve Lake, "Cecil Taylor in Berlin," in liner notes, *Cecil Taylor in Berlin '88* (FMP, 1989), 43.

99. Cecil Taylor European Orchestra, *Alms/Tiergarten (Spree)* (FMP, 1988).

100. Lake, "Cecil Taylor in Berlin," 45–46.

101. Stańko, "Statements," 58.

102. Wolter Wierbos, "Statements," in liner notes, *Cecil Taylor in Berlin '88* (FMP, 1989), 57.

103. Lake, "Cecil Taylor in Berlin," 49.

104. Parker interview, February 23, 2016.

105. Parker interview, February 23, 2016.

106. Peter Watrous, "Sounds around Town," *New York Times*, February 5, 1988; Jon Pareles, "Jazz: Cecil Taylor Quintet," *New York Times*, February 7, 1988; John Rockwell, "The Cecil Taylor Enigma Is Intact, Despite New LP's," *New York Times*, May 22, 1988.

107. Pareles, "Jazz: Cecil Taylor Quintet."

108. Lopez, *William Parker Sessionography*, 103–4.

109. The Cecil Taylor Unit had previously played a week at Sweet Basil in April 1986. Sweet Basil had been opened by Sharif Esmat in 1974 and gained a reputation as one of the premier jazz clubs in New York City. It closed in 2001. Jon Pareles, "Jazz: Cecil Taylor Unit," *New York Times*, April 27, 1986; *Cadence* 14, no. 12 (1988): 92; *New York*, January 30, 1989, 88; Peter Watrous, "Cecil Taylor, Clearinghouse of Jazz Ideas," *New York Times*, February 3, 1989; *DownBeat*, May 1989, 55; Lopez, *William Parker Sessionography*, 104–6. Watrous, "Cecil Taylor, Clearinghouse of Jazz Ideas."

110. Peter Watrous, "Cecil Taylor, Clearinghouse of Jazz Ideas."

111. Martinez, quoted in Lopez, *William Parker Sessionography*, 108.

112. William Parker, quoted by Andre Martinez in Lopez, *William Parker Sessionography*, 108.

113. Richard Cook, liner notes, Cecil Taylor Feel Trio, *2 Ts for a Lovely T* (Codanza, 2002), [3].

114. Cook, liner notes, Cecil Taylor Feel Trio, *2 Ts for a Lovely T*, [7].

115. Parker interview, January 27, 2017.

116. For more about the place of the Blue Note Tokyo in the Japanese jazz scene, see E. Taylor Atkins, *Blue Nippon: Authenticating Jazz in Japan* (Durham, NC: Duke University Press, 2001).

117. Lopez, *William Parker Sessionography*, 116.

118. Fernando Gonzalez, *Boston Globe*, September 16, 1990, October 12, 1990; Nels Nelson, *Philadelphia Daily News*, November 8, 1990; Lopez, *William Parker Sessionography*, 116–67.

119. Quoted in Watrous, "Cecil Taylor, Long a Rebel."

120. Andre Martinez made this argument. Lopez, *William Parker Sessionography*, 116.

121. William Parker, interview by author, digital recording, April 5, 2016.

Chapter 7: "It Is the Job of the Artist to Incite Political Revolution"

Epigraph: Quoted in William Parker, liner notes, *Sunrise in the Tone World* (AUM Fidelity, 1997), [9].

1. William Parker, *Who Owns Music? Notes from a Spiritual Journey*, 2nd ed. (Köln: Herausgeberin, 2006), 80.

2. The title of the piece originated in the longer statement "In order to survive, we must keep hope alive." William Parker, interview by author, digital recording, April 12, 2016.

3. The Nuyorican Poets Café had been founded around 1973 and moved locations to accommodate a growing audience over the decades of its existence. It was one of the primary stages for successive generations of poets of Puerto Rican and other backgrounds. It remains one of the few resilient Lower East Side cultural centers. Daniel Kane, *All Poets Welcome: The Lower East Side Poetry Scene in the 1960s* (Berkeley: University of California Press, 2003), 203–4; Harald Zapf, "Ethnicity and Performance: Bilingualism in Spanglish Verse Culture," in "Multilingualism and American Studies," special issue, *Amerikastudien* 51, no. 1 (2006): 13–16; Tyler Allen, "Nuyorican Poets Café," *World Literature Today* 82, no. 1 (2008): 34; Plexus International Forum Onlus, accessed October 22, 2018, http://plexusinternational.org.

4. In some ways the revolutionary spirit of *FIRE!!* was present in Parker's manifesto. Langston Hughes, another writer involved with *FIRE!!*, wrote that their vision for that magazine was to "to burn up a lot of the old, dead conventional Negro-white ideas of the past . . . into a realization of the existence of the younger Negro writers and artists, and provide us with an outlet for publication not available in the limited pages of the small Negro magazines then existing." W. Samuels, "From the Wild, Wild West to Harlem's Literary Salons," *Black Issues Book Review* 2, no. 5 (2000): 14. Among other things, *FIRE!!* had been a declaration of independence of that generation from their elders such as W. E. B. Du Bois and Alain Locke. Naomi Pabst, "An Unexpected Blackness," *Transition*, no. 100 (2008): 132; Suzanne W. Churchill, "Youth Culture in *The Crisis* and *FIRE!!*," *Journal of Modern Periodical Studies* 1, no. 1 (2010): 65–68.

5. Thomas H. Wirth, "Richard Bruce Nugent," in "Contemporary Black Visual Arts Issue," *Black American Literature Forum* 19, no. 1 (1985): 16.

6. In his own time, Nugent was a groundbreaking author, having written "the first literary work of an openly homosexual theme to be published by an Afro-American writer."

He also became highly regarded for his erotic art deco drawings. Wirth, "Richard Bruce Nugent," 16; Ellen McBreen, "Biblical Gender Bending in Harlem: The Queer Performance of Nugent's *Salome*," *Art Journal* 57, no. 3 (1998): 22; Tyler T. Schmidt, "'In the Glad Flesh of My Ear': Corporeal Inscriptions in Richard Bruce Nugent's 'Geisha Man,'" *African American Review* 40, no. 1 (2006): 161–62; Farah Jasmine Griffin, "On Time, in Time, through Time: Aaron Douglas, *FIRE!!* and the Writers of the Harlem Renaissance," in "Aaron Douglas and the Harlem Renaissance," special issue, *American Studies* 49, no. 1/2 (2008): 46; Darryl Dickson-Carr, *Spoofing the Modern: Satire in the Harlem Renaissance* (Chapel Hill: University of North Carolina Press, 2015), 53–54.

7. Rick Lopez, *The William Parker Sessionography: An Attempt at a Complete Historical Arc* (New York: Centering, 2014), 62–64.

8. Four issues of the *Cricket* were published in 1968–69, edited by LeRoi Jones, Larry Neal, and A. B. Spellman.

9. Lopez, *William Parker Sessionography*, 63.

10. Parker interview, April 12, 2016.

11. Parker, *Who Owns Music?*, 59.

12. Parker interview, April 12, 2016. Hooker had been on the scene since 1975, but his recordings as a bandleader did not take off until around 1988, when he signed with the Swedish label Silkheart, which was putting out records of a number of other figures on the scene, such as saxophonists David S. Ware and Charles Gayle. Hooker has gone on to put out more than two dozen of his own records, including collaborations with alternative rock band Sonic Youth's guitarist Lee Ronaldo. William Hooker Quartet, *Lifeline* (Silkheart, 1988); William Hooker and Lee Ronaldo, *Envisioning* (Knitting Factory Works, 1995); William Hooker, *Light: The Early Years 1975–1989* (NoBusiness Records, 2016).

13. Larry Neal, "Review: *New Grass* by Albert Ayler," *The Cricket: Black Music in Evolution* 3 (1969): 39.

14. LeRoi Jones, Larry Neal, and A. B. Spellman, "The Cricket," *The Cricket: Black Music in Evolution* 1 (1968): 1–2.

15. Quoted in Larry Neal, *Visions of a Liberated Future: Black Arts Movement Writings*, ed. Michael Schwartz (New York: Thunder's Mouth Publishing, 1989), xii–xv.

16. Others would also point to the failure of Black popular music to embrace Black nationalism, even if key figures within it were cultural icons of a certain type of Black progress. Michael Hanson, "Suppose James Brown Read Fanon: The Black Arts Movement, Cultural Nationalism and the Failure of Popular Musical Praxis," *Popular Music* 27, no. 3 (2008): 341–65.

17. Lopez, *William Parker Sessionography*, 63.

18. Parker, *Who Owns Music?*, 59.

19. Parker, *Who Owns Music?*, 59; Lopez, *William Parker Sessionography*, 63.

20. Parker, *Who Owns Music?*, 59.

21. "Free Jazz Quintet," *New York Times*, May 1, 1987; "William Parker," *New York Times*, July 3, 1987; "Jazz at St. Peter's," *New York Times*, August 1, 1987.

22. Cooper-Moore, interview by author, digital recording, September 30, 2016.

23. Moncur was most active in the 1960s and 1970s, with nine records as a leader, including *Evolution* (Blue Note, 1964); *Some Other Stuff* (Blue Note, 1965); *New Africa* (BYG Actuel, 1969); and *Echoes of Prayer* (JCOA, 1974). David H. Rosenthal, "Hard Bop and Its Critics," *Black Perspective in Music* 16, no. 1 (1988): 24; Amiri Baraka, *Digging: The Afro-American Soul of American Classical Music* (Berkeley: University of California Press, 2009), 227, 396; Amy C. Beal, *Carla Bley* (Champaign-Urbana: University of Illinois Press, 2011), 53; Kathy Lou Schultz, "Amiri Baraka's *Wise Why's Y's*: Lineages of the Afro-Modernist Epic," *Journal of Modern Literature* 35, no. 3 (2012): 30.

24. Parker interview, April 12, 2016.

25. Parker interview, April 12, 2016. Parker met Brown for the first time when Brown and drummer Frank Bambara wanted to play trio with Parker. They "called him and asked him to come over for rehearsal. He came and played and it was great." Rob Brown, interview by author, email transcript, February 14–March 26, 2017.

26. Parker interview, April 12, 2016.

27. Cooper-Moore interview, September 30, 2016.

28. Parker, *Who Owns Music?*, 60.

29. Brown interview, February 14–March 26, 2017.

30. Parker, *Who Owns Music?*, 60; Parker interview, April 12, 2016.

31. Parker, *Who Owns Music?*, 60.

32. Parker interview, April 12, 2016.

33. Peter Watrous, "Evolution and Festivals and Finding the Fittest," *New York Times*, June 18, 1993.

34. William Parker, *In Order to Survive* (Black Saint, 1995).

35. Ed Hazell, cited in Lopez, *William Parker Sessionography*, 138.

36. Lopez, *William Parker Sessionography*, 147.

37. *New York*, June 27–July 4, 1994, 174.

38. Lopez, *William Parker Sessionography*, 145.

39. Parker interview, April 12, 2016. Ibarra's highly praised work includes a dozen records as a leader beginning in 1998; Susie Ibarra and Denis Charles, *Drum Talk* (Wobbly Rail, 1998).

40. *De Volkskrant*, October 20, 1995.

41. William Parker, *Compassion Seizes Bed-Stuy* (Homestead Records, 1997).

42. Parker interview, April 12, 2016.

43. Parker interview, April 12, 2016.

44. In 2015 Parker performed the piece with the Raining on the Moon Sextet in Johannesburg, South Africa, including words, although the words were not recorded. William Parker, interview by author, digital recording, August 9, 2018.

45. *Mass for the Dakota Sioux*, directed by Bruce Baillie (Canyon Cinema Foundation, 1964).

46. Parker interview, August 9, 2018.

47. Steven Joerg, interview by author, digital recording, February 7, 2017.

48. Cooper-Moore interview, September 30, 2016.

49. Peter Watrous, "Jazz Review: Mood, Minor Melodies and Tributes to the Past," *New York Times*, June 10, 1996; *Signal to Noise* 58 (2010): 28.

50. Watrous, "Jazz Review."

51. Lopez, *William Parker Sessionography*, 174.

52. *New York Magazine*, October 14, 1996. The Cooler had been hosting music since at least 1989, when Homestead Records began a Monday-night series there. Lopez, *William Parker Sessionography*, 105.

53. *Courier News*, August 22, 1996: 38; *WIRE!!*, no. 157 (March 1997): 41; *Cadence* 23, no. 7 (1997): 28; William Parker's In Order to Survive, *The Peach Orchard*, 2 CDs (AUM Fidelity, 1998); Lopez, *William Parker Sessionography*, 184, 190.

54. William Parker, liner notes, *The Peach Orchard*; Lopez, *William Parker Sessionography*, 184, 190, 198.

55. Lopez, *William Parker Sessionography*, 196–97.

56. Parker, liner notes, *Peach Orchard*.

57. Parker, liner notes, *Peach Orchard*.

58. Parker, liner notes, *Peach Orchard*. Moholo recorded extensively for the FMP and Ogun labels, among others. Schweizer/Carl/Moholo, *Messer* (FMP, 1976); Louis Moholo-Moholo, *Mpumi* (Ogun, 2002). Ogun Records had been founded in London in 1973 by South African expatriates Harry Miller, Hazel Miller, and Keith Beal to record the music of British avant-garde jazz musicians and other African expatriates.

59. Parker, liner notes, *Peach Orchard*.

60. Parker, liner notes, *Peach Orchard*.

61. William Parker, liner notes, *Raincoat in the River*, vol. 1: *ICA Concert* (Eremite Records, 2001), [1]; Parker interview, August 9, 2018.

62. Parker, liner notes, *Peach Orchard*.

63. Parker interview, August 9, 2018.

64. The work was at least partially inspired by Parker's reading of Dee Brown's book *Bury My Heart at Wounded Knee: An Indian History of the American West* (New York: Holt, Rinehart and Winston, 1971). Parker, liner notes, *Peach Orchard*; Parker interview, August 9, 2018.

65. William Parker's In Order to Survive, *Posium Pendasem* (Free Music Productions, 1999).

66. Cooper-Moore interview, September 30, 2016.

67. Klaus Hübner, "Totale Musik, Triebgesteuert: Das Label 'Free Music Production' Steht für 40 Jahre Jazz und Improvisation in Deutschland," *Neue Zeitschrift für Musik* 172, no. 4: *Musik Verstehen?* (2011): 63.

68. Peter Brötzmann Group, *Alarm* (Free Music Productions, 1983); Cecil Taylor, *Olu Iwa* (Soul Note, 1994); Lopez, *William Parker Sessionography*, 73, 82–83.

69. The Feel Trio, *Celebrated Blazons* (Free Music Productions, 1993); Michael Marcus, *Here At!* (Soul Note, 1994); Lopez, *William Parker Sessionography*, 113, 140.

70. Susie Ibarra quoted in David Yaffe, "Holding Her Own among All the Guys," *New York Times*, May 30, 1999.

71. Steven Joerg, "What Struggle?," *New York Times*, June 12, 1999.

72. Cooper-Moore interview, September 30, 2016.

73. John Murph, "In Order to Survive: Beauty & Boredom," *Washington Post*, August 9, 1999.

74. "Jazz Listings for June 8–14," *New York Times*, June 7, 2012.

75. McIntyre began his career on Delmark and later worked with Cadence, among others, as he recorded ten records as a leader during his career. *Humility in the Light of the Creator* (Delmark, 1969); *Ram's Run* (Cadence, 1981).

76. William Parker, liner notes, *Wood Flute Songs* (AUM Fidelity, 2013), [14].

77. Tiwanaku, Dos Pilas, and Tenochtitlan are the historic sites of the Incan, Mayan, and Aztec peoples, respectively.

78. Parker, liner notes, *Wood Flute Songs*, [15].

79. Lopez, *William Parker Sessionography*, 417, 425.

80. Lopez, *William Parker Sessionography* online, accessed October 24, 2018, www.bb10k.com/PARKER.disc.html.

81. Parker also had a two-night debut concert at Dizzy's in July 2016. "Jazz Listings for July 22–28," *New York Times*, July 21, 2016; Café Oto, www.cafeoto.co.uk/events/black-top-residency-drake-parker; Sant' Anna Arresi Jazz Festiva, www.santannarresijazz.it/wordpress/en_US/peter-brotzmann-william-parker-hamid-drake-2.

82. William Parker, *Meditation/Resurrection* (AUM Fidelity, 2017); Giovanni Russonello, "Pop, Rock and Jazz in NYC this Week," *New York Times*, July 7, 2017. Systems Two was a recording studio and label that had been founded in Brooklyn in 1975 by Joe and Nancy Marciano and closed upon their retirement in 2018. It was one of the most active record studios during the period. "What's News," *New York City Jazz Record*, July 2018, 5.

83. Parker was born in 1952. William Parker, liner notes, *Meditation/Resurrection* (AUM Fidelity, 2017), [1].

84. Parker, liner notes, *Meditation/Resurrection*, [1], [3].

85. Oliver Lake has recorded thirty-eight records as a leader on the Black Saint, Gramavision, and Passin' Thru labels, among others.

86. Parker, liner notes, *Meditation/Resurrection*, [3].

87. Parker, liner notes, *Meditation/Resurrection*, [1], [2].

88. Giovanni Russonello, "13 Pop, Rock and Jazz Concerts to Check Out in N.Y.C. This Weekend," *New York Times*, August 24, 2018.

89. William Parker, interview by author, digital recording, January 27, 2019.

Chapter 8: Into the Tone World

Epigraph: William Parker, interview by author, digital recording, April 20, 2018.

1. William Parker, interview by author, digital recording, April 12, 2016.

2. William Parker, liner notes, *Sunrise in the Tone World* (AUM Fidelity, 1997), [3].

3. Parker by author, digital recording, interview, April 12, 2016.

4. Parker by author, digital recording, interview, April 12, 2016.

5. In addition to those mentioned above, Parker also participated in the Associated Big Band, which included many of Parker's longtime collaborators and performed at the Knitting Factory on October 27, 1991. He played in Europe in a big band led by Peter Brötzmann called März Combo on February 19, 1992. *New York Times*, February 18, 1982; FMP, accessed November 13, 2018, www.freemusicproduction.de/freemusicproduction/projekte/p_wfm_1983 .html; *Coda*, no. 197 (August 1984): 29; *Cecil Taylor: Berlin + NYC 1986*, directed by Ralph Quinke (1986); Bob Rusch, "William Parker Interview," *Cadence* 16, no. 12 (1990): 6; *New York Magazine*, October 28, 1991, 116; *Magnet* 34 (May/June 1998): 41; Rick Lopez, *William Parker Sessionography: Attempting a Complete Historical Arc* (New York: Centering, 2014), 1, 7–8, 22, 61, 83, 125.

6. Centering Big Band convened again for the Lower East Side Music, Poetry, and Arts Festival at the Shuttle Lab on September 28, 1984. "Jazz and Poetry Festival at Shuttle Lab," *New York Times*, September 28, 1984; William Parker, quoted in Ed Hazell, "A Different Architectural Blueprint for Each Situation," in liner notes, *Centering: Unreleased Early Recordings 1976–1987* (NoBusiness, 2012), 59.

7. William Parker, *Centering: Unreleased Early Recordings 1976–1987* (NoBusiness, 2012), CD 5. Sokolov has appeared on five records as a leader or featured artist, primarily on the Laughing Horse label.

8. Parker, quoted in Hazell, "A Different Architectural Blueprint," 59.

9. Dave Sewelson, interview by author, digital recording, March 21, 2017.

10. Wayne Horvitz, *Simple Facts* (Theater for Your Mother, 1980); *Coda*, no. 231 (April 1990): 35; "Afternoon Music," WKCR-FM broadcast, April 12, 1993; *New York*, December 6, 1993,

149; William Parker, *Long Hidden: The Olmec Series* (AUM Fidelity, 2006); Lopez, *William Parker Sessionography*, 39, 49, 73, 78, 108, 110, 132.

11. Parker, liner notes, *Sunrise in the Tone World*, [12].

12. Parker's work with Eneidi picked up considerably after 1991. Marco Eneidi, *Vermont, Spring, 1986* (Botticelli, 1986); Marco Eneidi, *The Marco Eneidi Collection* (Botticelli, 1994); Ben Young, *Dixonia: A Bio-discography of Bill Dixon* (Greenwood, 1998), 270, 274–76. Despite playing prolifically, Jackson Krall and the Secret Music Society never recorded. Lopez, *William Parker Sessionography*, 49, 62, 88.

13. Parker, liner notes, *Sunrise in the Tone World*, [13].

14. *Coda*, no. 197 (August 1984): 29; *New York*, August 22, 1988, 179; "Afternoon Music," WKCR-FM broadcast, April 12, 1993; Lopez, *William Parker Sessionography*, 74, 78, 108.

15. Moondoc's Jus Grew Orchestra did not record until 2000. "Jazz and Poetry Festival at the Shuttle Lab," *New York Times*, September 28, 1984; *Coda*, no. 201 (April 1985): 34; *East Village Eye*, June 1985, 56; *East Village Eye*, July 1985, 56; *Coda*, no. 205 (December 1985): 27–28; Masahiko Kono, "Brass Experiments in New York," *Jazz Hihyo* 74 (1992), reprinted on *Japan Improv*, accessed November 17, 2018, www.japanimprov.com/kono/essay.html; William Parker, *In Order to Survive* (Black Saint, 1994); Lopez, *William Parker Sessionography*, 78; William Parker, interview by author, digital recording, February 10, 2017.

16. Parker, liner notes, *Sunrise in the Tone World*, [13].

17. The lone exception was Bendian, who Parker began playing with in the Cecil Taylor Unit in 1989. *New York*, July 3, 1989, 196; *Coda*, no. 229 (December 1989): 21; *Coda*, no. 230 (February 1990): 12; *Cadence* 15, no. 12 (1989): 66–67; *Cadence* 16, no. 3 (1990): 4; Lopez, *William Parker Sessionography*, 107–8, 122, 143. Other than his work with Parker, Richard Keene's main recorded work was as a sideperson with drummer William Hooker in 1992–98. William Hooker Sextet, *Subconscious* (Ecstatic Peace!, 1992). Akira Ando is better known as a bassist and worked in bands led by Billy Bang. He later moved to Berlin, where he has worked with saxophonist Thomas Borgmann, among others. Billy Bang Quartet, *Spirits Gathering* (CIMP, 1996); Boom Box, *Jazz* (Jazzwerkstatt, 2011). Shoji Hano has an extensive discography as a leader and coleader, including work with Peter Brötzmann, Derek Bailey, and Billy Bang. Peter Brötzmann, Shoji Hano, Tetsu Yamauchi, and Haruhiko Gotsu, *Dare Devil* (DIW, 1992); Shoji Hano and Derek Bailey, *Fish* (P.S.F. Records, 2001); Billy Bang and Shoji Hano, *Four Seasons: East Meets West* (Heart Lord Studio Disc, 2009).

18. William Parker, liner notes, *Mayor of Punkville* (AUM Fidelity, 2000), [6].

19. Parker interview, February 10, 2017.

20. Rob Brown, interview by author, email transcript, February 14–March 26, 2017.

21. Jason Kao Hwang, interview by author, email transcript, February 21–March 29, 2017.

22. Sewelson interview, March 21, 2017.

23. Steve Swell, interview by author, email transcript, February 20, 2017.

24. James Brandon Lewis, interview by author, digital recording, April 1, 2017.

25. Ben Young, cited in Lopez, *William Parker Sessionography*, 142.

26. Following one of the concerts at CBGB's, the band went out into the streets, marched around the block, and came back into the venue. *New York*, February 14, 1994, 134; *New York*, June 20, 1994, 96; *New York*, July 18, 1994, 94; *New York*, July 25, 1994, 89; William Parker and the Little Huey Creative Music Orchestra, *Flowers Grow in My Room* (Centering Records, 1994); Lopez, *William Parker Sessionography*, 143, 145–47; Parker interview, February 10, 2017.

27. Parker interview, February 10, 2017.

28. *Coda*, no. 261 (1995): 16; Lopez, *William Parker Sessionography*, 157–59.

29. Parker, liner notes, *Sunrise in the Tone World*, [12].

30. *Coda*, no. 261 (1995): 16; William Parker and the Little Huey Creative Music Orchestra, *Sunrise in the Tone World* (AUM Fidelity, 1997); Lopez, *William Parker Sessionography*, 157.

31. Parker first came across the term *self sound* in a review of Bill Dixon and Alan Silva written by poet Ted Joans. Parker interview, February 10, 2017.

32. Parker, liner notes, *Sunrise in the Tone World*, [4].

33. Swell interview, February 20, 2017.

34. Sewelson interview, March 21, 2017.

35. Parker, liner notes, *Sunrise in the Tone World*, [4].

36. Ben Ratliff, "Not Grandpa's Big-Band Records," *New York Times*, December 23, 1997.

37. Parker, liner notes, *Sunrise in the Tone World*, [5].

38. Parker, liner notes, *Sunrise in the Tone World*, [6]. Kidd Jordan has more than a dozen records as a leader and has worked extensively with Hamid Drake, Kali Z. Fasteau, and Alvin Fielder, among others. Kidd Jordan, Hamid Drake, and William Parker, *Palm of Soul* (AUM Fidelity, 2006); Kali Z. Fasteau, Kidd Jordan, and Michael T. A. Thompson, *People of the Ninth (New Orleans and the Hurricane 2005)* (Flying Note, 2006); Kidd Jordan, Alvin Fielder, and Peter Kowald, *Live in New Orleans* (NoBusiness Records, 2013).

39. Dexter Gordon has dozens of records as a leader. See, for example, *Go!* (Blue Note, 1962); *The Tower of Power* (Prestige, 1969).

40. Parker, liner notes, *Sunrise in the Tone World*, [10].

41. Parker, liner notes, *Sunrise in the Tone World*, [9].

42. Parker, liner notes, *Sunrise in the Tone World*, [6].

43. Tens of thousands of people fled Cambodia in the 1970s after the rise of the genocidal Khmer Rouge. The compilation included only a thirteen-minute excerpt of "Hoang," drawn from a nearly forty-minute performance of the piece. Various artists, *Vision One— Vision Festival 1997 Compiled* (AUM Fidelity, 1998); Lopez, *William Parker Sessionography*,

187. The band played only one more time that year, a September 2, 1997, appearance at the Knitting Factory. *Soundboard* 1 (1997): 2.

44. "Pop and Jazz Guide," *New York Times*, May 22, 1998.

45. Lopez, *William Parker Sessionography*, 201.

46. William Parker and the Little Huey Creative Music Orchestra, *Mass for the Healing of the World* (Black Saint, 2003).

47. Alice Tully Hall had been built in 1969 to feature chamber music performances that had previously tended to appear in Town Hall. Lawrence Van Gelder, "Footlights," *New York Times*, January 27, 1999; "Pop and Jazz Guide," *New York Times*, January 29, 1999.

48. Fred Hopkins released dozens of records, working with figures such as Henry Threadgill, Peter Brötzmann, and Diedre Murray. Hopkins was also involved in a number of projects that fused jazz with poetry or theatre. Ntozake Shange, "Unrecovered Losses/Black Theatre Traditions," in "Black Theatre," special issue, *Black Scholar* 10, no. 10 (1979): 8; Barry Wallenstein, "The Jazz-Poetry Connection," *Performing Arts Journal* 4, no. 3 (1980): 134; Barry Wallenstein, "Poetry and Jazz: A Twentieth-Century Wedding," in "Literature of Jazz Issue," *Black American Literature Forum* 25, no. 3 (1991): 613, 615, 617n18; Travis A. Jackson, "'Always New and Centuries Old': Jazz, Poetry, and Tradition as Creative Adaptation," in *Uptown Conversation: The New Jazz Studies*, ed. Robert G. O'Meally et al. (New York: Columbia University Press, 2004), 364; George Lewis, "Experimental Music in Black and White: The AACM in New York, 1970–1985," in *Uptown Conversation: The New Jazz Studies*, ed. Robert G. O'Meally et al. (New York: Columbia University Press, 2004), 59, 66, 69–71; Amiri Baraka, *Digging: The Afro-American Soul of American Classical Music* (Berkeley: University of California Press, 2009), 265–66.

49. *Liberation*, March 23, 1999. The Banlieues Blues Festival was founded in 1984.

50. Lopez, *William Parker Sessionography*, 215.

51. Martin Williams, "Jazz: What Happened in Kansas City?" *American Music* 3, no. 2 (1985): 173–74, 176, 178; Gena Caponi-Tabery, *Jump for Joy: Jazz, Basketball, and Black Culture in 1930s America* (Amherst: University of Massachusetts Press, 2008), 68–69.

52. Lopez, *William Parker Sessionography*, 215.

53. "Pop and Jazz Guide," *New York Times*, August 20, 1999; "Pop and Jazz Guide," *New York Times*, September 3, 1999; Lopez, *William Parker Sessionography*, 216–17.

54. Lopez, *William Parker Sessionography*, 225; Andrew Barker, interview by author, email transcript, February 14–March 1, 2017.

55. Andrew Barker and Charles Waters were coleaders of Gold Sparkle Band, which put out seven records in 1994–2004. Barker had first met Parker through his association with Daniel Carter, and Gold Sparkle Band had opened for Other Dimensions in Music at the Cooler in 1997 or early 1998. After Barker and Waters relocated to New York in August 1998, Parker hired them for the pit orchestra for the Czech American Marionette Theatre at La MaMa and then hired them for Little Huey a few months later. Gold Sparkle Band, *Nu-Soul Zodiac* (Squealer, 1999).

56. Ori Kaplan later gained some mainstream pop music fame for iconic saxophone lines in "Talk Dirty" by R&B singer Jason Derulo and "Worth It" by Fifth Harmony.

57. Ellen Christi appeared in the William Parker Orchestra, an early big-band project, at the Holy Name Auditorium on April 12, 1975. The radio station WKCR aired an archival recording live during the "Loft Festival" in 1994. Lopez, *William Parker Sessionography*, 154.

58. Barker interview, February 14–March 1, 2017.

59. Parker, liner notes, *Mayor of Punkville*, [3].

60. Parker, liner notes, *Mayor of Punkville*, [8].

61. Parker, liner notes, *Mayor of Punkville*, [4].

62. Parker, liner notes, *Mayor of Punkville*, [4–5].

63. Crazy Horse was assassinated by U.S. agents just a year after his great victory over the American army at the Battle of the Little Bighorn in Montana. The other leaders survived but were confined to live on reservations.

64. Parker, liner notes, *Mayor of Punkville*, [5].

65. Sitting Bull was one of the Hunkpapa Lakota leaders who led their resistance to domination by the expansionist United States after the Civil War. He was murdered by U.S. agents on Standing Rock Indian Reservation, December 15, 1890.

66. Parker, liner notes, *Mayor of Punkville*, [5], [6], [8].

67. Parker, liner notes, *Mayor of Punkville*, [6].

68. Parker, liner notes, *Mayor of Punkville*, [7].

69. Steve Smith, "What's an Avant-Garde Evening without a Poet and Plush Toys?," *New York Times*, September 5, 2013.

70. Lopez, *William Parker Sessionography*, 223.

71. Ben Ratliff, "Pastoral Sounds Punctuated by Tensions," *New York Times*, March 15, 2000.

72. Program, Vision Festival 2000, May 19–29, 2000.

73. William Parker, interview by author, digital recording, December 21, 2018.

74. "Pop and Jazz Guide," *New York Times*, May 26, 2000; program, Vision Festival 2000.

75. Lopez, *William Parker Sessionography*, 235.

76. Bob Blumenthal, "William Parker, Bassist, Finds Inspiration in All Places," *Boston Globe*, February 23, 2001.

77. Bob Blumenthal, "Powerful Mix Defines Parker Show," *Boston Globe*, February 27, 2001.

78. Robert Garfias, "The Marimba of Mexico and Central America," *Latin American Music Review* 4, no. 2 (1983): 203–11.

79. Jay Keister, "The Shakuhachi as Spiritual Tool: A Japanese Buddhist Instrument in the West," *Asian Music* 35, no. 2 (2004): 118–22; Steven Casano, "From Fuke Shuu to Uduboo:

The Transnational Flow of the Shakuhachi to the West," in "The Music of 'Others' in the Western World," special issue, *World of Music* 47, no. 3 (2005): 21–22.

80. Fred Jung, "A Fireside Chat with William Parker," *Jazz Weekly*, April 3, 2003, http://jazzweekly.com/interviews/wparker.htm.

81. William Parker and the Little Huey Creative Music Orchestra, *Raincoat in the River*, vol. 1: ICA *Concert* (Eremite Records, 2001).

82. William Parker, liner notes, *Raincoat in the River*, vol. 1: ICA *Concert* (Eremite Records, 2001), [1].

83. Parker, liner notes, *Raincoat in the River*, [1]; William Parker, interview by author, digital recording, August 9, 2018.

84. Parker, liner notes, *Raincoat in the River*, [1].

85. Parker, liner notes, *Raincoat in the River*, [1–2].

86. Parker, liner notes, *Raincoat in the River*, [2].

87. Blumenthal, "Powerful Mix Defines Parker Show."

88. Parker, liner notes, *Raincoat in the River*, [2].

89. William Parker and the Little Huey Creative Music Orchestra, *Raincoat in the River*, vol. 1, track 4.

90. William Parker, liner notes, *Raincoat in the River*, [2].

91. Larry Blumenfeld, "A Father to the Followers of Free Jazz," *New York Times*, May 26, 2002.

92. Lopez, *William Parker Sessionography*, 248.

93. William Parker and the Little Huey Creative Music Orchestra, *Spontaneous* (Splasc[H], 2003). Mateen has released more than two dozen records as a leader or coleader on Eremite, Not Two, and other labels, working with a variety of figures. Lavelle has worked with Daniel Carter, among other collaborators.

94. Lopez, *William Parker Sessionography*, 135.

95. Jeanne Lee was a vocalist, poet, and composer. Lopez, *William Parker Sessionography*, 239, 152.

96. William Parker, liner notes, *Spontaneous*, [1].

97. Parker interview, February 10, 2017.

98. Parker, liner notes, *Spontaneous*, [1].

99. Parker interview, February 10, 2017.

100. The concerts were performed at a venue called the Center. "Classical Music and Dance Guide," *New York Times*, April 4, 2003; "Pop and Jazz Guide," *New York Times*, April 4, 2003.

101. Steve Smith, "Irving Stone Memorial Concert," AcousticLevitation.org, www.acousticlevitation.org/irvingstone.html.

102. Various Artists, *Irving Stone Memorial Concert* (Tzadik, 2004), disc 2, track 7.

103. "Pop and Jazz Guide," *New York Times*, February 27, 2004.

104. Favors had been Art Ensemble of Chicago's resident expert on the music of Africa. Ronald M. Radano, "Jazzin' the Classics: The AACM's Challenge to Mainstream Aesthetics," *Black Music Research Journal* 12, no. 1 (1992): 87–88; Lewis, "Experimental Music in Black and White," 51, 60–61, 71.

105. Lopez, *William Parker Sessionography*, 305.

106. "The Listings," *New York Times*, January 7, 2005; *The Wire* 253 (March 2005): 90.

107. William Parker, liner notes, *For Percy Heath* (Les Disques VICTO, 2007), [1–2].

108. Lopez, *William Parker Sessionography*, 325.

109. Iain Anderson, *This Is Our Music: Free Jazz, the Sixties, and American Culture* (Philadelphia: University of Pennsylvania Press, 2007), 84; Alex Stewart, *Making the Scene: Contemporary New York City Big Band Jazz* (Berkeley: University of California Press, 2007), 208.

110. John Sharpe, quoted in Lopez, *William Parker Sessionography*, 325.

111. Lopez, *William Parker Sessionography*, 327.

112. Nate Chinen, "Vision Artists for New Orleans," *New York Times*, September 16, 2005.

113. "Newsletter," Downtown Music Gallery, August 2, 2008.

114. Morris emerged in the Knitting Factory scene in the 1980s and 1990s, and he has released more than fifty records as a bandleader.

115. Lopez, *William Parker Sessionography*, 350. Swift's main band is Mazzmuse. Pavone has released over a dozen records, working with guitarist Mary Halvorson, among others. Jessica Pavone, *Knuckle Under* (Taiga Records, 2014). Dulberger has released several records under her own name.

116. William Parker, liner notes, *Double Sunrise over Neptune* (AUM Fidelity, 2008), [4].

117. Parker, liner notes, *Double Sunrise over Neptune*, [4].

118. Parker, liner notes, *Double Sunrise over Neptune*, [1].

119. Parker, liner notes, *Double Sunrise over Neptune*, [4], [3].

120. The performance was filmed by the David Lynch Foundation. Lopez, *William Parker Sessionography*, 379.

121. Lewis has acclaimed records as a leader, including *Days of FreeMan* (OKeh, 2015), and cofounded the jazz-poetry ensemble Heroes Are Gang Leaders. Kretzmer runs the Out Now label, on which he has released a number of his own records. Jones has released a number of records on the AUM Fidelity label in different formations. Lopez gained visibility in the Nate Wooley Quartet, leads his own trio, and is most prolific to date as a solo performer.

122. Rick Lopez, *William Parker Sessionography* online, www.bb10k.com/PARKER.disc.html.

123. Lopez, *William Parker Sessionography*, 418.

124. William Parker, interview by author, digital recording, January 27, 2019.

Epigraph: William Parker, liner notes, *Wood Flute Songs: Anthology/Live 2006–2012* (AUM Fidelity, 2013), [16].

1. *Jazzpodium* (1994, no. 9): 77; *Jazzpodium* (1994, no. 11): 64; *Jazzpodium* (1995, no. 2): 48; *Cadence 26*, no. 10 (2000): 35; David Keenan, Festival Review, *Wire*, no. 200 (2000): 98; Rick Lopez, *William Parker Sessionography: Attempting a Complete Historical Arc* (New York: Centering, 2014), 140, 149, 165, 195; Tempere Music Festival, accessed November 28, 2018, www.tamperemusicfestivals.fi/jazz/history.

2. Hamid Drake, interview by author, digital recording, January 15, 2019.

3. Peter Brötzmann's Die Like a Dog Quartet, *From Valley to Valley* (Eremite, 1999); Peter Brötzmann: Die Like a Dog, *The Complete FMP Recordings* (Jazzwerkstatt, 2007). The band did play some U.S. and Canadian dates in 1999 and 2000, including Vision Festival 4. Program, Vision Festival 1999; *Cadence 25*, no. 4 (2000): 2, 136; *Cadence 25*, no. 7 (2000): 139; Lopez, *William Parker Sessionography*, 212, 228–29, 233; "Chicago Now: Old Listings (2000)," Seth Tisue concert listings, accessed November 28, 2018, www.tisue.net/chicagonow/old2000.html.

4. William Parker, email to author, February 13, 2019.

5. David Keenan, Festival review, *Wire* 200 (2000): 98.

6. David Budbill, liner notes, *O'Neal's Porch* (Centering Records, 2001), [1].

7. *Cadence 24*, no. 6 (1998): 141; Frode Gjerstad with Hamid Drake and William Parker, *Frode Gjerstad with Hamid Drake and William Parker* (Cadence Jazz Records, 1999); *Cadence 25*, no. 1 (2000): 141; *One Final Note*, no. 2 (2000); Fred Anderson et al., *2 Days in April* (Eremite, 2000); Lopez, *William Parker Sessionography*, 193, 214, 218, 224–25; "Chicago Now: Old Listings (1998)," Seth Tisue concert listings, www.tisue.net/chicagonow/old1998.html, accessed November 28, 2018; "Chicago Now: Old Listings (2000)," Seth Tisue concert listings, www.tisue.net/chicagonow/old2000.html, accessed November 28, 2018; Creative Audio Archive, accessed November 28, 2018, www.creativeaudioarchive.org/xml/malachi-ritscher.xml.

8. Drake interview, January 15, 2019.

9. Steven Joerg, liner notes, *First Communion + Piercing the Veil* (AUM Fidelity, 2000, reissued in 2007), [2].

10. Steven Joerg, cited in Lopez, *William Parker Sessionography*, 226; Drake interview, January 15, 2019.

11. Drake interview, January 15, 2019.

12. William Parker and Hamid Drake, *Piercing the Veil* (AUM Fidelity, 2001); William Parker and Hamid Drake, *First Communion + Piercing the Veil* (AUM Fidelity, 2007).

13. William Parker and Hamid Drake, *Volume 2: Summer Snow* (AUM Fidelity, 2007).

14. William Parker, interview by author, digital recording, April 12, 2016.

15. William Parker Trio, *Painter's Spring* (Thirsty Ear Recordings, 2000); William Parker Quartet, *O'Neal's Porch* (Centering Records, 2001; reissued on AUM Fidelity, 2002).

16. Lewis Barnes, quoted in Budbill, liner notes, *O'Neal's Porch*, [1].

17. Drake interview, January 15, 2019.

18. Rob Brown, interview by author, email transcript, February 14–March 26, 2017.

19. Drake interview, January 15, 2019.

20. Budbill, liner notes, *O'Neal's Porch*, [1].

21. Budbill, liner notes, *O'Neal's Porch*, [1].

22. Budbill, liner notes, *O'Neal's Porch*, [1].

23. Lopez, *William Parker Sessionography*, 251, 258, 264, 274, 276, 308, 312.

24. William Parker Quartet, *Sound Unity* (AUM Fidelity, 2005).

25. William Parker, liner notes, *Sound Unity* (AUM Fidelity, 2005), [3].

26. Parker, liner notes, *Sound Unity*, [3–4].

27. Parker, liner notes, *Sound Unity*, [3], [5].

28. William Parker's Raining on the Moon, *Corn Meal Dance* (AUM Fidelity, 2007), track 3.

29. Parker, liner notes, *Sound Unity*, [4].

30. Lopez, *William Parker Sessionography*, 314.

31. "First on Capitol Records: Nature Boy," *Cash Box*, June 5, 1948, 14; "Green Hair Trouble," *Life*, December 6, 1948, 83; "Jack Patton," *Cash Box*, September 11, 1993, 21.

32. "Nature Boy," *Life*, May 10, 1948, 131–35.

33. *Wire*, no. 253 (2005): 94.

34. Lopez, *William Parker Sessionography*, 321–22, 326, 329.

35. Lee Hilderbrand, "Yoshi's Celebrates 40th Year," *San Francisco Chronicle*, August 12, 2012, www.sfgate.com/music/article/Yoshi-s-celebrates-40th-year-3778835.php.

36. Parker, liner notes, *Wood Flute Songs*, [4].

37. Parker, liner notes, *Wood Flute Songs*, [4].

38. William Parker Quartet, *Petit Oiseau* (AUM Fidelity, 2008).

39. Parker, liner notes, *Wood Flute Songs*, [5].

40. "Interview," *Coda*, no. 174 (1980): 7; Parker, liner notes, *Wood Flute Songs*, [5]; Lopez, *William Parker Sessionography*, 39.

41. Arthur Williams, *Forgiveness Suite* (NoBusiness Records, 2016).

42. Parker, liner notes, *Wood Flute Songs*, [5].

43. William Parker, liner notes, *Petit Oiseau* (AUM Fidelity, 2008), [2].

44. William Parker, liner notes, *Alphaville Suite: Music Inspired by the Jean-Luc Godard Film* (Rogue Art, 2007), [1].

45. Parker, liner notes, *Alphaville Suite*, [1].

46. Ed Hazell, quoted in Lopez, *William Parker Sessionography*, 343.

47. Lopez, *William Parker Sessionography*, 345, 347.

48. Parker, liner notes, *Wood Flute Songs*, [6].

49. Parker, liner notes, *Wood Flute Songs*, [7].

50. William Parker, interview by author, digital recording, January 3, 2019.

51. Parker, liner notes, *Petit Oiseau*, [2].

52. Parker, liner notes, *Wood Flute Songs*, [7].

53. Lopez, *William Parker Sessionography*, 347–48.

54. *Chicago Sun-Times*, July 13, 2007.

55. Parker, liner notes, *Wood Flute Songs*, [5].

56. Parker, liner notes, *Petit Oiseau*, [1].

57. Parker, liner notes, *Petit Oiseau*, [1].

58. Barnes, quoted in Parker, liner notes, *Petit Oiseau*, [1].

59. Parker, liner notes, *Petit Oiseau*, [2].

60. "Four Hearts," *Your Leisure* magazine, January 17, 2008; Lopez, *William Parker Sessionography*, 358.

61. Lopez, *William Parker Sessionography*, 361, 372.

62. Parker, liner notes, *Wood Flute Songs*, [8].

63. Parker, [9], [10].

64. Sons d'hiver, accessed December 4, 2018, www.sonsdhiver.org/media/static/files/programmes/sons-d-hiver-programme-2010.pdf.

65. Lopez, *William Parker Sessionography*, 382.

66. *Alphaville* (1965), directed by Jean-Luc Godard.

67. Lopez, *William Parker Sessionography*, 382.

68. Parker, liner notes, *Wood Flute Songs*, [10], [13].

69. Lee Mergner, "Jazz Violinist Billy Bang Dies," *Jazz Times*, April 12, 2011, https://jazztimes.com/news/jazz-violinist-billy-bang-dies.

70. The band also performed in Wroclaw, Poland, on June 23, 2012; the concert was recorded and released on the Polish record label For Tune. William Parker Quartet, *Live in Wroclaw* (For Tune, 2013); Lopez, *William Parker Sessionography*, 408, 411, 420.

71. David Budbill, quoted in Lopez, *William Parker Sessionography*, 426.

72. William Parker, email to author, January 7, 2019.

73. Lopez, *William Parker Sessionography* online, accessed December 5, 2018, www.bb10k .com/PARKER.disc.html.

74. William Parker Quartet, *Ao Vivo Na Fabrica* (Selo Sesc, 2016).

75. William Parker, liner notes, *Meditation/Resurrection* (AUM Fidelity, 2017), [2].

76. The debut of the piece with the quartet occurred at Winter Jazz Festival, January 9, 2010. Lopez, *William Parker Sessionography*, 382; Andy Schwartz, *New York Rocker*, accessed December 5, 2018, www.nyrocker.com/blog/2010/02/winter-jazz-fest.

77. Parker, liner notes, *Meditation/Resurrection*, [3].

78. Parker, liner notes, *Meditation/Resurrection*, [2].

79. Parker, liner notes, *Meditation/Resurrection*, [2], [3].

80. Drake interview, January 15, 2019.

81. Leena Conquest, interview by author, digital recording, March 24, 2017.

82. Parker, liner notes, *Wood Flute Songs*, [15].

83. Parker, liner notes, *Wood Flute Songs*, [15].

84. Lopez, *William Parker Sessionography* online.

85. Lopez, *William Parker Sessionography*, 226.

86. William Parker and the Little Huey Creative Music Orchestra, *Raincoat in the River*, vol. 1: *ICA Concert* (Eremite Records, 2001).

87. Conquest interview, March 24, 2017.

88. Parker, liner notes, *Wood Flute Songs*, [16].

89. William Parker, liner notes, *Raining on the Moon* (Thirsty Ear, 2002), [1].

90. Parker, liner notes, *Wood Flute Songs*, [16].

91. Conquest interview, March 24, 2017.

92. Drake interview, January 15, 2019.

93. Conquest interview, March 24, 2017.

94. Toma Jazz, accessed November 29, 2018, www.tomajazz.com/perfiles/temporada2004 /index.htm; Lopez, *William Parker Sessionography*, 268.

95. Lopez, *William Parker Sessionography*, 307.

96. Geoffrey Hunt et al., "Changes in Prison Culture: Prison Gangs and the Case of the 'Pepsi Generation,'" *Social Problems* 40, no. 3 (1993): 399.

97. In his will, Jackson left all of his book royalties and other funds to the Black Panther Party.

98. George Jackson, *Soledad Brother: The Prison Letters of George Jackson* (New York: Bantam, 1970), 86.

99. Peniel E. Joseph, *Waiting 'Til the Midnight Hour: A Narrative History of Black Power in America* (London: Routledge, 2006), 251–52; Larry Watani Stiner and Scot Brown, "The

US-Panther Conflict, Exile, and the Black Diaspora: The Plight of Larry Watani Stiner," in "New Black Power Studies: National, International, and Transnational Perspectives," special issue, *Journal of African American History* 92, no. 4 (2007): 541.

100. *Prisons on Fire* (1971), directed by Claude Marks; "Episodes from the Attica Massacre," in "Black Prisoner (II)," special issue, *Black Scholar* 4, no. 2 (1972): 34–39; Archie Shepp, *Attica Blues* (Impulse!, 1972); Stanley "Tookie" Williams, *Life in Prison* (SeaStar Books, 2001); Ja Rule, *Blood in My Eye* (Murder Inc., 2003); Claude Marks and Rob McBride, "Recovering, Amplifying, and Networking the Voices of the Disappeared—Political Prisoners on Internet Media," in "War, Dissent, and Justice: A Dialogue," special issue, *Social Justice* 30, no. 2: (2003): 139, 140n4; Lee Bernstein, *America Is the Prison: Arts and Politics in Prison in the 1970s* (Chapel Hill: University of North Carolina Press, 2010), 51–74; Greg Thomas, "Dragons! George Jackson in the Cinema with Haile Gerima—from the Watts Films to Teza," *Black Camera* 4, no. 2 (2013): 55–83.

101. Lopez, *William Parker Sessionography*, 307, 323, 309.

102. Media Wave Festival, www.mediawavefestival.hu/portal/archiv/katalogus/2004_prog-01–20.pdf, accessed December 4, 2016.

103. Lopez, *William Parker Sessionography*, 323–24, 326, 337–38.

104. The Stone, accessed November 29, 2018, www.thestonenyc.com.

105. Conquest interview, March 24, 2017.

106. Drake interview, January 15, 2019.

107. Parker, liner notes, *Wood Flute Songs*, [16].

108. William Parker's Raining on the Moon, *Corn Meal Dance* (AUM Fidelity, 2007); William Parker's Raining on the Moon, *Great Spirit* (AUM Fidelity, 2015).

109. Steven Joerg, liner notes, *Great Spirit* (AUM Fidelity, 2015), [1].

110. Greg Tate, liner notes, *Corn Meal Dance* (AUM Fidelity, 2007), [10].

111. William Parker, liner notes, *Corn Meal Dance* (AUM Fidelity, 2007), [5].

112. William Parker, liner notes, *Corn Meal Dance*, [14].

113. James Brandon Lewis, interview by author, digital recording, April 1, 2017.

114. Joerg, liner notes, *Great Spirit*, [2].

115. Lopez, *William Parker Sessionography*, 348; Alhambra Concert Hall, accessed November 30, 2018, http://archives.amr-geneve.ch; Bimhuis, accessed November 30, 2018, www.bimhuis.nl/archief; Combo Jazz Club, accessed November 30, 2018, www.combojazzclub.com/rassegna/cassero-jazz-2007; Musicus Concentus, accessed November 30, 2018, www.musicusconcentus.com/archivio.

116. Tunisia News, accessed November 30, 2018, www.tunisianews.org/april08/150408–3.htm; Tunisiana, "Jazz in Carthage," April 2008, http://2008.jazzacarthage.com.

117. Lopez, *William Parker Sessionography*, 361, 365; Angra Jazz, accessed November 30, 2018, www.angrajazz.com/2008; Euritmica, accessed November 30, 2018, www.euritmica.it/category/rassegne/udinjazz-rassegne/udinjazz-2008.

118. Lopez, *William Parker Sessionography*, 374, 392.

119. Parker, *Wood Flute Songs*, CD 7: *Raining on the Moon 2012*.

120. Parker, liner notes, *Wood Flute Songs*, [16].

121. Joerg, liner notes, *Great Spirit*, [2].

Chapter 10: Honoring the Elders

Epigraph: William Parker, liner notes, *Corn Meal Dance* (AUM Fidelity, 2007), [9].

1. Concert program, Context Studios, March 19–21, 1998, Centering Archive.

2. Lopez, *William Parker Sessionography*, 244.

3. William Parker, interview by author, digital recording, February 10, 2017.

4. William Parker, liner notes, *I Plan to Stay a Believer: The Inside Songs of Curtis Mayfield* (AUM Fidelity, 2010), [2]; Parker interview, February 10, 2017.

5. Steven Joerg, quoted in Lopez, *William Parker Sessionography*, 244.

6. Leena Conquest, interview by author, digital recording, March 24, 2017.

7. Hamid Drake, interview by author, digital recording, January 15, 2019.

8. Dave Burrell, *Echo* (BYG Records, 1969).

9. Lopez, *William Parker Sessionography*, 102.

10. Parker, liner notes, *I Plan to Stay a Believer*, [1].

11. Parker, liner notes, *I Plan to Stay a Believer*, [1].

12. Parker, liner notes, *I Plan to Stay a Believer*, [2].

13. Conquest interview, March 24, 2017.

14. Dave Burrell, interview by author, digital recording, February 14, 2017.

15. Burrell interview, February 14, 2017.

16. Drake interview, January 15, 2019.

17. Lopez, *William Parker Sessionography*, 264, 344, 366–67.

18. *El Periódico de Catalonia*, November 13, 2002; *William Parker's Inside Songs of Curtis Mayfield, Live in Rome* (rai Trade, 2007); Jazz Italia, accessed December 11, 2018, www.jazzitalia .net/iocero/Etnafest2008.asp#.XBAgenRKiUk; Lopez, *William Parker Sessionography*, 338, 348, 353, 358, 366–67, 369, 373, 379.

19. Drake interview, January 15, 2019.

20. Lopez, *William Parker Sessionography*, 395.

21. Luke Stewart, interview by author, text transcript, December 11, 2018.

22. Drake interview, January 15, 2019.

23. William Parker, interview by author, digital recording, February 2, 2016.

24. Lopez, *William Parker Sessionography*, 399, 400.

25. William Parker Orchestra, *Essence of Ellington with Special Guest Kidd Jordan: Live in Milano* (Centering Records, 2012).

26. Lopez, *William Parker Sessionography*, 408.

27. Burrell interview, February 14, 2017.

28. William Parker, liner notes, *Painter's Spring* (Thirsty Ear Recordings, 2000), [3].

29. The original poem, included in the liner notes, differed from the one above, but Parker updated the words in a private correspondence with the author. William Parker, email to author, January 3, 2019.

30. William Parker Clarinet Trio, *Bob's Pink Cadillac* (Eremite, 2002).

31. As noted above, Parker later used a gralla on the song "Red Desert" in 2007.

32. Lopez, *William Parker Sessionography*, 253.

33. William Parker Violin Trio, *Scrapbook* (Thirsty Ear Recordings, 2003).

34. Lopez, *William Parker Sessionography*, 291.

35. William Parker, *Luc's Lantern* (Thirsty Ear Recordings, 2005).

36. William Parker, liner notes, *Luc's Lantern* (Thirsty Ear Recordings, 2005), [1].

37. Parker, liner notes, *Luc's Lantern*, [1].

38. Parker, liner notes, *Luc's Lantern*, [3].

39. Parker, liner notes, *Luc's Lantern*, [2].

40. Lopez, *William Parker Sessionography*, 354.

41. *New York*, June 24, 1996, 156; Lopez, *William Parker Sessionography*, 178, 186, 189.

42. Lopez, *William Parker Sessionography*, 336, 338.

43. *The Record*, December 14, 2007.

44. Gerald Cleaver, William Parker, and Craig Taborn, *Farmers by Nature* (AUM Fidelity, 2009).

45. Bruce Gallanter, Downtown Music Gallery email newsletter, July 25, 2010; Lopez, *William Parker Sessionography*, 386.

46. Farmers by Nature, *Out of This World's Distortions* (AUM Fidelity, 2011).

47. Gerald Cleaver, liner notes, *Out of This World's Distortions* (AUM Fidelity, 2011), [1].

48. Lopez, *William Parker Sessionography*, 400.

49. "Farmers by Nature," Bimhuis, accessed December 12, 2018, www.bimhuis.com/gigs/farmers-by-nature; Lopez, *William Parker Sessionography*, 400.

50. Farmers by Nature, *Love and Ghosts* (AUM Fidelity, 2014), [1].

51. Lopez, *William Parker Sessionography*, 400.

52. Cisco Bradley, "Concerts Reviewed: Craig Taborn at the Stone, January 2016," *Jazz-rightnow.com*, February 1, 2016, https://www.jazzrightnow.com/concerts-reviewed-craig -taborn-at-the-stone-january-2016/.

53. William Parker, interview by author, digital recording, August 9, 2018.

54. William Parker, liner notes, *Uncle Joe's Spirit House* (Centering Music, 2010), [2].

55. William Parker Organ Quartet, *Uncle Joe's Spirit House* (Centering Music, 2010).

56. Parker, liner notes, *Uncle Joe's Spirit House*, [1], [2], [3].

57. Parker, liner notes, *Uncle Joe's Spirit House*, [2], [1].

58. Parker interview, August 9, 2018.

59. Lopez, *William Parker Sessionography*, 403.

60. Rick Lopez, *William Parker Sessionography* online, accessed December 12, 2018, www .bb10k.com/PARKER.disc.html.

61. The band returned to Europe for an appearance at the Sons d'hiver festival in Paris in January 2018 and to Groningen, Netherlands, in August 2018. Lopez, *William Parker Sessionography* online, accessed December 12, 2018.

62. James Brandon Lewis, interview by author, digital recording, April 1, 2017.

63. Lowell Davidson Trio, *Lowell Davidson Trio* (ESP-Disk, 1965); Giuseppi Logan Quartet, *Giuseppi Logan Quartet* (ESP-Disk, 1965); Milford Graves, *Bäbi* (IPS, 1977).

64. Ensemble Muntu, *First Feeding* (Muntu Records, 1977).

65. William Parker, email to author, February 13, 2019.

66. Lopez, *William Parker Sessionography*, 71, 100, 263.

67. Jeff Schlanger did a live painting of a performance by the trio in Graves's basement in Jamaica, New York, in 1993. Steve Dalachinsky, *The Final Nite and Other Poems: Complete Notes from a Charles Gayle Notebook 1987–2006* (Berkeley, CA: Ugly Duckling Presse, 2006), 142, 181; Lopez, *William Parker Sessionography*, 75, 120, 136, 173.

68. Charles Gayle, William Parker, and Rashied Ali, *Touchin' on Trane* (FMP, 1993).

69. Parker email, February 13, 2019.

70. Lopez, *William Parker Sessionography*, 305.

71. *Wire*, no. 275 (November 2006): 89, 92.

72. Lopez, *William Parker Sessionography*, 348.

73. Anthony Braxton, William Parker, and Milford Graves, *Beyond Quantum* (Tzadik, 2008).

74. *Wire*, no. 279 (March 2007): 11.

75. Lopez, *William Parker Sessionography*, 354.

76. *New York Times*, May 22, 1998.

77. Lopez, *William Parker Sessionography*, 266.

78. Parker email, February 13, 2019.

79. *Wire*, no. 288: 79; Lopez, *William Parker Sessionography*, 370.

80. Lopez, *William Parker Sessionography*, 23.

81. *Coda*, no. 237 (1991): 4; Lopez, *William Parker Sessionography*, 91–92, 97, 105, 117, 126.

82. William Parker, *Long Hidden: The Olmec Series* (AUM Fidelity, 2006).

83. William Parker, liner notes, *Long Hidden: The Olmec Series* (AUM Fidelity, 2006), [1], [3].

84. Lopez, *William Parker Sessionography*, 167, 170–71.

85. Parker had another bass that he now plays. The Dudek bass was never fully restored. Jeff Schlanger, quoted in Lopez, 71.

86. The version on the record was timed at just 3:46, but he performed extended versions of the piece at times, such as a performance at the Guelph Jazz Festival on September 12, 1999, with a version that lasted more than 37 minutes and one at Somewhere There in Toronto in 2008 that clocked at more than 51 minutes. Lopez, *William Parker Sessionography*, 16, 23, 218, 364.

87. William Parker, liner notes, *Long Hidden*, [2].

88. Lopez, *William Parker Sessionography*, 334, 374, 424.

89. "Jazz Listings for April 3–9," *New York Times*, April 2, 2015, www.nytimes.com/2015/04/03/arts/music/jazz-listings-for-april-3–9.html.

90. *Wire*, no. 277 (2007): 86; event poster, William Parker Solo at Point Éphémère in Paris, France, June 17, 2014; event poster, William Parker Solo at Ateliers Claus, Brussels, Belgium, June 18, 2014; Lopez, *William Parker Sessionography*, 352, 355, 359, 378, 390, 397, 400, 417; Lopez, *William Parker Sessionography* online.

91. Lopez, *William Parker Sessionography* online.

92. Lopez, *William Parker Sessionography*, 364.

93. William Parker, *At Somewhere There* (Barnyard Records, 2010).

94. Scott Thomson, liner notes, *At Somewhere There* (Barnyard Records, 2010), [1].

95. Valerie Wilmer, *As Serious as Your Life: The Story of the New Jazz* (Westport, CT: Lawrence Hill, 1977).

96. Thomson, liner notes, *At Somewhere There*, [1].

97. Joshua Abrams, interview by author, digital recording, May 10, 2017.

98. Lopez, *William Parker Sessionography*, 401.

99. Abrams interview, May 10, 2017.

100. William Parker, *Crumbling in the Shadows Is Fraulein Miller's Stale Cake* (Centering Records, 2011).

101. Abrams interview, May 10, 2017.

102. William Parker, liner notes, *Crumbling in the Shadows Is Fraulein Miller's Stale Cake*, [2].

103. Parker, liner notes, *Crumbling in the Shadows*, [10].

Chapter 11: All People Need Truth to Survive

Epigraph: William Parker, liner notes, *Wood Flute Songs* (AUM Fidelity, 2013), [8].

1. William Parker, *For Those Who Are, Still* (AUM Fidelity, 2015).

2. Fannie Lou Hamer, quoted in James MacGregor Burns, *The Crosswinds of Freedom: 1932–1988* (New York: Open Road Media, 2012), 3:636.

3. "About," The Kitchen, accessed December 17, 2018, www.thekitchen.org.

4. William Parker, liner notes, *For Those Who Are, Still* (AUM Fidelity, 2015), [21].

5. Philip Clark, liner notes, *For Those Who Are, Still* (AUM Fidelity, 2015), [7], [3].

6. Parker, liner notes, *For Those Who Are, Still*, [20].

7. Parker, liner notes, *For Those Who Are, Still*, [20].

8. William Parker, quoted in Clark, liner notes, *For Those Who Are, Still*, [4].

9. Clark, liner notes, *For Those Who Are, Still*, [4].

10. Parker, quoted in Clark, liner notes, *For Those Who Are, Still*, [4].

11. Clark, liner notes, *For Those Who Are, Still*, [5].

12. William Parker, liner notes, *Voices Fall from the Sky* (Centering Records, 2018), [1], [3].

13. William Parker, interview by author, digital recording, December 21, 2018.

14. Parker interview, December 21, 2018.

15. Parker, liner notes, *Voices Fall from the Sky*, [3], [8].

16. Parker, liner notes, *Voices Fall from the Sky*, [9].

17. Parker, liner notes, *Voices Fall from the Sky*, [5], [10].

18. Parker, liner notes, *Voices Fall from the Sky*, [12].

19. Parker, liner notes, *Voices Fall from the Sky*, [15], [13].

20. Parker, liner notes, *Voices Fall from the Sky*, [11].

21. Parker felt that the sextet live version fully realized his vision for the piece. William Parker, liner notes, *Flower in a Stained-Glass Window and the Blinking of the Ear* (Centering Records, 2018), [3].

22. Parker, liner notes, *Voices Fall from the Sky*, [20].

23. Parker, liner notes, *Flower in a Stained-Glass Window*, [2].

24. Kesivan Naidoo, quoted in Rick Lopez, *William Parker Sessionography* online, accessed February 12, 2019, www.bb10k.com/PARKER.disc.html.

25. Parker, liner notes, *Flower in a Stained-Glass Window*, [2], [3].

26. Parker, liner notes, *Flower in a Stained-Glass Window*, [3].

27. William Parker, interview by author, digital recording, January 27, 2019.

28. Arthur Jafa, quoted in Antwaun Sargent, "Arthur Jafa and the Future of Black Cinema," *Interview*, January 2017, www.interviewmagazine.com/art/arthur-jafa.

29. LeRoi Jones, "The Changing Same (R&B and New Black Music)," in *The Black Aesthetic*, ed. Addison Gayle Jr. (Garden City, NY: Doubleday, 1971), 126–27.

30. Matthew Shipp, interview by author, digital recording, July 29, 2016.

31. Jason Kao Hwang, interview by author, email transcript, February 21–March 29, 2017.

32. Shipp interview, July 29, 2016.

33. James Brandon Lewis, interview by author, digital recording, April 1, 2017.

34. Joshua Abrams, interview by author, digital recording, May 10, 2017.

35. William Parker, interview by author, digital recording, August 9, 2018.

36. Parker interview, August 9, 2018.

37. Parker interview, January 27, 2019.

38. Parker interview, August 9, 2018.

39. Larry Blumenfeld, "A Father to the Followers of Free Jazz," *New York Times*, May 26, 2002.

40. Lewis interview, April 1, 2017.

41. Patricia Nicholson Parker, interview by author, October 30, 2016.

42. Abrams interview, May 10, 2017.

43. Steve Swell, email interview by author, February 20, 2017.

44. Andrew Cyrille, interview by author, digital recording, April 22, 2017.

45. Hamid Drake, interview by author, digital recording, January 15, 2019.

46. Donald A. Sharif Graham, "Spreading the Wisdom of Sufism: The Career of Pir-o-Murshid Inayat Khan in the West," in *A Pearl in Wine*, ed. Pirzade Zia Inayat Khan (New Lebanon, NY: Omega, 2001), 128–29; Marcia Hermansen, "Common Themes, Uncommon Contexts: The Sufi Movement of Hazrat Inayat Khan (1882–1927) and Khawaja Hasan Nizāmī (1878–1955)," in *A Pearl in Wine*, ed. Pirzade Zia Inayat Khan (New Lebanon, NY: Omega, 2001), 325; Hülya Küçük, "A Brief History of Western Sufism," in "Transnationalizing Southeast Asia," special issue, *Asian Journal of Science* 36, no. 2 (2008): 301–2; Drake interview, January 15, 2019.

47. Swell interview, February 20, 2017.

48. Parker, liner notes, *Wood Flute Songs*, [5–6].

49. Swell interview, February 20, 2017.

50. Drake interview, January 15, 2019.

51. Shipp interview, June 29, 2016.

52. Synthesiaarts, "An Open Letter to Howard Mandel or William Parker Has Had It with Hacks," accessed January 18, 2019, http://synthesiaarts.blogspot.com/2014/04/an-open -letter-to-howard-mandel-or.html.

53. Andrew Barker, email interview by author, February 13–March 1, 2017.

54. Patricia Nicholson Parker, interview by author, November 5, 2016.

55. Dave Burrell, interview by author, February 14, 2017.

56. Drake interview, January 15, 2019.

57. William Parker, liner notes, *Sound Unity* (AUM Fidelity, 2005), [2].

58. Parker, liner notes, *Sound Unity*, [2].

Background Sources

1850 U.S. Census, Duplin County, North Carolina, population schedule, North Division, p. 10A (printed, 19 handwritten), dwelling 143, family 143, Elizabeth Parker. NARA microfilm publication M432, roll 629.

1860 U.S. Census, Cumberland County, North Carolina, population schedule, Cumberland East, p. 47, dwelling 318, family 322, Betsy Parker. NARA microfilm publication M653, roll 894.

1870 U.S. Census, Wayne County, North Carolina, population schedule, township of Brogden, p. 55, dwelling 436, family 436, Betsy Parker. NARA microfilm publication M593, roll 1165.

1880 U.S. Census, Orangeburg County, South Carolina, population schedule, township of Orange, p. 58, enumeration district 149, dwelling 577, family 481, Thomas Glover. NARA microfilm production T9, roll 1237.

1880 U.S. Census, Wayne County, North Carolina, population schedule, township of Brogden, enumeration district 295, p. 44, dwelling 400, family 400, Betsy Parker. NARA microfilm publication T9, roll 986.

1900 U.S. Census, Orangeburg County, South Carolina, population schedule, township of Orange, sheet 17, enumeration district 65, dwelling 319, family 321, Thomas Glover. NARA microfilm production T623.

1900 U.S. Census, Wayne County, North Carolina, population schedule, township of Goldsboro, enumeration district 101, sheet 20, dwelling 450, family 457, Dallas Dickson. NARA microfilm publication T623.

1910 U.S. Census, Wayne County, North Carolina, population schedule, enumeration district 103, sheet 19 B, dwelling 373, family 373, Dallas Dixon. NARA microfilm publication T674, roll 1137.

1920 U.S. Census, Orangeburg County, South Carolina, population schedule, township of Orange, enumeration district 70, sheet 11B, dwelling 216, family 217, Thomas M. Glover. NARA microfilm publication T625, roll 1705.

1930 U.S. Census, Wayne County, North Carolina, population schedule, city of Goldsboro, enumeration district 96–17, sheet 7A, dwelling 132, family 151, Dortch Parker. NARA microfilm publication T626.

1930 U.S. Census, Orangeburg County, South Carolina, population schedule, township of Orange, enumeration district 38–7, sheet 15A, dwelling 308, family 354, Thomas Glover. NARA microfilm publication T626.

1940 U.S. Census, New York County, New York, population schedule, Manhattan, enumeration district 31–1811, sheet 2B, household 22, Carrie Lee Jefferson. NARA microfilm publication T627, roll 2671.

1940 U.S. Census, New York County, New York, population schedule, Manhattan, enumeration district 31–1940, sheet 62B, household 212, Dortch Parker. NARA microfilm publication T627, roll 2667.

Adams, J. *Sketches Taken during Ten Voyages to Africa, between the Years 1786 and 1800; Including Observations on the Country between Cape Palmas and the River Congo; and Cursory Remarks on the Physical and Moral Character of the Inhabitants.* London: Hurst, Robinson, 1832.

Arnold, Robert. *The Dismal Swamp and Lake Drummond: Early Recollections.* Norfolk: Green, Burke and Gregory, 1888.

Clapp, Henry, Jr. *The Pioneer: or, Leaves from an Editor's Portfolio.* Lynn, MA: J. B. Tolman, 1846.

Davies, Reverend Ernest, and Gertrude Solomon, the Claremont Area Housing Committee, to Mayor Robert Wagner, April 14, 1954, box 137, folder 1990, Mayor Wagner Papers, New York City Municipal Archives.

Deed Book 16, Register of Deeds Office, Wayne County Courthouse, Goldsboro, NC: 16, 360. Duplin County Tax Records, North Carolina State Archive.

"The Dismal Swamp and Its Occupants." *Natural Science News* 1, no. 37 (1895).

Douglass, Frederick. *My Bondage and My Freedom.* New York: Miller, Orton and Mulligan, 1855.

Equiano, Olaudah. *The Interesting Narrative and Other Writings*, edited by Vincent Carretta. New York: Penguin, 2003.

"The Game of the Dismal Swamp." *Forest and Stream* 38, no. 21 (1892).

Grantee Book 1–5–10–14–15: 155. Duplin County Register of Deeds Office.

Grantee Book 7A: 97. Duplin County Register of Deeds Office.

Grantee Book 8A: 239. Duplin County Register of Deeds Office.

Grantee Book 8B: 128. Duplin County Register of Deeds Office.

Grantee Book 12: 70–2. Duplin County Register of Deeds Office.

Hunter, Alexander. "The Great Dismal Swamp." *Outing* 27, no. 1 (October 1895).

Hunter, Alexander. "Through the Dismal Swamp." *Potter's American Monthly* 17, no. 115 (1881).

Hutton, Catherine. *The Tour of Africa: Containing a Concise Account of All the Countries in That Quarter of the Globe, Hitherto Visited by Europeans; with the Manners and Customs of the Inhabitants.* Vol. 2. London: Baldwin, Cradock and Joy, 1821.

"Intergroup Relations in New York City: Progress and Problems, A Survey Summary." National Council of Christians and Jews, Manhattan-Westchester Region, February 1954, 7–11, box 59, folder 685, Mayor Wagner Papers, New York City Municipal Archives.

Jackson, Edmund. "The Virginia Maroons." *Liberty Bell*, January 1, 1852.

Johnson, Roy F. *Tales from Old Carolina: Traditional and Historical Sketches of the Area between and about the Chowan River and the Great Dismal Swamps*. Murfreesboro, NC: Johnson Publishing, 1965.

Laidlaw, Walter, ed. *Population of the City of New York, 1890–1930*. New York: Cities Census Committee, 1932.

Laidlaw, Walter, ed. *Statistical Sources for Demographic Studies of Greater New York, 1910*. New York: New York Federation of Churches, 1910.

Laidlaw, Walter, ed. *Statistical Sources for Demographic Studies of Greater New York, 1920*. New York: Cities Census Committee, 1922.

National Endowment for the Arts. *A Brief Chronology of Federal Support for the Arts: 1965–2000*. Washington, DC: National Endowment for the Arts, 2000.

New York City Housing Authority. *City-Wide Public Housing*. September 30, 1962.

New York City Housing Authority. Project Data. December 31, 1977.

Olmstead, Frederick Law. *A Journey in the Back Country*. New York: Mason Brothers, 1860.

Parker, Willie Tyson. Death Certificate. North Carolina State Board of Health, Bureau of Vital Statistics. North Carolina State Archives, Raleigh, NC.

"Peat in the Dismal Swamp." *DeBow's Review* 4, no. 4 (1867).

Redpath, James. *The Roving Editor, or Talks with Slaves in the Southern States*. New York: A. B. Burdick, 1859.

Roome, Henry Clay. *Southward in the Roamer: Being a Description of the Inside Route from New York to Florida*. New York: Rudder Publishing, 1907.

Schoepf, Johann David. *Travels in the Confederation, 1783–1784*. Translated and edited by Alfred J. Morrison. Philadelphia: William Campbell, 1911.

Street, Frederick. "In the Dismal Swamp." *Frank Leslie's Popular Monthly*, March 1903.

Stuart, John Ferdinand Smyth. *A Tour in the United States of America*. Vol. 2. London: G. Robinson, J. Robson, and J. Sewel, 1784.

Trumble, Alfred. "Through the Dismal Swamp." *Frank Leslie's Popular Monthly*, April 1881.

U.S. Bureau of the Census. *Census Tract Data on Population and Housing, New York City: 1940*. New York: Bureau of the Census, 1942.

U.S. Bureau of the Census. *Historical Statistics of the United States: Colonial Times to 1970*. Washington, DC: U.S. Government Printing Office, 1975.

Weld, Isaac. *Travels through the State of North America*. London: John Stockdale, 1799.

Film

Art of Vision, directed by Stan Brakhage, 1965.

Cecil Taylor: Berlin +NYC 1986, directed by Ralph Quinke.

Dog Star Man, directed by Stan Brakhage, 1961–64, originally released in five separate parts.

Jazz, directed by Ken Burns, 2001.

Little Stabs at Happiness, directed by Ken Jacobs, 1960.

The Loneliness of the Long-Distance Runner, directed by Tony Richardson, 1962.

Mass for the Dakota Sioux, directed by Bruce Baillie, 1964.

The Passion of Anna, directed by Ingmar Bergman, 1969.

Prisons on Fire, directed by Claude Marks, 1971.

Rising Tones Cross, directed by Ebba Jahn, 1985.

Shame, directed by Ingmar Bergman, 1968.

The Story of Film: An Odyssey, directed by Mark Cousins, 2011.

Super Fly, directed by Gordon Parks Jr., 1972.

Music Recordings

For William Parker's recordings as a leader, coleader, and sideperson, see Appendix A: Discography.

Anderson, Fred, et al. *2 Days in April*. Eremite, 2000.

Ayler, Albert. *Music Is the Healing Force of the Universe*. Impulse!, 1970.

Ayler, Albert. *Prophecy*. ESP-Disk, 1975.

Ayler, Albert. *Spirits*. ESP-Disk, 1965.

Ayler, Albert. *Spirits Rejoice*. ESP-Disk, 1970.

Ayler, Albert. *Spiritual Unity*. ESP-Disk, 1965.

Brötzmann, Peter. *Die Like a Dog: The Complete FMP Recordings*. Jazzwerkstatt, 2000.

Brötzmann, Peter. *Die Like a Dog Quartet: From Valley* to Valley. Eremite, 1999.

Brown, James. *Say It Loud—I'm Black and I'm Proud*. King Records, 1969.

Brown, Marion. *Afternoon of a Georgia Faun*. ECM, 1970.

Coleman, Ornette. *At the "Golden Circle" Stockholm*. Blue Note, 1965.

Coleman, Ornette. *Free Jazz*. Atlantic, 1961.

Coleman, Ornette. *The Shape of Jazz to Come*. Atlantic, 1959.

Coltrane, John. *Live in Seattle*. Impulse!, 1971.

Coltrane, John. *A Love Supreme*. Impulse!, 1965.

Coltrane, John. *Meditations*. Impulse!, 1966.

Coltrane, John. *Om*. Impulse!, 1967.

Dixon, Bill. *November 1981*. Soul Note, 1982.

Ellington, Duke. *Soul Call*. Verve Records, 1967.

Ellington, Duke, and His Orchestra. *Duke Ellington's Far East Suite*. RCA Victor, 1967.

Ellington, Duke, and His Orchestra. *Ellington at Newport*. Columbia, 1957.

Eneidi, Marco. *The Marco Eneidi Collection*. Botticelli, 1994.

Eneidi, Marco. *Vermont, Spring, 1986*. Botticelli, 1986.

Fitzgerald, Ella, and Duke Ellington. *Ella at Duke's Place*. Verve Records, 1966.

Graves, Milford. *Bäbi*. IPS, 1977.

Horvitz, Wayne. *Simple Facts*. Theater for Your Mother, 1980.

Ja Rule. *Blood in My Eye*. Murder Inc., 2003.

Jackson, Willis, and Brother Jack McDuff. *Together Again, Again*. Prestige, 1967.

Jarman, Joseph. *Song For*. Delmark, 1967.

Malik, Raphe. *Companions*. Eremite, 2002.

Malik, Raphe. *Last Set: Live at the 1369 Jazz Club*. Boxholder Records, 2004.

Malik, Raphe. *Looking East: A Suite in Three Parts*. Boxholder Records, 2001.

Mingus, Charles. *Mingus Ah Um*. Columbia, 1959.

Moondoc, Jemeel. *Muntu Recordings*. NoBusiness, 2009.

New York Art Quartet. *New York Art Quartet*. ESP-Disk, 1965.

Shepp, Archie. *Attica Blues*, Impulse!, 1972.

Shepp, Archie. *Fire Music*. Impulse!, 1965.

Spearman, Glenn. *Night after Night*. Musa-Physics, 1981.

Taylor, Cecil. *Air above Mountains*. Inner City Records, 1978.

Taylor, Cecil. *Calling It the 8th*. Hat Hut, 1983.

Taylor, Cecil. *Conquistador!* Blue Note, 1966.

Taylor, Cecil. *Dark to Themselves*. Enja, 1976.

Taylor, Cecil. *Double Holy House*. FMP, 1993.

Taylor, Cecil. *Erzulie Maketh Scent*. FMP, 1989.

Taylor, Cecil. *For Olim*. Soul Note, 1987.

Taylor, Cecil. *Garden*. Hat Hut Records, 1982.

Taylor, Cecil. *Looking (Berlin Version) Solo*. FMP, 1990.

Taylor, Cecil. *Looking Ahead!* Contemporary Records, 1959.

Taylor, Cecil. *Praxis*. Praxis, 1982.

Taylor, Cecil. *Silent Tongues: Live at Montreux '74*. Arista, 1975.

Taylor, Cecil. *Unit Structures*. Blue Note, 1966.

Taylor, Cecil. *The Willisau Concert*. Intakt Records, 2002.

Various artists. *FMP in Rückblick—In Retrospect*. FMP, 2010.

Liner Notes

Baird, Roger. Liner notes. *The Music Ensemble*. Roaratorio Records, 2001.

Bang, Billy. Liner notes. *The Music Ensemble*. Roaratorio Records, 2001.

Budbill, David. Liner notes. *O'Neal's Porch*. Centering Records, 2001.

Clark, Philip. Liner notes. *For Those Who Are, Still*. AUM Fidelity, 2015.

Cook, Richard. Liner notes. Cecil Taylor Feel Trio, *2 Ts for a Lovely T*. Codanza Records, 2002.

Hazell, Ed. "Carved Out of the Hard Dark Ebony of Africa: The Story of Jemeel Moondoc and Muntu." In liner notes, *Muntu Recordings*. NoBusiness Records, 2009.

Hazell, Ed. "Centering: Art Is the Process of Living." In liner notes, *Centering: Unreleased Early Recordings, 1976–1987*. NoBusiness, 2012.

Hazell, Ed. "A Different Architectural Blueprint in Each Section." In liner notes, *Centering: Unreleased Early Recordings, 1976–1987*. NoBusiness, 2012.

Hazell, Ed. Liner notes. *Centering: Unreleased Early Recordings 1976–1987*. NoBusiness Records, 2012.

Hazell, Ed. "A Muntu Sessionography." In liner notes, *Muntu Recordings*. NoBusiness, 2009.

Hazell, Ed. "A Place to Play What We Want." In liner notes, *Muntu Recordings*. NoBusiness, 2009.

Hertling, Nele. "A Few Words of Introduction." Translated by Barbara Fussmann. In liner notes, *Cecil Taylor in Berlin '88*, 5. FMP, 1989.

Joerg, Steven. Liner notes. *First Communion + Piercing the Veil*. AUM Fidelity, 2007.

Joerg, Steven. Liner notes. *Great Spirit*. AUM Fidelity, 2015.

Jost, Ekkehard. "Instant Composing as Body Language." In liner notes, *Cecil Taylor in Berlin '88*. FMP, 1989.

Kowald, Peter. Liner notes. Translated by Isabel Seeberg and Paul Lytton. *Posium Pendasem*. FMP, 1999.

Lake, Steve. "Cecil Taylor in Berlin." In liner notes, *Cecil Taylor in Berlin '88*. FMP, 1989.

Moondoc, Jemeel. "Muntu: The Essay." In liner notes, *Muntu Recordings*. NoBusiness Records, 2009.

Noglik, Bert. "A Light Ignited in the Open: Cecil Taylor—Both Sides of the Wall." In liner notes, *Cecil Taylor in Berlin '88*, 65–71. FMP, 1989.

Parker, William. Liner notes. *Corn Meal Dance*. AUM Fidelity, 2007.

Parker, William. Liner notes. *Flower in a Stained-Glass Window and the Blinking of the Ear*. Centering Records, 2018.

Parker, William. Liner notes. *For Those Who Are, Still*. AUM Fidelity, 2015.

Parker, William. Liner notes. *Meditation/Resurrection*. AUM Fidelity, 2017.

Parker, William. Liner notes. *The Peach Orchard*. AUM Fidelity, 1998.

Parker, William. Liner notes. *Petit Oiseau*. AUM Fidelity, 2008.

Parker, William. Liner notes. *Raining on the Moon*. Thirsty Ear, 2002.

Parker, William. Liner notes. *Sound Unity*. AUM Fidelity, 2004.

Parker, William. Liner notes. *Sunrise in the Tone World*. AUM Fidelity, 1997.

Parker, William. Liner notes. *Voices Fall from the Sky*. Centering, 2018.

Parker, William. Liner notes. *Wood Flute Songs*. AUM Fidelity, 2013.

Richards, Spencer A. Liner notes. Cecil Taylor Unit, *Live in Vienna*. Leo Records, 1988.

Stańko, Tomasz. "Statements." In liner notes, *Cecil Taylor in Berlin '88*, 58. FMP, 1989.

Tate, Greg. Liner notes. *Corn Meal Dance*. AUM Fidelity, 2007.

Taylor, Cecil. Liner notes. *Nicaragua: No Parasan*. Nica, 1984.

Thomson, Scott. Liner notes. *At Somewhere There*. Barnyard Records, 2010.

Wierbos, Wolter. "Statements." In liner notes, *Cecil Taylor in Berlin '88*, 57. FMP, 1989.

Radio

"Afternoon Music." WKCR-FM broadcast, April 12, 1993.

"The Great Proletariat Cultural Revolution." Hosted by Julius Lester. WBAI, 1968–75.

Television

For Blacks Only
Inside Bedford-Stuyvesant
Like It Is
Positively Black
Soul!

Secondary Sources

"About Books and Authors." *Black World*, January 1972, 75.

Achebe, Chinua. *Things Fall Apart*. 1958. Reprint, New York: Anchor, 1994.

"Action Exchange." *American Libraries* 10, no. 7 (1979): 400.

Afigbo, A. E. "The Anthropology and Historiography of Central-South Nigeria before and since Igbo-Ukwu." *History in Africa* 23 (1996): 1–15.

Alexander, Jane. *Commanding Performance*. New York: PublicAffairs, 2000.

Alexiou, Alice Sparberg. *Devil's Mile: The Rich, Gritty History of the Bowery*. New York: St. Martin's, 2018.

Alfaro, Kristen. "Access and the Experimental Film: New Technologies and the Anthology Film Archives' Institutionalization of the Avant-Garde." *Moving Image* 12, no. 1 (2012): 44–64.

Allen, Ernest, Jr. "The New Negro: Explorations in Identity and Social Consciousness, 1910–1922." In *1915, the Cultural Moment: The New Politics, the New Woman, the New Psychology, the New Art and the New Theatre in America*, edited by Adele Heller and Lois Rudnick, 48–68. New Brunswick, NJ: Rutgers University Press, 1991.

Allen, Tyler. "Nuyorican Poets Café." *World Literature Today* 82, no. 1 (2008): 34.

Alpern, Stanley B. *Amazons of Black Sparta: The Women Warriors of Dahomey*. New York: New York University Press, 1998.

Anderson, Eric. *Race and Politics in North Carolina 1872–1901: The Black Second*. Baton Rouge: Louisiana State University Press, 1981.

Anderson, Iain. "Jazz Outside the Marketplace: Free Improvisation and Nonprofit Sponsorship of the Arts, 1965–1980." *American Music* 20, no. 2 (2002): 131–67.

Anderson, Iain. *This Is Our Music: Free Jazz, the Sixties, and American Culture*. Philadelphia: University of Pennsylvania Press, 2007.

Anderson, Jervis. *This Was Harlem*. New York: Farrar, Straus and Giroux, 1982.

Andrews, W. D. E. "'All Is Permitted': The Poetry of LeRoi Jones/Amiri Baraka." *Southwest Review* 67, no. 2 (1982): 197–221.

Anker, Steve. "Obituary: Stan Brakhage." *Film Comment* 39, no. 3 (2003): 10–11.

Arthur, Paul. "The Chimeric Cinema of Ken Jacobs." *Film Comment* 33, no. 2 (1997): 58–63.

Atherton, Stanley S. "Alan Sillitoe's Battleground." *Dalhousie Review* 10 (1968): 324–31.

Atkins, E. Taylor. *Blue Nippon: Authenticating Jazz in Japan*. Durham, NC: Duke University Press, 2001.

Azuonye, Chukwuma. "Ìgbò ènwē ézè: Monarchical Power versus Democratic Values in Igbo Oral Narratives." In *Power, Marginality and African Oral Literature*, edited by Graham Furniss and Liz Gunner, 65–82. Cambridge: Cambridge University Press, 2008.

"Back Matter." In "Robert Creeley, a Gathering," special issue, *Boundary 2* 6, no. 3–7, no. 1 (1978): 565–70.

Bailey, Helen. Interview with the Bronx African American History Project. Digital Archive at Fordham University. October 13, 2015.

Baker, David, ed. *New Perspectives on Jazz*. Washington, DC: Smithsonian Institution, 1990.

Baraka, Amiri [LeRoi Jones]. "Black Art." In "Black American Culture in the Second Renaissance—1954–1970," special issue, *Black Scholar* 18, no. 1 (1987): 23–30.

Baraka, Amiri [LeRoi Jones]. *Digging: The Afro-American Soul of American Classical Music*. Berkeley: University of California Press, 2009.

Baraka, Amiri [LeRoi Jones]. "Jazz Criticism and Its Effect on the Art Form." In *New Perspectives on Jazz*, edited by David Baker, 56–70. Washington, DC: Smithsonian Institution, 1990.

Barlow, Barry H. "The Nicaraguan-Contra Negotiations of 1988: A Test of the Reagan Doctrine." *Canadian Journal of Latin American and Caribbean Studies* 18, no. 35 (1993): 67–85.

Bartlett, Andrew W. "Cecil Taylor, Identity Energy, and the Avant-Garde African American Body." *Perspectives on New Music* 33, nos. 1/2 (1995): 274–93.

Barzel, Tamar. "The Praxis of Composition-Improvisation and the Poetics of Creative Kinship." In *Jazz/Not Jazz: The Music and Its Boundaries*, edited by David Ake et al., 171–89. Music in America. Berkeley: University of California Press, 2012.

Baugher, Carl E. *Turning Corners: The Life and Music of Leroy Jenkins*. Redwood, NY: Cadence Jazz Books, 2000.

Bauman, Mark. "Southern Jewish Women and Their Social Service Organizations." *Journal of American Ethnic History* 22, no. 3 (2003): 34–78.

Beal, Amy C. *Carla Bley*. Champaign-Urbana: University of Illinois Press, 2011.

Benedict, Stephen, ed. *Public Money and the Muse*. New York: W. W. Norton, 1991.

Berg, Charles Merrell. "Cinema Sings the Blues." *Cinema Journal* 17, no. 2 (1978): 1–12.

Berger, Dan, ed. *The Hidden 1970s: Histories of Radicalism*. New Brunswick, NJ: Rutgers University Press, 2010.

Berman, Marshall. *All That Is Solid Melts into Thin Air*. New York: Simon and Schuster, 1982.

Bernardin, June. "My Reflections: Growing Up in Morrisania." *Bronx County Historical Society Journal* 42, no. 1 (2005): 16–18.

Bernstein, Lee. *America Is the Prison: Arts and Politics in Prison in the 1970s*. Chapel Hill: University of North Carolina Press, 2010.

Block, Steven. "Pitch-Class Transformation in Free Jazz." *Music Theory Spectrum* 12, no. 2 (1990): 181–202.

Blu, Karen I. *The Lumbee Problem: The Making of an American Indian People*. New York: Cambridge University Press, 1980.

Boughman, Arvis Locklear, and Loretta Oxendine. *Herbal Remedies of the Lumbee Indians.* Jefferson, NC: McFarland, 2003.

Bradley, Doug, and Craig Werner. *We Gotta Get Out of This Place: The Soundtrack of the Vietnam War.* Amherst: University of Massachusetts Press, 2015.

Braithwaite, John. Interview with the Bronx African American History Project. Digital Archive at Fordham University. December 4, 2015.

Brakhage, Stan. *Essential Brakhage: Selected Writings on Filmmaking.* Documentext series. Kingston, NY: McPherson, 2001.

Brakhage, Stan. *Film at Wit's End: Eight Avant-Garde Filmmakers.* Documentext series. Kingston, NY: McPherson, 1989.

Brenson, Michael. *Visionaries and Outcasts.* New York: New Press, 2001.

Briley, Ron, ed. *All-Stars and Movie Stars: Sports in Film and History.* Lexington: University Press of Kentucky, 2008.

Brower, Bill, and Willard Jenkins. "Bill Brower: Notes from a Keen Observer." In "Jazz in Washington," special issue, *Washington History* 26: (2014): 60–73.

Brown, Anna J. "The Language of the Incandescent Heart: Daniel Berrigan's and Etty Hillesum's Responses to a Culture of Death." In *Faith, Resistance, and the Future: Daniel Berrigan's Challenge to Catholic Social Thought,* edited by James L. Marsh and Anna J. Brown, 57–79. New York: Fordham University Press, 2012.

Brown, Dee. *Bury My Heart at Wounded Knee: An Indian History of the American West.* New York: Holt, Rinehart and Winston, 1971.

Browning, Judkin. "Vision of Freedom and Civilization Opening before Them: African Americans Search for Autonomy during Military Occupation in North Carolina." In *North Carolinians in the Era of the Civil War and Reconstruction,* edited by Paul D. Escott, 69–100. Chapel Hill: University of North Carolina Press, 2008.

Bryan, Sarah, and Beverly Patterson. *African American Music Trails of Eastern North Carolina.* Chapel Hill: North Carolina Arts Council, 2013.

Buholzer, Meinrad. "Cecil Taylor (Interview)." *Cadence* (December 1984): 5.

Burns, James MacGregor. *The Crosswinds of Freedom: 1932–1988.* Vol. 3. *The American Experiment.* New York: Open Road Media, 2012.

Bynum, Taylor Ho. "Guest Post: Taylor Ho Bynum on Bill Lowe." *Destination: Out.* February 1, 2012. http://destination-out.com/?p=3384.

Cameron, Lindsley, and Masao Miyoshi. "Hiroshima, Nagasaki, and the World Sixty Years Later." *Virginia Quarterly Review* 81, no. 4 (2005): 26–47.

Camper, Fred. "Brakhage's Contradictions." *Chicago Review* 47, no. 4/48, no. 1 (2001/2002): 69–96.

Capeci, Dominic J. *The Harlem Riot of 1943.* Philadelphia: Temple University Press, 1977.

Caponi-Tabery, Gena. *Jump for Joy: Jazz, Basketball, and Black Culture in 1930s America.* Amherst: University of Massachusetts Press, 2008.

Cardenal, Ernesto. *La Hora Cero y Otros Poemas.* Barcelona: Ediciones Saturno, 1971.

Carles, Philippe, and Jean-Louis Comolli. *Free Jazz/Black Power.* Rev. ed. Paris: Gallimard, 2000.

Caroline Zachry Institute of Human Development and the Common Council for American Unity. *Around the World in New York: A Guide to the City's Nationality Groups.* New York: Common Council for American Unity, 1950.

Cartwright, Katharine. "'Guess These People Wonder What I'm Singing': Quotation and Reference in Ella Fitzgerald's 'St. Louis Blues.'" In *Ramblin' on My Mind: New Perspectives on the Blues,* edited by David Evans, 281–327. Champaign-Urbana: University of Illinois Press, 2008.

Casano, Steven. "From Fuke Shuu to Uduboo: The Transnational Flow of the Shakuhachi to the West." In "The Music of 'Others' in the Western World," special issue, *World of Music* 47, no. 3 (2005): 17–33.

Cathey, Cornelius O. *Agriculture in North Carolina before the Civil War.* Raleigh, NC: State Department of Archives and History, 1966.

Ceynowa, Andrzej. "Black Theaters and Theater Organizations in America, 1961–1982: A Research List." In "Black Theatre Issue," *Black American Literature Forum* 17, no. 2 (1983): 84–93.

Chadbourne, Eugene. "Floyd Brady." Allmusic.com. Accessed January 30, 2019. www.allmusic.com/artist/floyd-brady-mn0001569697/biography.

Chambers, Douglas B. *Murder at Montpelier: Igbo Africans in Virginia.* Jackson: University Press of Mississippi, 2005.

Chambers, Douglas B. "'My Own Nation': Igbo Exiles in the Diaspora." *Slavery and Abolition* 18, no. 1 (1997): 72–97.

Chambet-Werner, Oriane. "Entre Jazz et 'Musique du Monde': Regards Croisés sur la Rencontre de l'Autre." *Cahiers de Musiques Traditionnelles* 13: *Métissages* (2000): 91–102.

"The Changing Scene." *Music Educators Journal* 65, no. 1 (1978): 85–87.

Child, Abigail. "Notes on Sincerity and Irony." In *Stan Brakhage: Filmmaker,* edited by David E. James. Philadelphia: Temple University Press, 2005.

Churchill, Suzanne W. "Youth Culture in *The Crisis* and *FIRE!!*" *Journal of Modern Periodical Studies* 1, no. 1 (2010): 64–99.

Clarke, John Henrik. *Harlem: A Community in Transition.* New York: Citadel, 1969.

Cleaver, Eldridge. *Soul on Ice.* New York: Dell, 1968.

"Commentary." *Black Perspective in Music* 3, no. 3 (1975): 346–49.

"Commentary." *Black Perspective in Music* 13, no. 1 (1985): 127–30.

Cook, Camille J., and Anne Rorimer. "Contemporary Film Art." *Bulletin of the Art Institute of Chicago* 67, no. 5 (September–October 1973): 14–15.

Craddock, Paul T., et al. "Metal Sources and the Bronzes of Igbo-Ukwu." *Journal of Field Archaeology* 24, no. 4 (1997): 405–29.

Creative Audio Archive. Accessed November 28, 2018. www.creativeaudioarchive.org/xml/malachi-ritscher.xml.

Crossman, E. J. "The Redfin Pickerel, Esox a. americanus in North Carolina." *Copeia,* no. 1 (1962): 114–23.

Cummings, Milton C., Jr. "Government and the Arts: An Overview." In *Public Money and the Muse,* edited by Stephen Benedict. New York: W. W. Norton, 1991.

"Czechoslovak Musical Instruments Co." *Music Supervisors' Journal* 17, no. 5 (1931): 75.

Dahl, Linda. *Stormy Weather: The Music and Lives of a Century of Jazz Women.* New York: Limelight Editions, 2004.

Dalachinsky, Steve. *The Final Nite and Other Poems: Complete Notes from a Charles Gayle Notebook 1987–2006.* Berkeley: Ugly Duckling Presse, 2006.

Dasgupta, Gautam. "Pinuccio Sciola: Sculptor in the Time of Stone." *Performing Arts Journal* 17, no. 1 (1995): 35–42.

De Jongh, James. *Vicious Modernism: Black Harlem and the Literary Imagination.* Cambridge: Cambridge University Press, 1990.

De Van Massey, Gregory. "The British Expedition to Wilmington, January-November, 1781." *North Carolina Historical Review* 66, no. 4 (October 1989): 387–411.

Delamothe, Tony. "Hiroshima: The Unforgettable Fire." *British Medical Journal* 299, no. 6706 (October 21, 1989): 1023–25.

Diawara, Manthia. "The Song of the Griot." *Transition,* no. 74 (1997): 16–30.

Dickson-Carr, Darryl. *Spoofing the Modern: Satire in the Harlem Renaissance.* Chapel Hill: University of North Carolina Press, 2015.

Diouf, Sylviane A. *Slavery's Exiles: The Story of the American Maroons.* New York: New York University Press, 2014.

Dongala, E. Boundzéki. "Le 'New Jazz': Une Interpretation." *Présence Africaine, Nouvelle Série,* no. 68 (1968): 141–48.

Driskell, Dana. Interview with the Bronx African American History Project. Digital Archive at Fordham University. October 29, 2015.

Duncan, Paul, and Bengt Wanselius, eds. *The Ingmar Bergman Archives.* Cologne: Taschen, 2008.

Edelman, Daniel. "DLA Statement: Squatting on East Seventh Street." In *Resistance: A Radical Political and Social History of the Lower East Side,* edited by Clayton Patterson et al., 187–88. New York: Seven Stories Press, 2007.

Effing, Mercè Mur. "The Origin and Development of Self-Help Literature in the United States: The Concept of Success and Happiness, an Overview." *Atlantis* 31, no. 2 (2009): 125–41.

Ehrhardt, Roy. *Violin Identification and Price Guide.* Vol. 1. Kansas City: Heart of America Press, 1977.

Emery, Lynne Fauley. *Black Dance from 1619 to Today.* 2nd ed. Hightstown, NJ: Princeton Book Co., 1988.

"Episodes from the Attica Massacre." In "Black Prisoner (II)," special issue, *Black Scholar* 4, no. 2 (1972): 34–39.

Escott, Paul D., ed. *North Carolinians in the Era of the Civil War and Reconstruction.* Chapel Hill: University of North Carolina Press, 2008.

Evans, David, ed. *Ramblin' on My Mind: New Perspectives on the Blues.* Champaign-Urbana: University of Illinois Press, 2008.

Evans, David, ed. "The Reinterpretation of African Musical Instruments in the United States." In *The African Diaspora: African Origins and New World Identities,* edited by Isidore Okpewho et al., 379–90. Bloomington: Indiana University Press, 2001.

Evans, Gareth. "The Eye and the Hand: Brakhage's Challenge to Ocularcentrism." In *Stan Brakhage: The Realm Buster*, edited by Marco Lori and Esther Leslie, 63–85. East Barnet, UK: John Libbey, 2018.

Evans, William McKee. *To Die Game: The Story of the Lowry Band, Indian Guerrillas of Reconstruction*. Syracuse, NY: Syracuse University Press, 1995.

Fabian, Imre. "Cologne." In *The New Grove Dictionary of Opera*, edited by Stanley Sadie, 904–5. London: Macmillan, 1998.

Ferguson, Sarah. "The Struggle for Space: 10 Years of Turf Battling on the Lower East Side." In *Resistance: A Radical Political and Social History of the Lower East Side*, edited by Clayton Patterson et al., 141–65. New York: Seven Stories Press, 2007.

"First on Capitol Records: Nature Boy." *Cash Box*, June 5, 1948, 14.

Fischer, David Hackett, and James C. Kelly. *Bound Away: Virginia and the Westward Movement*. Charlottesville: University Press of Virginia, 1994.

Flicker, Chris, and Thierry Trombert. "Qu-est-ce que la Loft Generation." *Jazz* (France) (June 1977): 13–23.

Fly. "Squatting on the Lower East Side." In *Resistance: A Radical Political and Social History of the Lower East Side*, edited by Clayton Patterson et al., 213–18. New York: Seven Stories Press, 2007.

Foley, Barbara. *Radical Representations: Politics and Form in U.S. Proletarian Fiction, 1929–1941*. Durham, NC: Duke University Press, 1993.

"Four Hearts." *Your Leisure* (Russia), November 17, 2008.

Fox, Hetty. Interview with the Bronx African American History Project. Digital Archive at Fordham University. October 1, 2015.

Franklin, John Hope. *The Free Negro in North Carolina, 1790–1860*. Chapel Hill: University of North Carolina Press, 1943. Reprint, New York: W. W. Norton, 1971.

Frölich, Stefan. "Wider die nukleare Bedrohung: Die Amerikanische 'Nuclear Freeze Campaign' 1980–84." *Vierteljahrshefte für Zeitgeschichte* 38, no. 4 (1990): 643–68.

Garfias, Robert. "The Marimba of Mexico and Latin America." *Latin American Music Review* 4, no. 2 (1983): 203–28.

Gayle, Addison, Jr., ed. *The Black Aesthetic*. Garden City, NY: Doubleday, 1971.

Gendron, Bernard. "The Downtown Music Scene." In *The Downtown Book: The New York Art Scene 1974–1984*, edited by Marvin J. Taylor, 41–65. Princeton, NJ: Princeton University Press, 2006.

Gennari, John. *Blowin' Hot and Cool: Jazz and Its Critics*. Chicago: University of Chicago Press, 2006.

Gill, W. W. "Residential Sections." In *The New North End: Bronx Borough*, edited by Taxpayers' Alliance. New York: Diagram, 1910.

Giordano, Richard William. "A History of the Morrisania Section of the Bronx in Three Periods: 1875, 1925, 1975." Master's thesis, Columbia University, 1981.

Glasco, Laurence A. *The WPA History of the Negro in Pittsburgh*. Pittsburgh: University of Pittsburgh Press, 2004.

Godard, Jean-Luc. "Review of Alexandre Astruc's Une Vie." *Cahiers du Cinéma*, no. 89 (1958), reprinted in *The French New Wave: Critical Landmarks*, edited by Peter Graham and Ginette Vincendeau, 155–61. London: Palgrave Macmillan, 2009.

Goldman, Danielle. *I Want to Be Ready: Improvised Dance as a Practice of Freedom*. Ann Arbor: University of Michigan Press, 2010.

Goldstein, Brian D. *The Roots of Urban Renaissance: Gentrification and the Struggle over Harlem*. Cambridge, MA: Harvard University Press, 2017.

Gomez, Michael A. "A Quality of Anguish: The Igbo Response to Enslavement in North America." In *Trans-Atlantic Dimensions of Ethnicity in the African Diaspora*, edited by Paul E. Lovejoy and David V. Trotman, 82–95. London: Continuum, 2003.

Gonzalez, Emma. *The Bronx. The Columbia History of Urban Life*. New York: Columbia University Press, 2004.

Goodson, Martia, et al., eds. "South Bronx Narratives." In *Devastation/Resurrection: The South Bronx*, ed. Robert Jensen. Bronx: Bronx Museum of Art, 1979.

Gourse, Leslie. "The Heyday of the Studio Musician: Thad Jones and Mel Lewis Start a Big Band at the Village Vanguard." *Massachusetts Review* 39, no. 4 (1998/1999): 585–95.

Gourse, Leslie. *Madame Jazz: Contemporary Women Instrumentalists*. New York: Oxford University Press, 1995.

Grant, Nathan L. "Caldwell, Ben." In *The Concise Oxford Companion to African American Literature*, edited by William L. Andrews et al., 64–65. New York: Oxford University Press, 2001.

"Green Hair Trouble." *Life*, December 6, 1948, 83.

Griffin, Farah Jasmine. "On Time, in Time, through Time: Aaron Douglas, *Fire!!* and the Writers of the Harlem Renaissance." In "Aaron Douglas and the Harlem Renaissance," special issue, *American Studies* 49, no. 1/2 (2008): 45–53.

Groover, Mark D. "Creolization and the Archaeology of Multiethnic Households in the American South." In "Evidence of Creolization in the Consumer Goods of an Enslaved Bahamian Family," special issue, *Historical Archaeology* 34, no. 3 (2000): 99–106.

Grotowski, Jerzy. *Towards a Poor Theatre*, edited by Eugenio Barba. A Theatre Arts Book. 1968. Reprint, New York: Routledge, 2002.

Hall, Gwendolyn M. *Slavery and African Ethnicities in the Americas: Restoring the Links*. Chapel Hill: University of North Carolina Press, 2005.

Hansen, Joyce. "A Place for Everyone." *Bronx County Historical Society Journal* 42, no. 2 (2005): 73–79.

Hanson, Michael. "Suppose James Brown Read Fanon: The Black Arts Movement, Cultural Nationalism and the Failure of Popular Musical Praxis." *Popular Music* 27, no. 3 (2008): 341–65.

Harless, Christopher. "Announcing the Impossible." In *Faith, Resistance, and the Future: Daniel Berrigan's Challenge to Catholic Social Thought*, edited by James L. Marsh and Anna J. Brown, 237–47. New York: Fordham University Press, 2012.

Harneit-Sievers, Axel. *Constructions of Belonging: Igbo Communities and the Nigerian State in the Twentieth Century*. Rochester, NY: Boydell and Brewer, 2006.

Hartman, Saidiya. *Lose Your Mother: A Journey along the Atlantic Slave Route*. New York: Farrar, Straus and Giroux, 2007.

Heitner, Devorah. *Black Power TV*. Durham, NC: Duke University Press, 2013.

Heller, Adele, and Lois Rudnick, eds. *1915, the Cultural Moment: The New Politics, the New Woman, the New Psychology, the New Art and the New Theatre in America*. New Brunswick, NJ: Rutgers University Press, 1991.

Heller, Michael C. *Loft Jazz: Improvising New York in the 1970s*. Berkeley: University of California Press, 2017.

Henderson, Lisa Y. "The Involuntary Apprenticeship of Free People of Color in Wayne County, North Carolina, 1830–1860." Master's thesis, Columbia University, 1990.

Hermes, Will. *Love Goes to Buildings on Fire: Five Years in New York That Changed Music Forever*. New York: Farrar, Straus and Giroux, 2012.

Hobbs, Stuart D. *The End of the American Avant Garde*. The American Social Experience. New York: New York University Press, 1997.

Hook, Glenn D. "Evolution of the Anti-Nuclear Discourse in Japan." In "War, Peace and Culture," special issue, *Current Research on Peace and Violence* 10, no. 1 (1987): 32–43.

Hoover, Edgar M., and Raymond Vernon. *Anatomy of a Metropolis: The Changing Distribution of People and Jobs within the New York Metropolitan Region*. Cambridge, MA: Harvard University Press, 1959.

Hübner, Klaus. "Totale Musik, Triebgesteuert: Das Label 'Free Music Productions' Steht 40 Jahre Jazz und Improvisation in Deutschland." *Neue Zeitschrift für Musik* 172, no. 4: Musik Verstehen? (2011): 60–63.

Hunt, Geoffrey, et al. "Changes in Prison Culture: Prison Gangs and the Case of the 'Pepsi Generation.'" *Social Problems* 40, no. 3 (August 1993): 398–409.

Insoll, Timothy A. "The Road to Timbuktu: Trade and Empire." *Archaeology* 53, no. 6 (2000): 48–52.

Isé, Claudine. "Considering the Art World Alternatives: LACE and Community Formation in Los Angeles." In *Sons and Daughters of Los: Culture and Community in L.A.*, edited by David E. James, 85–107. Philadelphia: Temple University Press, 2003.

Isichei, Elizabeth. *A History of African Societies to 1870*. Cambridge: Cambridge University Press, 1997.

"Jack Patton." *Cash Box*, September 11, 1993, 21.

Jack, Homer A. "The Second U.N. Special Session on Dismarmament." *Arms Control Today* (February 1982): 4–5.

Jackson, George. *Soledad Brother: The Prison Letters of George Jackson*. New York: Bantam, 1970.

Jackson, Travis A. "'Always New and Centuries Old': Jazz, Poetry, and Tradition as Creative Adaptation." In *Uptown Conversation: The New Jazz Studies*, edited by Robert G. O'Meally et al., 357–73. New York: Columbia University Press, 2004.

Jaffe, Aaron. "Frank Morales Interviewed by Aaron Jaffe in the Odessa Coffee Shop, Avenue A, Lower East Side." In *Resistance: A Radical Political and Social History of the Lower East Side*, edited by Clayton Patterson et al., 193–212. New York: Seven Stories Press, 2007.

Jalovec, Karel. *The Violin Makers of Bohemia: Including Craftsmen of Moravia and Slovakia.* London: Anglo-Italian Publications, 1959.

Jansen, Jan. "The Representation of Status in Mande: Did the Mali Empire Still Exist in the Nineteenth Century?" *History in Africa* 23 (1996): 87–109.

"Jazz." PBS.org. www.pbs.org/kenburns/jazz/home.

Jensen, Robert, ed. *Devastation/Resurrection: The South Bronx.* Bronx: Bronx Museum of Art, 1979.

Jones, Leroi, Larry Neal, and A. B. Spellman. "The Cricket." *Cricket: Black Music in Evolution* 1 (1968): 1–3.

Jones, LeRoi. *Blues People: Negro Music in White America and the Music That Developed from It.* New York: Morrow Quill, 1963.

Jones, LeRoi. "The Changing Same (R&B and New Black Music)." In *The Black Aesthetic,* edited by Addison Gayle Jr., 118–31. Garden City, NY: Doubleday, 1971.

Jones, LeRoi. *The Dead Lecturer.* New York: Grove, 1964.

Jones, LeRoi. "New Black Music: A Concert in Benefit of the Black Arts Repertory Theater/School Live," in LeRoi Jones, *Black Music.* New York: William Morrow, 1968.

Jones, Rhett S. "Community and Commentators: Black Theatre and Its Critics." *Black American Literature Forum* 14, no. 2 (1980): 69–76.

Jonnes, Jill. *South Bronx Rising: The Rise, Fall, and Resurrection of an American City.* New York: Fordham University Press, 2002.

Joseph, Peniel E. *Waiting 'Til the Midnight Hour: A Narrative History of Black Power in America.* London: Routledge, 2006.

Josephson, Barney, and Terry Trilling-Josephson. *Café Society: The Wrong Place for the Right People.* Champaign-Urbana: University of Illinois Press, 2009.

Jost, Ekkehard. *Free Jazz.* Graz: Universal Edition, 1975.

Jung, Fred. "A Fireside Chat with William Parker." *Jazz Weekly,* April 3, 2003. http://jazzweekly.com/interviews/wparker.htm.

Kane, Daniel. *All Poets Welcome: The Lower East Side Poetry Scene in the 1960s.* Berkeley: University of California Press, 2003.

Kane, Daniel. "Richard Hell, 'Genesis: Grasp,' and the Blank Generation: From Poetry to Punk in New York's Lower East Side." *Contemporary Literature* 52, no. 2 (2011): 330–69.

Kase, Carlos. "On the Importance of Anthology Film Archives: A Historical Overview and Endorsement." In *Captured: A Film/Video History of the Lower East Side,* edited by Clayton Patterson et al., 85–89. New York: Seven Stories Press, 1998.

Keenan, David. Festival review. *Wire,* no. 200 (2000): 98.

Keister, Jay. "The Shakuhachi as Spiritual Tool: A Japanese Buddhist Instrument in the West." *Asian Music* 35, no. 2 (2004): 99–131.

Kelley, Robin D. G. "New Monastery: Monk and the Jazz Avant-Garde." In "New Perspectives on Thelonious Monk," special issue, *Black Music Research Journal* 19, no. 2 (1999): 135–68.

Kelly, Robert. "On the Art of Vision." *Film Culture* 37 (1965): 14–15.

Kloza, Daniel. "African Origins of the Igbo Slave Resistance in the Americas." In *Olaudah Equiano and the Igbo World: History, Society and Atlantic Diaspora Connections,* edited by Chima J. Korieh, 349–68. Trenton, NJ: Africa World Press, 2009.

Knight, Roderic. "Review of *Kora Melodies from the Republic of Gambia*, by Alhaji Bai Konte." *African Arts* 8, no. 1 (1974): 78–79, 88.

Kominko, Maja, ed. *From Dust to Digital: Ten Years of the Endangered Archives Programme.* New York: Open Book, 2015.

Kono, Masahiko. "Brass Experiments in New York." *Jazz Hihyo* 74 (1992), reprinted in *Japan Improv.* Accessed November 17, 2018. www.japanimprov.com/kono/essay.html.

Korieh, Chima J. "Igbo Identity in Africa and the Atlantic Diaspora." In *Olaudah Equiano and the Igbo World: History, Society and Atlantic Diaspora Connections*, edited by Chima J. Korieh, 287–313. Trenton, NJ: Africa World Press, 2009.

Korieh, Chima J., ed. *Olaudah Equiano and the Igbo World: History, Society and Atlantic Diaspora Connections.* Trenton, NJ: Africa World Press, 2009.

Kornbluh, Peter. "Test Case for the Reagan Doctrine: The Covert Contra War." *Third World Quarterly* 9, no. 4 (1987): 1118–28.

Kourlas, Gia. "Dianne McIntyre Talks about Her Love Affair with Dance." August 20, 2012. www.timeout.com/newyork/dance/dianne-mcintyre-talks-about-her-love -affair-with-modern-dance.

Küçük, Hülya. "A Brief History of Western Sufism." In "Transnationalizing Southeast Asia," special issue, *Asian Journal of Science* 36, no. 2 (2008): 292–320.

Ladwing, Ronald V. "The Black Comedy of Ben Caldwell." *Players* 51, no. 3 (1976): 88–91.

Lamb, Brian. "The All-American Skin Game, or the Decoy of Race." *Booknotes*, C-SPAN, May 12, 1996.

Land, Jeff. *Active Radio: Pacifica's Brash Experiment.* Minneapolis: University of Minnesota Press, 1999.

Law, Robin. "'The Common People Were Divided': Monarchy, Aristocracy and Political Factionalism in the Kingdom of Whydah, 1671–1727." *International Journal of African Historical Studies* 23, no. 2 (1990): 201–29.

Law, Robin. "Dahomey and the Slave Trade: Reflections on the Historiography of the Rise of Dahomey." In "Special Issue in Honour of J. D. Fage," *Journal of African History* 27, no. 2 (1986): 237–67.

Law, Robin. "Ideologies of Royal Power: The Dissolution and Reconstruction of Political Authority on the 'Slave Coast,' 1680–1750." *Africa* 57, no. 3 (1987): 321–44.

Law, Robin. "Slave-Raiders and Middlemen, Monopolists and Free-Traders: The Supply of Slaves for the Atlantic Trade in Dahomey c. 1715–1850." *Journal of African History* 30, no. 1 (1989): 45–68.

Law, Robin. "The Slave Trade in Seventeenth-Century Allada: A Revision." *African Economic History*, no. 22 (1994): 59–92.

Lawrence, Robert C. *The State of Robeson.* New York: J. Little and Ives, 1939.

Levin, Robert. "The Jazz Composers' Guild: An Assertion of Dignity." *Down Beat*, May 6, 1965, 17–18.

Levy, Leonard. "The ABCs of Media." *Threepenny Review*, no. 2 (1980): 7–8.

Lewis, Edward S. "The Urban League, a Dynamic Instrument in Social Change: A Study of the Changing Role of the New York Urban League, 1910–1960." PhD diss., New York University, 1961.

Lewis, George. "Experimental Music in Black and White: The AACM in New York, 1970–1985." In *Uptown Conversation: The New Jazz Studies*, edited by Robert G. O'Meally et al., 50–101. New York: Columbia University Press, 2004.

Lewis, Gregory B., and Michael Rushton. "Understanding State Spending on the Arts, 1976–99." *State and Local Government Review* 39, no. 2 (2007): 107–14.

Lewis, Rodney. "Growing Up in Morrisania: A Recollection." *Bronx County Historical Society Journal* 42, no. 1 (2005): 19–22.

Lifton, Robert Jay. *Death in Life: Survivors of Hiroshima*. Chapel Hill: University of North Carolina Press, 1991.

Lo-Bamijoko, J. N. "Classification of Igbo Musical Instruments, Nigeria." *African Music* 6, no. 4 (1987): 19–41.

Lopez, Rick. *The William Parker Sessionography: Attempting a Complete Historical Arc*. New York: Centering, 2014.

Lovejoy, Paul E. "Ethnic Designations of the Slave Trade and the Reconstruction of the History of Trans-Atlantic Slavery." In *Trans-Atlantic Dimensions of Ethnicity in the African Diaspora*, edited by Paul E. Lovejoy and David V. Trotman, 9–42. London: Continuum, 2003.

Lovejoy, Paul E., and David V. Trotman, eds. *Trans-Atlantic Dimensions of Ethnicity in the African Diaspora*. London: Continuum, 2003.

Lowery, Malinda Maynor. *The Lumbee Indians: An American Struggle*. Chapel Hill: University of North Carolina Press, 2018.

Lowery, Malinda Maynor. *Lumbee Indians in the Jim Crow South: Race, Identity and the Making of a Nation*. First Peoples: New Directions in Indigenous Studies. Chapel Hill: University of North Carolina Press, 2010.

Lubell, Samuel. *The Future of American Politics*. 3rd ed. New York: Harper and Row, 1965.

Lusky, Louis, and Mary H. Lusky. "Columbia 1968: The Wound Unhealed." *Political Science Quarterly* 84, no. 2 (1969): 169–288.

Lynch, Kevin. "Cecil Taylor and the Poetics of Living." *Down Beat*, November 1986, 24.

MacKenzie, Scott. *Film Manifestos and Global Cinema Cultures: A Critical Anthology*. Berkeley: University of California Press, 2014.

Makhijani, Arjun, and Michio Kaku. "Nuclear Disarmament and Its Verification." *Economic and Political Weekly* 17, no. 38 (1982): 1531.

Maloff, Saul. "The Eccentricity of Alan Sillitoe." In *Contemporary British Novelists*, ed. Charles Shapiro. Carbondale: Southern Illinois University Press, 1965.

Mandel, Howard. "Beneath the Underdog." *Down Beat*, July 1998.

Marcoux, Jean-Philippe. "Troping and Groupings: Jazz Artistry, Activism and Cultural Memory in Lanston Hughes's 'Ask Your Mama.'" *CLA Journal* 53, no. 4 (2010): 387–409.

Marks, Claude, and Rob McBride. "Recovering, Amplifying, and Networking the Voices of the Disappeared—Political Prisoners on Internet Media." In "War, Dissent, and Justice: A Dialogue," special issue, *Social Justice* 30, no. 2 (2003): 135–42.

Massey, Gerald. *A Book of the Beginnings: Containing an Attempt to Recover and Reconstitute the Lost Origines of the Myths and Mysteries, Types and Symbols, Religion* and Language, with Egypt for the Mouthpiece and Africa as the Birthplace. London: Williams and Norgate, 1881.

Mastro, Victor, and John Hogrogian. "Bronx, Blacks, and the NFL." *Coffin Corner* 15, no. 1 (1993): 1–5.

Maxwell, William J. *New Negro, Old Left: African-American Writing and Communism between the Wars*. New York: Columbia University Press, 1999.

Mayfield, Todd, and Travis Astria. *Traveling Soul: The Life of Curtis Mayfield*. Chicago: Chicago Review Press, 2017.

McBreen, Ellen. "Biblical Gender Bending in Harlem: The Queer Performance of Nugent's *Salome*." *Art Journal* 57, no. 3 (1998): 22–28.

McIntosh, Roderick J., and Susan Keech McIntosh. "The Inland Niger Delta before the Empire of Mali: Evidence from Jenne-Jeno." *Journal of African History* 22, no. 1 (1981): 1–22.

McIntyre, Dianne. www.DianneMcIntyrecom. Accessed October 3, 2018.

McLean, Robert C., ed. "A Yankee Tutor in the Old South." *North Carolina Historical Review* 48, no. 1 (1970): 51–85.

McVeigh, Rory. *The Rise of the Ku Klux Klan: Right-Wing Movements and National Politics*. Minneapolis: University of Minnesota Press, 2009.

Mekas, Jonas, and Gerald R. Barrett. "Jonas Mekas Interview October 10, 1972." *Literature/Film Quarterly* 1, no. 2 (1973): 103–12.

Mergner, Lee. "Jazz Violinist Billy Bang Dies." *Jazz Times*, April 12, 2011.

Merrell, James H. *The Indians' New World: Catawbas and Their Neighbors from European Contact through the Era of Removal*. Chapel Hill: University of North Carolina Press, 1989.

Meyer, Herbert E. "How Government Helped Ruin the South Bronx." *Fortune*, November 1975, 144–45.

Meyer, Katherine Jeannette. "A Study of Tenant Associations in New York City with Particular Reference to the Bronx, 1920–1927." Master's thesis, Columbia University, 1928.

Meyer, Matt, and Paul Magno. "Hard to Find: Building for Nonviolent Revolution and the Pacifist Underground." In *The Hidden 1970s: Histories of Radicalism*, edited by Dan Berger, 250–66. New Brunswick, NJ: Rutgers University Press, 2010.

Milteer, Warren. "The Complications of Liberty: Free People of Color in North Carolina from the Colonial Period through Reconstruction." PhD diss., University of North Carolina, 2013.

Morgan, Stacy I. *Rethinking Social Realism: African American Art and Literature, 1930–1953*. Athens: University of Georgia Press, 2004.

Morgenstern, Dan, and Ira Gitler. "Newport '67." *Down Beat*, August 1967, 20–22, 37–39.

Morris-Crowther, Jayne. "An Economic Study of the Substantial Slaveholders of Orangeburg County, 1860–1880." *South Carolina Historical Magazine* 86, no. 4 (1985): 296–314.

Muller, Ada H. "A Study of a Bronx Community." Master's thesis, Columbia University, 1915.

Naar-Obed, Michele. "Nonviolent Peace Activism." In "War, Dissent, and Justice: A Dialogue," special issue, *Social Justice* 30, no. 2 (2003): 119–22.

Naison, Mark. *Communists in Harlem during the Depression.* Urbana: University of Illinois Press, 1983.

Naison, Mark. "Introduction." In *Before the Fires: An Oral History of African American Life in the Bronx from the 1930s to the 1960s,* edited by Mark Naison and Bob Gumbs. New York: Fordham University Press, 2016.

Naison, Mark. "'It Takes a Village to Raise a Child': Growing Up in the Patterson Houses in the 1950s and Early 1960s, an Interview with Victoria Archibald-Good." *Bronx County Historical Society Journal* 40, no. 1 (2003): 4–22.

Naison, Mark, and Bob Gumbs, eds. *Before the Fires: An Oral History of African American Life in the Bronx from the 1930s to the 1960s.* New York: Fordham University Press, 2016.

"Nature Boy." *Life,* May 10, 1948.

Neaher, Nancy C. "Igbo Metalsmiths among the Southern Edo." *African Arts* 9, no. 4 (1976): 46–49, 91–92.

Neal, Larry. "The Black Arts Movement." *Drama Review* 12, no. 4 (1968): 28–39.

Neal, Larry. "Review: New Grass by Albert Ayler." *Cricket: Black Music in Evolution* 3 (1969): 37–40.

Neal, Larry. "The Social Background of the Black Arts Movement." In "Black American Culture in the Second Renaissance—1954–1970," special issue, *Black Scholar* 18, no. 1 (1987): 11–22.

Neal, Larry. *Visions of a Liberated Future: Black Arts Movement Writings,* edited by Michael Schwartz. New York: Thunder's Mouth Press, 1989.

Neal, Larry, and LeRoi Jones, eds. *Black Fire! An Anthology of Afro-American Writing.* New York: William Morrow, 1968.

Needs, Kris. "Hendrix: The Gigs That Changed History—#9 The Harlem Street Fair." October 30, 2015. www.loudersound.com/features/hendrix-the-gigs-that-changed -history-9-the-harlem-street-fair.

Nepstad, Sharon Erickson. "Disruptive Action and the Prophetic Tradition: War and Resistance in the Plowshares Movement." In "War and Peace," special issue, *U.S. Catholic Historian* 27, no. 2 (2009): 97–113.

Nepstad, Sharon Erickson. "Persistent Resistance: Commitment and Community in the Plowshares Movement." *Social Problems* 51, no. 1 (2004): 43–60.

Nepstad, Sharon Erickson, and Stellan Vinthagen. "Strategic Changes and Cultural Adaptations: Explaining Differential Outcomes in the International Plowshares Movement." In "Special Issue: Antiwar Movements," *International Journal of Peace Studies* 13, no. 1 (2008): 15–42.

Nevader, Arun. "John Coltrane: Music and Metaphysics." *Threepenny Review,* no. 10 (1982): 26–27.

Njoku, J. Akuma-Kalu. "Establishing Igbo Community Tradition in the United States: Lessons from Folkloristics." *Journal of American Folklore* 125, no. 497 (2012): 327–42.

"North Atlantic Treaty Organization: Documents from the Bonn Summit." *International Legal Materials* 21, no. 4 (1982): 905–7.

Northrup, David. "The Growth of Trade among the Igbo before 1800." *Journal of African History* 13, no. 2 (1972): 217–36.

Nwokeji, G. Ugo. "The Atlantic Slave Trade and Population Density: A Historical Demography of the Biafran Hinterland." In "Special Issue: On Slavery and Islam in African History: A Tribute to Martin Klein," *Canadian Journal of African Studies* 34, no. 3 (2003): 616–55.

Nzewi, Meki. "Ancestral Polyphony." *African Arts* 11, no. 4 (1978): 74, 92–94.

Ocejo, Richard E. *Upscaling Downtown: From Bowery Saloons to Cocktail Bars in New York City*. Princeton, NJ: Princeton University Press, 2014.

Oguagha, P. A. "The Impact of European Trade on Igbo-Igala Commercial Relations in the Lower Niger, c. 1650–1850 A.D." *Journal of the Historical Society of Nigeria* 11, nos. 3/4 (1982–83): 11–27.

Okpewho, Isidore, Carole Boyce Davies, and Ali A. Mazrui, eds. *The African Diaspora: African Origins and New World Identities*. Bloomington: Indiana University Press, 2001.

Oliver, Paul. *Savannah Syncopators: African Retentions in the Blues*. Worthing, UK: Littlehampton Book Services, 1970.

O'Meally, Robert G., et al., eds. *Uptown Conversation: The New Jazz Studies*. New York: Columbia University Press, 2004.

Ongiri, Amy Abugo. *Spectacular Blackness: The Cultural Politics of the Black Power Movement and the Search for a Black Aesthetic*. Charlottesville: University of Virginia Press, 2010.

Osofsky, Gilbert. "Harlem: The Making of a Ghetto." In *Harlem: A Community in Transition*, edited by John Henrik Clarke. New York: Citadel, 1969.

Ouellette, Laurie. *Viewers Like You: How Public TV Failed the People*. New York: Columbia University Press, 2002.

Pabst, Naomi. "An Unexpected Blackness." *Transition*, no. 100 (2008): 112–32.

Panke, Werner. "New York Loft Scene." *Jazz Forum* (United Kingdom) (February 1978): 56–59.

Parker, William. "Introduction." *Bill Collector*, no. 1 (August 1984): [1–4].

Parker, William. *Who Owns Music? Notes from a Spiritual Journey*. 2nd ed. Cologne: Herausgeberin, 2013.

Patterson, Clayton, ed. *Resistance: A Radical Political and Social History of the Lower East Side*. New York: Seven Stories Press, 2007.

Peavy, Charles D. "Satire and Contemporary Black Drama." *Satire Newsletter* 7 (1969): 40–49.

Penner, Allen R., and Alan Sillitoe. "Human Dignity and Social Anarchy: Sillitoe's 'The Loneliness of the Long-Distance Runner.'" *Contemporary Literature* 10, no. 2 (1969): 253–65.

Perdue, Theda, and Michael D. Green. *The Columbia Guide to American Indians of the Southeast*. New York: Columbia University Press, 2001.

Perpener, John, III. "Dance, Difference, and Racial Dualism at the Turn of the Century." *Dance Research Journal* 32, no. 1 (2000): 63–69.

Pierce, Julian T., et al. *The Lumbee Petition*. Vol. 1. Pembroke, NC: Lumbee River Legal Services, 1987.

Porter, Eric. *What Is This Thing Called Jazz? African American Musicians as Artists, Critics, and Activists.* Berkeley: University of California Press, 2002.

Powell, Anna. "The Occult: A Torch for Lucifer." In *Black Leather Lucifer: The Films of Kenneth Anger,* ed. Jack Hunter, 59–129. Glitter Books, 2012.

Pressly, Thomas J. "The Known World of Free Black Slaveholders: A Research Note on the Scholarship of Carter G. Woodson." In "The African American Experience in the Western States," *Journal of African American History* 91, no. 1 (2006): 81–87.

"Pursuit of Peace." Atomic Bomb Museum. Accessed June 19, 2017. www .atomicbombmuseum.org/5_timetable.shtml.

Quirk, Eugene F. "Social Class as Audience: Sillitoe's Story and Screenplay 'The Loneliness of the Long-Distance Runner.'" *Literature/Film Quarterly* 9, no. 3 (1981): 161–71.

Radano, Ronald M. "Jazzin' the Classics: The AACM's Challenge to Mainstream Aesthetics." *Black Music Research Journal* 12, no. 1 (1992): 79–95.

Ramsey, Andrea Butler. "Growing Up 'Bronx' 1943–1960: Poor but Privileged." *Bronx County Historical Society Journal* 42, no. 1 (2005): 11–15.

Randall, Duncan P. "Wilmington, North Carolina: The Historical Development of a Port City." *Annals of the Association of American Geographers* 58, no. 3 (1968): 441–51.

"Reagan's Rag-Tag Mob." *Economic and Political Weekly,* March 14, 1987, 429–30.

Record and Guide (New York, NY), September 3, 1898; November 4, November 18, 1911; January 2, 1915.

Rees, Linda W. "A Thousand Cranes: A Curriculum of Peace." In "A Curriculum of Peace," special issue, *English Journal* 89, no. 5 (2000): 95–99.

Rodriguez, Clara. "Growing Up in the Forties and Fifties." In *Devastation/Resurrection: The South Bronx,* ed. Robert Jensen. Bronx: Bronx Museum of the Arts, 1979.

Rogoff, Leonard. *Down Home: Jewish Life in North Carolina.* Chapel Hill: University of North Carolina Press, 2010.

Roney, Patrick. "The Paradox of Experience: Black Art and Black Idiom in the Work of Amiri Baraka." In "Amiri Baraka Issue," *African American Review* 37, nos. 2/3 (2003): 407–27.

Rosenthal, David H. "Hard Bop and Its Critics." *Black Perspective in Music* 16, no. 1 (1988): 21–29.

Rosenthal, Josh. "Hangin' on the Bowery: Observations on the Accomplishment of Authenticity at CBGB." *Ethnography* 9, no. 2 (2008): 139–74.

Rosenthal, M. L. "Some Thoughts on American Poetry Today." In "Contemporary Poetry in America," special issue, *Salmagundi,* nos 22/23 (1973): 57–70.

Ross, David. "Robert Norris, Agaja, and the Dahomean Conquest of Allada and Whydah." *History in Africa* 16 (1989): 311–24.

Ross, Thomas E. *One Land, Three Peoples: An Atlas of Robeson County, North Carolina.* Private printing, 1992.

Rout, Leslie B., Jr. "Reflections on the Evolution of Post-War Jazz." In *The Black Aesthetic,* edited by Addison Gayle Jr., 150–60. Garden City, NY: Doubleday, 1971.

Rowe, Carel. "Myth and Symbolism: Blue Velvet." In *Black Leather Lucifer*, edited by Jack Hunter, 13–57. Glitter Books, 2012.

Rowell, Charles H., and Brent Hayes Edwards. "An Interview with Brent Hayes Edwards." *Callaloo* 22, no. 4 (1999): 784–97.

Rusch, Bob. "William Parker Interview." *Cadence* 16, no. 12 (1990).

Salaam, Kalamu Ya. *The Magic of Juju: An Appreciation of the Black Arts Movement*. Chicago: Third World Press Foundation, 2016.

Samuels, W. "From the Wild, Wild West to Harlem's Literary Salons." *Black Issues Book Review* 2, no. 5 (2000): 14.

Sanchez, Sonia. "poem at thirty." In *Black Fire! An Anthology of Afro-American Writing*, edited by Larry Neal and LeRoi Jones. New York: William Morrow, 1968.

Sargent, Antwaun. "Arthur Jafa and the Future of Black Cinema." *Interview*, January 2017. www.interviewmagazine.com/art/arthur-jafa.

Sarin, Sophie. "In the Shadow of Timbuktu: The Manuscripts of Djenné." In *From Dust to Digital: Ten Years of the Endangered Archives Programme*, edited by Maja Kominko, 173–87. New York: Open Book, 2015.

Schmidt, Tyler T. "'In the Glad Flesh of My Ear': Corporeal Inscriptions in Richard Bruce Nugent's 'Geisha Man.'" *African American Review* 40, no. 1 (2006): 161–73.

Schultz, Kathy Lou. "Amiri Baraka's Wise Why's Y's: Lineages of the Afro-Modernist Epic." *Journal of Modern Literature* 35, no. 3 (2012): 25–50.

Schwartz, Andy. *New York Rocker*. Accessed December 5, 2018. www.nyrocker.com/blog/2010/02/winter-jazz-fest.

Schwartz, Joel. *The New York Approach: Robert Moses, Urban Liberals, and Redevelopment of the Inner City*. Columbus: Ohio University Press, 1993.

Scott, Britain, and Christiane Harrassowitz. "Beyond Beethoven and the Boyz: Women's Music in Relation to History and Culture." *Music Educators Journal* 90, no. 4 (2004): 50–56.

Seib, Rebecca S. *Settlement Pattern Study of the Indians of Robeson County, N.C., 1735–87*. Pembroke, NC: Lumbee Regional Development Association, 1983.

Shange, Ntozake. "Unrecovered Losses/Black Theatre Traditions." In "Black Theatre," special issue, *Black Scholar* 10, no. 10 (1979): 7–9.

Sharpe, Christina. *In the Wake: On Blackness and Being*. Durham, NC: Duke University Press, 2016.

Shaw, Arnold. *The Street That Never Slept: New York's Fabled 52nd Street*. New York: Coward, McCann and Geoghegan, 1971.

Shepherd, Verene A. "Ethnicity, Colour and Gender in the Experiences of Enslaved Women on Non-sugar Properties in Jamaica." In *Trans-Atlantic Dimensions of Ethnicity in the African Diaspora*, edited by Paul E. Lovejoy and David V. Trotman, 195–217. London: Continuum, 2003.

Simpson, John. "Global Non-proliferation Policies: Retrospect and Prospect." *Review of International Studies* 8, no. 2 (1982): 69–88.

Smethurst, James. "'Don't Say Goodbye to the Porkpie Hat': Langston Hughes, the Left, and the Black Arts Movement." *Callaloo* 25, no. 4 (2002): 1224–37.

Smethurst, James Edward. *The New Red Negro: The Literary Left and African American Poetry, 1930–1946*. Race and American Culture. New York: Oxford University Press, 1999.

Smith, Carolyn, and Jack Smith. Interview with the Bronx African American History Project. Digital Archive at Fordham University. September 16, 2015.

Smith, Robert S. *Warfare and Diplomacy in Pre-colonial West Africa*. 2nd ed. Madison: University of Wisconsin Press, 1989.

Smith, Steve. "Irving Stone Memorial Concert." AcousticLevitation.org. Accessed December 8, 2018. www.acousticlevitation.org/irvingstone.html.

Solis, Gabriel. *Monk's Music: Thelonious Monk and Jazz History in the Making*. Berkeley: University of California Press, 2008.

Sollors, Werner. *Amiri Baraka/LeRoi Jones: The Quest for a "Modern Populism."* New York: Columbia University Press, 1978.

Sorrie, Bruce A., et al. "Noteworthy Plants from Fort Bragg and Camp McKall, North Carolina." *Castanea* 62, no. 4 (1997): 239–59.

Soulodre-La France, Renee. "'I, Francisco Castañeda, Negro Esclavo Caravali': Caravali/Ethnicity in Colonial New Granada." In *Trans-Atlantic Dimensions of Ethnicity in the African Diaspora*, edited by Paul E. Lovejoy and David V. Trotman, 96–114. London: Continuum, 2003.

Spellman, A. B. *Four Lives in the Bebop Business*. New York: Limelight Editions, 1985.

Spellman, A. B. "Not Just Whistling Dixie." In *Black Fire! An Anthology of Afro-American Writing*, edited by Larry Neal and LeRoi Jones, 159–68. New York: William Morrow, 1968.

St. Clair, Jeffrey. "The Aesthetic Crimes of Ken Burns: Now That's Not Jazz." Counterpunch.org. Accessed January 26, 2016.

Starr, Douglas P. "Private and Government Sources: Funding the Arts." *Music Educators Journal* 69, no. 8 (1983): 43–45.

Stefanile, Felix. "Letter to the Editor." *Georgia Review* 35, no. 4 (1981): 900–901.

Stegman, Michael A. *The Dynamics of Rental Housing in New York City*. Piscataway, NJ: Center for Urban Policy Research, 1982.

Stephen, Curtis. "New York 1977: The Night the Lights Went Out." Curtisstephen.com. July 12, 2017. http://curtisstephen.com/new-york-1977-the-night-the-lights-went-out.

Stevens, Jan. "On Ken Burns Jazz Documentary and Bill Evans." Accessed October 4, 2018. www.billevanswebpages.com/burns.html.

Stewart, Alex. *Making the Scene: Contemporary New York City Big Band Jazz*. Berkeley: University of California Press, 2007.

Stewart-Nuñez, Christine. "Filaments of Prayer." *North American Review* 298, no. 1 (2013): 40–43.

Stiglitz, Joseph E., and Mary Kandor, eds. *The Quest for Security: Protection without Protectionism and the Challenge of Global Governance*. New York: Columbia University Press, 2013.

Stiner, Larry Watani, and Scot Brown. "The US-Panther Conflict, Exile, and the Black Diaspora: The Plight of Larry Watani Stiner." In "New Black Power Studies:

National, International, and Transnational Perspectives," special issue, *Journal of African American History* 92, no. 4 (2007): 540–52.

Strozier, Charles B. *Until the Fires Stopped Burning: 9/11 and New York City in the Words and Experiences of Survivors and Witnesses*. New York: Columbia University Press, 2011.

Stuckert, Robert P. "Free Black Populations of the Southern Appalachian Mountains: 1860." *Journal of Black Studies* 23, no. 3 (1993): 358–70.

Sullivan, Donald G. "1940–1965: Population Mobility in the South Bronx." In *Devastation/Resurrection: The South Bronx*, edited by Robert Jensen, 37–44. Bronx: Bronx Museum of Art, 1979.

Sun Ra. "'The Visitation.'" In *Black Fire! An Anthology of Afro-American Writing*, edited by Larry Neal and LeRoi Jones. New York: William Morrow, 1968.

Sutton, J. E. G. "The International Factor at Igbo-Ukwu." *African Archaeological Review* 9 (1991): 145–60.

Taxpayers' Alliance, ed. *The New North End: Bronx Borough*. New York: Diagram, 1910.

Taylor, Marvin J., ed. *The Downtown Book: The New York Art Scene 1974–1984*. Princeton, NJ: Princeton University Press, 2006.

Theoharis, Jeanne, and Komozi Woodard, eds. *Freedom North: Black Freedom Struggles outside the South, 1940–1980*. New York: Palgrave Macmillan, 2003.

Thomas, Greg. "Dragons!: George Jackson in the Cinema with Haile Gerima—from the Watts Films to Teza." *Black Camera* 4, no. 2 (2013): 55–83.

Thomas, Lorenzo. "'Classical Jazz' and the Black Arts Movement." In "Special Issues on the Music," *African American Review* 29, no. 2 (1995): 237–40.

Thomas, Lorenzo. "'Communication by Horns': Jazz and Redemption in the Poetry of the Beats and the Black Arts Movement." In "Poetry and Theatre Issue," *African American Review* 26, no. 2 (1992): 291–98.

Thomas, Lorenzo. "Neon Griot: The Functional Role of Poetry Readings in the Black Arts Movement." In *Close Listening: Poetry and the Performed Word*, edited by Charles Bernstein, 300–323. New York: Oxford University Press, 1998.

Thomas, Lorenzo. "The Shadow World: New York's Umbra Workshop and Origins of the Black Arts Movement." *Callaloo*, no. 4 (1978): 53–72.

Thornton, John K. *Warfare in Atlantic Africa 1500–1800*. London: Routledge, 1999.

Travers, Tony. "Cities and Conflict Resolution." In *The Quest for Security: Protection without Protectionism and the Challenge of Global Governance*, edited by Joseph E. Stiglitz and Mary Kandor, 276–87. New York: Columbia University Press, 2013.

Truffaut, François. "A Certain Tendency in French Cinema." *Cahiers du Cinéma*, no. 31 (1954), reprinted in *The French New Wave: Critical Landmarks*, edited by Peter Graham and Ginette Vincendeau, 39–63. London: Palgrave Macmillan, 2009.

Turner, Darwin W. "Retrospective of a Renaissance." In "Black American Culture in the Second Renaissance—1954–1970," special issue, *Black Scholar* 18, no. 1 (1987): 2–10.

Van Deburg, William L. *New Day in Babylon: The Black Power Movement and American Culture, 1965–1975*. Chicago: University of Chicago Press, 1992.

"Violins by Juzek." *Etude* 71 (1953): 52.

Wagner, Christoph. "C. T.—der Ausserirdische: Cecil Taylor, Wegbereiter des Freien Jazz, wird 75." *Neue Zeitschrift für Musik* 165, no. 2: Soundscapes (2004): 56–58.

Wagner, Christoph. "Im Maschinenraum der Avantgarde: Die New Yorker Loft-Szene." *Neue Zeitschrift für Musik* 168, no. 5: Artmix and Electronics (2007): 66–68.

Wald, Gayle. "Black Music and Black Freedom in Sound and Space." In "Sound Clash: Listening to American Studies," special issue, *American Quarterly* 63, no. 3 (2011): 673–96.

Wald, Gayle. *It's Been Beautiful: Soul! and Black Power Television.* Durham, NC: Duke University Press, 2015.

Wald, Gayle. "Soul Vibrations: Black Music and Black Freedom in Sound and Space." In "Sound Clash: Listening to American Studies," special issue, *American Quarterly* 63, no. 3 (2011): 673–96.

Walden, Daniel. "Black Music and Cultural Nationalism: The Maturation of Archie Shepp." *Negro American Literature Forum* 5, no. 4 (1971): 150–54.

Wallenstein, Barry. "Poetry and Jazz: A Twentieth-Century Wedding." In "Literature of Jazz Issue," *Black American Literature Forum* 25, no. 3 (1991): 595–620.

Wallenstein, Barry. "The Poetry-Jazz Connection." *Performing Arts Journal* 4, no. 3 (1980): 122–34.

Walton, Ortiz. *Music: Black, White, and Blue.* New York: Morrow, 1972.

Watson, Steven. *The Harlem Renaissance: Hub of African-American Culture, 1920–1930.* Circles of the Twentieth Century. New York: Pantheon, 1995.

Watts, Jerry Gafio. *Amiri Baraka: The Politics and Art of a Black Intellectual.* New York: New York University Press, 2001.

Weiss, Allen S. "An Eye for an I: On the Art of Fascination." In "Issue 51: Recent Film Theory in Europe," *SubStance* 15, no. 3 (1986): 87–95.

Wellburn, Ron. "The Black Aesthetic Imperative." In *The Black Aesthetic,* edited by Gayle Addison Jr., 132–49. Garden City, NY: Doubleday, 1971.

Wellburn, Ron. "The SoHo Loft Jazz." *Music Journal* (March 1977): 26–28.

Westendorf, Lynette. "Cecil Taylor: Indent—'Second Layer.'" *Perspectives on New Music* 33, nos. 1/2 (1995): 294–326.

"What's News." *New York City Jazz Record,* July 2018, 5.

White, Jerry. "Brakhage's Tarkovsky and Tarkovsky's Brakhage: Collectivity, Subjectivity, and the Dream of Cinema." In "A Sense of Sight: Special Issue Devoted to Stan Brakhage," *Revue Canadienne d'Études Cinématographiques/Canadian Journal of Film Studies* 14, no. 1 (2005): 69–83.

Wild, Nicole. *Dictionnaire des Théâtres Parisiens au XIXe Siècle: Les Théâtres et la Musique.* Paris: Aux Amateurs de Livres, 1989.

Williams, Martin. "Jazz: What Happened in Kansas City?" *American Music* 3, no. 2 (1985): 171–79.

Williams, Stanley "Tookie." *Life in Prison.* SeaStar Books, 2001.

Wilmer, Valerie. *As Serious as Your Life: The Story of the New Jazz.* Westport, CT: Lawrence Hill, 1977.

Wirth, Thomas H. "Richard Bruce Nugent." In "Contemporary Black Visual Arts Issue," *Black American Literature Forum* 19, no. 1 (1985): 16–17.

Woodard, Komozi. "It's Nation Time in NewArk: Amiri Baraka and the Black Power Experiment in Newark, New Jersey." In *Freedom North: Black Freedom Struggles Outside the South, 1940–1980*, edited by Jeanne Theoharis and Komozi Woodard. New York: Palgrave Macmillan, 2003.

Wright, Mary F., and Sandra Kowalczyk. "Peace by Piece: The Freeing Power of Language and Literacy through the Arts." In "A Curriculum of Peace," special issue, *English Journal* 89, no. 5 (2000): 55–63.

Wunsch, James L. "From Burning to Rebuilding: The Revival of the South Bronx 1970–1999." *Bronx County Historical Society Journal* 38, no. 1 (2001): 4–22.

Yearns, W. Buck, and John G. Barrett, eds. *North Carolina Civil War Documentary*. Chapel Hill: University of North Carolina Press, 2002.

Young, Ben. *Dixonia: A Bio-discography of Bill Dixon*. Discographies no. 77, edited by Michael Gray. Westport, CT: Greenwood, 1998.

Zanetti, Vincent. "Le Griot et le Pouvoir: Une Relation Ambiguë." *Cahiers de Musiques Traditionnelles* 3: Musique et Pouvoir (1990): 161–72.

Zapf, Harald. "Ethnicity and Performance: Bilingualism in Spanglish Verse Culture." In "Multilingualism and American Studies," special issue, *Amerikastudien* 51, no. 1 (2006): 13–27.

Page numbers followed by f indicate illustrations.

9/11, 247, 258

recordings (continued)

Punkville, 204, 208; *Meditation/Resurrection*, 190–91; *Olmec Series, The*, 197; *O'Neal's Porch*, 5, 219–20; *Painter's Spring*, 245–46f; *Peach Orchard, The*, 185–87, *Posium Pendasem*, 188; *Petit Oiseau*, 223, 226; *Raincoat in the River*, 209–11, 232; *Raining on the Moon*, 232–33; *Red Giraffe with Dreadlocks*, 263–64; *Scrapbook*, 247; *Sound Unity*, 221–22; *Spontaneous*, 211; *Sunrise in the Tone World*, 200–202; *Through Acceptance of the Mystery Peace*, 113; *Two Days in April*, 275–76; *Voices Fall from the Sky*, 265; William Parker Organ Quartet, 250–51, 353n61; William Parker Quartet: Diverse World concert, 225–26; "William Parker Vocal Series," 270; *Wood Flute Songs*, 189–90, 229

recordings (collaborations): *Beyond Quantum*, 253; *Dawn Voice*, 129–31; Farmers by Nature, 248; *Out of This World's Distortions*, 249; *Love and Ghosts*, 249; *Touchin' on Trane*, 253; with Hamid Drake, 218

recordings (sideperson): *Black Beings*, 118, 221, 322n110; *Calling It the 8th*, 153–54; *Evening of the Blue Men*, 122; *First Feeding*, 121; performances with Cecil Taylor, 169; *Nicaragua: No Parasan*, 141; *Winged Serpent (Sliding Quadrants)*, 163

recordings (solo performances), 255–60; "Cathedral of Light," 133, 257f; *Corn Meal Suite*, 136; *Crumbling in the Shadows Is Fraulein Miller's Stale Cake* and *Testimony*, 258–60; *Long Hidden: The Olmec Series*, 255–56; "Sunrise in the Tone World," 226; *Wood Flute Songs*, 221, 323n1

records: early favorites, 72; shopping for, 49–50, 52. *See also* recordings

Red Giraffe with Dreadlocks, 263–64

reeds, 268

relationships, 125. *See also* Nicholson, Patricia

religion, 85; and spirituality, 118

rent, 103, 106, 111. *See also* economy of music

residencies: Bohemian Caverns, 242–43; Decidedly Jazz Danceworks, 230; International Improvised Music Workshop, 235; Stone, the, 250; Total Music Meeting, 253

revolution, 173–74, 181, 185, 232, 240, 266, 269

Rising Tones Cross, 142–43

Rivers, Sam, 96, 106, 115–16, 206

Robeson, Paul, 183

rock music, 175, 178

Rodea, Jean Carla, 266

Rodriguez, Richard, 2, 198

Rollins, Sonny, 135

Rome, 223, 242

Roney, Kojo, 256

Roulette, 181; 20th anniversary performance, 203; Farmers by Nature, 250f; Little Huey Creative Music Orchestra, 211; Parker, Milford Graves and Patricia Nicholson, 255; William Parker Essential Orchestra, 215; William Parker's Tone Motion Theater, 268

Rozie, Mixashawn, 190

Rudd, Roswell, 69, 101, 105–6

Russell, George, 215

Russia, 227. *See also* Moscow

sacred music, 101

Sadako Sasaki, 139. *See also* Thousand Cranes project

Sami people, 227

Sandinistas, 141

Sanders, Pharoah, 85, 107–8

Sandy, AnnMarie, 266, 268

Savoy Ballroom, 40, 222, 252

scatting, 232

Schlanger, Jeff: artwork, 181, 186, 353n67; Somewhere There collaboration, 256–58

school, 54, 84, 88–89. *See also* education (music)

Sciola, Pinuccio, 158

Scrapbook, 247

Scrootable Labs, 249

seasonal change, 187, 202

self-expression, 195, 273